Mastering
Autodesk®Navisworks®2013

Jason Dodds

Scott Johnson

WILEY

John Wiley & Sons, Inc.

Senior Acquisitions Editor: Willem Knibbe

Development Editor: Kelly Talbot

Technical Editor: Michael N. Smith

Production Editor: Elizabeth Britten

Copy Editor: Linda Recktenwald

Editorial Manager: Pete Gaughan

Production Manager: Tim Tate

Vice President and Executive Group Publisher: Richard Swadley

Vice President and Publisher: Neil Edde

Book Designer: Judy Fung and Maureen Forys, Happenstance Type-O-Rama

Proofreader: Paul Sagan, Word One New York

Indexer: Ted Laux

Project Coordinator, Cover: Katherine Crocker

Cover Designer: Ryan Sneed

Cover Image: © Pete Gardner/DigitalVision/Getty Images

Dear Reader,

Thank you for choosing *Mastering Autodesk Navisworks 2013*. This book is part of a family of premium-quality Sybex books, all of which are written by outstanding authors who combine practical experience with a gift for teaching.

Sybex was founded in 1976. More than 30 years later, we're still committed to producing consistently exceptional books. With each of our titles, we're working hard to set a new standard for the industry. From the paper we print on to the authors we work with, our goal is to bring you the best books available.

I hope you see all that reflected in these pages. I'd be very interested to hear your comments and get your feedback on how we're doing. Feel free to let me know what you think about this or any other Sybex book by sending me an email at nedde@wiley.com. If you think you've found a technical error in this book, please visit http://sybex.custhelp.com. Customer feedback is critical to our efforts at Sybex.

Best regards,

Neil Edde
Vice President and Publisher
Sybex, an Imprint of Wiley

Wow, what an adventure! I don't think it would have been possible without someone on the other end. Thank you, sweetheart, for the patience and understanding you have provided. There are many times I may have lost my sanity along the way. To my many colleagues who have been able to add ideas as well, I have appreciated the support all along journey. I have appreciated writing this book with you as well, Scott. Thank you.
—Jason

First and foremost, to my best friend and partner in crime, Jojo—I could not have done this without you. You always believe in me.

Special thanks go to Mom, Dad, and my family for their love and support, C&J for their unwavering company, and my many colleagues at Autodesk who have challenged and inspired me.
—Scott

Acknowledgments

First, we want to thank Autodesk and the Navisworks team for creating such a great product. Product development can be a long, drawn-out process, but it has been particularly satisfying to watch Navisworks grow and mature over the years. Thank you for listening to all of the users and helping advance this wonderful piece of technology.

Second, we want to thank those have made personal contributions to this book, including John Mack from Herrero Contractors, Art Theusch from The Christman Company, Roberta Oldenburg from Mortenson Construction, Chris Bushong from Gensler, C.W. Driver, and many others too numerous to mention. Thank you for your valuable case studies and other contributions. They have helped to make this a Mastering book.

Finally, we would like to thank some of the behind-the-scenes team members. Thanks to Michael Smith, our technical editor, for sharing his expertise and insight on numerous chapters. We also want to thank Willem Knibbe for helping develop the idea of this book, but more importantly, for his tenacity and perseverance in keeping us on track.

And, of course, to all of our friends and colleagues who have shared in this great adventure: Thank you!

About the Authors

Jason Dodds has been actively involved in the design and building technology community for over 15 years. During his career, Jason's focus and experience have been on construction, architecture, interiors, structures, MEP, construction administration, and using Navisworks on projects. He has been involved in all facets of design and building processes and understands what it takes to complete projects from design, to estimating, to coordination, and to fabrication. Jason is also a nationally recognized speaker at industry associations such as the BIMForum, Construction Management Association of America (CMAA), and Associated General Contractors of America (AGC), as well as a speaker at Autodesk University.

When not working, Jason enjoys off roading in his Jeep, playing golf, and spending time in the kitchen.

Scott Johnson is a senior technical account manager supporting key construction accounts at Autodesk. His broad background includes over 15 years of experience in the design/build, manufacturing, and architecture, engineering, and construction (AEC) industries. Scott has spoken and lectured at Autodesk University, BIMForum, and Autodesk Users Group International (AUGI) events as well as at numerous university settings. His educational background includes a Bachelor of Arts in Pipe Organ Design and Construction from Lewis and Clark College as well as a master's in Construction Management from Washington University in St. Louis.

In his spare time, Scott enjoys biking and camping in the Pacific Northwest, travel, woodworking, cooking, good beer, and music.

Michael N. Smith, Technical Editor, is a BIM manager for C.W. Driver, a general contracting and construction management firm headquartered in Pasadena, California. His areas of focus include scheduling and coordination, creating site studies and project simulations, and integrating 5D practices. He has a wealth of knowledge of current software capabilities and limitations. Michael has been a speaker at several BIM conventions and user groups, including Autodesk University, the Coalition for Adequate Student Housing (C.A.S.H.) Conference, and American Society for Healthcare Engineering (ASHE). He is the content manager for *AUGIWorld* magazine and has written numerous articles documenting Navisworks best practices. Michael is also the instructor for CAD Learning's Navisworks 2012 and 2013 courses and founder of Blink Forward LLC. Michael graduated from Brigham Young University with a Bachelor of Science in Construction Management.

In his free time, Michael enjoys mentoring students, writing software, and providing service through the Church of Jesus Christ of Latter-day Saints.

Contents at a Glance

Contents

Foreword

During a long career within the construction industry, I have developed, authored, and implemented software solutions and new business processes for what is now called building information modeling (BIM). The projects have been as small as a few houses to prestigious multibillion programs. A common problem on all projects has been the ability to engage the whole project team and to have ready access to information and the virtual construction models—not just the designers and CAD operators, but also the CAD/BIM users.

In the early 1990s, a major collapse of the rail tunnels into the London Heathrow Airport during the construction phase demanded a new approach to construction and the collaboration of the entire supply chain to rectify and deliver the project on time. One of the innovative solutions suggested for the reconstruction project was to deliver a zero-defect, fit-first-time project, risk-free-from-delay set of production documentation. The use of a 3D project model (BIM) was part of the innovation; computer capability and power at that time was limited and what was needed to view the models was a powerful browser tool with a minimum power requirement.

As always in history, luck and timing came together with the availability of Navisworks. This was the only solution with the power and capability to do what we needed to allow the designers and construction managers to review and plan the project before construction was started. The success of the project is well documented, as was the very successful application of the solution on the London Heathrow Express and Terminal 5 projects, the first and largest truly BIM ever produced.

The current state of the world economy and our industry is such that we need to produce and construct in the most economic fashion possible with reduced risk, at cost and on time. The use of the BIM processes and the technologies to support the delivery of projects at least 25–30 percent less than previously by removing the inaccuracy, incompleteness, and ambiguity in the traditional documentation is gaining traction in the global marketplace. Effectively build four and get another free is what will be needed to compete.

We should see this as an exciting time for change; we know it is required and we have the environment to do it. What is needed is guidance on how to get the best out of the processes and technologies and to engage the total supply chain, client included, throughout the project life-cycle. This book can educate you in the possibilities of virtual construction: to see it before you build it, sell it before you complete it, and manage and maintain it after it has been completed. This means the information as well as the graphical representation.

Training and guidance from experts is required to get the best out of any tool. The authors of this book have been involved in the use of Navisworks from its inception and have a wealth of experience on its use in real-world contracts. They have accumulated some 30 years of experience in construction and on major projects.

This book has been written to leave no doubt as to how the Navisworks tools can be used to manage and deliver the best-quality information at the right time.

Each chapter and topic is logically and simply explained so that even the most experienced user will find something new to enhance their abilities. Everything here is essential. As a user of the solution since it was first available, I thought I had little or even nothing to learn, but I was wrong! No matter your skill level, this book will improve your skills and management potential.

With the global acceptance and acceleration in the use of BIM, I hope to see many of you at the conferences or on the Internet forums furthering the knowledge and experiences we all need to share.

Good luck with your endeavors.

—*Mervyn Richards*
Director, MR1 Consulting

Introduction

Welcome to *Mastering Autodesk Navisworks 2013*. This book is based on the 2013 release of Navisworks and covers tools for the three different versions of Navisworks: Simulate, Manage, and Freedom.

Autodesk® Navisworks® 2013 pushes the boundaries of BIM technology and boldly takes construction and design to new levels. *Mastering Autodesk Navisworks 2013* is the comprehensive guide to the software, and in it we present practical industry applications. We begin with the foundation basics such as interface and file aggregation. Beyond mastering the basics, we focus on exploring complex workflows, clash detection, Presenter, and TimeLiner.

While there are many aspects of this book that go into detail on a technical level, there are also many accessible case studies, exercises, and examples to help you develop your skills and fully exercise the benefits of Navisworks. We hope you find this book well balanced with technical knowledge and real workflow methodologies.

All of the tutorial files to complete the book's exercises are located at www.sybex.com/go/masteringnavisworks2013. To download a trial version of Navisworks, go to www.autodesk.com/navisworks, where you will also be able to find complete system requirements for running Navisworks.

Who Should Read this Book?

This book is for anyone who wants to master and apply Navisworks to the AEC industry. That includes the BIM or VDC manager who needs to learn just a little more about Navisworks, as well as the project manager trying to learn more about this application.

This book can serve as a simple refresher course if you already know Navisworks but need to perfect a workflow or solve a persistent problem. For these advanced users, we wrote the book in such as way that you can jump into a chapter, search for the information you need, and solve your problem or workflow issue. If you know the basics of Navisworks, but you need to learn an advanced skill such as Presenter, or if you need help finding the motivation to dive further into this wonderful piece of BIM technology, *Mastering Autodesk Navisworks 2013* is for you.

What You Will Learn

This book starts with the basics including navigation and file aggregation. Building on those skills, you'll explore advanced topics of clash detection, site logistics and scheduling with TimeLiner, and creating visualizations with Presenter. In the "Bottom Line" section of each chapter, you can test your mastery of the skills you have learned along the way. Take a look at the following chapter descriptions for a preview.

Chapter 1, "Getting to Know Autodesk Navisworks," introduces you to the interfaces and features of Navisworks.

Chapter 2, "Files and File Types," helps you understand the various file types and how to begin bringing them into Navisworks, a process sometimes referred to as file aggregation.

Chapter 3, "Moving around the Model," is about navigation techniques and tools.

Chapter 4, "Climbing the Selection Tree," familiarizes you with the selection tree and other project organization tools such as search and selection sets.

Chapter 5, "Model Snapshots: Viewpoints, Animations, and Sections," gives you the opportunity to learn more about creating viewpoints and animations in Navisworks as well as skills needed to section your model.

Chapter 6, "Documenting Your Project," teaches you skills to redline, mark up, and dimension your projects, which are essential for conveying information to users.

Chapter 7, "4D Sequencing with TimeLiner," focuses on the TimeLiner tool, its features, and functions.

Chapter 8, "Clash Detection," focuses on the ins and outs of clash detection along with the specific workflows for effectively clashing your projects.

Chapter 9, "Creating Visualizations," helps you to unlock the mystery of visualizations and learn the skills necessary to create them with Presenter in Navisworks.

Chapter 10, "Animating Objects," shows you how to create rich presentations that enhance your model.

Chapter 11, "Giving Objects Life and Action with Scripter," explores adding realism and interaction to your animations.

Chapter 12, "Collaborating outside of Navisworks," looks at external applications and tools that allow you to leverage and extend the value of Navisworks beyond the core application.

Chapter 13, "Other Useful Navisworks Tools," explores some of the lesser-known features of this program.

Chapter 14, "Managing BIM Workflows," gives several different perspectives on workflows that use Navisworks.

Appendix A, "The Bottom Line," gathers together all the "Master It" problems from the chapters and provides a solution for each.

Appendix B, "Best Practices and Supplementary Information," covers some of the additional tips, tricks, and resources available for Navisworks.

The Mastering Series

The *Mastering* series from Sybex provides outstanding instruction for readers with intermediate and advanced skills, in the form of top-notch training and development for those already working in their field and clear, serious education for those aspiring to become pros. Every *Mastering* book features:

◆ The Sybex "by professionals for professionals" commitment: *Mastering* authors are themselves practitioners, with plenty of credentials in their areas of specialty.

◆ A practical perspective for a reader who already knows the basics—someone who needs solutions, not a primer.

◆ Real-World Scenarios, ranging from case studies to interviews that show how the tool, technique, or knowledge presented is applied in actual practice.

◆ Skill-based instruction, with chapters organized around real tasks rather than abstract concepts or subjects.

◆ Self-review test containing "Master It" problems and questions, so you can be certain you're equipped to do the job right.

How to Contact the Authors

We welcome feedback from you about this book or about books you'd like to see from us in the future. You can reach Jason Dodds by writing to jason@masteringnavisworks.com. For more information about Jason's work, please visit his blog at http://doddsandends.typepad.com/.

You can reach Scott Johnson by writing to scott@masteringnavisworks.com.

Sybex strives to keep you supplied with the latest tools and information you need for your work. Please check our website at www.sybex.com, where we'll post additional content and updates that supplement this book if the need arises. Enter **Mastering Navisworks** in the Search box (or type the book's ISBN—**9781118281710**) and click Go to get to the book's update page.

Part 1

Navisworks Basics

Chapter 1

Getting to Know Autodesk Navisworks

This chapter explains the Autodesk® Navisworks® 2013 interface, its tools, capabilities, recommended settings, and basic operating features. By understanding the interface, you will create a solid foundation for tool locations, understand each individual function, and increase your overall knowledge of Navisworks.

In this chapter, you'll learn to:

◆ Understand the ribbon

◆ Use the Measure and Redline tools

Interface Organization

Over the years, the Navisworks interface has remained relatively unchanged—until the 2011 release. Autodesk introduced a new interface based on tabs and panels, all the while keeping some of the features from the previous versions. With the Navisworks 2013 release, new tools have been added to take advantage of the native Revit® file, Grid tools, and a new interface for the Clash Detective.

Application Menu: The Blue N

A basic starting point within Navisworks, the Application menu, or blue N, contains operations like New, Open, and Save. Several other useful operations that can be performed from here are shown in Figure 1.1.

FIGURE 1.1
The blue N, or
Application menu

TOOLTIP

If you pause and hover your mouse cursor over any area in Navisworks, you get a tooltip, as shown here. Tooltips briefly explain the tool and may contain information about shortcuts (such as pressing Ctrl+A for Append). Also, if you leave your mouse in place a little longer, you will gain a longer explanation of the tool—the tooltip will expand into a definition from the help file.

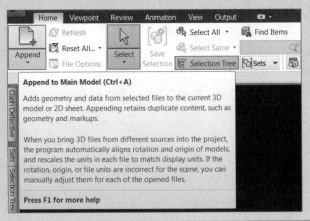

New   Closes the currently open file and opens a new file.

Open   Opens a new file (see Figure 1.2). Note that using Open while another file is already open will close that currently open file. You want to use Append and Merge to add additional files. Options include:

Open   Opens a new file while closing the currently open file.

Open URL   Opens a file from a URL, usually a website location.

Append   Appends additional files into already open files and merges duplicate geometry.

Merge   Merges a selected file into other files and adds only new information such as new geometry, new viewpoints, and new clashes.

FIGURE 1.2
Additional Open
operations

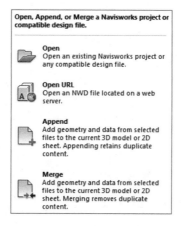

Open, Append, or Merge a Navisworks project or compatible design file.

Open
Open an existing Navisworks project or any compatible design file.

Open URL
Open an NWD file located on a web server.

Append
Add geometry and data from selected files to the current 3D model or 2D sheet. Appending retains duplicate content.

Merge
Add geometry and data from selected files to the current 3D model or 2D sheet. Merging removes duplicate content.

Save   Saves the current file.

Save As   Allows you to save the file in a different location or as a different file type (for example, as an NWD or NWF file). It allows you to save up to three versions back.

Export   Contains the Export operations (see Figure 1.3). Many of the other operations are located on the Output tab, explained later in this chapter.

Publish   Creates an NWD file. (An NWD file contains all model geometry together with Navisworks-specific data, such as review markups, viewpoints, or timeline sequence.) Also available on the Output tab.

Print   Contains Print, Print Preview, and Print Setup operations. Also available on the Output tab.

Send By Email   Saves the current file as an NWD and uses your default email application to prepare an email to send. Also available on the Output tab.

Recent Documents   This list shows all of the recently opened documents. You can control the order by Size, Access Date, Type, or Ordered List (default). Projects are only added to this list with the Normal view selected. If Classic view is used to open a file, no project will be added to this list. All appended files will be added to this list when brought into a project.

Options   Opens the Options Editor. You can also access the Options Editor by using Ctrl+F12.

FIGURE 1.3
Export flyout

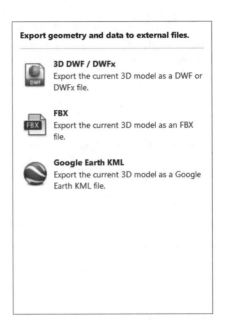

Quick Access Toolbar

The Quick Access toolbar (Figure 1.4), located adjacent to the Application menu, is a series of predefined operations. By default, you can find New, Open, Append, Merge, Save, Print, Refresh, Undo, and Redo.

FIGURE 1.4
Quick Access
toolbar

The Quick Access toolbar is customizable. You can remove tools by right-clicking the item you wish to remove or by clicking the down arrow to the right of the bar and clicking the option you wish to remove. You can add tools by selecting them from the tab and panel locations, right-clicking, and then choosing Add To Quick Access Toolbar.

Help Toolbar

Another useful toolbar in Navisworks, the Help toolbar (Figure 1.5), provides a central location for Search, Subscription Center access, Communication Center, Favorites, general Help, and the About page. This menu cannot be customized.

FIGURE 1.5
Help toolbar

Search Enter information in the search field to begin searching within Navisworks, online, and within the help file. You can customize the locations with additional sites.

Subscription Center By clicking the key icon, you can get access to the Subscription Center (membership required), where you can create support requests and view the e-learning catalog as well as other Subscription Center items.

Communication Center By clicking the satellite dish icon, you can access controls to get Navisworks product updates and announcements.

Favorites Click the star icon to store information from Search and the Subscription and Communication Centers.

Help The question mark icon connects you to Help, the Getting Started Guide, and the New Features Workshop. Help also contains information about the version of Navisworks you are using in addition to providing access to the license checkout function, if you are using a networked license.

About The small drop-down arrow at the right end of the Help toolbar connects you to information about the current version of Navisworks you are running. About also allows you to check out or return a license file on a network license.

Navisworks Options

Options, or the Options Editor (sometimes referred to as Global Options), is used to adjust the program settings for Navisworks. The settings that you change here are retained across different Navisworks sessions. Settings can also be shared across a project team via the import/export feature (Figure 1.6).

FIGURE 1.6
Navisworks Options
Editor

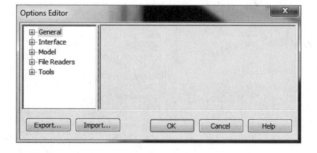

Let's look at each page of the Options Editor.

GENERAL

Use the General settings (see Figure 1.7) to adjust the buffer size, file locations, number of recent file shortcuts you want Navisworks to store, and the Auto-Save options. Additional options include:

Undo Specifies the amount of space Navisworks uses for undo/redo operations.

Locations Enables the sharing of centralized project information for the project directory and site directory.

FIGURE 1.7
General options,
with the Auto-Save
settings shown

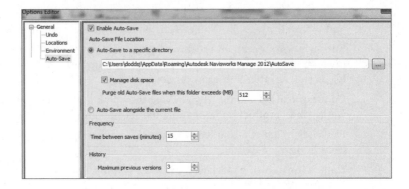

Environment   Specifies the maximum number of recently opened files for Navisworks to display. The default setting is 4 with a maximum of 16.

Auto-Save   Controls the settings for the Navisworks Auto-Save feature. From here, you can specify the save interval (30 minutes is recommended), the save location, and the number of save versions you want to maintain.

INTERFACE

Use the settings on the Interface page (see Figure 1.8) to customize the behavior of Navisworks. Additional information includes:

FIGURE 1.8
Interface options,
with the Snapping
options shown

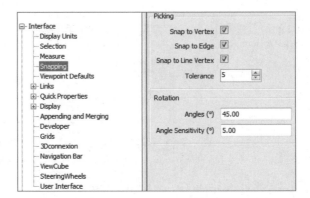

Display Units   Changes the Navisworks display units. Meters are the default setting for new Navisworks files.

Selection   Configures the way geometry is selected and highlighted within Navisworks.

Pick Radius   Specifies the radius that an object has to be within to be selected.

Resolution   Specifies the level of selection. If you have problems selecting objects, you might try changing these settings.

Compact Tree Specifies the level of detail to display on the Compact tab of the selection tree.

Highlight Controls the Highlight settings. When the Enabled box is unchecked, selected items are no longer highlighted.

Measure Use these options to adjust the settings for the Measure tools.

In 3D Allows accurate measurements in 3D. This tool allows you to find the distance of 3D objects in a view. When 3D is not selected, Navisworks defaults to a 2D object defined by the points you select. In 3D changes the way the measurements are shown. If the measurement line is obscured by model geometry, it will be hidden when In 3D is selected.

Use Center Lines With this check box selected, the Shortest Distance measurements snap to the center lines of the selected object. When Use Center Lines is not selected, the surface of the object is used.

Snapping Enables Snaps within Navisworks (Vertex, Edge, and Line Vertex). Enabling this tool is useful in conjunction with Measure tools.

Viewpoint Defaults These options define the attributes that are saved with saved viewpoints.

Settings Opens the Default Collision dialog box. Allows you to control settings from the Third Person avatar. This dialog box can also be accessed from the Viewpoint tab under Edit Viewpoints.

Links This page allows you to customize how links are displayed within Navisworks.

Quick Properties Customizes the way Quick Properties are displayed. Use this page to set up additional Quick Properties categories or choose to hide Quick Properties using this tab.

Developer Select this option if you want to enable the Geometry tab and the Transform tab within the Properties palette. This tab also enables the use of Hard Conservative clash tests.

Display Adjusts display performance.

Occlusion Culling Select this check box to enable or disable the Culling feature. Enabling Culling means that Navisworks draws only visible objects and ignores other objects.

Grids Grids allow you to change the options for the Grids and Levels tool found on the View tab. Here, you can change options such as color, font size, and grid transparency (X-Ray mode).

3Dconnexion Controls the settings for a 3D mouse or motion controller mouse, often referred to as a space mouse (including speed). A space mouse can be used as an alternative (or in addition) to the mouse to move around the scene view.

Navigation Bar Used for customizing the Navigation Bar and legacy navigation tools.

ViewCube Customizes the behavior of the ViewCube® tool.

SteeringWheels Customizes the behavior of the SteeringWheels® tool.

User Interface Used to switch between Standard (ribbon) and Classic (toolbars) interface mode.

MODEL

Use the Model settings (see Figure 1.9) to optimize the performance of Navisworks and to customize parameters for NWD and NWC files. Additional options include:

FIGURE 1.9
Model options, with Performance options shown

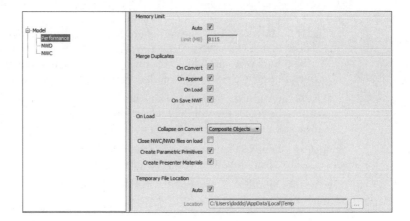

Performance   Optimizes the performance of Navisworks.

> **Memory Limit**   Specifies the amount of physical memory that Navisworks uses.
>
> **Merge Duplicates**   Allows you to control how and when information is merged into Navisworks.
>
> **On Load**   Optimizes the performance of Navisworks when loading files into Navisworks.
>
> > ◆ **Collapse On Convert:** Collapses the tree structure.
> >
> > ◆ **Close NWC/NWD Files On Load:** Controls whether or not the NWC/NWD files are locked for editing. When this box is unchecked, the files will be locked for editing. Checked means that these files are closed once loaded into memory and can be edited.
> >
> > ◆ **Create Parametric Primitives:** Improves speed and performance by using Parametric objects.
> >
> > ◆ **Create Presenter Materials:** Allows you to create and use materials when an NWC file is loaded.

NWD   Enables and disables geometry compression for the NWD file format.

NWC   Use this page to manage the file options for the NWC file format.

> **Caching**   With these boxes checked, Navisworks creates and saves to a cache file, or NWC. This is a recommended setting because NWC files are typically smaller than their original files.

THE CLOSE NWC/NWD FILES ON LOAD OPTION

Depending on your workflow and what your needs are, you should give this check box careful consideration. If you leave Close NWC/NWD Files On Load unchecked, you will not be able to update your NWC/NWD files on the fly. In other words, if you are working on an active project (coordination meetings, for example) and find yourself updating files often, you would have to close Navisworks in order to update the NWC/NWD files loaded in the project. With this box checked, you can modify your files during the project.

FILE READERS

Use the File Readers settings (see Figure 1.10) to configure the file readers required to open native CAD, BIM, and scanning application file formats in Navisworks.

FIGURE 1.10
File Readers page, with options for DWG/DXF shown

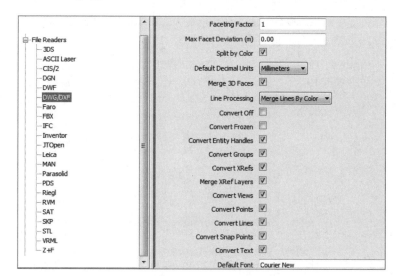

DWG/DXF   Adjust options for the DWG™/DXF™ file reader.

Merge 3D Faces   Allows the file reader to merge the 3D faces of DWG/DXF objects into a single item in the selection tree. This helps to lessen the number of items selected.

DWG Loader Version   Allows Navisworks to select which version of the Autodesk object enablers to use when loading a DWG file. If the DWG Loader Version needs to change, Navisworks must be restarted for this setting to take effect.

Advanced   Use the Convert Object Properties dialog box (click Advanced to open this dialog) to select third-party applications for the file reader to read additional options from (Figure 1.11).

FIGURE 1.11
Convert Object
Properties
dialog box

All other file readers adjust the options for the file type they are associated with.

TOOLS

Use the Tools settings (see Figure 1.12) to adjust the options for Clash Detective, Presenter, TimeLiner, Scripter, and Animator. Options include:

FIGURE 1.12
Tools options,
with settings for
TimeLiner shown

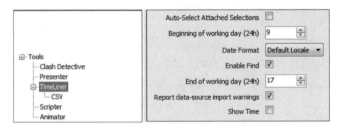

Clash Detective   Customizes Clash Detective options.

Presenter   Customizes Presenter options.

> **Profile**   You can adjust Presenter profiles to reflect your level of comfort or knowledge. The Basic setting is the Navisworks default and has a limited editing functionality. Standard has some advanced Presenter features. Advanced gives you access to such features as extra materials, lights, and render styles.
>
> **Interactive Materials**   When this check box is cleared, materials are not displayed during navigation. This decreases the load on the video card and can improve performance.
>
> **Interactive Lighting**   When this check box is cleared, lights are not displayed during navigation. This decreases the load on the video card and can improve performance.

TimeLiner   Customizes TimeLiner options.

> **Auto Select Attached Selections**   When enabled, automatically selects attached objects in TimeLiner.
>
> **Display Synchronization Errors**   When enabled, indicates that error messages will display when synchronizing tasks from eternal links in TimeLiner.

CSV File: Read and Write Encoding   Specifies the file format of the imported or exported CSV file.

Scripter   Use these options to customize the Scripter settings.

Animator   A check box indicates whether or not a manual entry is shown in the Animator.

IMPORT AND EXPORT

These settings allow you to export the current Options settings into an Options XML file; you can choose which categories are exported. These items may also be imported using the Import feature.

From a workflow perspective, it may be useful to save individual files for each category (General, Interface, and so forth) per project. This way, specific settings are retained as needed and can be shared among users quickly and easily.

For additional information on the Options Editor, see "External Options Editor" in Appendix B, "Additional Resources and Tips."

SHIFT + GLOBAL OPTIONS = ADVANCED OPTIONS

There might come a time when you need to expose more options than you are given by the standard Options Editor. To access more Global Options, right-click, hold down the Shift key, and select Options.

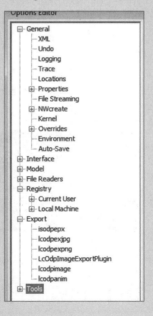

This will expose additional tools like the Navisworks Windows Registry. But be warned you will be making changes to the Windows Registry at this level. This should be reserved for only the advanced users.

You can find other useful additions here like changing the default image size to the Clash Detective so you are able to export larger images when sending out clash reports.

Exploring the Ribbon

The ribbon, located at the top of the user interface, is a palette that groups the entire Navisworks toolset into an easy-to-find and -use location. The ribbon is divided into tabs, with each tab supporting a specific activity or task. Within each tab is a series of panels that contain the available tools.

While you are not able to add to or remove custom commands from the ribbon, you can customize the appearance and location of the panels using these methods:

- Right-click the tab or panel to open the context menu. From here, you can turn tabs or panels on or off.

- Left-click and hold a specific panel to move its location. You can change its location to a new place within the tab or drag it out into the workspace to make it more accessible. Panels may not be moved to other tabs.

- To reset the panel to its default position, right-click on an empty location on the panel and click Restore Default Ribbon.

PUSHPINS

Any time you see a pushpin icon, you can click it to pin an item to the screen. This will allow the panel or palette to stay on top and remain open as you move to other tools in Navisworks.

Home

The Home tab contains Project, Select & Search, Visibility, Display, and Tools panels (Figure 1.13 and Figure 1.15).

FIGURE 1.13
Home tab, showing additional tools enabled

PROJECT

Append   Appends, or combines, files. The drop-down also contains Merge.

Refresh   To ensure that you are working with the most current information, Navisworks contains a Refresh feature.

Reset All   Uses the various tools to reset changes applied in Navisworks.

Appearance   Returns all color and transparency overrides to their original state.

Transforms   Resets all Transforms overrides to their original state.

Links   Resets all links applied to their original state. Deletes all links made in Navisworks and retains only links inherited from the original files.

File Options   This dialog box (see Figure 1.14) controls the appearance of the model as well as the speed of navigation around it. Changes made in this dialog box are for the current session only, and options are returned to the defaults when the model is closed.

FIGURE 1.14
File Options
dialog box

Culling   Use this tab to adjust geometry culling (that is, the ability to navigate large areas) in the open Navisworks file.

Orientation   Use this tab to adjust the real-world orientation of your model.

Speed   Use this tab to adjust the frame rate speed to reduce the amount of dropout during navigation.

Headlight   Use this tab to change the intensity of the scene's ambient light and headlight for Headlight mode. This setting is useful to customize the lighting as you navigate.

Scene Lights   Use this tab to change the intensity of the scene's ambient light for Scene Lights mode. This setting is useful to define a different lighting scheme as you navigate the model.

Data Tools   Use this tab to create and manage links between open Navisworks files and external databases. You will not likely use this setting often.

Scene Statistics An extremely useful tool, Scene Statistics lists all of the files contributing to aggregated elements, or the "scene." It also shows the various graphic elements that help to make up the scene. Use Scene Statistics when an object enabler appears to be missing or when certain objects are not showing up properly.

SELECT & SEARCH

Select Allows you to select objects with your mouse. Also available within the drop-down list is Select Box, which allows you to select all items within a defined box.

Select All Selects all objects within the model.

Select None Deselects the current selection. Pressing the Esc key has the same function.

Invert Selection Deselects the currently selected items and selects the currently unselected items. In short, it selects the opposite of what you had selected.

Save Selection Saves the currently selected objects as a selection set and opens the Sets window. The set can then be renamed and modified.

Select Same Allows you to select multiple instances of the selected item or group of items. Also opens to the Select Same drop-down for additional selection criteria and options.

Selection Tree Toggles the selection tree on and off. The selection tree is a palette that displays a variety of categorized views of the structure of the model depending on the loaded model.

Find Items Toggles the Find Items palette on and off.

Quick Find A simplified version of Find Items, Quick Find allows you to search the scene using the Quick Find dialog box.

Sets Displays a list of defined search and selection sets. You can access the Sets palette from this drop-down.

Selection Inspector Displays a list of all selected objects showing their Quick Properties information. Quick Properties information can be customized in the Options Editor.

VISIBILITY

Hide Hides selected items from display. You can select multiple items to hide them and at different intervals. The items also appear grayed out in the selection tree to represent hidden.

Require Forces an item to remain visible regardless of performance settings, such as culling. When an item is set to Required, it will appear red in the selection tree. Required items can still be hidden; the Required setting is mainly to help ensure that items will not be dropped from view when you have to change your performance settings.

Hide Unselected Hides all items except those that are currently selected. This tool is useful when you're trying to build a selection set and ensure the items that you have selected.

Unhide All Reveals all hidden items in the scene. The drop-down also contains Unrequire All, which sets required items back to optional.

FIGURE 1.15
Home tab
continued

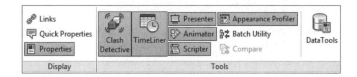

DISPLAY

Links   Displays or hides links. Several types of links display in Navisworks: Hyperlink, Label, Viewpoints, Clash Detective, TimeLiner, Sets, Redline tags, and user-defined links. You can use the Options Editor to toggle the display of each of the link categories and also to control their appearance.

Quick Properties   When enabled, Quick Properties displays brief information about the object in a tooltip type of display. You can edit the type of information that is displayed in the Options Editor.

Properties   Toggles the Properties palette on and off. The Properties palette displays available properties for a selected item. If more than one item is selected, the Properties palette will display only the total number of selected items and no additional property information.

TOOLS

Clash Detective   Toggles the Clash Detective palette on and off. Clash Detective enables you to interactively search your model for clashes or interferences.

TimeLiner   Toggles the TimeLiner palette on and off. TimeLiner allows you to create 4D simulations of your project, linking time with modeled objects.

Presenter   Toggles the Presenter palette on and off. Presenter allows you to apply materials and lighting to your model to aid in creating renderings.

Animator   Toggles the Animator palette on and off. Animator allows you to animate objects to bring realism to your project.

Scripter   Toggles the Scripter palette on and off. Scripter adds interactivity to your animated objects.

Batch Utility   Opens the Batch Utility dialog box. From here, you can create a list of all design files, append multiple design files into a single NWD or NWF file, and convert multiple design files into individual NWDs.

Appearance Profiler   Toggles the Appearance Profile palette on and off. This tool lets you create custom appearance profiles for items based on properties or sets (Search and Selection). Then you can use the appearance profiles to essentially color-code the objects in your model to help identify or differentiate status or type.

Compare   Opens the Compare dialog box. You can look for differences between any two items selected in the model. These items can be files, layers, instances, groups, or geometry.

Data Tools   Opens the Data Tools dialog box. From here, you can connect Navisworks to external databases and create links to objects within the model.

Viewpoint

The Viewpoint tab contains the Save, Load & Playback panel as well as the Camera, Navigate, Render Style, Sectioning, and Export panels (Figure 1.16 and Figure 1.17).

FIGURE 1.16
Viewpoint tab

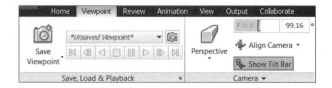

SAVE, LOAD & PLAYBACK

Save Viewpoint   Saves a viewpoint of the current view. The saved viewpoint retains the properties and attributes of the current view when the Save Attributes setting in the Options is selected. There is also a Record feature to record your actions (Walk, Fly, Zoom, and other actions in Navisworks). The recording is saved in the Saved Viewpoints window.

Animation Controls   See "Playback" in the section "Animation."

Edit Viewpoint   Opens the Edit Viewpoint dialog box. This dialog box allows you to edit any viewpoints attributes, including camera position, field of view, speed of motion, and saved attributes. The Collision dialog box is located within the Edit Viewpoint dialog box, allowing you to adjust collision settings for the current viewpoint.

Saved Viewpoints Dialog Launcher   Toggles the Saved Viewpoints palette.

CAMERA

Perspective   Allows you to choose between Orthographic or Perspective mode. Walk and Fly navigation tools are not available in Orthographic mode. Tip: If the view becomes distorted when you switch between modes, undo the switch, use the Focus tool, and then switch modes.

Field Of View (F.O.V.)   Defines the area of the scene that the camera can view. The lower the number, the narrower the camera angle or the closer you are to the object being viewed. You can you edit existing or saved Field Of View settings using the Edit Viewpoint dialog box. The higher the number is, the more distorted the model looks.

Align Camera   Opens the Align Camera drop-down, which allows you to use these tools to align the camera to the chosen axis:

Align X   Aligns the camera to the x-axis.

Align Y   Aligns the camera to the y-axis.

Align Z   Aligns the camera to the z-axis.

Straighten   A useful tool to straighten the view when you find yourself askew, which can often occur when using some of the navigation tools such as Fly and Orbit. It works only when the view is within 13 degrees of a face of the ViewCube.

Show Tilt Bar   Toggles the Tilt Bar off and on. Tilt adjusts the vertical angle of the camera.

FIGURE 1.17
Viewpoint tab
continued

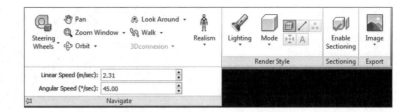

NAVIGATE

Navigate Tools   Included on the Viewpoint tab are Navigation tools to help to move around the model. Here, you can find tools for Pan, Zoom Window, Orbit, Look Around, Walk, and SteeringWheels. Most of these tools can also be found on the Navigation Bar.

Realism   Toggles the Realism settings on and off for the following options. Figure 1.18 shows one result of working with Realism settings: a construction worker avatar in a crouching position.

> **Collision**   Enabling Collision allows you to navigate the model with mass. As you interact with the model and come into contact with objects like doors or columns, you stop or are unable to pass through that object. You can change or customize the size of the Collision Volume to reflect the needs of the user or collision requirements. Collision can only be used with the Walk and Fly tools.
>
> **Gravity**   This tool gives you the appearance of weight. When you are using the Walk tool and you begin to move, you will "fall" until you reach a surface. Gravity works best when Collision is also active so that when a surface is contacted, the falling stops. Use Gravity in conjunction with Collision to walk up or down stairs. Gravity can only be used with the Walk tools. If Gravity is selected, Collision is automatically turned on. You cannot have Gravity without Collision.
>
> **Crouch**   With Crouch activated, you will automatically crouch under any objects that you cannot freely walk under at the specified avatar height. This can be useful for checking clearance heights under pipes and other equipment.
>
> **Third Person**   When Third Person is active, it turns on Third Person view, or an avatar, which you can use as a representation of yourself while navigating the model. Third Person has other added benefits like working with Gravity, Collision, and Crouch. When you're using the avatar for Collision, it will turn red when it approaches another item. Also, you can customize Third Person by changing the avatar selection and dimensions.

Linear Speed   Sets the linear speed, which is the speed the Walk and Fly tools use when navigating through the model. The 5–10 ft/sec range is ideal for an average walking pace. This is a temporary setting specific to the view. If you change views, this setting will go back to the project default.

Angular Speed   Sets the angular speed, which is the speed at which the Walk and Fly tools turn when navigating through the model. The 45–60 deg/sec range is ideal for an average walking pace.

FIGURE 1.18
Third Person with
Gravity, Collision,
and Crouch enabled

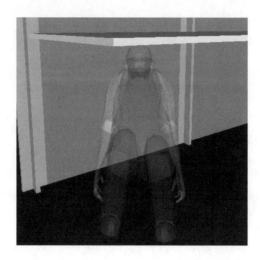

RENDER STYLE

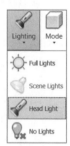

Lighting   Changes the Lighting mode within Navisworks to control how the 3D scene lighting is displayed.

Full Lights   Uses the highest quality lighting available. Controlled by Presenter.

Scene Lights   Uses the lights supplied with the appended files. If no lights are added, Navisworks will add two opposing lights. You can change the ambient lighting options using the File Options tool.

Headlights   Uses a light that comes from the camera location. You can change the ambient lighting option using the File Options tool.

No Lights   Does not use any lights in the view; geometry is rendered with flat lights.

Mode   The Mode drop-down controls the options for displaying the scene geometry rendering and the level of materials to display.

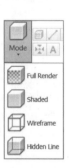

Full Render   In Full Render mode, the model is shown with materials and textures along with edges and smooth shading.

Shaded   The model is shown with additional edges and smooth shading. Materials and textures are not included in this mode.

Wireframe   The model is shown in Wireframe mode only. Materials and textures are not included in this mode.

Hidden Line   The model is shown in Wireframe mode but only outline and facet edges are displayed; this hides additional lines over Wireframe mode. Materials and textures are not included in this mode.

Surfaces   Toggles 3D surface geometry on and off.

Lines   Toggles on and off the 2D lines that come from an appended file.

Points   Toggles on and off the points that come from appended files. When you are inserting point cloud or laser scan data, it may be necessary to have the points enabled.

Snap Points   Toggles on and off the rendering of snap points within the model.

Text   Toggles on and off 2D or 3D text that comes from appended files.

Using a combination of these tools when bringing in an AutoCAD® file or other vector-based file types helps to clean up the scene in Navisworks and create a display of only 3D geometry.

SECTIONING

Enable Sectioning   Opens the Sectioning Tools tab (Figure 1.19). The Sectioning tools allow you to create cross-sections of your model. Sections can enabled and disabled as needed.

FIGURE 1.19
Sectioning Tools tab

EXPORT

Image   Saves an image file of the current view.

Rendered Image   Saves a rendered image of the current view.

Piranasi EPix   Saves a Piranasi EPix file of the current view.

Review

The Review tab contains Measure, Redline, Tags, Comments, and Collaborate panels (Figure 1.20).

FIGURE 1.20
Review tab

MEASURE

Measure   Navisworks has tools that allow you to measure between points, calculate area, and convert measurements to redlines. The Measure tools are independent of Navigation tools. If you activate the Navigation tools (walk, fly, orbit, pan), you will have to go back to your Measure tools after using any of the Navigation tools. However, you can use the mouse tools for navigation (mouse orbit, pan and zoom) without affecting the Measure tools. Using the mouse tools can help you to also move to better align your measurement.

Use right-click or the Esc key to cancel any of the Measure tools. To clear the screen of the measurement after placement, use Clean as explained below.

Point To Point   Measures the distance between two points.

Point To Multiple Points   Measures the distance between a starting point or base point and any number of additional selected points.

Point Line   Measures consecutive linear distances.

Accumulate   Measures the total length of nonconsecutive linear measurements (keeps a running total of the linear measurements) until cleared or canceled.

Angle   Measures the angular distance as defined by three selected points.

Area   Measures the area of selected points.

Shortest Distance   Measures the shortest distance between two selected objects (two objects must be selected; use the Ctrl key to select the objects as needed).

Convert To Redline   Clears the measurement and converts it to a redline. The redline will be saved as part of the active viewpoint. If no viewpoint is selected, the Convert To Redline tool will create a new viewpoint automatically.

Clear   Clears the current measurement from the screen.

Transform Selected Items   Moves or rotates the currently selected object the distance specified by a measuring tool. Use Transform Selected Items to move the object in the direction that you specified. For example, if you selected the bottom of an object and then the top of an object with a measuring tool, your object will be moved up. Keep in mind that this is not a temporary transform that can be reset by using Reset Transform, but that it affects the file units and transforms; this is a permanent change to the object.

MOVING AN INCORRECT ELEMENT

Learning to use the Measure Transform tool can sometimes mean the difference between a project moving smoothly and a project with additional conflicts because of a misplaced appended item. There are times during an Append or Merge operation when objects could be improperly aligned, even given the best efforts of the project team. There is good news, though; all items in Navisworks can be moved. In most cases, entire file sets are selected and transformed to a new location.

Using the Measure Transform tool in conjunction with the selection tree lets you specify a distance to relocate the object. It helps to know a good reference or common location between the items when selecting your points. Another good idea is to have your snaps enabled when using the Measure Transform tool to help with selecting points.

REDLINE

Draw   Allows you to add redline shapes and text notes to your model. Redlines can only be added to a saved viewpoint or to a clash, which has a saved viewpoint. If there are no saved viewpoints, adding a tag will automatically create and save a viewpoint for you. Otherwise, you will receive an error, and you'll have to save a viewpoint before adding any redlines.

Color   Allows you to change the color of redlines.

Thickness   Changes the line thickness of the redlines being added; 9 is the maximum thickness.

TAGS

Add Tag   Inserts a tag into your model. If you have a viewpoint selected, the tag will be created within that viewpoint; otherwise, the tag will create its own viewpoint.

Tag ID   Allows you to enter the tag ID or number to use with Go To Tag.

Go To Tag   Once you enter the desired number, you can use the Go To Tag tool to take you to the tag.

Tag Selection   Scrolls through the tag and its associated viewpoints.

Renumber Tag IDs   Used to renumber the tag IDs; removes duplicates. This tool is useful when you're appending or merging files that may have existing tag IDs.

COMMENTS

View Comments   Toggles the Comments palette on and off. From here, you can manage the comments created throughout the model.

Find Comments   Opens the Find Comments palette. You can search through both comments and tags for text, author, comment ID, status, comment, and date modified.

Renumber Comment IDs   Used to renumber the comment IDs; removes duplicates. This tool is useful when you're appending or merging files that may have existing comment IDs.

COLLABORATE

Collaborate   Enables a collaboration session using Windows NetMeeting.

Drive   Enables the user to become the driver of a remote computer.

Refresh   Shares model updates with each member of the team.

Animation

This tab contains the Create, Playback, Script, and Export panels (Figure 1.21).

FIGURE 1.21
Animation tab

CREATE

Animator Toggles the Animator palette on and off (same as the Animator located on the Home tab). Animator allows for the animation of objects to bring realism to your project.

Record Begins to record your actions (Walk, Fly, Zoom, and other actions in Navisworks). The recording is saved as an animation in saved viewpoints that you can later edit or add to as needed.

PLAYBACK

After an animation has been created, you gain access to the Playback tools. From the drop-down, select the animation that you wish to play, and use the tools available to play the animation. You can also use the slide at the bottom of Playback to manually change the display of the playback.

SCRIPT

Enable Scripts Enables and disables scripts. Once a script has been created, it has to be enabled before the action created can be utilized. For example, if you created a script to operate a door on approach, enabling scripts will allow this to occur.

Scripter Toggles the Scripter palette on and off (same as the Scripter located on the Home tab). The Scripter adds interactivity to your animated objects.

EXPORT

Export Animation Exports the current animation.

View

The View tab contains Stereo, Navigation Aids, Grids & Levels, Scene View, and Workspace panels (Figure 1.22).

FIGURE 1.22
View tab

STEREO

Enable Stereo Stereo, or stereoscopic viewing, allows you to view the 3D model through stereo-enabled hardware (i.e., in true 3D), including active and passive stereo viewing glasses. This option is only available if you have the required hardware as well as the correct driver and display settings.

Navigation Aids

Navigation Bar   Toggles the Navigation Bar on and off. Contains ViewCube, SteeringWheels, Pan, Zoom, Orbit, Look, Walk, and Fly tools.

ViewCube   Toggles the ViewCube on and off. The ViewCube allows you to switch between views of your model. Use ViewCube to set a Home view that you can easily get back as you navigate around your model.

HUD   In Head Up Display, or HUD for short, the x-, y-, and z-axes, the position readout, and the grids display on and off. All of the HUDs are displayed in the lower-left corner of the screen.

> **XYZ Axes**   As you can see in Figure 1.23, this option shows the X, Y, Z visual orientation of the camera (or the Third Person position if Third Person has been enabled).
>
> **Position Readout**   As you can see in Figure 1.23, this option shows the X, Y, Z textual position of the camera (or the Third Person position if Third Person has been enabled).
>
> **Grids**   Displays the Grid location HUD, as shown in Figure 1.23. With the Grid HUD turned on, you can see your level as well as the grid reference.

FIGURE 1.23
XYZ axes, position
readout, and grids

F(2)-4(1) : Ground Floor
X: 2.87 m   Y: -7.26 m   Z: 0.67 m

Reference Views   Toggles the Plan and Section views on and off. Both reference views allow you to gain perspective and location within your model, especially in large models. To use this feature, drag the white triangle to move yourself around. Additional tools are available on the context menu to aid in navigation.

Grids & Levels

Show Grid   Toggles the grid on or off.

Mode   Allows you to change how the grid is displayed in Navisworks. Choose from Fixed, Below, Above, or Above And Below.

File   Permits you to choose the active file and change settings for the grids as needed.

Level   Controls the default level based on the active file.

Scene View

Full Screen   Clears away all tabs and palettes and displays Navisworks in Full Screen mode. Press F11 to exit Full Screen mode and return to your tools.

Split View   Allows you to add horizontal and vertical screen splits. Each view can be set to represent a different view of the model. Only one view can be active at a time.

Background   Opens the Background Settings dialog box, which allows you to change the background color and scheme.

Window Size   Opens the Window Size dialog box, which allows you change the size of the Navisworks canvas. If you change the size and want to return to the default, change back to Use View.

Show Title Bars   Show or hides the title bars on secondary display view windows.

Workspace

Windows   Serves as a central list all of the palettes and toggles them on and off.

Load Workspace   Workspaces retain information about which windows are open, their positions, and the size of the application window. The Load Workspaces drop-down contains predefined workspaces as well as any custom workspaces. Workspaces do not maintain changes to the ribbon but do include changes made to the Quick Access toolbar.

>   **Safe Mode**   Opens the workspace with minimal features.
>
>   **Navisworks Minimal**   Loads the workspace with the fewest tools and most space in the scene.
>
>   **Navisworks Standard**   Loads the workspace with the most commonly used tools and palettes.
>
>   **Navisworks Extended**   Opens the workspace with the most tools. This workspace is recommended for advanced users.
>
>   **More Workspaces**   Opens previously saved workspaces.

Save Workspace   Saves the current workspace as an XML file.

Output

The Output tab contains Print, Send, Publish, Export Scene, Visuals, and Export Data panels (Figure 1.24 and Figure 1.26).

FIGURE 1.24
Output tab

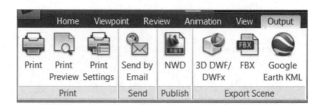

Print

Print   Sends the current view to a printer.

Print Preview   Creates a preview of the view to be printed.

Print Settings   Allows you to specify the printer settings.

SEND

Send By Email   Saves the current file and uses your default email application to prepare an email to send. It can be used to send either an NWF or NWD file, but an NWD
file is considerably larger. Make sure the file size meets the requirements of the email
provider.

PUBLISH

NWD   Creates an NWD file (NWD is a file that contains all model geometry together with
Navisworks-specific data, such as review markups, viewpoints, or timeline sequence). You
can also set options such as May Be Re-saved or set the file to expire within a certain timeframe (Figure 1.25).

FIGURE 1.25
Publish dialog box

When using Publish to create an NWD file, you can't save to previous versions of
Navisworks, but you have access to all the other features and functions of Publish. If you need
to create an NWD file for an older version of Navisworks, you will have to use Save As instead.
The downside is that you will no longer have access to the Publish options.

EXPORT SCENE

3D DWF   Exports all materials and geometry into a 3D DWF file.

FBX   Exports an FBX® file out of Navisworks. Allows you to include things like lights, cameras, and textures in your export.

Google Earth KML   Google Earth KML files can be exported from Navisworks. The exporter creates a compressed KML file with the extension .kmz.

VISUALS

FIGURE 1.26
Output tab
continued

Image   Opens the Export Image dialog box. This dialog box allows you to export an image of the current scene.

Rendered Image   Opens the Rendered Image dialog box, which allows you to export a rendered image.

Animation   Opens the Animation Export dialog box. You can choose from Source, Renderer, Output Type, and Size.

Piranesi EPix   Exports an EPX file for rendering in Piranesi from Informatix.

EXPORT DATA

Clash Tests   Exports the settings for all of the clash tests created in Clash Detective into an XML file.

TimeLiner CSV   Exports the current TimeLiner tasks into a CSV file.

Current Search   Saved Find Items criteria can be exported from Navisworks into an XML file and imported into other sessions of Navisworks.

Search Sets   Saved search sets can be exported from Navisworks into an XML file and imported into other sessions of Navisworks.

Viewpoints   Exports all of the viewpoints into an XML file. This is a text-based XML file and the images are not exported. This file contains all associated data, including camera positions, sections, hidden items, material overrides, redlines, comments, tags, and collision-detection settings. The XML file can be imported into other Navisworks files, and it creates all the views from the original project.

Viewpoints Report   Creates an HTML file or report of JPEG files of all saved viewpoints. The report contains camera position, comments, and other associated data. If you have created an animation, the report will also include the animation frames as individual images as part of the report.

PDS Tags   Exports all PDS tag data from the model into a TAG file.

Item Tools

The Item Tools tab (Figure 1.27) gives you a centralized location for several useful tools, such as Hold, Zoom, and SwitchBack. When you select an item from the selection tree or canvas, Item Tools will appear and let you take advantage of the following tools:

FIGURE 1.27
Item Tools tab

SwitchBack   SwitchBack allows you to select an object and open a similar view for editing in its authoring program; in this case, it would be Revit, AutoCAD and AutoCAD-based programs, and MicroStation and MicroStation-based programs. You must have the corresponding program installed on the same computer as Navisworks in order for SwitchBack to work.

In Navisworks 2011 and earlier, you could only access SwitchBack from the Clash Detective Results tab. It was added to the Item Tools tab in Navisworks 2012 to improve workflow.

Hold   The Hold function allows you to pick an object and physically "hold" onto it as you navigate through your model. That means that when you have an object selected and you're using a tool like Walk or Fly, you could have an object Walk along your path with you.

The object itself does not respect things like Gravity and Collision, but at least you have a visual representation of your item as your navigate through the model.

The Hold function can be useful for things like equipment moving down a hallway or moving a duct run briefly to understand the impact farther down the line. Let's briefly explore the concept of how to use Hold:

1. Select an object.
2. Select Hold from the Item Tools tab.
3. Use a Navigation tool (Walk, Fly, Orbit, Pan, Zoom, etc.) to move around your model. Your object will move with you.
4. When you are finished, you can select the object again and use Reset Transform to return the object to its original location.

Look At   Provides quick and easy access to the Focus On Item and Zoom tools, which are also located on the Navigation Bar.

Visibility   Provides additional access to Hide and Require, which are also located on the Home tab.

Transform   Within Navisworks, you have the ability to both visually and dimensionally move objects. The Transform tools located here allow for moving, rotating, and scaling objects. You also have access to the Dimensional drop-down as well.

When objects have been transformed, you can select the object later and use Reset Transform to return the object to its original position.

Appearance   Gives you access to object appearance tools so you can change things like color and transparency of your objects. Use Reset Appearance to restore an object to its original state.

Links   Gives you a centralized location for the Link tools, where you can add, edit, and reset the links for your model.

Status Bar, Performance Indicators, and Context Menus

Located in the bottom-right corner of the screen is the status bar, which contains four performance indicators that give you feedback on the performance of your computer and currently loaded Navisworks model (Figure 1.28).

FIGURE 1.28
Status bar

Pencil Bar Indicates how much of the current view is drawn, that is, how much image dropout there is in the current view. When the progress bar is at 100 percent, the scene is completely drawn, with no dropout. The icon changes color when a redraw is in progress. While the scene is being drawn, the pencil changes to yellow. If there is too much data to handle and your computer cannot process this quickly enough for Navisworks, then the pencil changes to red, indicating dropout.

Disk Bar Indicates how much of the current model is loaded from the local hard drive. When the progress bar is at 100 percent, the entire model, including geometry and property information, is loaded into memory. The icon changes color when a file load is in progress. While the data is being read, the disk changes to yellow. If there is too much data to handle and your machine cannot process it quickly enough for Navisworks, then the disk changes to red, indicating a potential problem.

Web Server Bar Indicates how much of the current model is downloaded from a web server. When the progress bar is at 100 percent, the entire model has been downloaded. The icon changes color when a file load is in progress. While data is being downloaded, the web server changes to yellow. If there is too much data to handle and your computer cannot process it quickly enough for Navisworks, then the web server changes to red, indicating a potential problem.

Memory Bar Indicates the amount of system memory being utilized by Navisworks.

Navisworks uses a few context menus that contain various tools. These tools can help you save time once you master when and how to leverage them.

No Item Selected This context menu (Figure 1.29) has a variety of tools that are found across various tabs and toolbars within Navisworks but that have been centralized for easy access. Access this menu by right-clicking in white space away from geometry. Once the menu is open, select your tool.

FIGURE 1.29
Context menu, with
no items selected

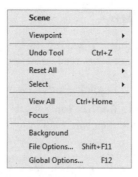

With Item Selected   The With Item Selected context menu contains even more tools to help you along your way. Access this menu (Figure 1.30) by right-clicking once you've selected the geometry. If you right-click when no geometry is selected (right-clicking on the object instead of selecting it first), Navisworks will select that single piece of geometry and open this context menu as well, saving you the step of having to select the object first.

FIGURE 1.30
Context menu, with
an item selected

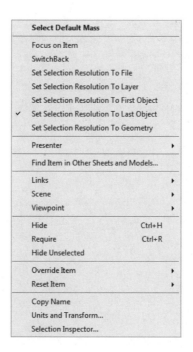

Notice that under the Scene flyout, the No Item Selected context menu can still be accessed. Take note of the additional flyout tools available as well: Links, Viewpoint, Override Item, and Reset Item.

The Bottom Line

Understand the ribbon.   Knowing the locations of various tools within the Ribbon provides a good foundation for being able to quickly access items across the Navisworks interface.

Master It   Can you quickly locate Gravity and Collision?

Use the Measure and Redline tools.   The Measure and Redline tools are useful in Navisworks throughout a project, and having a basic understanding of these tools is essential.

Master It   Locate two columns and use the Measure Shortest Distance tool. Can you create a viewpoint and convert this to a redline?

Chapter 2

Files and File Types

Chapter 1, "Getting to Know Autodesk Navisworks," introduced you to the basics of the Autodesk® Navisworks® 2013 interface. In this chapter, we'll cover the principles of the various file types and the process of aggregating these disparate files to create a single whole-project view of your model. By bringing together geometry and data from multidisciplinary teams, you can explore and review complex models in real time.

One of the most important things you can do to become proficient at Navisworks is get a firm grasp on file types and the process of how they are aggregated. File aggregation is one of the core strengths of Navisworks and one that is the foundation for all the features you'll discover in the following chapters. After all, this is how you bring your project together. Spend some time with these concepts and you'll be far more successful!

In this chapter, you'll learn to:

◆ Understand Navisworks file formats

◆ Open and append various files

◆ Configure object enablers

Navisworks File Types

The power of Navisworks rests in its ability to open files originated from a variety of design and engineering applications and its capacity to then share and coordinate these different file types into a single data-rich, intelligent model. The composite model of aggregated files can then be selectively available or viewed by all parties involved to enhance the design review and coordination process. In addition, Navisworks converts and compresses most files up to 80 percent of their original size, so sharing and collaborating are greatly improved. This section will cover the numerous file types and explain the differences. We will also explore some of the standard workflows and provide best practices for file sharing and aggregation.

Native File Formats

Navisworks utilizes three native file formats: NWD, NWC, and NWF. This section will explain the differences and explore some of the various workflows.

NWD File Format

An NWD, or Navisworks Document, file is the basic file format that contains all geometry, relevant object properties, and clash tests, as well as any markup, comments, and viewpoint information. As the project evolves, an NWD can be thought of as a snapshot of the model that captures the current conditions or milestone events. This also includes clash tests and 4D simulations, which will be covered in subsequent chapters. The file size of most NWDs is considerably smaller compared to the corresponding CAD/BIM formats.

NWC File Format

NWC, or Navisworks Cache, files are generated by default when CAD/BIM files or laser scans are opened, merged, or appended in Navisworks. They can also be created by using a designated file exporter, which we'll cover later, in the section "File Exporters." NWC files are read-only files and can be thought of as a transfer mechanism to convert CAD/BIM and other model data into a format that Navisworks recognizes. All geometry, relevant object property information, and display settings from the original source files will carry over with the NWC export. Once the file is opened in Navisworks, any changes made—such as redlines, markups, viewpoints, or display overrides—cannot be saved back to this format.

By default, when the native CAD/BIM format files are first brought in, Navisworks creates a file with the same name but with the .nwc file extension in the same directory as the original source file. This is an intentional behavior and an important concept for a successful Navisworks project. Keep in mind that good model-management skills can help your projects run more smoothly.

When NWC files are opened, merged, or appended, Navisworks compares the original data to the newly created NWC file and re-caches the file if data in the original file is newer than the NWC. This ensures that as changes are made to the project design, they are reflected in your Navisworks project. If no changes are detected, Navisworks opens from the original NWC file, resulting in quicker loading.

> **UPDATING NWC FILES**
>
> To ensure changes to your CAD/BIM files are updated correctly in your Navisworks model, the filename *must* remain the same. If the source filename changes, a new NWC file will be created.

NWF File Format

NWF files host no 3D geometry but rather contain links to the geometry from the original native source files (see Figure 2.1). Besides the links, NWF files contain such items as markup data, viewpoints, comments, graphical overrides, search/selection sets, and TimeLiner and Clash Detective data. We'll explore these topics in more detail in future chapters.

When working with the NWF file format, you'll notice the file size for NWFs is extremely small as compared to the NWC and NWD formats; however, remember that the user must have access to the original source files to view them properly. As you work toward mastery of Navisworks, consider using the NWF as the standard file format during your project. While NWD files can be thought of as static snapshots that capture specific milestones, the NWF workflow is dynamic and allows for easy updating of design changes from the original source files. Later in the book, you'll explore clash detection, 4D simulation, and other concepts, so having a good grasp of the file formats is crucial.

FIGURE 2.1
Source files linked to the NWF file format

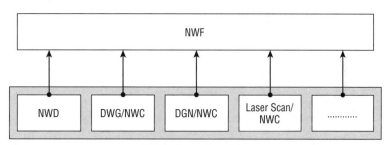

Original Source Data Files

USING NWF AND NWD FORMATS IN A TYPICAL WORKFLOW

Now that we've covered the basic file formats, let's look at a typical workflow. Typical Navisworks workflows utilize a combination of NWD, NWC, and NWF files. At the start of the project, the project coordinator opens Navisworks and appends the original source 3D data files from the specific trades on the project (e.g., Architecture, MEPF, Structure, Civil 3D®, or Existing Conditions files). Navisworks converts these files to the NWC format and places the NWC files in the same directory as the original source files.

When the project coordinator saves the Navisworks session, the project is saved as an NWF format, which captures the link to the saved source and NWC files. In the meantime, the architect, MEPF coordinator, structural engineer, and civil engineer all make changes, such as moving objects or adding/removing components, to their original 3D data files. When the project coordinator opens the project saved as an NWF, Navisworks will look for the linked files and do a quick comparison to determine if any of the original 3D data files are newer than the NWC files. In our sample workflow, all of these original data sources were modified, so Navisworks re-caches those files and overwrites the original NWC files with the new data. Periodically, the project coordinator will save or publish the model to the NWD file format to archive specific milestone events or share with external users who do not have access to the original source data files (see Figure 2.2).

In the event the original source files are renamed or moved, Navisworks prompts you for their location, as shown in Figure 2.3. If the accompanying NWC files are moved or deleted, Navisworks automatically re-caches the files and creates a new NWC file.

FIGURE 2.2
Typical project
workflow

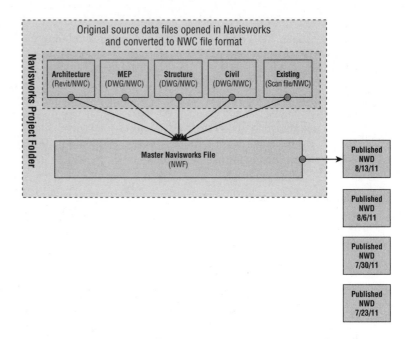

FIGURE 2.3
The Resolve
dialog box

To manually locate original source data files click the Browse button and navigate to the new location. When the NWF file is resaved, it will remember the new location for these files. Also, it should be noted that Navisworks uses a relative path structure when saving files. If your project folder contains several subfolders for the various disciplines (Architect, MEP Engineer, Structural Engineer, etc.), you can share this project folder without breaking any of the links.

WORKING WITH NWF FILES

Dynamic work environments sometimes require that changes be made to the CAD/BIM source files while users are also referencing them in an active Navisworks session. By default, Navisworks locks down the source files so they are read-only when the NWF file is open. You can override this setting in the Options Editor to modify and save the source files while keeping your initial Navisworks session open.

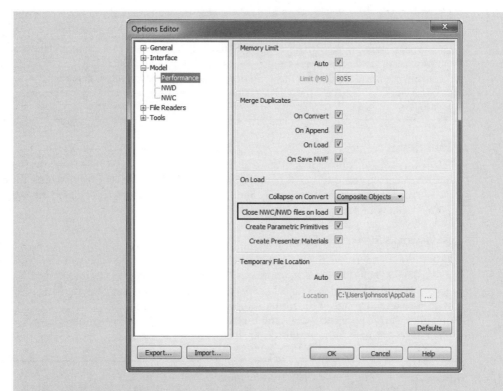

The Options Editor can be accessed via Application ➤ Options ➤ Model ➤ Performance. Uncheck the Close NWC/NWD Files On Load setting. If this setting is unchecked, users can make changes to all subsequent design source files, regardless of whether the NWF file is open.

As a best practice, it's recommended that during an ongoing project, the NWF file format be utilized so that the original source files can be updated and re-cached. Remember, the NWF format is strictly a container that links to the different source files. Graphical overrides such as changing model element colors and transparency are captured and stored in the NWF file. As a result, when updated cache files are loaded, Navisworks will remember your graphical settings and apply them to the updated files. This principle is similar to the concept of external references (Xrefs) in Autodesk® AutoCAD® files, whereas changes made to the original source files will update the NWF file.

Similar to the NWC format, the NWD format includes all geometry and object property data but can save changes and graphical overrides to the model. The primary difference is that NWD files do not update or re-cache if changes have been made to the original source data. Sometimes, having a static representation of your model is useful if you need to archive specific milestone events. Also, since this format has all of the geometry "baked" into the file, it is a perfect format to share with other users without worrying about supplying the accompanying source files. The NWD file format is also compatible with the free viewer, Navisworks Freedom. Additional detail on Navisworks Freedom is covered in Chapter 12, "Collaborating Outside of Navisworks."

RESOLVING MODEL UPDATES

The benefit of working with NWF files is that as changes are made to the source files, these changes are reflected in the Navisworks model. Occasionally, you might find that Navisworks isn't re-caching the source file to display these changes. If this happens, simply delete the NWC and reopen Navisworks. A new NWC file will be created, and the latest geometry will be uploaded into your project.

File Readers

File readers allow Navisworks to open and append additional file types from a variety of design and engineering applications. When you open a CAD/BIM model in Navisworks, the appropriate file reader is loaded automatically and all model geometry and associated metadata is incorporated into your scene.

NAVISWORKS SUPPORTED FORMATS

In addition to the native file formats (NWD, NWC, and NWF), Navisworks can read over 40 different 3D CAD/BIM formats, as shown in Table 2.1. Model entities contained in both 2D and 3D geometry and all associated object property data are typically supported. Being able to work with such a wide range of file formats allows Navisworks to accommodate almost every design and engineering application. Having this level of file compatibility in turn allows you to collaborate, coordinate, and communicate effectively.

TABLE 2.1:   Supported CAD/BIM formats

FORMAT	EXTENSIONS
Navisworks	.nwd, .nwf, .nwc
AutoCAD	.dwg, .dwf
MicroStation (SE, J, V8, XM)	.dgn, .prp, .prw
3D Studio	.3ds, .prj
ACIS SAT	.sat, .sab
CATIA	.model, .session, .exp, .dlv3, .CATPart, .CATProduct, .cgr
CIS/2	.stp
DWF™	.dwf, .dwfx, .w2d
FBX®	.fbx
IFC	.ifc
IGES	.igs, .iges
Inventor®	.ipt, .iam, .ipj

TABLE 2.1:   Supported CAD/BIM formats   *(CONTINUED)*

FORMAT	EXTENSIONS
Informatix MAN	`.man, .cv7`
JT Open	`.jt`
NX	`.prt`
PDS Design Review	`.dri`
Parasolids	`.x_b`
Pro/ENGINEER	`.prt, .asm, .g, .neu`
Revit®	`.rvt, .rfa, .rte`
RVM	`.rvm`
SketchUp	`.skp`
SolidWorks	`.prt, .sldprt, .asm, .sldasm`
STEP	`.stp, .step`
STL	`.stl`
VRML	`.wrl, .wrz`

In addition to the CAD/BIM formats, Navisworks is a powerful tool for viewing laser scan files, sometimes referred to as point clouds. These files are made up of millions, even billions, of geo-referenced points that typically define the surface of an object. The benefit is that existing conditions such as older building structures or civil site plans can now be captured easily and displayed inside Navisworks to compare against proposed designs. Table 2.2 lists the supported laser scan formats.

TABLE 2.2:   Supported laser scan formats

FORMAT	EXTENSIONS
ASCII laser file	`.asc, .txt`
Faro	`.fls, .fws, .iQscan, .iQmod, .iQwsp`
Leica	`.pts, .ptx`
Riegl	`.3dd`
Trimble	Native file not supported; convert to ASCII laser file
Z+F	`.zfc, .zfs`

CONFIGURING FILE READERS

Configuring file readers is mostly automatic, but there are times when you need to adjust settings depending on the file type. Navisworks provides a full menu for each native file reader. Options vary depending on the file utilized, but the more common file types (DWG™/DXF™ and DGN™ file types) have a robust menu with options to configure visibility settings. Here are the basic steps:

1. To access the native file reader's menu, navigate to the Application button ➢ Options ➢ File Readers.

2. In the Options Editor, expand the File Readers hierarchy on the left, as shown in Figure 2.4.

FIGURE 2.4
File reader's
Options Editor

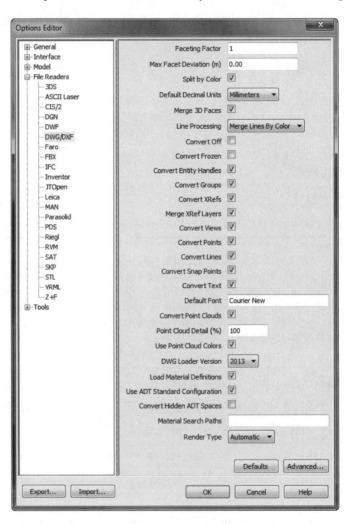

3. Select the appropriate file reader and modify the settings as necessary.

4. Click OK to return to the main Navisworks application.

Since the DWG file format is one of the most recognized file reader formats in Navisworks, let's investigate these options in greater detail. The DWG/DXF file reader uses Autodesk ObjectDBX™ technology, which is guaranteed to read all object geometry and information from all applications that utilize this framework. A partial snapshot of the supported object entities includes the following:

- All 2D and 3D geometry
- Points and snap points
- Named views
- Layers
- Colors
- Blocks, groups, and Xrefs
- Text
- Attributes
- Object properties

Looking at the DWG/DXF file reader, you can see a number of options that allow you to configure the settings of this file reader. Let's take a deeper look at these options:

Faceting Factor   This option allows you to control the level of faceting. The default value is 1. Greater values produce smoother results but add additional polygons and increase the file size.

Max Facet Deviation   This option controls the maximum distance between the facet and the actual geometry. If the distance is greater than the specified value, Navisworks adds more facets to meet this value. If the value is set to 0, this function is ignored.

Split By Color   Certain compound objects are displayed as one entity in Navisworks. Checking this box will split these compound objects into individual components based on their color. An example is a door assembly that can be split into the individual door frame and door.

Default Decimal Units   This option specifies the type of units used to open the DWG/DXF file.

Merge 3D Faces   Occasionally, some 3D models will have adjoining faces that consist of the same color, layer, and parent. This option allows Navisworks to interpret those faces as a single object.

Line Processing   When converting lines and polylines, Navisworks provides three options for processing them:

Merge Lines By Color   Navisworks will merge any lines on the same layer or proxy entity that contain the same color. This option is useful because it helps speed up navigation and overall conversion. This option is checked by default.

As Provided   With this option, no additional conversion takes place. All lines and polyline elements are displayed as they are specified in their native DWG file.

Separate All Lines   Use this option if you want to split all line elements into their respective nodes for each segment of the line.

Convert Off This option allows Navisworks to convert certain layers that are switched off in the DWG file. When checked, any file that contains hidden layers will be marked as hidden in Navisworks.

Convert Frozen Keeping this option checked will convert layers that are frozen in the DWG file. Any file that contains frozen layers will be marked as hidden in Navisworks when open or appended.

Convert Entity Handles Keeping entity handles is an important aspect of object selection. This option will attach entity handle information to the object properties in your Navisworks model.

Convert Groups This option allows you to retain your group settings in the DWG file. Files that have this option enabled gain an additional selection level in the selection tree.

Convert Xrefs For those who want a seamless opening/appending of their DWG file with all Xrefs, this feature allows you to convert all reference files automatically. If left unchecked, you need to append the files manually.

Merge Xref Layers This option allows you to merge the layers in an Xref file with the main DWG file in the selection tree.

Convert Views Keep this option checked if you want to convert your named views in AutoCAD to viewpoints in Navisworks.

Convert Points This option will convert all points in your DWG file.

Convert Lines Select this option to convert lines and arcs in your DWG file.

Convert Snap Points This option will convert snap points in your DWG file.

Convert Text As its name implies, this option will convert text in your DWG file.

Default Font This option allows you to define which font you want to use for the converted text. There is no predefined list for this option; rather, you need to type in the name of the font you wish to use.

Convert Point Clouds DWG files that have embedded point cloud entities will only display if this box is checked. This option is separate from the laser scan/point cloud readers.

Point Cloud Detail This option allows you to specify the density of the point cloud. Values are between 1 and 100, where 100 is the maximum density. To assist with performance issues when working with larger point clouds, you might want to reduce this value to speed the conversion process.

Use Point Cloud Colors Certain point clouds contain native color coding of points. Unchecking this box will ignore these colors and default to the color profile specified in AutoCAD.

DWG Loader Version When working with DWG files that utilize ObjectDBX, this option allows you to specify which version to use when loading files. This feature is useful when configuring certain DWG object enablers. You'll learn more later in this chapter in the section "Object Enablers."

Load Material Definitions Select this option to extract material definitions from DWG files.

Use ADT Standard Configuration This option converts geometry and materials in your DWG file using the standard display configuration.

Convert Hidden ADT Spaces In certain modeling conventions, objects such as floors or ceilings may be drawn without proper thickness and thus lack any true visible 3D geometry. Select this option to display the hidden geometry.

Material Search Paths   When files with applied materials are opened or appended in Navisworks, the application will search for all material paths automatically. If additional materials are defined, you can manually specify the path in this field. Be sure to use a semicolon to separate the paths.

Render Type   These options define how the DWG file is displayed in Navisworks:

> **Automatic**   This option is selected by default and will read the DWG file with the settings that were saved in the DWG file.
>
> **Rendered, Shaded, or Wireframe**   Use these options to override the original settings in your DWG file if the file is not displaying correctly. We recommend that you save your DWG file with the proper display settings to avoid having to manually override these settings.

File Exporters

File exporters allow you to create native Navisworks NWC files directly from your original source data files for applications that aren't read natively in Navisworks. This section will explain why you need a file exporter, where to locate file exporters, and the typical workflow for exporting NWC files to Navisworks.

WHY YOU NEED A FILE EXPORTER

Certain file types, such as 3ds Max® (MAX) and ArchiCAD (PLN, PLA) files, are not recognized by Navisworks in their native format. Navisworks also installs file exporters for AutoCAD-based applications in addition to natively reading the DWG file format. When Navisworks is initially installed, it searches throughout your computer and identifies all compatible design and engineering applications. If a valid installation is detected, it installs the appropriate file exporter for that application. Since the file formats for most applications are unique, most file exporters are product and release year specific, so you may have multiple file exporters for the same product family. An example of this is having an AutoCAD file exporter for the 2012 release in addition to one for the 2013 release.

For users who do not have access to Navisworks, another option to consider is the NWC File Export Utility (a separate download), which converts the model geometry and any relevant object intelligence into the NWC file format for Navisworks to display. File exporters are also useful for individuals who want to publish their content to the smaller NWC file format for ease in sharing and collaborating. Furthermore, certain CAD applications have custom objects and external referenced files, which if not shared or configured properly, can lead to missing geometry in your Navisworks model display. The NWC File Export Utility removes all of these barriers and creates an easy and effective way to share your model data with other Navisworks users.

LOCATING AND INSTALLING FILE EXPORTERS

When a new application is installed *after* the original Navisworks installation, the file exporters for that application will need to be reinstalled. They can easily be added afterward in a few simple steps. Let's explore:

1. Depending on what operating system you're using, go to your Control Panel and select Add/Remove Software or Uninstall/Change Program.

2. Select Autodesk Navisworks 2013 32 Bit Exporter Plug-ins or Autodesk Navisworks 2013 64 Bit Exporter Plug-ins from the list. If you're running a 64-bit OS, you may have both.

3. Double-click the appropriate file exporter.

4. In the Navisworks Exporter dialog box, select Add Or Remove Features.

5. Select the appropriate applications for which to install an exporter, as shown in Figure 2.5.

FIGURE 2.5
Navisworks
Exporter list

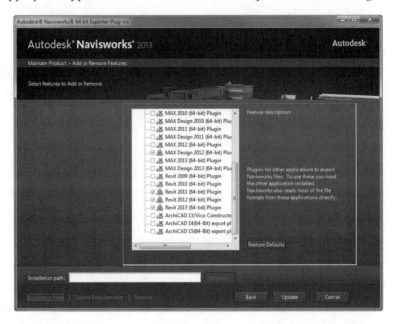

6. Click Update. Navisworks will install the new exporters for the selected applications.

7. Select Finish to close the Exporter dialog box.

In addition to these steps, you can use the Repair or Reinstall functions from the main Navisworks Exporter dialog box to install the file exporters. When you're reinstalling Navisworks, it may take longer than using the Repair feature.

For users without Navisworks, Autodesk provides the NWC File Export Utility free of charge for all users. You can download it from the Autodesk website at www.autodesk.com/navisworks. Once you've downloaded and installed the EXE file, follow all onscreen instructions to complete the installation process. This process will install the NWC File Export Utility on all relevant installed applications.

EXPORTING NWC FILES FROM SOURCE FILES

New to Navisworks 2013 is the ability to import native Revit® files into your Navisworks scene. Although this is the most direct option, there may be times where you want to have more control over what parts of your Revit model are imported into Navisworks. To accommodate these workflows, you will still need to use the NWC exporter. To export NWC files from Revit-based applications, follow these steps:

1. In Revit, navigate to the Add-ins tab and select Navisworks 2013 from the External Tools panel (Figure 2.6).

FIGURE 2.6
Choose Navisworks
2013 from the
External Tools
panel in Revit.

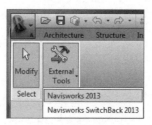

EXPORTER NOT FUNCTIONING?

If the Export button for the Navisworks exporter is not displayed properly in the Add-ins tab, check to make sure the NWC File Export Utility is installed correctly. For an unavailable (grayed-out) button, make sure you have exited from all active commands in Revit. Also, make sure you're in a 3D model view. The export feature will not work when you're viewing schedules, quantities, or other non-graphical data.

If you installed any AutoCAD-based application after installing the NWC File Export Utility, you need to update the exporter plug-ins to reflect these changes.

---

2. In the Export Scene As dialog box, specify the filename and select the desired storage location.

3. To adjust the export settings, select the Navisworks Settings button at the bottom of the Export Scene As dialog box.

4. In the Navisworks Options Editor, expand the File Readers hierarchy and select Revit, as shown in Figure 2.7.

5. Adjust the settings and click OK to accept the changes, or click Cancel to return to the Export Scene As dialog box.

FIGURE 2.7
Navisworks Options
Editor for Revit

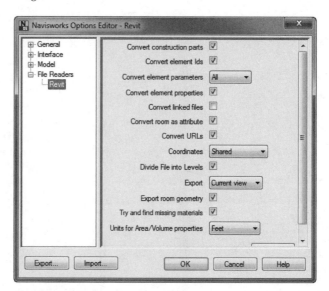

To export NWC files from AutoCAD-based applications, the NWC File Export Utility installs ARX plug-ins for any AutoCAD-based product such as AutoCAD Civil 3D, AutoCAD MEP, AutoCAD Plant 3D, or AutoCAD Architecture. This utility is available for any AutoCAD platform from the 2004 release on.

To use the AutoCAD command line to export NWC files, follow these steps:

1. Type **NWCOUT** in the command line of your AutoCAD model.

2. In the Export To Navisworks dialog box, specify the filename, select the desired storage location, and click Save.

3. To adjust the export settings, type **NWOPT** at the command line in AutoCAD.

4. In the Navisworks Options Editor, expand the File Readers hierarchy and select DWG, as shown in Figure 2.8.

5. Adjust the settings and click OK to accept the changes, or click Cancel to return to the AutoCAD main window.

FIGURE 2.8
Navisworks Options
Editor for AutoCAD

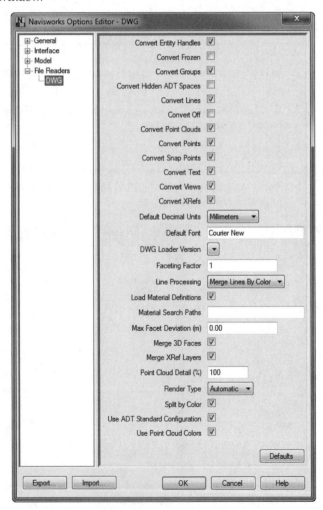

File Aggregation

The building industry has expanded and become more technically diverse over the last few decades. As a result, there are a plethora of design and engineering applications aimed at solving their own small piece of the building puzzle. Couple that with the fact that each of these applications has its own unique file format, and you can quickly see how managing these files becomes a challenge. This is where Navisworks shines by allowing the user to combine these disparate files into a composite model, thereby removing the interoperability challenges of the numerous formats.

In this section, we'll explore the concept of aggregating these various file formats and ways to automate the creation of the composite model. As you read through this section, think about a current, or past, project and start to identify the different file types or disciplines that make up the model. Doing so will help you understand all of the moving pieces in most projects—and will also make the exercises much more relevant and speed up your mastery of Navisworks.

Whether you're using a native NWC or NWD file or bringing in one of the numerous CAD formats, opening files is the first step to creating your composite model. Navisworks is an intuitive program, so you'll notice that there is more than one way to accomplish most tasks. By design, this flexibility is designed to accommodate most users' habits and keep the learning curve minimal.

Opening Files

We'll explore a couple of methods for opening files in Navisworks. Navisworks will keep a list of your recently opened files in the Open dialog box. By default, this list is limited to 4 files; however, you can change this amount up to a maximum of 16. To override the default, choose the Application button ➤ Global Options ➤ General ➤ Environment and adjust the value for Maximum Recently Used Files.

NEW FILES

To open a new file, follow these steps:

1. Click the blue application icon in the upper-left corner.

2. If your file is listed in the Recent Documents list, select the file you want to open.

3. If your file is not listed, click the small arrow to the right of the Open icon and choose Open, as shown in Figure 2.9.

   If you hover your cursor over the Open command, the Recent Documents list will change to reflect the various open options.

4. Select the appropriate file type from the drop-down list (see Figure 2.10).

5. Navigate to the file location, select the file, and click Open.

   You can also use the default keyboard shortcut Ctrl+O to access the Open dialog box.

FIGURE 2.9
The Navisworks
Open menu

FIGURE 2.10
List of all file
formats Navisworks
can read

When opening multiple files at once, you can use the Shift and Ctrl keys to access several files in the Open dialog box. Also, you can bypass the Open dialog box by simply dragging and dropping your file directly into the Navisworks model space window. Be careful, though, if you have an existing file already open; dragging a new file into Navisworks will close the old file without saving changes and open the new file.

Open via URL

In addition to opening files from a local or network drive, you can open files from a web server using the Open URL command. Here's how:

1. Select the Open command under the blue application icon in the upper-left corner. Choose Open URL from the list.

2. In the Open URL dialog box shown in Figure 2.11, enter the appropriate web server address and click OK. A sample model is available for training purposes here:

   `http://download.autodesk.com/us/navisworks/Brewery.nwd`

FIGURE 2.11
Open URL
dialog box

Currently, this function only works with web servers that require no authentication, so only unsecured files can be accessed via the URL command at this time.

Appending Files

Complex models may consist of multiple files from a variety of file formats and disciplines. The Append command allows you to build up your scene and create a composite model, which will provide the whole project view of your plan.

The Append command functions almost identically to the Open command, but instead of opening a new file, all existing files remain open in Navisworks while the new model is added to the overall scene. To use the Append command, do the following:

1. Start Navisworks and open a file.

2. To append another file to this scene, click the Append button on the left side of the Home tab (Figure 2.12).

FIGURE 2.12
Append button

3. In the Append dialog box, select the appropriate file type from the drop-down box.

4. Navigate to the file location and select the file (or hold down the Shift or Ctrl key to select multiple files). Click Open to append files into the existing scene. Remember, drag and drop does not append additional files but functions only as the Open command.

When files are appended into Navisworks, the application will attempt to align, rotate, and scale the subsequent files to reflect the current coordinate system of the existing model. This includes rescaling models with different units of measurement to match the current display. However, models that are designed in an entirely different coordinate system or view plane will not align properly. For information on translating models, see Chapter 6, "Documenting Your Project."

Merging Files

In the current geographically dispersed environment, it's feasible that multiple users will need access to the same Navisworks model at identical times for model review and coordination. The Merge feature allows multiple copies of the same model to be combined without any duplication.

When model design reviews are conducted with the various disciplines (Architect, MEP Engineer, Structural Engineer, etc.), having access to the Navisworks composite data model becomes paramount. Typically, most current Navisworks models are shared among the entire team as an NWD or NWF file with the associated source files for the external design reviews. Navisworks assists with the review process by providing markup tools such as redline and comments (which will be covered in Chapter 6). Since the models all contain the same model geometry, the only differences are any comments made by the different disciplines. The Merge command allows these multiple reviewed models to be combined into a single file. Any duplication of geometry is automatically removed, so the final file contains one set of geometry and all of the markups and comments from the different reviewers. It's important to note that this scenario works only with NWF files. The Merge command will function like the Append command with NWD files and ultimately display duplicates. Figure 2.13 shows a typical workflow where the master Navisworks file is shared with the various disciplines for the mechanical, structural, and architectural design reviews. After any comments, redlines, and markup data are recorded, the files are then returned to the project coordinator, who merges the three files into the single NWF file. Because all three files are copies and contain the same geometry, all duplication is removed in the merging process and only the unique comments and markup data are preserved.

All unique items such as non-duplicated geometry, redlines, comments, and viewpoints are merged into the single model. For information on merging models with embedded TimeLiner schedules, see Chapter 7, "4D Sequencing with TimeLiner."

To create a merged file, follow these steps:

1. Open Navisworks with one of the original files.

2. Click the drop-down arrow on the Append button and choose the Merge command, as shown in Figure 2.14. You can also use the default keyboard shortcut Ctrl+M.

3. In the Merge dialog box, select the appropriate file type from the drop-down box.

4. Select the appropriate file(s) and click Open.

5. All files without any duplicated elements are successfully merged into a single file.

FIGURE 2.13
Typical file-merging process

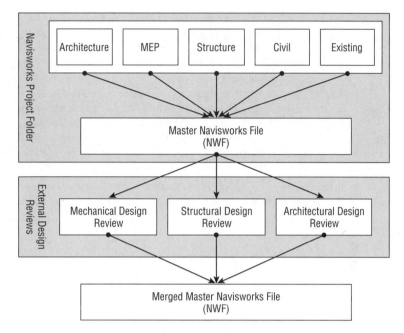

FIGURE 2.14
Merge command

Real World Scenario

TRACKING NAVISWORKS FILE VERSIONS

Inevitably, changes to designs will occur and require the master Navisworks model to be updated. The questions that arise are how to manage this process and what is the best practice for archiving the older files. On one job, a project team was receiving updated models from their subcontractors (subs) on a weekly basis. Originally, the subs were labeling their drawings with a date in the file-name. While this allowed us to identify the latest file easily, it kept breaking the links to our NWF master file since Navisworks was looking for the absolute path to a particular file. The workaround was to create a series of working folders with the name of each discipline (e.g., Architect, MEP, Structural, etc.).

We asked that the subs drop the date from the naming convention on their models and provide all updates using the same filename as the original submission. When they initially submitted their models, we created a new folder named after their discipline and placed their file in that folder. When the file was read into Navisworks, the generated NWC file was saved in the same folder as the original data source. As updated files were received from the subs, we renamed the working folder with the date to designate the date it was archived. This also became the date of the current model in the project. The new models were then saved in the discipline-named working folder; thus, the links in the NWF file remained intact. When the NWF file was opened, the new models were loaded and a new NWC file was generated and placed in the folder. Any changes such as display overrides, viewpoints, and markups were retained and applied to the new models.

In addition to the archiving of the NWC files, we made a weekly NWD file, which was a snapshot of the project. Since this was an archive of the project to date, we used the date in the naming convention for easy identification.

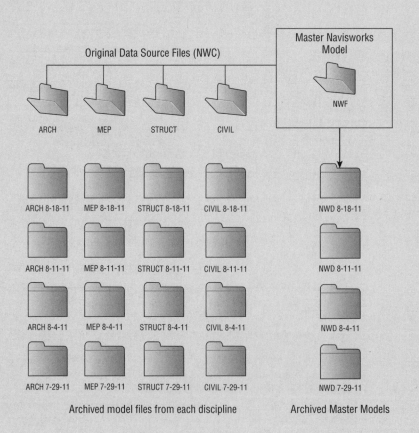

Refreshing Files

Because of the collaborative nature of Navisworks, it's possible that other users will be modifying the original source files during your current session. If you're using an NWF file that is referencing the NWC design files, you can refresh the model to update any changes made to the original source files while your current Navisworks session is still open. By default, this setting is disabled. To enable this feature, you need to make sure that the Close NWC/NWD Files On Load option is selected. You can set this option by choosing the Application button ➢ Options ➢ Model ➢ Performance ➢ On Load.

To refresh the model, click the Refresh button in the Project area of the Home tab, as shown in Figure 2.15, or use the default keyboard shortcut F5. Navisworks will compare the original source files to the existing NWC files and update if the source files are newer.

FIGURE 2.15
Refresh button

Deleting Files

Occasionally, you may want to delete files that are appended to your scene. You can delete files as long as they meet the following criteria:

◆ They are not saved or published into the NWD format.

◆ They contain at least one file in the scene.

To delete an appended file:

1. Open your Navisworks scene and locate the file to be deleted in the selection tree. (For more on the selection tree, review Chapter 4, "Climbing the Selection Tree.")

2. Right-click the file to be deleted.

3. Select Delete toward the bottom of the context menu. You can also select the file in the selection tree and press Delete on your keyboard.

   If you make a mistake and accidentally delete the wrong file, you'll need to re-append the file because the Undo command does not function in this mode.

Saving Files

When you're finished with your Navisworks session, you can either save your work as an NWF and maintain active links to your source files or save it as an NWD to capture a snapshot of your project. As you'll recall, NWC files are read-only and cannot be saved. We recommend that you maintain the NWF format while the project is under way to facilitate easy updates to the model. However, if you need to share the model with users who are using Navisworks Freedom or don't have access to the source files, you may want to consider saving as an NWD to lock the geometry into a single file.

Historically, Navisworks has been updated on a yearly development cycle that also includes updating the file format. While Navisworks can read older versions, users who haven't yet updated to the newer release may not be able to open the most current file format. To allow these users to view the newer files, you need to save down to an earlier version. Here's how:

1. Select the blue application icon in the upper-left corner of the screen and choose Save As from the list.

2. In the Save As dialog box, choose the appropriate file type (NWF or NWD) and version (Figure 2.16).

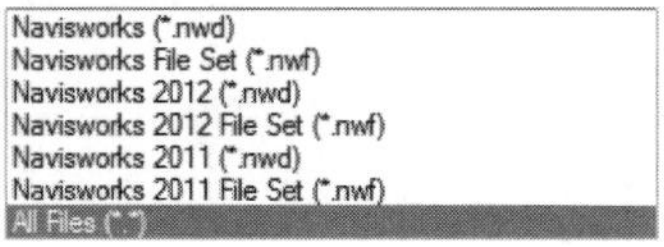

FIGURE 2.16
Navisworks formats
available for
saving to

| Navisworks (*.nwd) |
| Navisworks File Set (*.nwf) |
| Navisworks 2012 (*.nwd) |
| Navisworks 2012 File Set (*.nwf) |
| Navisworks 2011 (*.nwd) |
| Navisworks 2011 File Set (*.nwf) |
| All Files (*.*) |

3. Enter the appropriate filename and location, and choose Save.

Publishing Files

Periodically, you may want to share your Navisworks file with others. As an added layer of reassurance, Navisworks has several security features that should put to rest any fears about your file falling into the wrong hands. The Publish command in Navisworks allows users to embed additional document information, including file password protection and file expiration.

WHY YOU SHOULD USE THE PUBLISH COMMAND

The Publish feature is primarily used when sharing files outside an organization's regular ecosystem. The security features allow the file to be accessed only with the proper password and/or for a designated timeframe before expiring and becoming useless. Published files are only available as an NWD, so there is no need to worry about your source files being mishandled.

In our collaborative environment, published files are becoming an integral part of the design-review process to help manage the multiple versions of documents. By limiting the timeframe for access to these models, you can greatly reduce the chance that users will accidentally reference an out-of-date model. Also, publishing files is an extremely useful procedure for periodic archiving of the project files to ensure that no changes are made to the project snapshot.

PUBLISHING OPTIONS

Navisworks provides several options for users who want to publish their files. Here are the basic steps:

1. Select the blue application icon in the upper-left corner, and from the drop-down list, choose Publish.

   Alternatively, you can access the Publish command from the Output tab in the ribbon, as shown in Figure 2.17.

FIGURE 2.17
Accessing the
Publish command
from the ribbon

FIGURE 2.17
Accessing the
Publish command
from the ribbon

2. In the Publish dialog box, fill in the appropriate settings, as shown in Figure 2.18.

FIGURE 2.18
The Publish
dialog box

The following options are available in the Publish dialog box. In the first eight sections on the list, Navisworks will remember the last five entries for each of those fields.

Title   Users can create a title for the document. It can be different from the filename.

Subject   Users can enter a subject for the published document.

Author   Lists the author of the document.

Publisher   Lists the publisher of the document.

Published For   Lists for whom the document is published.

Copyright   Users can list any copyright information.

Keywords   Contains a selection of words that can be used to help search the document.

Comments   Allows you to enter supplementary information about the published document.

Password   The Password field can contain any combination of letters, numbers, spaces, and other keyboard characters. You must confirm your password before publishing the file. Also, if you lose or forget the password, there is no way to recover it, so select carefully!

Display At Password   This option allows you to toggle on/off the Publish dialog box when opening a password-protected file. If the box is left checked, all users who do not have the password to open the file will have read-only access to the document properties. This allows users to locate the resource that might assist with the password.

Expires   This option opens a calendar box and asks you to choose a specific expiration date. The expiration date can reference any future dates, but once the date has passed, the file cannot be opened.

May Be Re-saved   Check this option if you want to allow individuals to save changes to the published NWD file. If this option is left unchecked, users can only save changes as an NWF file.

Display On Open   This option displays the Publish dialog box every time the file is opened. The user has to acknowledge the message by clicking OK. Clicking the Cancel button or clicking the X in the upper-right corner of the window will cancel the loading of the file. If the file is password protected, the user must successfully supply the password before the dialog box is displayed.

Embed Textures   This option allows material assignments in the model to be embedded in the published file and available for other users.

Embed Database Properties   This option allows data from external databases to be accessible in published files for users without access to the database.

Prevent Object Property Export   This option masks the object properties of the file when published. You can share model geometry without fear of disclosing sensitive metadata that might compromise your intellectual property.

Emailing Files

Working in a collaborative environment sometimes requires that files be distributed to diverse groups. Email is an efficient way to quickly reach out to external project teams and third-party consultants who may not have access to a corporate network or server. The Navisworks file format, while useful for collaboration and security features, is also ideal for email because of its small file size.

Sending Files

In Navisworks, you can send your current scene, either NWD or NWF, to a dispersed group very efficiently, using these steps:

1. Select the blue application icon in the upper-left corner of the screen.

2. Choose Send By Email from the drop-down menu. You can also access this command in the Send area of the Output tab on the ribbon, as shown in Figure 2.19.

Navisworks will first save your file and then open a blank message from your current mail-delivery application. The Navisworks file will be attached to this message and ready to be sent off.

If you're working with NWF files, the send feature will transmit just the NWF portion of your project. Make sure all email recipients have access to the original source files when you send your project; otherwise, they won't be able to reference any of the geometry. As a best practice, you may want to standardize on NWD files when sending via email. Not only does this ensure that users can see all referenced geometry, but if the end users don't have access to a core version of Navisworks, they can still view the file using the Freedom viewer.

RECEIVING FILES

Receiving Navisworks files is similar to receiving most types of email attachments. Follow these steps to configure and open emailed files:

1. Download the attached Navisworks file to a designated storage space on your computer.

2. Double-click the File icon to start Navisworks, or open Navisworks and open the file using the Open command.

3. If you're receiving an NWF file, Navisworks will search for the referenced original source data files using the relative path that was saved in the original NWF file. As a best practice, consider using a common convention with the file hierarchy and drive letter on all projects. Even without a server to distribute files, Navisworks can still locate files based on the common naming conventions in the local folders.

4. If Navisworks can't locate the referenced files, you can either manually browse for the reference files and update the NWF or save the NWF file in the same directory with all the reference files. Navisworks will search for the reference files relative to the master NWF location.

Batch Utility

The Batch utility allows you to automate the import and conversion process of standard Navisworks file formats, such as appending multiple design files into a single NWD or NWF file. Furthermore, you can schedule these conversions to take place at a set time to avoid tying up resources during working hours. This is one of the many exciting features in Navisworks that allow you to automate repetitive tasks. There are four areas where the Batch utility can assist you:

File List This option produces a text file containing a list of the paths and filenames of all design source files used in the model.

File Combine This option enables you to automatically import a batch of files from any supported format into a single model.

File Convert This option enables you to automatically convert a batch of supported files into individual Navisworks files.

Batch Schedule This option allows you to access the Windows Scheduler and run batches at a specific time/date.

Exploring the Batch Utility

The Batch utility interface is made up of three distinct areas that will be used in different scenarios, including creating model reports and automating the file-conversion process. In the ribbon, navigate to the Home tab and select the Batch Utility button from the Tools panel, as shown in Figure 2.20. Let's explore this utility in greater detail:

FIGURE 2.20
Batch Utility button
in the ribbon

Input The Input area, as shown in Figure 2.21, lets you specify the files for inclusion in the Batch utility. Select the appropriate drive and folder to navigate to the specific files. Once you've selected them, notice how all applicable files are now shown in the field to the right. To filter the file list by specific file formats, choose the File Type drop-down located just above the Add File Spec button and select the appropriate format.

When adding files to the Batch utility, you can add the contents of the whole folder by selecting the Add File Spec button. This option will add all files from the folder depending on which file type is selected from the File Type drop-down. If you want to choose specific files from the project folder, highlight the individual files in the list and click the Add Files button. If you need to remove a specific file, highlight the file in the conversion list and click the Remove Item button. Click Remove All to remove all files. Note that the removal action only removes the files from the Batch utility and does not delete the files from their respective storage locations.

Output The Output area specifies where the completed file will be saved. In Navisworks, you have two options for this output. The first, the As Single File tab, allows for a single file to be saved to a specific folder, as shown in Figure 2.22. This tab lets you save your file as an NWD file, an NWF file, or a file list (TXT).

The second tab allows you to save multiple design files as individual NWD files only. Options for this output include saving to a specified folder or saving the NWD files to the same directory as the original source data files (Figure 2.23).

FIGURE 2.21
The Input area of
the Batch Utility
dialog box

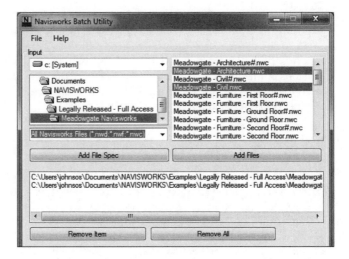

FIGURE 2.22
As Single File out-
put options

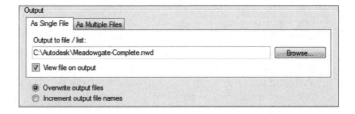

FIGURE 2.23
As Multiple Files
output options

In addition, Navisworks provides the option of overwriting existing output files or incrementing the filenames. You can specify these options by selecting the appropriate button at
the bottom of the output section.

Depending on your workflow, it may behoove you to explore these options in detail.
Exporting as an exclusive NWD file is useful if you're trying to convert and merge multiple
source files into a single file that can easily be shared or emailed to users without worrying
about the associated reference files, or for the user who is planning to use the Freedom viewer.
However, if you're working with multiple files, you have two export options: output to the same
directory as source files and output to a specific directory. This is useful if you want to maintain

the links to the source files, especially if they're located in different directories. Note that when exporting as multiple files, your only option is to save as NWD files.

In addition, the option to overwrite the output or increment is beneficial to the BIM workflow. You may find it useful to overwrite the output names so that you're not dealing with multiple versions of the files. Thus, all users are accessing the same data. Moreover, certain workflows need to document changes with a file history trail. The ability to increment the filenames allows you to create unique references to past revisions.

BATCHING PUBLISHED FILES

You can use any of the currently supported file formats when you append or convert files with the Batch utility. However, if you use any published NWD files as input, they must have been created with the May Be Resaved option selected. Otherwise, when you run the Batch utility, no NWD output files will be saved. However, you can still create an NWF output file. If you're incrementing the output filenames, Navisworks will append a four-digit number to the end of each filename. By default, the setting is configured so that previous output files are overwritten.

Log   The Log area allows you to capture all events and save as a text (.txt) file when you execute a batch process. You can specify the location of the log file for reference, as shown in Figure 2.24. You need to check the Log Events To box to activate this feature. If you're running consecutive batches, there is an option to overwrite any log files with newer ones by checking the Overwrite Existing Log File check box. If this setting remains unchecked, all subsequent log file events are appended to the original log file.

FIGURE 2.24
Log output options

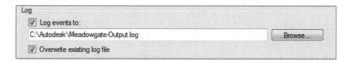

CREATING MODEL REPORTS

The Batch utility allows you to create a list of all design files in use in the current model. This list can then be saved out as a TXT file for future reference. The fundamental steps are as follows:

1. Open a project file in Navisworks.

2. In the ribbon, navigate to the Home tab and click the Batch Utility button in the Tools panel.

3. Select the files you want to use for your model report.

4. In the Output section, select As Single File and click the Browse button.

5. In the Save Output As dialog box, select File List (.txt) from the File Type drop-down. Specify the desired save location for the file.

6. After saving the file, click the Run Command button at the bottom of the Batch Utility dialog box. After Navisworks processes this request, you should be able to navigate to the file and get the listing of all the filenames and locations of the original data source files. When you're sharing NWF files, this type of information makes it easy to track down and locate files for collaboration.

Automating File Importing/Conversions

In addition, the Batch utility can append multiple design files into either a single Navisworks file (NWD or NWF) or separately as individual NWD files. Use the following steps to create a single NWD file:

1. Open a project file in Navisworks.

2. In the ribbon, navigate to the Home tab and click the Batch Utility button in the Tools panel.

3. In the Batch Utility dialog box, navigate to your model location and select the files you wish to append. Click the Add Files button to add them to the conversion list. If necessary, use the File Type drop-down to filter the results.

4. Double-click the filename in the upper-right queue to add the file to the output list, or use the buttons to add or remove files from this list.

5. When all models have been specified, select As Single File from the Output area and click the Browse button.

6. In the Save Output dialog box, choose NWD from the File Type drop-down box. Select the desired location for the file output. Click Save.

7. Check View On Output if you wish to view the appended model immediately after completion.

8. By default, all outputs will overwrite any existing files with the same name. If you want to maintain an archive of previous versions, check the Increment Output File Names radio button.

9. Additionally, you can create a log of your different batches for future reference. In the Log section of the Batch Utility dialog box, select the Log Events To button and browse to your desired location.

10. Click the Run Command button to execute the Batch utility.

To create an output of multiple files, repeat the process but choose the As Multiple Files tab in the Output section.

Using the Batch utility is a great way to use tools already in Navisworks to perform automation of certain tasks, such as creating model reports and file aggregation. However, you can further add value by scheduling batch runs to occur after hours so you're not tying up resources during business operations. To do this, set up your batch tests using the previous steps, but before running the command, configure the scheduling component. Here's how:

1. Now that your batch test is fully configured, click the Schedule Command button toward the bottom of the Batch Utility dialog box.

2. Before configuring the schedule tasks, Navisworks wants you to save your task file. In the Save Task File As dialog box, select your desired location and enter a name for this file. Click Save.

3. The Schedule Task dialog box opens, and depending on your computer's security profile, it may ask for your username and password. You can also change the task name to suit your own naming conventions (Figure 2.25).

FIGURE 2.25
Schedule Task login

4. Once your login is validated, Navisworks displays a separate window where you'll configure the schedule.

5. Choose the Schedule tab. Click the New button to define a new task, as shown in Figure 2.26.

FIGURE 2.26
Click New on the
Schedule tab.

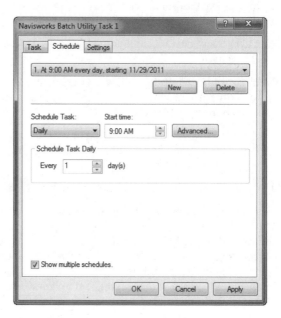

6. Specify the time and frequency for the batch test runs, and then click OK.

SCHEDULING WITH THE BATCH UTILITY

The Batch utility scheduling window contains several tabs that allow you to modify the default settings. If you've used the standard Windows Task Scheduler in the past, you'll notice some similarities between these applications.

Task Tab The Task tab displays information such as the Run and Start In destinations for the Batch utility. It also includes an option for defining and setting a password.

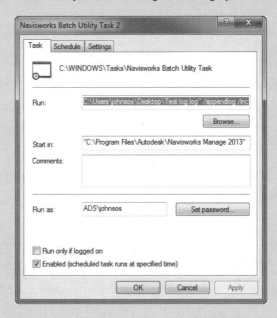

Schedule Tab This tab displays the features for defining the dates and times when a task is scheduled. The Advanced button allows for additional settings such as defining specific start and end dates in addition to options for repeating this task.

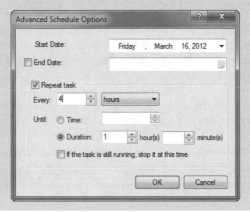

Settings Tab   The Settings tab contains several options for advanced users who want to manage the performance of their system when the tasks are scheduled to run. Some of these options include settings to stop the task after a certain period of time or only if the computer is idle or connected to a power source.

In addition to the standard Batch utility interface, Navisworks allows you to use DOS command-line switches to convert files. This feature will be discussed in Chapter 12.

Real World Scenario

EXPLORING BIM WORKFLOWS WITH THE BATCH UTILITY

In a standard project workflow, the models for the unique disciplines are modeled by different trade subcontractors and consultants. These models are then aggregated into the Navisworks scene to create a composite or project model. Since these files are typically authored in remote locations, files are shared via FTP sites, networked drives, or collaboration tools such as Buzzsaw®*, Autodesk's data management solution. In most cases, the native design files are shared so the project team can create a master NWF. This allows the team to accommodate updates from the source files as they occur. The challenge arises when working with large project datasets since the time to update and re-cache files can be lengthy. This is an opportunity to explore using the Batch utility to automate the conversion of these files and save them in a specific location.

In the following graphic, the specific trades upload their models to a common location. This is usually accomplished through a document management system or FTP site for version control and secure access. In most cases, these files are then downloaded to a specific folder structure or automatically mirrored to a replicate file hierarchy such as the Sync feature in Autodesk that Buzzsaw provides.

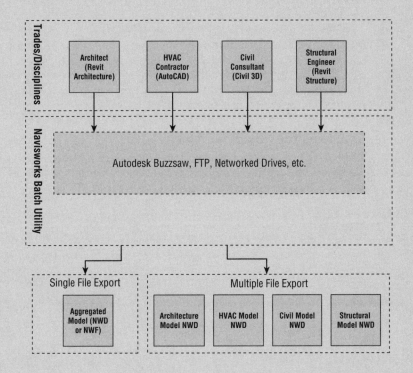

With the Navisworks Batch utility, users can specify the files from whichever discipline they want to aggregate and schedule a time for this action to occur. Users can then automate the aggregation and export of a single file or multiple files. When saving as a single file, you can export as an NWD, which will contain all of the converted and aggregated files. This is useful for users who do not have access to the source files or who only have access to the Freedom viewer. However, some workflows are based on incorporating updates into the Navisworks scene periodically. In this case, you can export as a single file but save as an NWF. When you do so, the Batch utility will first convert the source files into an NWC and then link them to the NWF.

With some project teams, the responsibilities are shared across numerous geographies. The Batch utility allows users to schedule to the completion of one team's workday and have an aggregated NWD or NWF file awaiting the beginning of the next team's work session. Users can automate and schedule the retrieval, aggregation, and export of project files to align with team updates. Furthermore, they can save the files to a specific location for group access.

* *Additional information on Buzzsaw is available at* www.autodesk.com/buzzsaw.

Object Enablers

Opening and appending different file types is fundamental to working productively in Navisworks. As discussed earlier, certain file types require additional translators to display properly. In this section, we will explore object enablers and review methods for configuring and modifying them.

Autodesk applications such as the AutoCAD platform (Architecture, MEP, Civil 3D, and Plant 3D) and other software vendors use the ObjectARX® (AutoCAD Runtime Extension) application to generate graphical and non-graphical custom objects such as piping and architectural/ civil elements that are saved in the DWG format. While these objects can be viewed in the native authoring application, they will not display properly in Navisworks unless an object enabler is installed to convert the custom objects into a format that Navisworks can read.

Exploring the Object Enabler

Think of an object enabler as a translator that converts custom objects into a format that Navisworks recognizes. Without this translation, files may display as a wireframe geometry/ bounding box or proxy graphic, as shown in Figure 2.27.

FIGURE 2.27
Proxy graphic view

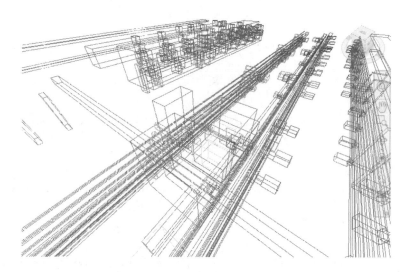

Any time you load a DWG-based file with custom objects, Navisworks will require an object enabler to display the geometry properly. This requirement tends to be consistent for most DWG files generated in applications other than standard AutoCAD. Your scene statistics will also indicate whether any object enablers are missing in your model.

You can access the Scene Statistics dialog box by doing the following. In the ribbon, navigate to the Home tab and, in the Project panel, select the Scene Statistics button, as shown in Figure 2.28.

Navisworks opens the Scene Statistics dialog box. If object enablers are missing from the current scene, they will be recorded in the list along with which file they are missing from (Figure 2.29).

FIGURE 2.28
Accessing Scene Statistics from the ribbon

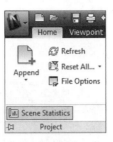

FIGURE 2.29
Missing object enablers listed in the Scene Statistics dialog box

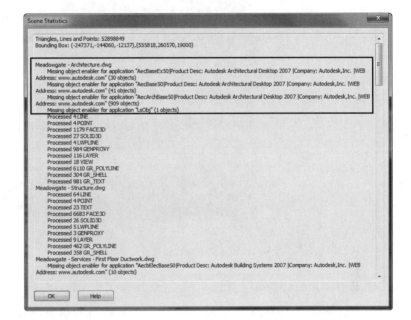

Locating and Configuring an Object Enabler

Object enablers can usually be located from the appropriate software vendors. For Autodesk products, the object enablers can be found here: www.autodesk.com/oe.

Selecting object enablers can be a little tricky. When downloading the object enabler, choose the enabler that best matches the program you wish to view the file with. For Navisworks, this will be vanilla, or plain, AutoCAD. As you'll recall, Navisworks can view DWG files without any custom objects, so you want to create a translator that allows AutoCAD to view those files. In turn, Navisworks will also be able to view those files.

To locate the proper object enabler for Navisworks, choose AutoCAD from the list of applications. Choose the product year to match up with your DWG file. Then choose the appropriate operating system and download the enabler to your computer.

Once you've downloaded the appropriate object enablers, follow these steps to install and configure them:

1. Unzip the file and double-click to start the installation.

2. When you arrive at the Object Enabler setup page, as shown in Figure 2.30, make sure you select the Navisworks products shown in the list.

FIGURE 2.30
Object Enabler
setup page

3. When you've finished selecting, click Install.

INSTALLING ENABLERS

Some object enablers have dependencies on other enablers; therefore, you must install them in a specific order. This is the case with the older enablers, especially the AutoCAD MEP 2009 enabler, which was dependent on the AutoCAD Architecture 2009 enabler. As a result, you *must* install the AutoCAD MEP enabler after the AutoCAD Architecture enabler. The 2010 and more recent versions of the MEP/Architecture enablers have been combined, so this issue has been addressed.

Once the object enabler is installed, you need to configure Navisworks to recognize this file. These next steps will guide you through the process of configuring for the DWG file:

1. Open Navisworks, but don't open any files just yet.

2. Select the blue application icon in the upper-left corner; click the Options button toward the bottom.

3. In the Options Editor, choose File Readers from the hierarchy and expand it, as shown in Figure 2.31.

4. Select DWG/DXF from the list.

FIGURE 2.31
Options Editor

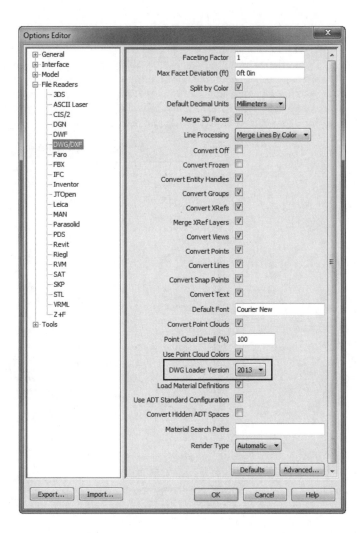

5. In the area on the right, select the appropriate DWG loader version or the file version of your DWG.

   Here's an easy way to think about this: Say the DWG file you're trying to load in Navisworks was created in AutoCAD MEP 2010. To open the file, install the AutoCAD MEP & Architecture 2010 Enabler. In Navisworks, set the DWG loader version to 2010.

6. Before opening the model in Navisworks, make sure that all previous NWC files that are referencing the DWG files have been deleted. Remember, Navisworks will load the NWC file if there are no changes to the DWG file. In other words, even if you have the object enabler configured properly, Navisworks will ignore it as long as the NWC file is current. Deleting the NWC files will force Navisworks to read the DWG file with the proper object enablers and re-cache the NWC files.

CONFIGURING OBJECT ENABLERS

In addition to installing the object enabler, you still need to configure your AutoCAD file to display properly. In the command line in AutoCAD, enter **proxygraphics** and set the value to **1** and save your file. Remember to delete any NWC files. Otherwise, Navisworks will reference the old data. If you're still getting a wireframe view, change the Render Type setting in the File Readers settings to Shaded. Delete any NWC files and reopen the DWG file.

The Bottom Line

Understand Navisworks file formats. Having a complete understanding of the different file formats is important. The 3D files are the building blocks for any successful Navisworks project. Take time to fully understand file formats before moving ahead.

Master It What are the three native file formats that Navisworks uses? What is the advantage of using the NWF format rather than the NWD?

Open and append various files. Appending and merging files is the proper way to create highly complex yet intelligent 3D models. Aggregating and sharing this information with a larger audience helps drive efficiency and increase project awareness.

Master It   How can the Merge feature complement the design review process with an extended team?

Configure object enablers.   Not all files types are created equally. Proper planning and understanding of the various file types will help you identify where object enablers are required and configure the proper setup to ensure uninterrupted access.

Master It   How do you display a custom object in Navisworks?

Chapter 3

Moving around the Model

In Chapter 1, "Getting to Know Autodesk Navisworks," we introduced you to some of the tools and features of the Autodesk® Navisworks® 2013 interface. This chapter will go beyond that and leverage the Navigation tools inside Navisworks, allowing you to easily traverse through a model, set locations, and examine objects. For example, you'll find that the Walk and Fly tools have Collision capabilities and that the Orbit tools can be used in conjunction with the Pan tools. In addition, there are mouse controls that help you navigate around the model. These tools, while not complicated to use, are essential to being able to utilize Navisworks to its greatest potential, greatly extending the user experience. You will find that once you master the Navigation tools, you will be able to easily move around your Navisworks model.

In this chapter, you'll learn to:

◆ Use the mouse to navigate inside Navisworks

◆ Walk and fly through the model

◆ Understand the ViewCube and SteeringWheels

Using the Navigation Bar

The Navigation Bar, as shown in Figure 3.1, was created as a shared storage location for the ViewCube®, SteeringWheels®, Pan, Zoom, Orbit, Look, and Walk/Fly tools. You can customize the tools that are displayed on the Navigation Bar as well as control the docking position.

Clicking the Navigation Bar Options located on the drop-down arrow on the Navigation Bar gives you the ability to control the behavior of the Orbit and Walk tools. Changing the Orbit settings allows you to change the Orbit tools back to tools that were available in previous versions of Navisworks—Examine, Turntable, and Classic Orbit—should you need access to them. These settings can be accessed through the Options dialog box as well. Options for the Walk tools include controls for things like walk angle constraints and walk speed. These options can also be accessed through the File Options dialog box by choosing Options ➢ Interface ➢ Navigation Bar.

Having the Navigation Bar on your screen allows you to quickly change between Navigation tools without having to search for them on the ribbon or other locations. Imagine being able to quickly access the Pan tool to move across the model, then selecting the Orbit tool to further examine your space, and then clicking the Walk tool to move through your model—all without having to leave the screen and from an easily accessible Navigation Bar.

FIGURE 3.1
Navigation Bar

If you need to customize the Navigation Bar, click the arrow at the bottom of the Navigation Bar. This will open a drop-down list to select from. Here, you can control which tools are shown on the Navigation Bar as well as where the Navigation Bar is docked (Figure 3.2). Should you need to reset the Navigation Bar to its original settings, choose Options ➤ Interface ➤ Navigation Bar ➤ Defaults.

FIGURE 3.2
Customizing the
Navigation Bar

Panning and Zooming

Pan and Zoom are essential tools for navigating around your model. While these two tools can be used as independent actions, they can also be combined with other tools and actions to create "helper" tools. For example, while using the Orbit tool, you can use the middle mouse button to pan and zoom around the model without having to access an additional tool. There even may be times when you find yourself using these two tools in parallel with each other, improving your workflow and giving you access to additional tools without having to stop and select a secondary tool.

Pan Tool

With the Pan tool active (you'll have a four-sided cursor), you can pan or move about the model left, right, up, and down. The Pan tool moves the model itself and not the camera. To use this tool, follow these steps:

1. Access the Pan tool from the Navigation Bar (pressing Ctrl+6 also activates the tool).

2. Use the left mouse button to pan or move around the model in the desired direction (left, right, up, down).

The middle mouse button can be used as a pan tool in most cases while other tools are active—Selection, Orbit, or Look Around, for example. Having the ability to pan at will grants you the capability to gain additional perspective on the model or move around to see a specific part of the view. To use the middle mouse button to pan, do the following:

1. Select the Selection, Orbit, or Look Around tool.

2. Press and hold the middle mouse button (or wheel) to access the Pan tool.

3. Move or pan as needed.

4. Release the middle mouse button to return to your previous tool.

Zoom Tools

Similar to the Pan tool, Zoom allows you to change the magnification level of the model in several different ways. The Zoom tool contains a few subtools that allow you to control the model and navigate in your own way.

The zoom direction is based on the current pivot point or zoom location. If you move the location of the mouse cursor prior to using the Zoom tool, it will move the pivot point. While using the Zoom tool, you can choose among four different ways to change the magnification level of the model:

◆ After selecting the Zoom tool from the Navigation Bar, click the left mouse button to advance (zoom in) the magnification by a factor of 25 percent.

◆ After selecting the Zoom tool from the Navigation Bar, click the left mouse button while holding the Shift key down to reverse (zoom out) the magnification by a factor of 25 percent.

◆ After selecting the Zoom tool from the Navigation Bar, click the left mouse button and hold it to change the zoom level as needed. Move the mouse up (zoom in) and down (zoom out) to change the magnification level without a defined factor.

◆ After selecting the Zoom tool from the Navigation Bar, roll your middle mouse button or wheel to change the magnification level at your discretion.

ZOOM WINDOW

The Zoom Window tool lets you identify a specific window to zoom within. There are two types of Zoom Window tools. The default selection lets you select corners to create a rectangle to specify the area you wish to zoom into (Figure 3.3); the other option defines a center point for creating the Zoom window. To create a Zoom window by selecting corners, do the following:

FIGURE 3.3
Identify a Zoom window by selecting corners.

1. Select the Zoom Window tool from the Navigation Bar or press Ctrl+5.

2. Left-click the first corner of the window at your desired location and hold the button down.

3. Move the mouse cursor to the second location and release the left mouse button. The view zooms to the selected window.

When the Zoom Window tool is active, pressing Ctrl before selecting points gives you the chance to select your point from the center instead of selecting corners, ensuring that your zoom area and the items you contained in your window will be centered within the zoom. Zoom Window becomes a valuable tool when you are working on larger projects because the model may not always know where you are in space.

ZOOM SELECTED

Zoom Selected, as shown in Figure 3.4 and Figure 3.5, is a great tool for selecting an object or group of objects and zooming in or focusing on the object or objects. (The Zoom Selected tool replaced the View Selected tool [the mountain icon] in previous versions of Navisworks.) If no items are selected, the Zoom Selected tool will work the same way as Zoom All and zoom to the furthest magnification of the model. (We'll discuss Zoom All in a bit.) Here's how to use Zoom Selected:

1. Select the item or group of items you want to zoom to.

2. Select Zoom Selected from the Navigation Bar; you can also press the Page Down key on your keyboard. The view will move to focus on the item or group of items. You will be returned to the last used tool.

FIGURE 3.4
Scene with an item selected before using Zoom Selected

FIGURE 3.5
After selecting Zoom Selected

ZOOM SELECTED TIP

You can use the Zoom Selected tool when an object is selected in the selection tree.

ZOOM ALL

Zoom All is used to zoom to the extents of all items in the model, meaning it will show the limits of all the included items loaded in the model. The Page Up key also works as a shortcut key for this tool. For large models, using Zoom All may zoom you too far out from the view. Sometimes, the best alternative is to create a Home view instead (see the section "ViewCube" later in this chapter to learn more about the Home view).

Pan and Zoom in Action Together

In many cases, Pan and Zoom are used in combination with each other. As you are learning to navigate your way around your model, you will find many instances where these tools fit together nicely.

If you have selected Pan (or Zoom) from the Navigation Bar and you are using the left mouse button to navigate your model, you can still use the middle mouse button to access the other tool. For instance, if you have Pan active, you can roll the middle mouse button to change the view magnification; if Zoom is active, you can press the middle mouse button to pan at any point.

You can easily access the Pan and Zoom tools from the middle mouse button or wheel and use them in combination when you have other tools such as Select or Orbit active. For instance, if you are panning across a section (holding the middle mouse button down) and need to zoom out for a better view, you can roll the button backward and you will zoom out.

Learning to Walk and Fly

Walk and Fly (see Figure 3.6) are essential tools for moving around Navisworks and are especially important to give the user the experience of realism during navigation. With Walk and Fly, additional functions exist to enhance the experience and make navigation easier: Collision, Gravity, Crouch, and Third Person.

Here's a common workflow you might encounter with these tools. Say you're using the Fly tool to move around a large building to get a sense of the site. You then use the Walk tool to navigate inside your project and combine it with Gravity and Collision to "walk" up a set of stairs and further into the building. While navigating with these tools, you are gaining valuable perspectives on the project, all in front of the building owner or in a coordination meeting, perhaps.

FIGURE 3.6
Walk and Fly tools, with options

At first, these tools may seem cumbersome or slightly difficult to use, but with practice, you will find them easy to control, and they will likely become crucial to most of your projects. Mastering the Walk and Fly tools will allow you to explore your Navisworks model with greater ease. Think of using these tools as playing a first-person video game with you in the driver's seat.

Walk Tool

With the Walk tool, you can navigate through a model as if you were walking through it. There are different ways that you can utilize its features and various methods of navigation. Here are the basic steps:

1. Select Walk from the Navigation Bar (Ctrl+2); the "feet" will appear on the screen.

2. With the left mouse button pressed, move your mouse in the direction you wish to go.

3. Move the mouse forward to go forward and move it left or right to turn.

4. Stop moving forward and only move the mouse left or right to look around; be sure to keep the left mouse button pressed to continue navigation.

5. Pull the mouse backward to move in reverse.

6. Let go of the mouse button to stop walking.

ALTERNATE WALKING METHOD

Some people prefer to use the keyboard instead of the mouse when they are first starting to learn to navigate with the Walk tool. You can use the arrow keys (left, right, up, down) on the keyboard to help you with navigation.

Learning the arrow keys helps you get into tight places. Sometimes, you need to make fine adjustments, and it can be a little easier with the keyboard than with the mouse.

Some of the options for walking include Tilt Angle, Glide, and Walk Speed. To access these options, choose Viewpoint ➢ Save, Load & Playback panel, and click the Edit Current Viewpoint button.

Tilt Angle   Tilt Angle controls the vertical angle where the camera looks or the head position when walking. A Tilt Angle value of 0 is usually looking straight ahead. You can use the middle mouse button to roll forward to look down or backward to look up while navigating. Alternatively, you can use the slider on the Tilt window to adjust the angle up or down (Figure 3.7). For a finer level of control, you can enter a number at the bottom of the Tilt Angle window to change the angle. Enter **0** to return to a straight-ahead view.

Glide (Walking Pan)   While similar to the Pan tool (the symbol is different), Glide moves the camera instead of the model. This tool is useful for doing things like changing elevation or traversing left, right, up, or down only instead of walking. For example, Figure 3.8 shows Glide being used to move up between floors to examine mechanical equipment. If you have Gravity and Collision enabled, you will be able to move left or right efficiently, but moving up and down can be tricky. You can still glide down with Gravity and even glide up—you will just fall down again if you start to glide up. Gliding down with Gravity lets you fall right where you want to fall. To enable Glide, press and hold the middle mouse button while Walk is active. A second option for accessing Glide is to press Ctrl while pressing the left mouse button.

Walk Speed   Walk speed can be controlled in two different ways. First, you can use the Shift key while walking to temporarily double your current walk speed. Release Shift to return to your original walk speed.

Or, you can change the overall Navisworks Walk/Fly speed by selecting the Viewpoint ➢ Save, Load & Playback panel ➢ Edit Current Viewpoint button. Then change the Linear Speed value in the Motion section. Usually, 10 is a good speed for walking; 30 can be a little fast but is considered good for flying. Linear Speed is included within the viewpoint, meaning that if you change to a saved viewpoint, it will revert to the originally saved speed. You can edit it later. You can also change this speed by clicking the Viewpoints tab ➢ Navigate ➢ down arrow ➢ Linear Speed.

FIGURE 3.7
Tilt Angle slider

FIGURE 3.8
Examining
mechanical
equipment using
Glide

Realism Realism settings, found in the Walk and Fly drop-down on the Navigation Bar as well as on the Viewpoint tab, give you additional controls while walking (and flying) through Navisworks. These tools can be combined in several ways, depending on your needs.

Collision Enabling Collision (Ctrl+D) allows you to navigate the model with mass. As you interact with the model and come into contact with objects like doors or columns, you stop or are unable to pass through that object. The Collision Volume value can be changed or customized to reflect the needs of the user or collision requirements. Collision can be used with the Walk and Fly tools.

Gravity This tool (Ctrl+G) gives you the appearance of weight. When you are using the Walk tool and you begin to move, you will "fall" until you reach a surface. Gravity works best when Collision is also active so that when a surface is contacted, the falling stops. Use Gravity in conjunction with Collision to walk up and down stairs, for example. When you disable Collision, Gravity will also be disabled. However, you can enable Collision without enabling Gravity. While you are able to use Collision on its own, Gravity must always be paired with Collision. Gravity can be used with the Walk tool but not with the Fly tool.

Crouch With Crouch activated, you will automatically crouch under any objects that you cannot freely walk under at the specified avatar height. This tool can be useful for checking clearance heights under pipes and other equipment. Not all avatars can crouch.

Third Person When Third Person (Ctrl+T) is active, it turns on Third Person view, or an avatar, which may be used as a representation of you while navigating the model. Third Person has other added benefits, such as working with Gravity, Collision, and Crouch. When you're using the avatar for Collision, it will turn red when it collides with another item. Also, Third Person can be customized by changing the avatar (Figure 3.9) selection and dimensions.

FIGURE 3.9
Example of
Navisworks avatars
and customizable
features

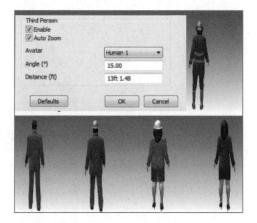

Being able to switch between avatars quickly lets you provide context to the environment that you are exploring. For example, if you are considering a hazardous environment, it might make more sense to utilize a firefighter rather than an office worker. To change the avatar quickly, follow these steps:

1. With Third Person active, select the Viewpoint tab.

2. Click the Edit Current Viewpoint button on the Save, Load & Playback panel.

3. At the bottom right under Collision, click Settings to open the Collision dialog box.

4. Select the desired avatar from the drop-down list and click OK. The new avatar will now display and you can use it.

🌐 Real World Scenario

CREATING YOUR OWN AVATARS

Imagine you have a piece of machinery or equipment that needs to be added to an existing project or building, and you want to check to make sure it will fit down the hallway and make corridor turns. Creating the machine as your own avatar in this case works well since it respects gravity and collision but is not able to crouch. Here's how to do it:

1. Save the item in its own NWD file.

2. Locate the `C:\Program Files\Autodesk\Navisworks Manage 2013\avatars` directory.

3. Create a folder in this directory.

4. Place your saved NWD file in this folder.

5. Restart Navisworks, and the new avatar should be available for use.

One key point to consider when creating avatars is the orientation in which they are saved. You don't want them to come in upside down or backward, as in this image. It never hurts to take a look at a few of the other avatars as well to understand how they were created. Keep in mind that when creating an avatar, it may take a few tries to place it correctly.

Fly Tool

Flying allows you to gain perspective from a birds-eye view of your model or project, all the while enabling the use of functions like Collision, Crouch, and Third Person. This tool is used often in animations of entire projects to showcase large sites or to easily navigate the exterior of a building. Much like the Walk tool, the Fly tool can be difficult to master and, in some cases, a little tougher to grasp. With some practice, though, this tool can be easily incorporated into your Navisworks skill set. Let's try it out:

1. Select Fly from the Navigation Bar; the "paper airplane" will appear on the screen.

2. Press and hold the left mouse button to start flying forward, similar to a flight simulator. To fly straight, hold the mouse button down without moving in any direction.

3. Move the mouse left or right to bank the movement. Move up or down to change elevation.

4. Use the arrow keys to change the zoom magnification and location. Use the up- and down-arrow keys to zoom in and out and the left- and right-arrow keys to spin the camera around the respective axis. These are tools you'll find useful when you want to readjust the view while using the Fly tool.

Roll Angle Roll Angle controls how the camera rotates around its own axis while moving forward. This allows you to rotate left or right as you move so that you are no longer parallel to the model, as shown in Figure 3.10. Use the Ctrl key or middle mouse button to change the roll angle while flying. To reset the roll angle back to 0, click the Edit Current Viewpoint button on the Save, Load & Playback panel on the Viewpoint tab. Then change the Roll Angle value to **0**. Doing so can be a real asset when you have found yourself upside down or far out of alignment from the view.

FIGURE 3.10
Roll Angle

Fly Speed Similar to walk speed, the fly speed can be controlled in two ways. One is to use the Shift key while flying to temporarily double your current fly speed. Release Shift to return to the original fly speed.

Or you can change the overall Navisworks Walk/Fly speed by choosing the Edit Current Viewpoint button on the Save, Load & Playback panel on the Viewpoint tab. Change the

Linear Speed value under Motion. Usually, 30 to 40 is a good speed for flying, but you may want to change it back to 10 to 15 for walking.

Walking around the Model

Effective navigation is essential to mastering Navisworks. The Walk tool can be a valuable asset in navigating through a project.

Say you are in a meeting and have assembled the project team. You need to walk through the project to make sure that the changes to an interior stairwell have been reflected and then do a quick visual inspection for possible mechanical interferences in the ceiling space on the second floor. From there, you can begin to have additional discussions about the changes that may need to occur based on your findings.

1. Launch the Navisworks application, Navisworks Simulate, or Navisworks Manage (not Navisworks Freedom).

2. Open the file c03-walking.nwd.

3. From the Navigation Bar, select Walk, or press Ctrl+2.

4. From the Navigation Bar or the Viewpoint tab in the Realism panel, enable Collision, Gravity, Crouch, and Third Person.

5. Using your Walk tool, walk to the revolving door at the front of the building, as shown in Figure 3.11.

FIGURE 3.11
Avatar at the front
of the building

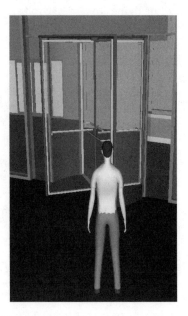

6. Disable Collision (Ctrl+D) long enough to enter the building and walk through the front.

7. Reenable Collision (Ctrl+D) and walk toward the stairs on the left.

8. Walk up the stairs (Figure 3.12) to the top of the landing. Continue navigating through the double doors at the top of the stairs, and follow the hallway left after entering the door.

FIGURE 3.12
Avatar walking up
the stairs

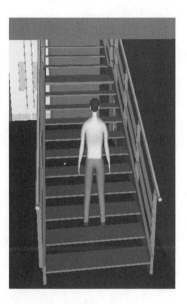

9. Navigate down the corridor to the office area at the end of the hallway. Position yourself near a desk (Figure 3.13) and get the avatar to crouch (ensure that Crouch is enabled). Notice how the tool reacts when it is near an object that it is unable to walk under cleanly. Keep in mind that custom avatars will not crouch.

FIGURE 3.13
Avatar crouching
under a desk

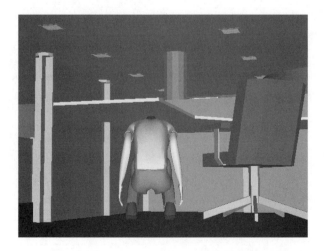

10. Disable Third Person, Crouch, Collision, and Gravity.

11. Using Glide (the middle mouse button or Ctrl key), change your elevation (up) to move between the floors. Navigate using the Walk tool until you can find the piping that interferes with the ductwork, as shown in Figure 3.14. Hint: You might have to turn around or walk around the ceiling space beyond the area you're standing in to find the clash.

FIGURE 3.14
Using the Walk tool to locate potential mechanical equipment interferences

12. Feel free to continue to use the Walk tool. If you wish, return to the Home view by choosing Saved Viewpoints and selecting Home View (or any of the other saved viewpoints). Practice using the Fly tool. When you've finished, close the file without saving.

In this example, you used the Walk tools in conjunction with the associated helper items: Collision, Gravity, Crouch, and Third Person. Taking the time to master this exercise and the navigation components will go a long way to getting you comfortable with the Walk tool. These same skills can also be applied to the Fly tool (except for Gravity, since it does not work with Fly).

NAVIGATE WITH LEVELS AND GRIDS

Having Grids and Levels from your Revit® model can greatly help with navigation and location in Navisworks.

As you move through the model, the Grids tool will update your location in reference to where you are on the model grid. Notice also as you navigate that the Grid Location from the HUD (View tab ➤ Navigation Aids panel ➤ HUD ➤ Grid Location) will update as well. This gives you two references (visual and HUD) to better understand your location during navigation.

Using the Orbit and Look Tools

Orbit and Look are indispensable tools for moving around a model and continuing to build your navigation skill set. These tools allow you to focus on specific items, look around from a fixed point, and orbit (revolve) around a pivot point.

Orbit Tools

Orbit and its associated tools affect the overall orientation of the model. As you move the cursor, the model reacts to your movement around a pivot point. Only the Free Orbit tool moves the model (model centric). All the other tools move the camera (camera centric).

Orbit　The Orbit tool changes the camera location in the model. As you move in any direction, you can explore the various directions in the model. Drag the mouse cursor to move the Orbit tool in the desired direction. You can use Pan and Zoom in conjunction with Orbit as needed.

Pivot Point　You can change the pivot point that the Orbit tool is based on (see Figure 3.15) by pressing the Ctrl key while using the left mouse button and moving the mouse to locate a new pivot point. From there, you can orbit from a new location or pivot point.

FIGURE 3.15
A pivot point being moved

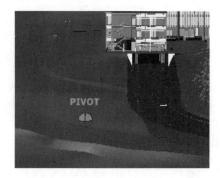

Maintain Horizontal Or Up Direction　To maintain an up or horizontal direction, use the tilt angle to reset the view back to 0. Doing so enables you to look from a level view direction. However, as soon as you start to orbit the model, the tilt angle will change again.

Free Orbit　The Free Orbit tool moves the model in the scene view. This allows you to position the model in the scene in any way you desire. The same motions and options apply. You can use Ctrl to move the pivot point.

Constrained Orbit　Constrained Orbit allows for camera movement around the pivot point. You can move left and right but not up and down. This tool is similar to the compass of the ViewCube. Use Ctrl to move the pivot point.

COMBINATION TOOLS: PAN, ZOOM, AND ORBIT

As explained earlier, you can use the Orbit tool in combination with the Pan and Zoom tools. This helps you extend and improve on your available toolset. Usually, these tools can be found when you have the Selection, Orbit, and Zoom tools already selected. To use them in combination, try the following:

1. With one of the tools active—Orbit, Zoom, or Selection—use the middle mouse button to pan around the model; press and hold the Ctrl key on the keyboard. (The Selection tool works best as you navigate since you are free to select objects and take full advantage of these tools.)

2. Roll the middle mouse button forward or backward to activate the Zoom tool.

3. Press the Shift key while pressing the middle mouse button to activate the Orbit tool.

Now, you have three tools available from the middle mouse button without having to go back to the Navigation Bar to activate them. Although you may still encounter instances when you need the actual tools themselves, having this skill set should serve you well.

Look Tools

With Look and its associated tools, you can rotate the current view. When rotating the view, your line of sight rotates about the current eye position, as when you turn your head. Think of these tools as standing in a fixed location and being able to look around or focus on an item.

Look Around   Look Around (Ctrl+3) lets you "stand" in a stationary position and examine the model or look around. You can look in both horizontal and vertical directions without moving from your current position. A good example of when to use this tool might be when you're examining a new space design to ensure all the elements are included. Use your mouse to navigate this tool and look around your position.

Look At   The Look At tool lets you select a specific object to examine. Once you select the object, your view will be adjusted to look at that specific object head on. Look At will adjust where your camera is looking but will not adjust the zoom factor. Look At will help to adjust the angle to align with the item selected. To use Look At, do the following:

1. Select the Look At tool from the Navigation Bar.

2. Determine the item to look at and select it.

3. Notice that your view is adjusted to look straight at the item.

4. Use the Pan and Zoom tools (middle mouse button) to adjust as needed.

Focus   Similar to Look At, Focus lets you select an object and will change the view based on the selected item (the camera will swivel based on the point you select). After focusing on the item, you can use the Pan and Zoom tools to further adjust as needed. On large projects, the Focus tool allows the selection box to focus on the correct area of the building. Using this tool will help Navisworks keep itself on track when locating and focusing on objects. It also lets you use the pivot point for the Constrained Orbit in Classic mode should you wish to switch back to that tool.

Using the ViewCube and SteeringWheels

Found in most other Autodesk programs, the ViewCube and SteeringWheels can greatly aid in the navigation of your model. SteeringWheels includes many of the tools we've already discussed, such as Pan, Zoom, and Orbit, allowing for quick and easy access. The ViewCube is used to improve the workflow by allowing you to set a Home view and change the overall direction of the model view.

ViewCube

The ViewCube (Figure 3.16) is a tool used to aid in setting up and navigating between views. The ViewCube provides visual feedback and allows for instant changes to the view of the model. You can drag or click the ViewCube, switch to one of the available preset views, roll the current view, or change to the Home view of the model.

The ViewCube usually remains open at the top corner of the screen. If you need to close the ViewCube (or if it is closed and you need to open it), you can do so by selecting the View tab ➢ Navigation Aids panel.

FIGURE 3.16
ViewCube with compass and corner highlighted

Views   When you're using the ViewCube and select any of the views, the model will orient itself to the selected view. You have options for Top, Front, Left, Right, Bottom, and all the views in between. With the ViewCube, you can select on top, bottom, and middle areas to further adjust your view.

LOST IN THE VIEWCUBE

Often, you may find yourself lost in the model because the ViewCube disappears for one reason or another. Well, don't fret about not being able to find your way out. You can always use the Navigation tools with Zoom All, utilize previously saved viewpoints, or use the Camera Position in the Camera panel on the Viewpoint tab. Also, don't forget about the Home button (small house) at the top of the ViewCube.

Compass   The Compass behaves similarly to the Constrained Orbit discussed earlier. The difference is instead of clicking in the screen to move, you click on the compass you drag around the model. Using the compass saves time since you do not have to stop to access an additional tool, and it will not cancel the tool that you have active. For example, if you are walking through the model with the Walk tool and then use the Compass to move around, it will return you to the Walk tool. Using Constrained Orbit will cancel your Walk tool. In some cases, the Compass can save you time and effort and act as a shortcut for some tools.

ViewCube Pivot Point   The pivot point for the ViewCube is set by the last selected item or tool to use a pivot point. If you need to change the pivot point for the ViewCube, select another point or use a tool that will allow you to move the pivot point—Orbit, for example.

The ViewCube's context menu, shown in Figure 3.17, contains a few useful options. You can, for example, change the view between Perspective and Orthographic and access the Help and ViewCube options.

FIGURE 3.17
ViewCube context menu

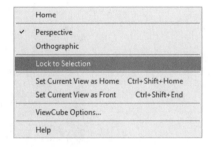

Something that does not appear by default is the ability to select an object or group of objects and then lock that item to the ViewCube as a selection. This will allow you to set a permanent pivot point for the view and compass direction until you release the lock. A lock icon will appear at the top, next to the Home button. Lock To Selection is available only when items are selected. To use Lock To Selection, follow these steps:

1. Select the object or group of objects. Selecting multiple objects will cause the ViewCube to divide the difference between them, and it will use the center point as the pivot point.

2. Right-click the ViewCube and choose Lock To Selection from the context menu.

3. Use the ViewCube to pivot around the item or selected items.

4. To return to a normal pivot point, right-click and select Lock To Selection again to toggle it off.

Home View   The Home view is a great tool that lets you return to a saved view. Usually, this is an often-used view that represents the home of the project or maybe a specific location that may change from time to time based on the needs of the Navisworks session. What's important is that it's easy to access: you click Home View (Home icon) at the top of the ViewCube to return to the Home view. To create a Home view, do the following:

1. Set up the required view that is to be used for the Home view, using the various tools in Navisworks.

2. Right-click the ViewCube and select Set Current View As Home, or press Ctrl+Shift+Home to set the Home view.

3. Navigate your model and return to the Home view as needed.

SteeringWheels

SteeringWheels is a combination of tools that provides the ability to access various 3D Navigation tools from a single tool. For many users, SteeringWheels saves time because it combines many commonly used tools into a single interface.

At first, some of the SteeringWheels tools (see Figure 3.18) may seem cumbersome and difficult to use. But with practice, they can be an aid in Navisworks navigation. The SteeringWheels tools are meant to follow your cursor as you move your mouse until you close the tools.

Access SteeringWheels from the Navigation Bar or by pressing Ctrl+W. Click the X in the upper-right corner to close it (or press Ctrl+W again). Here's a list of the various SteeringWheels options:

FIGURE 3.18
SteeringWheels with the full navigation wheel

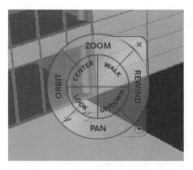

Pan SteeringWheels Pan operates the same as the Orbit tool from the Navigation Bar. The benefit is that this tool is heads up, meaning it's always on the screen, saving you the time of having to search for additional tools when using this tool or other SteeringWheels tools. It also moves with the cursor.

Zoom SteeringWheels Zoom operates the same as the Orbit tool from the Navigation Bar. Again, the benefit is that this tool is heads up, meaning it's always on the screen, saving you the time of having to search for additional tools when using this tool or other SteeringWheels tools. It also moves with the cursor.

Orbit SteeringWheels Orbit also operates the same as the Orbit tool from the Navigation Bar. Again, it saves you the time of having to search for additional tools when using this tool or other SteeringWheels tools. It also moves with the cursor.

Rewind With the Rewind tool (Figure 3.19), you can locate views from the navigation history, and you can restore a previous view or scroll through all of the saved views. As you use SteeringWheels, it maintains a running total of view history and allows you to rewind to those views. Those views are not retained from session to session.

FIGURE 3.19
SteeringWheels
Rewind tool

Center   With the Center tool, you can define the center of the current view of a model. This tool will redefine the pivot point based on where the cursor is pointing when you select the Center tool. This tool can be used in conjunction with the ViewCube.

Walk   SteeringWheels Walk operates similar to the Walk tool from the Navigation Bar. Again, the benefit is that this tool is heads up and moves with the cursor. One of the key differences is that pressing the Shift key allows you to change the up and down elevation (even if you have Gravity and Collision turned on). You cannot slide with this tool or modify the camera angle.

Look   SteeringWheels Look operates the same as the Look Around tool from the Navigation Bar. Again, the benefit is that this tool is heads up and moves with the cursor.

Up/Down   This option changes the elevation, similar to the Tilt Angle tool, which is not available while you're using SteeringWheels.

The SteeringWheels context menu contains a few valuable tools to aid in navigation and functionality of SteeringWheels:

Wheel Views   The Wheel Views option allows you to change the view level of SteeringWheels. Changing the view level limits the number of tools that display on the wheel. In most cases, the full navigation wheel is utilized.

Home and Fit To Window   Selecting Home from the menu returns you to the Home view specified in the ViewCube. Fit To Window does the same thing as Zoom All from the Navigation Bar and zooms you to the extent of the model.

Camera Controls   With the Camera Controls, you are able to increase or decrease the Walk tool speed. The Level Camera tool sets the Tilt Angle value back to 0 so that you are looking at a level angle when using the Walk tool.

Using the ViewCube and SteeringWheels Together

There are many instances when you will use the ViewCube and SteeringWheels together. You can access any of the ViewCube tools while you still have SteeringWheels open. That way, you don't have to close SteeringWheels every time you need to adjust the view with the ViewCube. The first reaction for many users is to close SteeringWheels when they need to select something from the ViewCube, when, in fact, the tools work hand in hand.

Imagine being able to walk, orbit, and zoom right from the same tool—SteeringWheels. Then, you can move over to the ViewCube to select a new view, or navigate quickly to the other side of the building, all without having to take your hand off the mouse or search for additional tools.

Some users employ the ViewCube and SteeringWheels for most of their navigation in Navisworks. As an added benefit, these navigation skills can extend into other Autodesk software because they have similar versions of the ViewCube and SteeringWheels.

The Bottom Line

Use the mouse to navigate inside Navisworks.   Learning to use the mouse to navigate is critical to understanding and mastering the tools in Navisworks. Almost every Navigation tool utilizes the mouse for navigation in some way. There are shortcuts for tools like Orbit, Zoom, and Pan that can aid in your navigation.

Master It   Explain the process for using the mouse controls with Zoom, Pan, and Orbit.

Walk and fly through the model.   As with the Walk tool, learning the Fly tool is essential. While at first, this tool may seem difficult to understand, it has great potential for navigating large sites and covering great distances.

Master It   Where do you go to reset the roll angle of the Fly tool?

Understand the ViewCube and SteeringWheels.   For some users, these tools can be difficult to master; others find them to be useful time-savers because of the heads-up type of use, meaning they're always on the screen, saving you the time of having to search for additional tools when using these tools. You also have the ability to utilize the two sets of tools together. Having at least a basic understanding will help improve your workflow.

Master It   How can the ViewCube and SteeringWheels be utilized in conjunction with each other? Give an example.

Chapter 4

Climbing the Selection Tree

Now that you've become proficient at aggregating, appending models, and moving around with the various navigation tools, let's look at the different ways that Autodesk® Navisworks® 2013 software manages these models. This chapter will cover object properties and explore ways to fully leverage this embedded metadata for use in model searches to identify specific objects. We'll also focus on the selection tree and project browser, both dockable windows that display the file structure of your appended models.

In addition, we'll explore the new Selection Inspector tool, which displays a list of all of the selected objects in your scene. Finally, we'll explore the selection tree display options that control visibility and object selection. These features are useful for hiding and overriding colors of specific model elements in your Navisworks scene.

The concepts covered in this chapter will lay out some additional foundation elements necessary for mastery in Navisworks. Future chapters will assume an understanding of these principles, so devote some time to strengthening your knowledge of these concepts.

In this chapter, you'll learn to:

◆ Create search and selection sets

◆ Export and reuse search sets

◆ Navigate the selection tree

Discovering Object Properties

Object properties are without a doubt one of the most important aspects of your Navisworks model. While the 3D geometry is useful for visually exploring the design and understanding the full scope of the project, having access to the underlying data allows you to leverage your project for further analysis and simulations inside Navisworks. In this section, we'll explore the types of data that Navisworks can read and ways to leverage this metadata with model searches.

Properties

When Navisworks opens a model file, any unnecessary information is stripped out and the geometry is converted to a surface model for easy visualization and navigation. In addition, any embedded metadata or object properties, including parametric properties in the source files, are converted as well. This conversion process allows Navisworks to work with data-rich models that become more than just pretty pictures. This object property information becomes the basis for a building information model (BIM) where the *I* is paramount to the virtual design and construction (VDC) workflow by enabling intelligent interaction and exploration. Since Navisworks can read numerous file types, the object properties created by these different authoring applications will vary, with certain applications embedding more information than others. However, every object has some type of embedded property information. This can range from basic data such as the source filename, CAD layer/BIM group information, or object ID to data such as quantities, calculations, and materials. When models are appended to Navisworks, all object properties are displayed in the Properties window based on the hierarchy shown in Figure 4.1.

FIGURE 4.1
Typical object
property hierarchy
in Navisworks

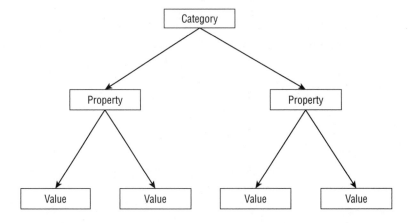

To better understand how Navisworks displays object properties, look in the `Chapter 4` folder, open the file `c04_Meadowgate 2013.nwd`, and follow these steps:

1. Open the Properties window, which you can access from the Display panel of the Home tab. Alternatively, you can open the Properties window by pressing Shift+F7.

2. Select the roof of the building. The Item tab of your Properties window will list the information shown in Figure 4.2.

FIGURE 4.2
Navisworks
Properties window
showing standard
properties

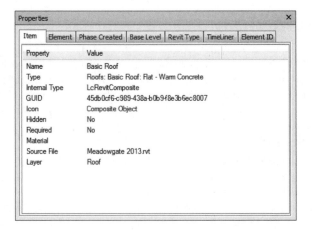

3. Cycle through the tabs and notice the different types of properties and how they are laid out.

4. Press Esc to deselect the element.

If more than one object is selected, the Properties window will not show any property data but will indicate how many objects are currently selected (Figure 4.3).

FIGURE 4.3
Properties window displaying the number of objects selected

Properties   ×

5 Items Selected

 Real World Scenario

WORKING WITH REVIT FILES

With the new native Autodesk® Revit® file import capability in Navisworks 2013, you aren't required to export your Revit file as an NWC file to open the geometry in Navisworks; however, there may be times when you still want to use the NWC format.

When exporting from Revit, you can configure several settings for the NWC export. Clicking the Navisworks Settings icon at the bottom of the Export dialog box opens another dialog box where you can configure Revit to export additional element properties. In the following image, you'll notice the default for this option has the Convert Element Properties check box deselected.

The result is that Revit will export the basic categories of data to Navisworks. If you export with this check box selected, Revit will include additional categories. In addition, when importing native Revit files, the Convert Element Properties option is also available in the Revit file reader in the Options Editor.

The following table shows the differences between the two settings. Exporting as an NWC or importing a native Revit file will produce the same list of properties depending on which Convert Element Properties option is selected. The categories listed are those available when we select the roof of our model.

CONVERT ELEMENT PROPERTIES UNCHECKED	CONVERT ELEMENT PROPERTIES CHECKED
Item	Item
Element	Element
Element ID	Element ID
Phase Created	Phase Created
Base Level	Base Level
Revit Type	Revit Type
	Element Properties

CONVERT ELEMENT PROPERTIES UNCHECKED	CONVERT ELEMENT PROPERTIES CHECKED
	SlabShapeEditor
	RoofType
	OwnerViewID
	WorksetID
	Materials
	SimilarObjectTypes
	ObjectType
	Level
	Document
	ParametersMap
	Parameters
	Category
	ID

There are some additional items to consider when working with native Revit files. Grid lines are now active for the NWC Exporter and Revit File Reader. Also, you can configure the Revit file conversion parameters to change the way the file is displayed in the selection tree. For example, you can divide the file into levels to organize the model hierarchy by File at the top level, down to Category, Family, Type, and Instance. See the section "Navigating the Selection Tree" later in this chapter for more information.

Also, for Revit files, subparts are named according to the material from which they are made. For example, a wall may be broken up into subparts composed of asphalt or aluminum. When using the 2013 version of Revit, you have the option of using either the original room geometry or converting it into construction subparts in Navisworks. Also, room items within the Revit file have their own Rooms category in the Properties window.

The NWC Exporter was useful as it allowed you to export only the visible geometry in your Revit model. To accommodate this workflow when importing the native Revit file, the Revit File Reader has three options that allow you to control how the model is displayed when opened or appended in Navisworks.

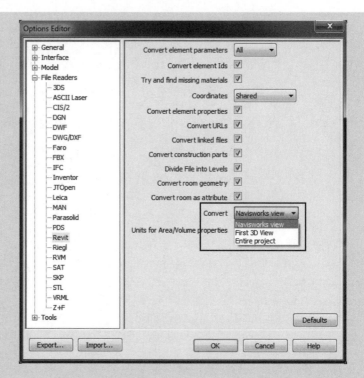

Navisworks View   In this setting, the first 3D view that contains the text "Navisworks" or "Navis" in the view name is selected. The text is not case sensitive. If this option is chosen and no views in the Revit model meet these naming criteria, the first available 3D view is selected. Note that using all caps is not supported (for example, NAVISWORKS, NAVIS).

First 3D View   This setting selects the first listed 3D view as the basis for what is displayed from the Revit file.

Entire Project   This setting will display all geometry from the Revit file regardless of whether items are hidden.

The Navisworks View option is probably the most useful setting because it allows you to create a specific 3D view for your Navisworks model without overriding any of the other visibility settings or views in Revit.

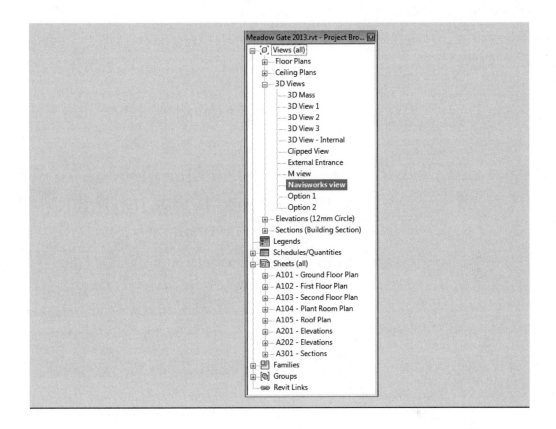

Quick Properties

The Quick Properties command is useful when you're interacting with the model to quickly gain access to the object properties without having to highlight the element or open the Properties window. You simply hover over the element, and Navisworks displays the property data in a pop-up window, similar to a tooltip. By default, this window displays the item name and type, but you can configure it to display any property that is listed in the Properties window. Here are the steps to configure Quick Properties using the model c04_Meadowgate 2013.nwd:

1. Open Quick Properties from the Display panel on the Home tab (Figure 4.4).

FIGURE 4.4
Click Quick
Properties on the
Display panel.

2. Hover your cursor over the roof of the model, and you should see the item name and type (Figure 4.5).

FIGURE 4.5
Navisworks scene
showing the Quick
Properties pop-up

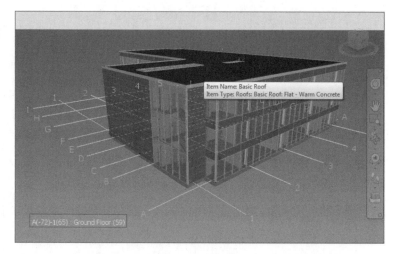

3. To configure this pop-up for additional properties or different ones, open the Global Options Editor and select Interface ➤ Quick Properties ➤ Definitions (Figure 4.6).

FIGURE 4.6
Use the Global
Options Editor
to modify Quick
Properties settings

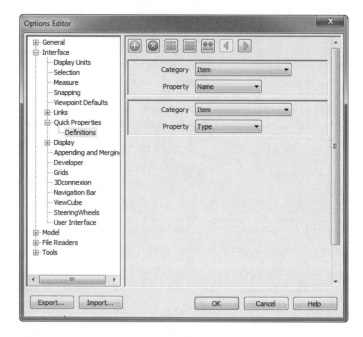

4. To add more properties, select the green plus sign near the top. A new Quick Properties field will be added.

5. From the Category drop-down, select Revit Type. For Property, select Default Thickness. Click OK.

6. Make sure Quick Properties is enabled, and hover over the roof element. You should now have three properties displaying data about the roof (Figure 4.7).

FIGURE 4.7
Revised Quick
Properties

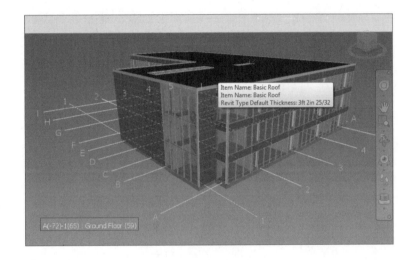

Item Name: Basic Roof
Item Name: Basic Roof
Revit Type Default Thickness: 3ft 2in 25/32

A(-72)-1(65) : Ground Floor (59)

QUICKLY ACCESSING FIELDS FOR QUICK PROPERTIES

When selecting the category and property values for your Quick Properties definitions, you can type in the first letter of the value you're looking for rather than scrolling through the long list.

Using Quick Properties is an efficient way to view property information. The benefit of this feature is that you can navigate through the model and still access the properties without having to change from Navigation mode to Select mode and back. You can keep moving, stopping only long enough to hover over the model element to retrieve the data. Also, since the data in your scene is dynamic, any new updates to the model are reflected once they're loaded in Navisworks. If an object has no associated property values, Navisworks will leave the fields blank.

You can also export your Options Editor settings for use on other projects. Simply select the Export button and specify what options you wish to export. The file is saved as XML and can be queried or edited in a standard editing tool. Experiment with configuring other Quick Properties and think about where you can use this technique.

EXPLORING QUICK PROPERTIES WORKFLOWS

One of the benefits of Navisworks is the large number of file types that can be read. The downside to this is that each of these file types typically contains a different property name and syntax. As a result, configuring the Quick Properties can be time consuming since each file type needs to be configured for the particular nomenclature.

You can maximize your efficiency with the Quick Properties by creating a master XML file and sharing it on all projects. Load a model and create the Quick Property definitions for that particular file type. Click the Export icon and select Definitions in the Quick Properties option.

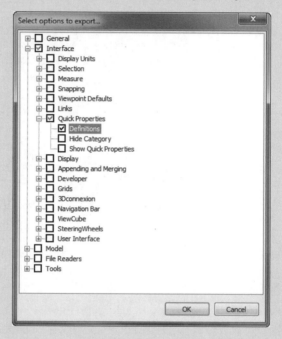

Go ahead and create additional XML exports for the other file types you typically work with (e.g., Revit, AutoCAD®, Civil 3D®, Inventor®, and other file types). In a text editor or Notepad, open the XML file and note the file structure. You'll see the structure comprises an optionset name, option name, data type, and internal name. Copy and paste the relevant properties from the individual files into a master XML file.

```
<?xml version="1.0" encoding="UTF-8"?>
<exchange xsi:noNamespaceSchemaLocation="http://download.autodesk.com/us/navisworks/schemas/nw-exchange-8.0.xsd" xmlns:xsi="http:
  <optionset name="">
    <optionset name="interface">
      <optionset name="smart_tags">
        <optionarray name="definitions">
          <optionset name="">
            <option name="category">
              <data type="name">
                <name internal="LcOaNode">Item</name>
              </data>
            </option>
            <option name="property">
              <data type="name">
                <name internal="LcOaPartitionFilename">File Name</name>
              </data>
            </option>
          </optionset>
          <optionset name="">
            <option name="category">
              <data type="name">
                <name internal="LcRevitData">Element</name>
              </data>
            </option>
            <option name="property">
              <data type="name">
                <name internal="revit_Door Panel Offset">Door Panel Offset</name>
              </data>
            </option>
          </optionset>
          <optionset name="">
            <option name="category">
              <data type="name">
                <name internal="LcOaNode">Item</name>
              </data>
            </option>
            <option name="property">
              <data type="name">
                <name internal="LcOaNodeLayer">Layer</name>
              </data>
            </option>
          </optionset>
          <optionset name="">
            <option name="category">
              <data type="name">
                <name internal="LcRevitData">Revit Type</name>
```

Import the master XML file back into Navisworks using the Import button at the bottom of the Options Editor. Recall that if an object has no associated property, it will remain blank when you hover over the object. Navisworks will only display those that are available for that particular file type. In addition to creating a "one size fits all" approach for your Navisworks sessions, you can share this file among your project team so everyone can leverage the Quick Properties features.

Exploring Object Properties of Multiple Elements

When selecting multiple objects, the Properties window will not show any property data but will indicate how many objects are currently selected. New to Navisworks 2013 is the Selection Inspector function. This tool allows you to view the object properties for selections of multiple elements. To better understand how Navisworks displays these multiple selections, look in the Chapter 4 folder, open the file c04_Meadowgate-Selection Inspector.nwd, and follow these steps:

1. Open the Selection Inspector by selecting the icon in the bottom-right corner of the Select & Search panel of the Home tab, as shown in Figure 4.8.

FIGURE 4.8

Selection Inspector icon in the Select & Search panel

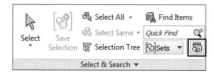

2. Select the Doors search set.

3. By default, Navisworks will list the current Quick Properties setting. To configure additional properties or different ones, select the Quick Property Definitions icon on the upper right of the Selection Inspector window.

4. To add more properties, select the green plus sign near the top. A new field will be added to the Selection Inspector. In the drop-down menu, select a new category and property value. Depending on the details of the model, the lists of available options will differ.

5. To see the list of all available properties associated with the categories in your Navisworks scene, select the Records view icon ⚏. In this view, you can use the left and right arrows to toggle between all of your currently defined Quick Properties definitions. Any changes made will override your original settings. When finished, select either the Grid view ▤ or List view ▤ icon to return to the main listing of properties.

6. Select OK when finished to return to the Selection Inspector window.

In addition to inspecting the object properties of search and selection sets, you can also inspect a selection from the selection tree or Scene view. By holding down the Ctrl key and selecting the object in your Scene view, you can quickly assemble detailed selection sets. Furthermore, you can then zoom to the selection to display it within the model or modify the contents by removing individual components from the set. When you save a selection, it appears in the Selection Sets window. You can then rename your selection set. Table 4.1 provides an overview of the different icons and buttons in the Selection Inspector.

TABLE 4.1:   Selection Inspector Overview

ICON	NAME	DESCRIPTION
	Model	This icon represents a model or design file.
	Layer	This icon signifies a layer or level.
	Group	This icon represents a group such as a block definition from a CAD/BIM application.
	Instanced Group	This icon represents an instanced group, such as an inserted block from AutoCAD. (If in the imported file the instance was unnamed, Navisworks renames the instance to match the child's object name.)
	Geometry	This icon signifies geometry such as linework or closed polylines/polygons.
	Instanced Geometry	This icon represents an instanced item of geometry such as items of instances from 3D Studio or other applications.
	Composite Object	This icon represents a composite object. Items include single CAD objects that are defined and represented in Navisworks as a series of individual geometry items.
	Collection	This icon signifies a collection of items. This typically refers to a Revit model with numerous objects within. It may also include other geometry and groups, subgroups, and/or instanced groups.
	Deselect	This button deselects an object or group of objects from the Selection Inspector window.
	Show Item	This button zooms to the selected object in the main Scene window.
	Export	This button exports the selection listing into a .csv file for reference outside the Navisworks application.

With the Selection Inspector, it's easy to quickly reference the object properties of multiple elements. Moreover, you can create customized selection sets based on specific properties by simply adding and deselecting objects to the set and saving it as a selection set for later use. Note that the Quick Properties settings in the Options Editor are used to define both the Selection Inspector and Quick Properties definitions.

User-Defined Properties

Earlier, our Properties window displayed several category tabs. It's important to note that these tabs can vary depending on the file format and the level of object properties that are embedded in the file. In addition, you can create your own tab to attach supplemental data to the different model elements. You might do so if you want to add a property for tracking who has reviewed the model or to enter milestone dates for a piece of equipment that has been delivered to a job-site. Let's go through an example and add a few custom tabs to the Properties window using the file c04_Meadowgate-User Properties.nwd:

1. Select the roof in your model.

2. In the Properties window, right-click anywhere in the area below the tabs. Then select the Add New User Data Tab option.

3. You should now have a new tab named User Data. Go ahead and select the tab to activate it.

4. Right-click again anywhere in the body of the box and choose Rename Tab.

5. Rename the data tab **Reviewers**.

6. Right-click again and select Insert New Property. You will be prompted to choose String, Boolean, Float, or Integer. Select the String property. Here is a quick overview of each property:

   String   Choose this option if your property value is a string (such as John Doe). String values can be any combination of alphanumeric characters.

   Boolean   This option provides you with a yes/no property value only.

   Float   This property is used for decimal values (such as 3.141).

   Integer   Use this property for both positive and negative real numbers (including 0).

7. A blank field will be added to the tab. Go ahead and enter **Name**. If you click elsewhere, you'll need to right-click the blank field and select the Rename command.

8. Double-click the blank Value field or right-click the Name property you just created and select Edit Property Value. A separate dialog box will open, as shown in Figure 4.9.

FIGURE 4.9
Custom property dialog box for user-defined properties

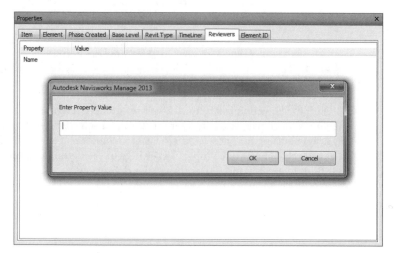

9. Enter the name of the reviewer and click OK.

10. Close the file without saving.

In this exercise, you added a custom user tab to the Properties window. For our example, you created a Reviewer tab for the roof selection; however, consider what other data you could incorporate here or in other parts of your model.

Managing Models

While Navisworks can handle extremely large models with ease, it can sometimes become a burden to locate objects, especially ones that are occluded or obscured behind other elements. Also, with larger projects, similar-type objects may be spread out across a larger expanse, making it troublesome to locate them. This section will focus on features such as search and selection sets to break down the complex model into more manageable pieces. We'll also cover ways to locate specific groupings of items by referencing their object properties as well as ways to reuse these search criteria on future projects.

The main area for accessing this data is the Sets window. Like other Navisworks functions, this too contains a dockable window that can be pinned to specific areas in your Navisworks interface. If you're familiar with this feature in older releases, you'll be happy to know that in the 2013 release, there were some changes to this window. Most notable is the addition of icons at the top of this window for accessing features such as saving search and selection sets. There are also icons for creating folders, duplicating sets, and adding comments. In addition, the context menu for the Sets window has been simplified, so you can now hide/unhide groups of objects.

Using Selection Sets

Selection sets are one of the easiest ways to remember groupings of objects in your model. You select the object(s) from your model and save them as a grouping that you can recall at a later date. The benefit is that instead of manually searching for a specific object, you select the selection set and Navisworks will highlight the saved grouping of objects in your model. Selection sets are static collections, meaning that if portions of the model change or are updated, they will only remember what objects were originally saved. Using the c04_Meadowgate 2013.nwd file, let's create some selection sets in this file:

1. Open the Sets window by selecting the Home tab.

2. In the Select & Search area, select Manage Sets from the bottom of the drop-down menu to open the Sets window, as shown in Figure 4.10. This is a dockable window, so you can pin it open or have it floating in your Navisworks scene.

FIGURE 4.10
Click Sets ➤ Manage Sets in the Select & Search panel.

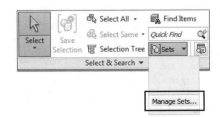

3. Use the revolving door on the main entrance to the building as the object for your selection set. Navigate to the front of the structure and select the main revolving door assembly; then, while holding down the Ctrl key, select the surrounding glazing and mullions of the main entrance, as shown in Figure 4.11.

FIGURE 4.11
Display window showing the selected revolving door assemblies

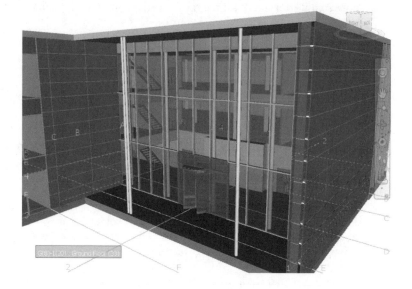

4. In the Sets window, right-click and select Save Selection. Navisworks will add an icon of a circle with a blue square. You can also click the Save Selection button in the Select & Search area of the Home tab in the ribbon.

5. Rename the generic selection set **Revolving Door** and press Enter to save your selection.

6. Press Esc to clear any selection on the screen.

You can think of selection sets as groups in a CAD/BIM application or as categories in Revit. They are groupings of objects by similar discipline, display, phasing, or any other classification. Spend some time becoming familiar with selection sets because you'll use them to break your model into "bite-sized" pieces for easier access and navigation. When naming the different selection sets, use a consistent naming convention because Navisworks allows duplicate names.

DRAG AND DROP SELECTION SETS

New to Navisworks 2013 is the ability to create selection sets by dragging model components directly into the Sets window. Open the Sets window and highlight all of the model elements you wish to capture in your main scene. Using the Select tool, left-click at least one of the highlighted elements and drag it/them over the Sets window. The mouse selector icon will change to a pointer, and when you release the mouse button, a new set named Selection Set will be created. In addition to dragging model components from the Scene view, you can also drag and drop elements from the selection tree hierarchy.

Creating Search Sets

Search sets are similar to selection sets, but instead of manually selecting the objects in your Navisworks scene, you can leverage the object properties of the model to identify specific objects. When you run a query of the model with specific criteria, Navisworks will highlight all relevant objects. You can then save this grouping as a search set.

The main benefit of a search set is that every time you highlight the grouping, Navisworks will conduct a search of the model to identify any components that match your criteria. In effect, this allows the search sets to identify changes and updates to the model. Since this is a dynamic feature, you'll find it extremely useful while your model is still in development because it lets you capture changes without having to manually adjust your existing selection set.

To create a search set, you'll use the Find Items tool. The Find Items tool is another dockable window that you will use to define the search criteria for your search set. In the Find Items dialog box, you can specify which properties you want to use in the search. Search options are based on the same object properties hierarchy we discussed earlier in this chapter (Category, Property, and Value). Let's go through a few examples of using Find Items to identify the interior doors in our model. We'll be using the c04_Meadowgate 2013.nwd file for this exercise. Follow these steps:

1. Open the Sets and Properties windows.

2. Locate the Find Items command on the Select & Search panel of the Home tab. Make sure the Find Items and Properties windows are pinned open so you can access them easily.

3. Navigate to the inside of the model and select any of the interior doors. Make sure you select the door body and not the handle.

4. Keep the door selected, and in the Properties window, select the Element tab and note the value for the property labeled Category (Figure 4.12). If you're not seeing the Element tab, look in the selection tree to make sure you're referencing the parent object and not the geometry subobjects (Figure 4.13). Selection resolution will be covered later in this chapter in the section "Exploring Selection Tree Options."

FIGURE 4.12

Properties window showing the interior door properties

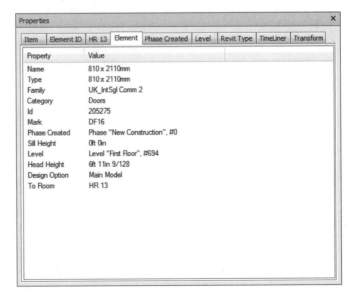

FIGURE 4.13
Expanded selection tree

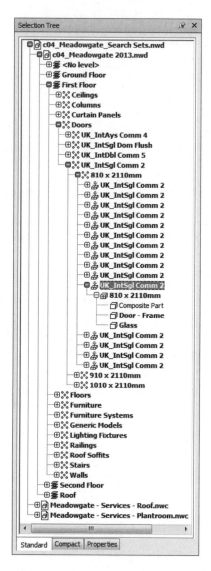

You should see Doors as the value for your selection. The next steps involve using this information for your search criteria. It's important to note that some model objects may not have as much property information, so you may need to identify other property categories to use for identification. Spend a few minutes looking at other components in the model and the level of embedded object properties.

The Find Items window contains some duplicate elements from the Navisworks interface. Let's explore these in detail before you finish the search set. On the left side of the window is a listing of all the appended models in our scene. When you conduct a search for a specific item, you can direct Navisworks to focus on a specific file (Figure 4.14). If no file is specified from the list, Navisworks will search through all models in the scene.

FIGURE 4.14
Find Items window
showing the list of
appended models

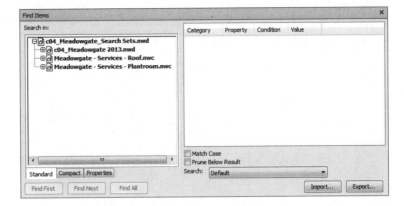

The area on the right contains the search fields for our query. Note the standard object property hierarchy but with the addition of the Condition tab, which will be used as an operator for our search. Let's break out these tabs in more detail and explain how they relate to the Properties window:

Category   The first part of our object property hierarchy is the category. If you expand the drop-down for this option, Navisworks lists all of the available categories from your entire model, unless you've selected specific models from the selection tree on the left side. In our Properties window, the category refers to the tabs along the top (Figure 4.15).

FIGURE 4.15
Hierarchy
layout between
the Find Items and
Properties windows

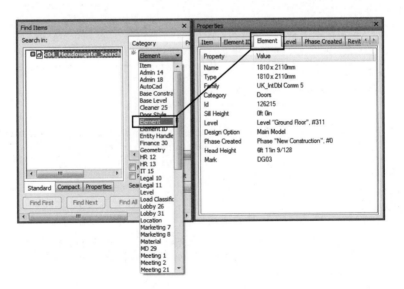

Property   The Property tab lists all of the available property names. This list varies and is determined by the selected category. In our Properties window, this corresponds to the listing under the Property heading, as shown in Figure 4.16.

FIGURE 4.16
Property
mapping between
the Find Items and
Properties windows

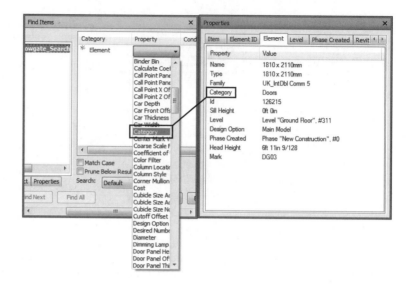

Condition This option lets you select a condition operator for your search. Table 4.2 provides a more in-depth look at the operators.

TABLE 4.2: Search Condition Operators

OPERATOR	DESCRIPTION
=	This operator refers to an equal match between the object property and the specified value. This will be the most common operator in your searches.
Not Equals	The Not Equals operator can be used to negate the values in a search. This is usually used in conjunction with other statements.
>–	The Greater Than operator can only be used with numerical values. This operator is useful when you're referencing dates and other sequential values where you need to identify components beyond the specified value.
>=	The Greater Than or Equals operator is used with numerical values. Similar to the Greater Than operator, it allows you to specify items that are equal to or greater than the specified value.
<–	The Less Than option can only be used with numerical values. Similar to the Greater Than operator, Less Than is useful for referencing values less than the specified value.
<=	The Less Than or Equals operator is used with numerical values. Similar to the Greater Than operator, it allows you to specify items that are equal to or less than the specified value.

TABLE 4.2: Search Condition Operators *(CONTINUED)*

OPERATOR	DESCRIPTION
Contains	The Contains operator allows you to search based on a partial value. This operator is useful when you're trying to select multiple items that contain a common sequence of characters. Examples include using just Window instead of specifying Window1, Window2, etc.
Wildcard	The Wildcard operator allows you to use both ? and * in your specified value. The ? will match one unspecified character, while the * will match multiple characters.
Defined	The Defined operator allows you to qualify a search, assuming there is a defined value in the search string.
Undefined	The Undefined operator functions similar to Defined, except you must not have any defined values in your search string.

Value The Value tab lists all property values for your search criteria. Just like the Property options, the Value drop-down entries will vary depending on the selection (Figure 4.17).

FIGURE 4.17
Value mapping between the Find Items and Properties windows

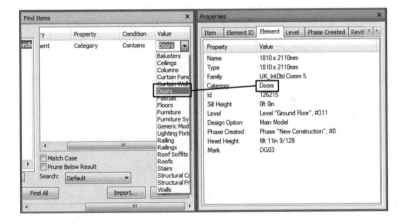

Now, let's run through an exercise using the Door values we just explained. Here are the steps:

1. Enter the following values in the drop-down menus of the Find Items window, as shown in Figure 4.18.

   ◆ Category: **Element**

   ◆ Property: **Category**

   ◆ Condition: = (equals)

   ◆ Value: **Doors**

FIGURE 4.18
Find Items window
showing the search
criteria for the
interior doors

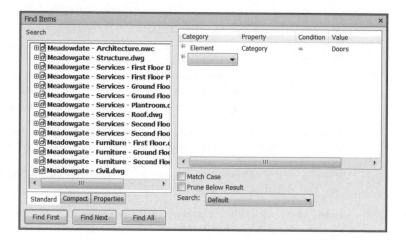

2. Uncheck the Match Case check box, unless you want to respect the capitalization of the model properties.

3. Keep your search as Default in the drop-down box.

4. On the lower left of the Find Items window are three options for initiating the Find feature. For this exercise, you want to locate all doors in the model, so select the Find All button.

   Navisworks will search the model and highlight any objects that contain the Element category of Doors.

5. To save this as a search set, in the Sets window, right-click and select Save Search. Name the Search Set **Interior Doors**.

If you select Save Selection, Navisworks will capture just the highlighted objects in your scene. This is identical to creating a selection set, as discussed earlier in this chapter. An easy way to distinguish between search and selection sets is that selection sets use a circle with a blue square, while search sets use a small blue square with binoculars (Figure 4.19).

FIGURE 4.19
Search and
Selection Set icons

At this point, you've created a search set that identifies all of the interior doors in this model. Now let's use a second search to pinpoint a smaller set of the doors. This technique is useful if, for example, the doors in our model are referenced in both the interior and exterior of the model. In the Find Items window, you can layer multiple searches to further isolate the objects and create an exact grouping of the model elements.

In our next exercise, you want to create a series of search sets for the interior doors but isolate them by level. In the Properties window, you see that the Item tab lists layer information, which in this model refers to Ground Floor, First Floor, and Second Floor. Using the same principles for isolating the doors, let's create a second part to our query to isolate by levels. Here's how:

1. Using the same search criteria from the earlier exercise, add a second search query. Let's use the following search criteria, as shown in Figure 4.20.

   ◆ Category: **Item**

   ◆ Property: **Layer**

   ◆ Condition: = (equals)

   ◆ Value: **Ground Floor**

FIGURE 4.20
Search criteria mapping between the Find Items and Properties windows

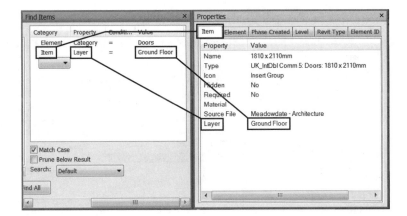

2. Select Find All, and note that only the doors listed on the Ground Floor are selected.

3. Create a search set and name it **Ground Floor Doors**.

4. Repeat this exercise for creating search sets for **First Floor Doors** and **Second Floor Doors**.

The previous example is useful when you're working with a large grouping of similar items and narrowing it down to a smaller subset. However, there are times when you want to create search sets that consist of dissimilar objects. Examples include window assemblies where there are the pane, mullions, and possibly additional elements. Since these objects are unique and don't share the same object properties, you'll get zero results in your search unless you direct Navisworks to recognize these criteria. When you create a search query, there is an option to include an Or statement. This statement tells Navisworks to identify objects from either search criteria but not to look for objects that contain both. Let's use the windows example and try this out:

1. Right-click in the search window and select Delete All Conditions. This clears the old search criteria.

2. Create a search set that is based on the following criteria:

◆ Category: **Element**

◆ Property: **Name**

◆ Condition: = (equals)

◆ Value: **Glazed**

3. Add a second search criteria using the following:

◆ Category: **Element**

◆ Property: **Category**

◆ Condition: = (equals)

◆ Value: **Curtain Wall Mullions**

4. Select Find All. You should get an error message indicating that there are no objects found. Click OK.

5. Right-click the second search criteria in the Find Items window and select Or Condition from the context menu (see Figure 4.21).

FIGURE 4.21
Choose the Or condition from the context menu

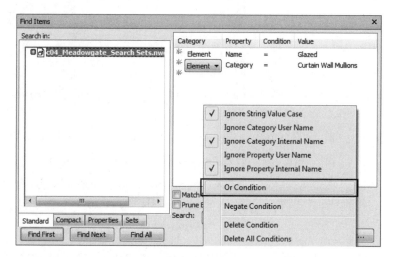

6. Navisworks will display a small black + sign next to the search string indicating that it will read both strings as separate searches.

7. Select Find All and notice that Navisworks has identified both the glazing and the mullions.

8. Save this as a search set named **Glazing Assembly**.

In addition to the Or condition, there is also an option to use negative conditions for certain searches where you want to negate the values. As you develop skills for using the Find

Items functions and search sets, you'll start to realize the benefit of using intelligent models as opposed to strictly a 3D model with no object properties. In this exercise, we leveraged the metadata or embedded object properties to isolate model elements and save groupings for future use. This concept allows even the most complex of models to easily be divided or broken down into smaller pieces. In future chapters, you'll use search sets to configure colors, link model elements to project schedules, and more. Spend time becoming comfortable with search sets to speed your mastery of Navisworks.

Using Select Commands

The Select commands are useful tools that let you quickly select model elements by common property types or naming conventions. Let's look in the Select & Search panel of the Home tab and examine the Select All (Figure 4.22) and Select Same drop-downs.

FIGURE 4.22
The Select All
drop-down menu

In the Select All drop-down, you can choose from three options:

◆ Select All

◆ Select None

◆ Invert Selection

Select All, as its name implies, will highlight all elements in your Navisworks scene. Select None will deselect all objects in your model. Pressing the Esc key will also deselect all highlighted objects. Invert Selection will reverse which items are selected and deselected. This is a useful feature when you're trying to select a group of objects within a scene. Sometimes, it's easier to select what you don't want and invert the selection to capture the selections.

The Select Same drop-down contains additional selection features, but the values in the drop-down will vary depending on what item(s) are selected. If nothing is currently selected, the drop-down is unavailable. Open the Meadowgate model, c04_Meadowgate 2013.nwd, and select just one interior door. In the Select Same drop-down, notice the broad range of choices you can use to further select additional model elements (Figure 4.23).

FIGURE 4.23
Select Same
drop-down menu

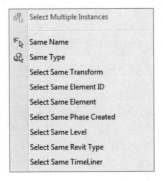

This feature allows you to select objects by name, type, or a series of object properties. Experiment with selecting different commands and note which items are highlighted. Choose a different object and note how the selection commands vary. Selection commands function similarly to search sets but are not as flexible; nonetheless, these commands still provide you with an easy way to select similar objects with a limited amount of interaction.

Exploring the Quick Find

Sometimes, you're in a hurry to locate a specific item and don't want to go through the process of using the Find Items command. The Quick Find (shortcut key Ctrl+F) tool allows you to enter any word or combination of words from the object properties. Navisworks will search through the model and highlight the first instance of your search string. You can also use the Quick Find tool located in the Select & Search panel. To advance to the next match, type in your search term and click the magnifying glass icon to the right of the text field (see Figure 4.24).

FIGURE 4.24
Quick Find appears
in the Select &
Search menu

Adding, Removing, and Updating Items

When working with selection sets, you may want to add more elements. Remember, selection sets are static and do not update with changes to the model. To add items to an existing selection set, do the following:

1. Select the appropriate selection set to which you wish to add items.

2. Hold down the Ctrl key and select the additional items.

3. Right-click the set in the Sets window.

4. Choose Update from the context menu. The new additions are now part of the selection set.

Updating search sets is slightly different since they are already dynamic and will update accordingly with any changes to the model; however, you may want to adjust the search criteria to include or remove additional elements. Here's how:

1. Select the appropriate search set from the Sets window.

2. Open the Find Items window and modify the search criteria.

3. Right-click in the Sets window and choose Update from the menu. The new search criteria are now saved under the existing search set.

Updating items in your search and selection sets is an easy process that is aimed at quickly resolving changes to your scene. Depending on your model, you may have a combination of search and selection sets.

Adding sets together is also possible. Simply select the first set in the Sets window, and then hold down Ctrl and select the next set. Once the two sets are selected, press and hold Ctrl again, select any item in the project, and right-click it twice. One click selects it and the second click deselects it. Now you can save the new set.

Exporting and Reusing Search Sets

In addition to automatic updates when you're working with search sets, a bonus is that you can reuse them on future projects. Recall that a search set is a data query that is executed every time that particular set is highlighted. In Navisworks, you can export these queries and import in other projects. This allows you to build up a library of search sets and avoid having to create them with every new project. One limitation with search sets is that your naming conventions must remain the same; otherwise, the search criteria will be looking for object properties that are listed under a different name and return no results. To export search sets, do the following:

1. Open the file c04_Meadowgate_Search_Set_Export.nwd.

2. In the Output tab, choose Search Sets from the Export Data panel (Figure 4.25).

FIGURE 4.25
Choose Search Sets from the Export Data panel

Alternatively, you can select the Import/Export icon on the top right of the Sets window and select Export Sets from the drop-down menu.

3. Specify the filename and location for saving.

4. Close the file without saving and open c04_Meadowgate_Search_Set_Import.nwd.

5. Choose Import ➢ Search Sets from the Application menu or the Import/Export icon at the top of the Sets window.

6. Select the saved XML file.

7. Open the file and note how the search sets are added back to the Sets window.

8. Close the file without saving.

MASTERING THE FIND ITEMS FEATURE

The power of search sets extends well beyond the current model since you can reuse them on future projects. To maximize the effectiveness of your search set queries, let's explore some best practices that will speed up the creation process but allow you to utilize them on additional Navisworks projects.

When selecting the values for your search query, you can type in the first letter of the value you're looking for, rather than scrolling through the long list. This is useful on large projects where there are hundreds of different categories to choose from.

Also, when defining the Condition statement, you may find that using Contains instead of = will help you define your results much quicker. If you plan on reusing the search sets queries on additional projects, the = statement will require the Value entry to be an exact match. When working with the Contains operator, you can utilize wildcards (*) before and after the entered value. In the following image, we're looking for items that are part of a Hydronic Piping system. By using a series of Contains statements and partial Value entries, we can capture all of the items for our search set. More important, this query is loose enough to capture variables in naming conventions, so this query could be used on additional projects.

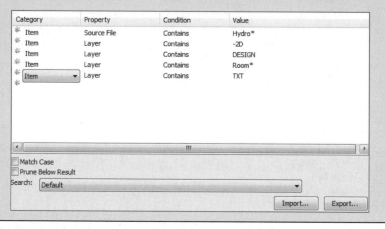

Navigating the Selection Tree

The selection tree displays the hierarchical listing of all files in your Navisworks scene based on the format they were originally saved in. Items in the selection tree are bidirectional with the model display, so when an element is selected in the selection tree, the corresponding model object is highlighted, and vice versa. This feature allows for quick and easy identification of the numerous objects in your scene.

Since the selection tree is a dockable window, you may need to pin it open or open it from the Home tab on the ribbon. Knowing your way around the selection tree is the first step to success in reaping the benefits of Navisworks. Let's explore the different areas of the selection tree and highlight the functions of the different tabs.

Standard

There are a total of four tabs in the selection tree, but by default, only Standard, Compact, and Properties are initially displayed. The Standard tab, as its name implies, displays the default model hierarchy. In Figure 4.26, you see that all appended models are listed by their filenames and type. The order shown is based on the loading sequence of the models. To follow along with these examples, look in the Chapter 4 folder for the file c04_Meadowgate-Selection Tree.nwd.

Expand the hierarchy by clicking the plus sign to the left of the filename, and you can drill into the structure of the file. In Figure 4.27, you see that the first model, Meadowgate - Architecture - Shell.rvt, is broken down by floor levels, as they were originally referenced in Revit, but with the components for each floor listed. The second model listed, Meadowgate

`- Services - First Floor Ductwork.dwg`, is an AutoCAD file and has a structure that is based on layers.

FIGURE 4.26
The selection tree showing all appended files

FIGURE 4.27
Expanded selection tree showing the different hierarchy between AutoCAD and Revit files

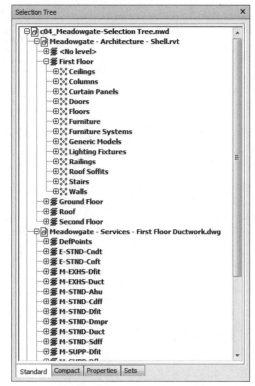

If you continue drilling down into hierarchy of the Architecture model, you start to uncover the individual components that reside on the First Floor. As you can see in Figure 4.28, one of the components listed on the First Floor is a 450 mm diameter round column. If you continue expanding the list, you will finish up by listing the basic geometry that composes an element.

FIGURE 4.28
Fully expanded selection tree showing the hierarchies of a Revit file

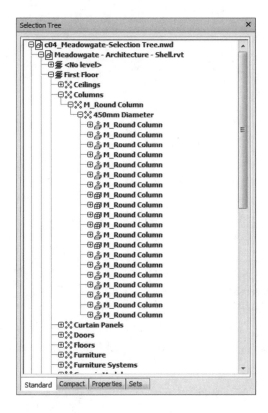

Expanding the AutoCAD model `Meadowgate - Services - Ground Floor Pipework.dwg`, you see a similar taxonomy; however, this hierarchy is based on layers in the AutoCAD model and not the level, as listed for the Revit model (Figure 4.29). It's important to note how these various file structures affect your selection decisions.

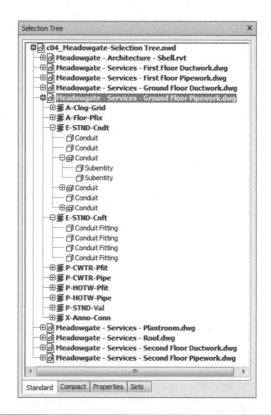

WHAT'S IN A FILENAME?

As was mentioned earlier in the book, Navisworks 2013 allows for the direct importation of native Revit files (.rvt, .rfa, .rte). There are times when you'll need to export the Revit model to either the NWC or other formats. It's important to note that even though the geometry and underlying data is mostly identical, the hierarchical structure varies greatly between the different formats.

Using the standard NWC export from Revit, you get a hierarchy based on the levels as defined in the Revit model shown in the following graphic. Typically, components that are constrained to a base level are listed in that same level in the Navisworks selection tree. Here's an example: Say you create a column in Revit that spans between the first and second floors of your model. In Navisworks, the column will be listed under the First Floor of the selection tree. Where this gets tricky is when objects aren't "based" on any particular level or span multiple levels. If your column were to span from the First Level to the roof of this multistory building, it would still be listed as being located on the First Floor in your selection tree. Items that are located between floors and aren't constrained to a level will sometimes appear in the <No Level> hierarchy.

Using the same Revit model but exporting to the DWF™/DWFx file format, you get an entirely different model hierarchy when appended into Navisworks. All the model elements are now structured as a component list that breaks down the Revit model by components such as Walls, Doors, and Windows.

The FBX® format is another format that is occasionally used to exchange information from Revit to other rendering applications. In the selection tree, you see that there is a limited structure with only a listing of the components in the model.

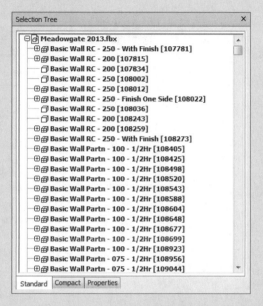

If we look at the native Revit file import, by default, we get a mixture of these results. Most noticeable is the combination of the levels as shown in the NWC import, but we also get the component listing as shown in the DWF/DWFx file import.

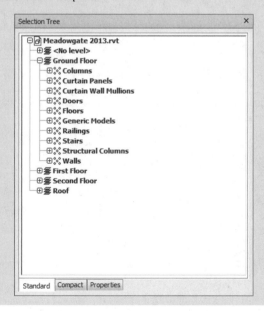

To parse the native Revit file by components only without any level designations, you can modify the file reader in the Global options. If you uncheck the Divide File Into Levels box, Navisworks will ignore dividing the file into individual levels. Note: These changes won't take effect until you reload the Revit file. Make sure you delete the existing cached NWC file; otherwise, Navisworks will reload the older hierarchy.

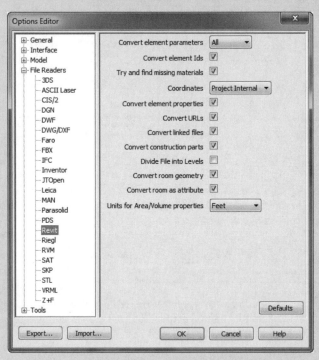

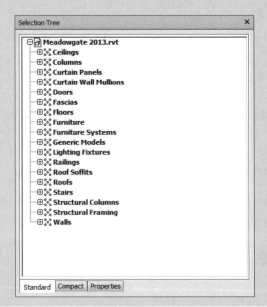

While there is no one format that is considered the best for Navisworks, remember that one of the strengths of Navisworks is the numerous file formats it can read. You should be familiar with interacting with the various types and the limitations of each.

The Standard tab in the selection tree is the principal location for most users. It's important to note that filenames cannot be modified once imported into Navisworks. If you're using an NWF file, you can delete the individual files and reappend the updated or modified files. If you're working with an NWD file, you can't make any changes to the hierarchy.

Compact

The Compact tab in the selection tree displays roughly the same information as the Standard tab, albeit a simplified version that omits some of the complexity. In Figure 4.30, the Compact tab display is showing the filename and the first level in the file structure only.

FIGURE 4.30

The Compact tab showing the abridged hierarchy of the selection tree

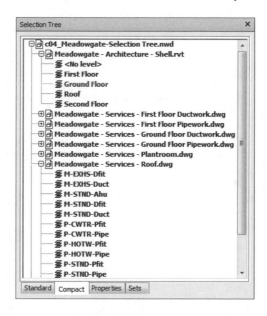

In Global Options, you can specify the level of compacting to include the following:

◆ Models

◆ Layers

◆ Objects

This feature is useful if your model contains numerous blocks or instanced groups that add more levels to your hierarchy. By reducing the complexity, it becomes much easier to navigate within the selection tree. Follow these steps to change the Compact tab properties:

1. Navigate to the Options Editor and select Interface ➢ Selection.

2. In the Compact Tree drop-down, select the appropriate level (see Figure 4.31).

3. Click OK when finished to close the Options Editor.

FIGURE 4.31
The Compact tab settings in the Options Editor

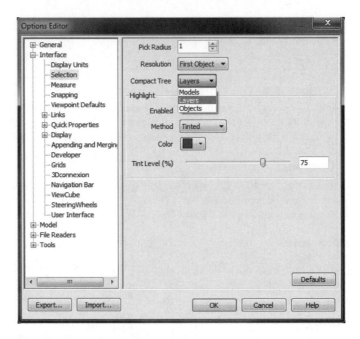

Let's do a quick comparison to see what information is truncated from the Compact tab. These series of figures show the Standard tab on the left and the Compact tab setting on the right. In Figure 4.32, with the Compact tab option set to Model, you cannot select any individual components.

FIGURE 4.32
Comparison between the Standard and Compact tabs

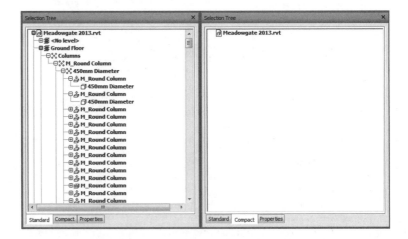

In Figure 4.33, the Compact tab option has been set to Layer. Notice how you can now choose the individual layers, but you're still missing individual model elements.

FIGURE 4.33
Comparison using the Layer option

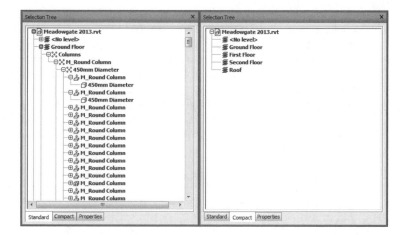

In Figure 4.34, the Compact tab has been set to Object. You can select individual objects down to the basic geometry. Notice the fewer number of levels the user needs to expand to reach the geometry layer. In this case, it would require seven clicks to reach the Line Set element using the Standard tab and only five using the Compact setting.

FIGURE 4.34
Comparison using the Object option

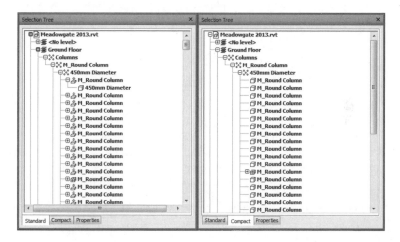

Depending on your file type, the Compact tab may provide an easier avenue to access the various levels of your model's hierarchy.

Properties

The Properties tab provides a different type of model organization. In Chapter 2, "Files and File Types," we mentioned the file aggregation process where geometry and the associated metadata are brought into Navisworks. Similar to the Standard and Compact tabs, the object properties metadata has a hierarchy of its own and uses the Properties tab to display this logic. Depending on the authoring application of your source files, this will vary, with certain applications embedding more than others. When models are appended to Navisworks, all object properties are displayed in the Properties tab. There is also a Properties window, which can be opened from the ribbon's Home tab. The data displayed in the selection tree is based on the hierarchy of the Properties window.

To explain this process a little more succinctly, look in the Chapter 4 folder for the file c04_Meadowgate 2013.nwd and select the roof of the main structure. Pin open or activate the Properties window. You should see a series of tabs: Item, Element, Phase Created, Base Level, Revit Type, TimeLiner, Reviewers, and Element ID, as shown in Figure 4.35.

FIGURE 4.35
Object Properties window showing roof data

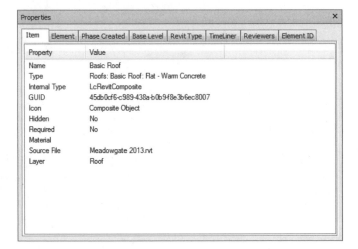

Select the Base Level tab for the Properties window. In the selection tree, select the Properties tab and expand the Base Level. You'll notice that the names in the Properties tab of the selection tree correspond to the tabs in the Properties window. However, the tabs in the Properties window are referencing *only* the roof object you selected, whereas the property hierarchy in the selection tree refers to all the object properties in the whole model (Figure 4.36).

FIGURE 4.36
Comparison between the Properties tab and the selection tree

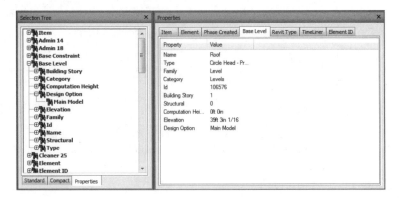

Selecting any of the objects in the selection tree will highlight all of the items corresponding to that particular object property. This enables quick and efficient searching of the model by property. Pressing Esc removes the highlighting.

Sets

The Sets tab displays a list of search and selection sets. This tab is identical to the information contained in the Sets window. If no search or selection sets have been defined, this tab is not shown. Search and selection sets cannot be added, deleted, or modified in the selection tree's Set tab; they can only be added, deleted, or modified in the Sets window.

Exploring Selection Tree Options

In this section, we'll explore the options available for the selection tree and ways to control the visibility of the various model elements. These concepts will be useful throughout the book as you develop your own methods for interacting with the model.

Configuring Model Visibility

As your project progresses and you continue to append and add files to your Navisworks scene, your model can get quite complex and detailed. While having access to this rich information is useful for a whole project view, there are times when you need to display certain elements that might be obstructed from view by other elements. An example to consider is the mechanical components in the interstitial space of a building that are typically bordered by walls, floors, and ceilings. In this section, we'll delve into the options that let you control the visibility of the model elements. You'll learn how to configure these settings to increase the performance of your navigation within larger models.

HIDE

The Hide command allows you to temporarily remove objects from your Navisworks scene to aid in viewing the obscured parts of the model. In later chapters, when we discuss design review workflows, this command will become useful when you need to isolate portions of the model. Navisworks is an intuitive program that is easy for users to learn. To illustrate this, the Hide command is accessible from no less than four different locations throughout the Navisworks interface. This allows you to work productively with your particular preference. Let's try out this command with the Meadowgate model from our earlier exercises, using the following steps:

1. Open c04_Meadowgate 2013.rvt.

2. In the selection tree, choose the Standard tab and expand the root node.

3. Expand the Ground Floor node and select Curtain Panels, and holding down the Ctrl key, select Curtain Wall Mullions.

4. In the Visibility panel located in the Home tab of the ribbon, select the Hide command, as shown in Figure 4.37. The curtain wall of the model will now be hidden, allowing you to see some of the structure and interior components of the model.

5. To unhide the elements, simply click the Hide icon again.

6. Expand the selection tree and try hiding a combination of elements using the Ctrl and Shift keys to select different groups of objects.

7. Close the file without saving.

FIGURE 4.37
Visibility icons in
the Home tab

When items are hidden, the list in the selection tree will turn gray to indicate which items are impacted. If you expand the selection tree hierarchy, you'll see that all the subelements of that model appear to be displayed as unhidden. Remember, any changes that happen to the parent node in the selection tree relationship flow down to the children nodes.

If you select another command, you can still unhide the now-hidden elements by clicking the Hide button again. However, if you select another object, the Hide icon will become grayed out and you won't be able to unhide your model elements. Don't worry—if you reselect the currently hidden objects from the selection tree, the icon will reappear and you can select it to unhide the elements.

HIDE UNSELECTED

Unlike the Hide command, which temporarily removes objects that are selected from your scene, the Hide Unselected function does just the opposite by hiding objects that aren't currently selected. This function is extremely useful when you select an object and want to isolate it from the rest of the model. Instead of trying to locate the adjacent objects to hide, you simply click the Hide Unselected icon to hide the surrounding objects. To unhide, click the icon again to display all objects.

USING THE HIDE UNSELECTED COMMAND

Deselecting the Hide Unselected command will reveal all objects in the project, including any previously hidden objects and files. A note of warning: If there are objects you wish to keep hidden, make a selection set of them so you can easily rehide them. Another way to unhide all objects previously hidden is to use the Undo command. This will retain any previously hidden objects.

REQUIRE

The Require function is useful when you're working with large models that are a drain on system resources. Depending on the complexity of your model and system resources, when navigating a large model, you may see flickering or, in some instances, portions of the model dropping out. The purpose of the Require command involves the way Navisworks processes data. When employing large models that demand considerable RAM to load and review the scene, Navisworks optimizes the available RAM by paging unnecessary data to the hard disk to speed up the loading process. This process allows you to continue navigating the model, even if it isn't completely loaded. Also, similar to gaming technology, Navisworks will display the objects deemed most important to the viewer and continuously load additional elements as RAM opens up. Sometimes, this on-demand rendering has unintended results: Model elements that are necessary for model navigation may drop out. The Require function allows you to specify which items will be prioritized when you're navigating through the model. The function will shift any dropout or flickering to other items and allow you to navigate through the model with better precision.

In our Meadowgate project, we noticed that the glazing is dropping out when we navigate around the model. Let's walk through the process of setting this up. You'll use the c04_Meadowgate 2013.rvt file again for this exercise:

1. Expand the Ground Floor level and select the Curtain Panels group from the Standard tab in the selection tree.

2. In the Visibility panel of the Home tab, click the Require button (see Figure 4.37 earlier).

3. If you move around the model, you'll notice that the glazing is rendered in full with no dropout or flickering.

4. When finished, do not save the changes.

When items are set to Require, the elements in the selection tree will be listed in a red font for easy identification. You can set any combination of items as Required, but keep in mind that this feature overrides the guaranteed frame rate and will slow down performance if your computer can't keep up. For more information on guaranteed frame rates, see the section on performance optimization in Appendix B, "Additional Resources and Tips."

In addition to using the Hide and Require icons in the Home tab, you can use the contextual tab that appears when you select any object. Figure 4.38 shows the contextual tab with the Hide and Require commands. You can also access this functionality by right-clicking the object name in the selection tree or by using the default keyboard shortcuts, Ctrl+H and Ctrl+R, respectively.

FIGURE 4.38
The contextual tab with the Hide and Require commands

UNHIDE ALL/UNREQUIRE ALL

The Unhide All and Unrequire All functions are a quick way to undo any of the changes you've made to the model. This functionality becomes useful when you've hidden various groups of objects and have moved on to other tasks. Recall that to unhide the elements, you must reselect all the names in the selection tree. Selecting the Unhide All icon reverts your model to a fully visible state without you having to identify which items were originally hidden. The drop-down for this function, shown in Figure 4.39, lets you access the Unrequire All command, which removes the object required feature from all instances in the selection tree.

FIGURE 4.39
Expanded Unhide All menu

Controlling Object Display Using Display Overrides

When displaying geometry, Navisworks will use the settings that were saved in the original source files. However, you may need to occasionally modify these settings to change colors or move objects in your model. This section will guide you through the various display configurations and discuss strategies for incorporating them in your standard workflows.

Display override refers to a collection of tools aimed at modifying the display properties of your Navisworks model to gain a better understanding. For most of these commands, we will be using the Item Tools contextual tab. As you'll recall, this tab is displayed only when an object in either the selection tree or model space is selected.

COLOR

Overriding colors is one of the easiest ways to transform your Navisworks scene for quick identification of the different disciplines in your scene. The process involves selecting the object(s) to override either from the selection tree or the model display and assigning a color from the drop-down in the Appearance panel in the Item Tools tab, as shown in Figure 4.40.

FIGURE 4.40

Appearance panel
of the Item Tools tab

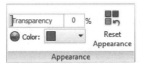

By default, Navisworks provides 40 basic colors to choose from in the initial drop-down menu; however, you can expand this selection by selecting More Colors at the bottom of the menu. Doing so opens a new dialog box with additional palettes of color and options for defining your own custom colors by mixing the RGB values (0–255), as shown in Figure 4.41.

FIGURE 4.41

Color selector in the
Appearance panel

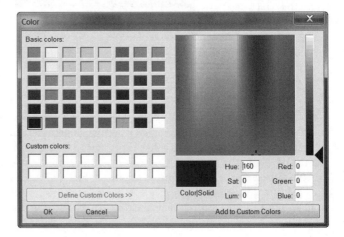

TRANSPARENCY

Similar to the color override feature, Navisworks also provides the ability to override the transparency of objects in your scene for a more realistic interaction. Items such as glazing can be configured as semitransparent, allowing you to see additional objects that had been occluded before. This feature is also useful when you're focusing on internal elements such as HVAC systems or other MEP objects by overriding the walls, ceilings, and other structures to a semitransparent view rather than hiding those elements (Figure 4.42). The advantage is that you still have a faint outline of the wall elements to help establish your components' location and context.

FIGURE 4.42
Display view with transparency showing hidden components

Depending on your system, performance may be impacted if you use excessive amounts of transparency because items that were previously occluded in the display must now be rendered. This extra rendering can put additional demand on your computer.

CHANGING THE SELECTION HIGHLIGHTING

By default, Navisworks highlights selected objects with a semitransparent green tint. While this is useful and quickly aids in identifying which objects are currently selected, there are times when you need to use a color other than green. In the Global Options Editor, you can specify the color as well as the method of the selection. Navigate to Global Options ➤ Interface ➤ Selection to access the options for changing the selection highlights. In the Method drop-down, you have three options to choose from:

◆ Shaded

◆ Wireframe

◆ Tinted

In the images that follow, we'll explore these settings. First, you see the original model with color-coded objects:

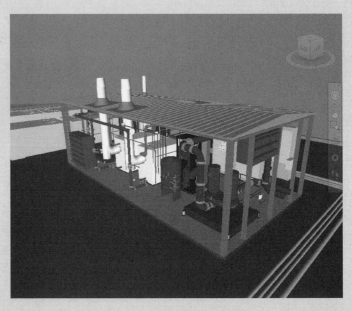

Shaded provides a consistent opaque color to the selected object. Use this option if you need to be able to identify objects and are not concerned about surface details.

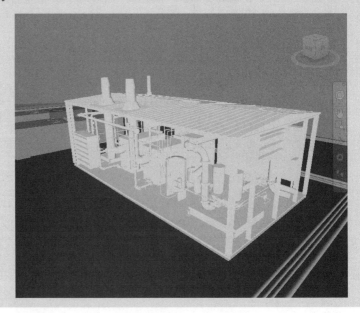

The Wireframe option overlays a series of colored lines. Since the colored lines don't mask your original objects, you can still reference surface features. This feature is also useful if you are using a variety of colors in your model so you can identify the selection by the wire appearance.

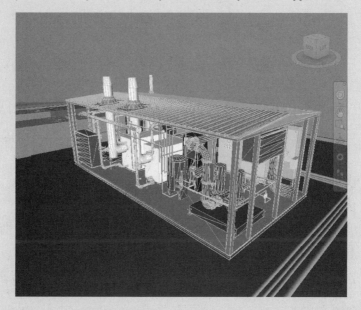

The Tinted option allows you to apply a specific level of transparency to the selection highlighting. This gives you a balance between the opaque shading selection and surface details.

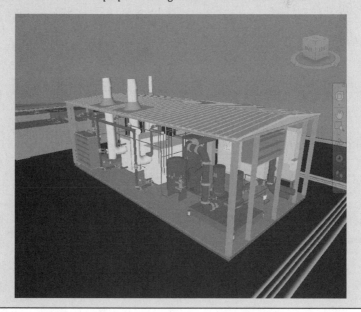

Transform

In addition to the basic color and transparency overrides, you can transform objects in your Navisworks scene by using the following overrides:

◆ Move

◆ Rotate

◆ Scale

◆ Reset Transform

Transformations become useful when you need to adjust the model to validate "what if" scenarios without impacting the original source data files.

To practice a transformation, let's walk through the steps to move the plant room model on the roof of our Meadowgate project:

1. Open c04_Meadowgate-Selection Tree.nwd.

2. Select Meadowgate - Services - Plantroom.dwg in the selection tree.

3. In the Item Tools contextual tab, select Move from the Transform panel (Figure 4.43).

FIGURE 4.43
Transform panel
showing the Move,
Rotate, Scale, and
Reset Transform
commands

4. In your display, Navisworks will display a gizmo in the geographic center of your selected geometry. The red, green, and blue lines refer to X-, Y-, and Z-axes (Figure 4.44). If you hover your mouse over the ends of these lines, the pointer will change to a hand that lets you drag the model along that specific axis. If you hover over the yellow planes that bridge the axis lines, you can drag the model in two different axes at once. When you select this box, the color will turn to white, indicating that you've selected that particular plane.

5. In addition to manually moving the model with the gizmo, you can specify the transform in numerical values by using the Transform drop-down menu in the ribbon, as shown in Figure 4.45.

The Rotate transform is executed in a similar fashion, except that you can specify the rotation axis by dragging the gizmo by the planes between the X-, Y-, or Z-axis markers. To rotate the model, hover over the curved red, green, and blue planes and drag your mouse in the appropriate direction (Figure 4.46). You can rotate in only one plane at a time. You can also specify the rotation in the Transform drop-down menu.

FIGURE 4.44
Plant room model
showing the Move
gizmo

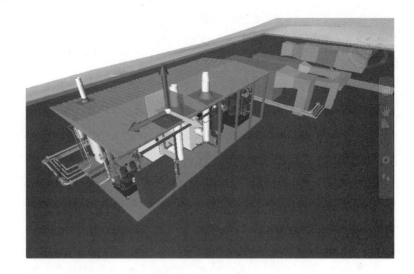

FIGURE 4.45
Transform
drop-down menu
showing area
to apply values
manually

FIGURE 4.46
Plant room model
showing the Rotate
gizmo

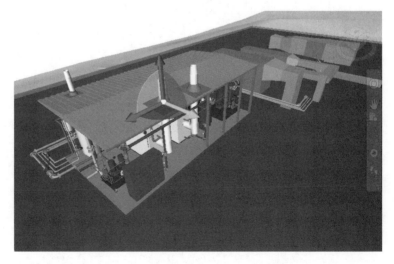

With the Scale transform, you can stretch the model in any axis or use a combination of axes. The gizmo is identical to the Move command and allows you to easily pick multiple axes to scale the model. If you select a plane between the arrows, the model will scale equally between the two arrows you selected. If you select the center ball, the entire model will be scaled the same. You can also manually enter a scale by clicking the drop-down menu.

 Real World Scenario

SITE LOGISTICS PLANNING WITH NAVISWORKS

One of the benefits of Navisworks is being able to fully understand your design before moving forward. This allows you to identify any challenges that might otherwise cause conflicts, and you can rectify them early in the design phase. Construction site logistics is an area where Navisworks is being used to fully understand the site and discover ways to mitigate risks associated with the construction process.

A recent publication discussed using cardboard cutouts of typical construction equipment (such as a jobsite trailer, material storage boxes, or portable toilets) on top of a 2D site drawing to plan the layout of an upcoming project. After the coordination was complete, you could then tape the cardboard outlines to the site plan and pin it up on the wall for reference.

Navisworks can re-create this concept in a much more beneficial way by using accurate 3D models of construction equipment in your model. Using navigation tools like Walk and the Third Person avatar, you can create virtual walkthroughs that are superior to trying to conceptualize the cardboard cutouts in 3D.

One of the ideas I like to share with my construction clients is to keep a library of construction equipment on hand for such planning purposes. With the variety of file formats that Navisworks can recognize, there are numerous websites that offer free content. I typically create a library that is broken down by the various equipment categories and populate it with the most common items.

Using the Append and Transform tools, it's easy to introduce this construction equipment into your model for realistic planning and coordination. On a tight site, it's important to introduce the context of the site. Doing so will ensure that material laydown areas are properly identified and safety is not compromised. In the next image, you see that the construction site is in a dense urban environment. Having the surrounding buildings in your Navisworks scene allows you to consider material delivery routes and laydown areas as well as emergency access.

Using the same model, you can get a bird's-eye view showing the placement of the various components within the perimeter of the site. In the next image, the turning radius of the tower crane has been displayed to aid in the proper placement of the crane. Note the tight proximity of the neighboring buildings. You could also verify that any material loads necessary for the project fall within the lifting capacity of the crane.

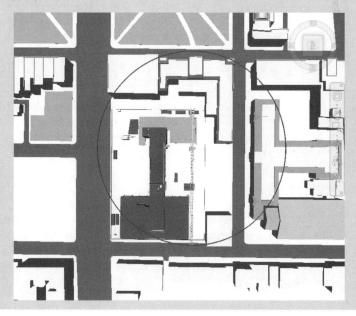

Using the Third Person avatar and Walk navigation tools, you can re-create the experience for the construction worker and identify any potential pitfalls that might cause injury. With safety being paramount at all jobsites, the desire to uncover hazards and modify the logistics plan to mitigate risk presents enormous opportunities to use Navisworks for site logistics planning.

FOCUS

To use the Focus tool, you first select an object. When you click the Focus icon in the Look At panel of the Item Tools tab, Navisworks will move that object to the center of your display window. The navigation tools will treat that object as the focal point and use the center of the selected object as the main orbital axis, or center of view.

ZOOM

In the same panel as the Focus command, you'll find the Zoom function, which allows you to zoom into the extents of any selected object. When working with a complex model, you can easily select any object(s) and engage the Zoom command to move the model so the selected object is in view in your display window.

SWITCHBACK

Occasionally, you may need to make changes to the source data in your scene and save the changes back into Navisworks. Instead of opening your design files and manually navigating to the components to modify, you can use the SwitchBack feature to re-create your current view in Navisworks inside your CAD or Revit model. This feature is currently limited to AutoCAD, Revit, and MicroStation file formats. To use this feature, you must have both Navisworks and the Revit or CAD application installed on the same machine. Let's examine the steps to create this workflow with CAD-based applications:

1. In your AutoCAD application, type **nwload** in the command line (MicroStation users, type **mdl load nwexport9**).

2. In Navisworks, select an object in your display window.

3. In the Item Tools contextual tab, select SwitchBack.

4. Your current view in Navisworks is re-created in your CAD application, and the same item is selected. Make any necessary changes to your source file and save.

5. In Navisworks, refresh the model to update the changes.

For Revit models, you'll need to work with any of the Revit platforms (Architecture, MEP, and Structure) from Navisworks release 2012 or newer for this feature to work. Here are the steps for this workflow:

1. In Revit, navigate to a 3D view.

2. Select Navisworks SwitchBack from the External Tools drop-down menu in the Add-Ins tab.

3. In Navisworks, select an object in your display window.

4. In the Item Tools contextual tab, select SwitchBack.

5. Your current view in Navisworks is re-created in Revit. Make any necessary changes to your source file and save. If you are working on an exported .nwc file, you will need to re-export the file.

6. In Navisworks, refresh the model to update the changes.

In Chapter 8, "Clash Detection," we'll explore more workflows with the SwitchBack feature and Clash Detection.

Hold

The Hold command allows you to constrain, or hold, any object to the display screen while continuing to move around the model. Any objects that are selected will be locked in their current location onscreen, while using the navigation tools will cause the other elements to change. The Hold command is useful if you need to pin an object in place and want to move the surrounding elements.

Let's say you're installing a large pump and want to mimic the delivery path. You can lock the pump in place and, using any of the navigation commands, move the pump through the scene for evaluation purposes. To release the pump, click the Hold icon again. Once you've completed your analysis, click the Reset Transform icon to return the pump to its original location.

Appearance Profiler

The Appearance Profiler allows you to override colors and transparencies by using selection or search sets and object properties to define which objects are impacted by this change. In versions of Navisworks older than 2012, changes to color or transparency could only be made from objects selected in the display window or selection tree. If your search set updated to reflect changes to the model, you had to manually update the color or transparency on any new items. With the Appearance Profiler, you can specify a color override for search and/or selection sets so that changes to the model are captured and updated.

This feature has some added benefits because it allows you to easily manage the color scheme of your Navisworks model. When working with complex models, it's easier to color-code items by discipline to aid in quick recognition. This ability becomes important when you're working in a dense area of the model and you're faced with a variety of disciplines. Another added benefit is that you can reuse these color profiles on future jobs.

Much like reusing selection sets, if you have a common naming convention, you can save an enormous amount of time. Table 4.3 lists sample color configurations for the various disciplines in a typical AEC workflow.

TABLE 4.3:   Sample Color Configurations by Discipline

DISCIPLINE	COLOR	TRANSPARENCY
Architectural	White	50%
Structural Steel	Brown	
Structural Slabs	Gray	50%
HVAC Equipment	Gold	
HVAC Supply Ducts	Blue	
HVAC Return Ducts	Magenta	
HVAC Pipe	Light Blue	
Electrical Equipment	Yellow	
Conduits	Yellow	
Cable Tray	Orange	
Low Voltage	Pink	
Lighting	Light Yellow	50%
P-Tube	Green	
Plumbing-Water	Cyan	
Plumbing-Sewer	Dark Orange	
Plumbing-Storm	Light Green	
Fire Protection	Red	

Let's create a color configuration using the Appearance Profiler. For this exercise, we'll use the c04_Meadowgate_Appearance_Profiler.nwd file. There are two options for assigning colors. You can use the embedded object properties or leverage your search and selection sets. We'll cover both functions in the following exercise. Here are the steps:

1. Open the Appearance Profiler from the Tools window in the Home tab.

2. In the Selector area on the left, you can select between using object properties or sets. We'll use By Property for this first exercise.

3. Remember the object properties hierarchy from earlier in this chapter? The three fields allow you to enter any search string using the Category, Property, and Value data.

   Let's use the example of coloring all the doors in our model. In the Category box, enter **Element**. For the Property value, enter **Category**, and finally, enter **Doors** for the value (be sure to choose Equals from the accompanying drop-down); see Figure 4.47.

FIGURE 4.47
The Appearance Profiler window

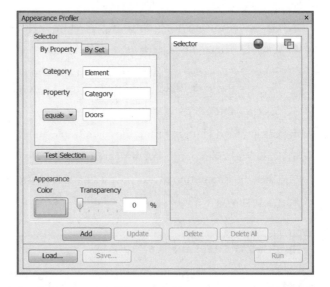

4. To validate that this selection works, click the Test Selection button. You should see all the doors in your model highlight. If you receive an error message, check your spelling and capitalization, because this tool is case sensitive.

5. Once you've verified that the logic is correct, you can apply a color and/or transparency to these model elements. In the Appearance section of the Profiler, choose a specific color and transparency setting.

6. Click the Add button; you should now have a line item on the right side indicating Element: Category Equals "Doors" and the appropriate color and transparency settings (Figure 4.48).

FIGURE 4.48
Selection value displayed in the Appearance Profiler

7. Continue to add more elements. When finished, click the Run icon in the lower-right corner. All of the doors in the model should be updated with the new color code.

8. To change an existing color or transparency setting, update your preferences in the Appearance section, and then click the Update button. Click the Run button again to update the model with your new appearances.

9. To remove an item, highlight the profile in the selection list on the right side and click the Delete button.

10. To save this profile for future use or use in other models, click the Save button and specify a name and location for the DAT file.

In addition to the object properties, you can leverage your existing search sets for managing the appearance of your model. Here's how:

1. Open the Appearance Profiler and select By Set from the Selector area.

2. Click Refresh to update the listing of search and selection sets.

3. Select the Doors search set from the list and choose Test Selection to validate. All interior doors in the model should highlight. Press Esc to deselect all items.

4. Specify your color and/or transparency.

5. Click the Add button to add the color/transparency to the Selector list on the right.

6. Continue to add more sets until your changes are complete.

7. Click the Run button to execute the changes in your model.

8. Close the file without saving.

RUNNING THE APPEARANCE PROFILER

When using the Appearance Profiler, the colors will only update once the Run command is executed. If changes are made to any model components, they will not be colored automatically until after the profiler is run. In both of these exercises, you used the intelligence in the BIM to aid in your exploration and interaction. Having access to a 3D model is useful for visually understanding the space, and the embedded object properties further elevate the benefits by allowing you to quickly identify, isolate, and interact with the model.

Selection Resolution

When models are appended in Navisworks, their hierarchy can vary depending on the file type and whether there are groups, blocks, or other assemblies in the source data file. This factor poses a challenge when you're selecting an object in your display window; Navisworks doesn't know which level of the selection tree hierarchy you're trying to access. To alleviate this issue, the Selection Resolution menu allows you to specify where in the selection tree Navisworks should reference when you're selecting objects. There are a total of six settings for configuring the selection resolution. Let's look at each setting in more detail:

File   When this option is selected, any item selected in the model will highlight all objects in the appended model.

Layer   When the layer node is selected, any selection will highlight all objects in that particular layer of the selection tree hierarchy.

First Object   The First Object selection option looks for any objects that are listed below the parent node (for instance, the layer node).

Last Unique   When the Last Unique option is selected, Navisworks will look for any object that is not multi-instanced in the selection tree and highlight the start of this unique level.

Last Object   By default, Last Object is the initial setting for the selection resolution. This option selects any objects at the lowest level of objects in your selection tree. Navisworks will first search for composite objects and substitute geometry if none are found.

Geometry   The Geometry option is typically the lowest level in the selection tree hierarchy. Choose this option to have your search path start at this level.

Similar to other commands in Navisworks, there are multiple ways to access the Selection Resolution Editor. The first option is to right-click in the selection tree window and choose from the available resolutions (Figure 4.49).

FIGURE 4.49
Context menu
from the selection
tree showing the
various Selection
Resolution options

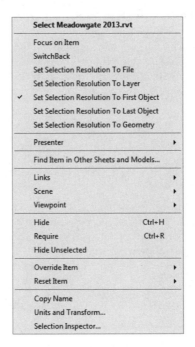

The second option is to access the selection resolution from the drop-down menu in the Select & Search panel of the Home tab. This panel also shows what your current resolution is set to (Figure 4.50).

Lastly, you can also access the selection resolution by opening the Global Options Editor and choosing Interface and then Selection. For any of these settings, keep in mind that different file types will require a different resolution to effectively navigate the selection tree. Having a good grasp of this concept will help you with your interaction between the display window and the selection tree.

File Units and Transform

When files are brought into Navisworks, any files containing different units of measurement are rescaled to match the other appended files. This makes working with metric and Imperial units much easier, but sometimes, you may need to modify your scene because a file didn't scale properly or is out of alignment. In Navisworks, the File Units And Transform feature allows you to modify these items:

◆ File Units

◆ Origin

◆ Rotation

◆ Scale

To access this feature, right-click the file you want to modify in your selection tree window and select Units And Transform. A separate dialog box will open in Navisworks, as shown in Figure 4.51.

The Model Units option lets you manually override the units for the loaded file. You can choose from the following options:

◆ Centimeters

◆ Feet

◆ Inches

◆ Kilometers

- ◆ Meters

- ◆ MicroInches

- ◆ Micrometers

- ◆ Miles

- ◆ Millimeters

- ◆ Mils

- ◆ Yards

FIGURE 4.51

The Units And Transform dialog box

Changing the unit of measurement affects the entire file. Even if you select a child element, Navisworks will apply these settings to the parent file.

The Origin area lets you enter the X, Y, and Z coordinates to move the model to a new position. This feature is useful if you know the values of the transform. If the values are unknown, you can use the Measuring tool to transform the model. This topic will be covered in greater detail in Chapter 6, "Documenting Your Project."

To rotate a model, you enter the value in the Rotation field. By default, Navisworks uses two decimal places for accuracy. You can expand this up to 17 decimal places for increased accuracy. When rotating the model, Navisworks will use the origin point as specified in the Units And Transform dialog box.

The Scale command allows you to modify the scaling of the X-, Y-, and Z-axes. By default, 1 is the current size; 0.5 is half and 2 is double. The Transform tools mentioned earlier in this chapter emulate some of this functionality, except that they can modify individual components and be reset, whereas the options listed in the Units And Transform dialog box affect the entire file only and can only be changed through the dialog box, shown in Figure 4.51. These are both useful features and need to be leveraged accordingly.

Compare

In the typical workflow with the NWF file format and source data files, your model may be published and shared with numerous members of the whole project team. Using the Merge command, you can aggregate these duplicate files and capture any changes to the models. However, it's nice to know what was modified in these files before beginning the merge. The Compare tool allows you to identify any changes between the two versions and either highlight the changes in the display window or save the results for future reference. Navisworks will look for differences in the following properties:

◆ Type

◆ Unique IDs

◆ Name

◆ Properties

◆ Path

◆ Geometry

◆ Tree

◆ Overridden Material

◆ Overridden Transform

Let's explore a typical comparison of two similar files, following these steps:

1. Open `c04_Meadowgate 2013.rvt`.

2. Use the Append function and add the `c04_Meadowgate 2013 update.rvt` file to your scene.

3. In the selection tree, hold down the Ctrl key and select both files.

4. Click the Compare icon in the Tools panel of the Home tab.

5. In the Compare dialog box, select the items in which you want to look for differences (Figure 4.52). Let's uncheck everything in the Find Difference In column except for Geometry.

6. In the Results area, check everything except for Hide Matches. Click OK.

   Navigate to the front entrance of the model. You should see a pair of the structural columns highlighted showing the differences in location, as shown in Figure 4.53.

   Open the Search/Selection Sets window and you'll notice that there are new selection sets that are linked to these differences as well (Figure 4.54).

7. To bring back the original model appearance, highlight both model files in the selection tree and click Reset Appearance in the Item Tools tab.

FIGURE 4.52
Compare dialog box

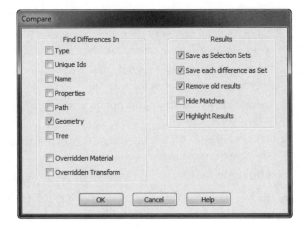

FIGURE 4.53
Differences
between the two
models

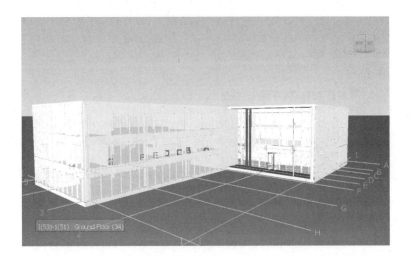

FIGURE 4.54
Selection sets
showing differences
in the model

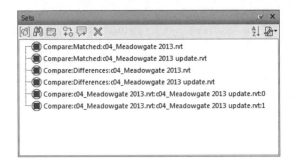

Following are the different options and the resultant outputs:

Save As Selection Sets   This option saves any comparison results as a selection set in your model. All changes are bundled together into one set.

Save Each Difference As Set   Use this option if you want to capture each resulting difference as a selection set.

Remove Old Results   This option removes any previous selection sets when conducting a new comparison.

Hide Matches   To help identify the differences, this option allows you to hide all items that are the same between the two files.

Highlight Results   This option highlights the differences with a color override.

8. Experiment with different results settings. Note that the selection sets will have comments associated with each set that provide additional detail.

9. If you're using the Highlight Results option, you can reset the colors in your model by clicking the Rest Appearance button in the Appearance panel of the Item Tools contextual tab.

10. Close the file without saving when finished.

The Bottom Line

Create search and selection sets.   The ability to break down your model into intelligent groupings is one of the key areas of Navisworks that help expand the benefits of coordinating large models.

Master It   How are search sets created, and what other tools are required?

Export and reuse search sets.   The strength of Navisworks lies in its ability to reuse search strings. This allows you to build a library of search criteria that will drastically cut down the amount of time it takes to configure new projects.

Master It   How can a search set be reused on another project?

Navigate the selection tree.   The selection tree maintains the list of all models in your current scene. In addition, there are numerous options for controlling visibility and selections.

Master It   How do you change the color and/or transparency of one of the appended files?

Chapter 5

Model Snapshots: Viewpoints, Animations, and Sections

This chapter will focus on saving and viewing the data you have created and changed. The tools in this chapter are essential: they allow you to embellish parts of the model, save views to explore later, change visibility (hide, transparency, color, etc.), and restore views at the click of a button. With viewpoints, you have the chance to save views or snapshots of your model for use later. Animations help you give your projects life and movement. With the Section tool, you can explore parts of your model from different perspectives.

In this chapter, you'll learn to:

- ◆ Create and save animations
- ◆ Link sections
- ◆ Save and edit viewpoints

Understanding Viewpoints

Viewpoints allow you to take snapshots of scenes in your model. This way, you can save information to use at a later date or return to a saved point of reference in the model. More important, viewpoints can contain information like redline markups, comments, tags, and measurements (see Chapter 6, "Documenting Your Project"). In addition, a saved viewpoint serves as a navigation aid in that it can remember when you change things like transparency, color, and item displays (hide/unhide); see Figure 5.1. Viewpoints are also retained or transferred when you produce an NWD file for use with Autodesk® Navisworks® 2013 Freedom.

You'll find the Remember Transparency And Hidden Items Between Views option under Options ➢ Interface ➢ Viewpoint Defaults ➢ Override Material. This option is not set by default. Note that saving views in this way increases the amount of memory used.

Another advantage of creating viewpoints is that each viewpoint retains the navigation mode that was used or set up when it was created. For example, if you were using the Fly tool with Third Person and Collision turned on when you saved the viewpoint, the navigation settings are retained when you return to the saved viewpoint.

FIGURE 5.1
Restoring a saved
viewpoint with
items hidden and
materials applied

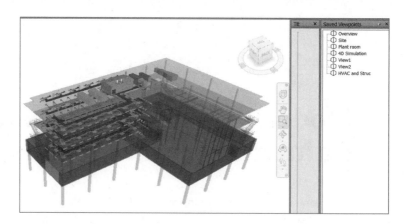

VIEWPOINTS TO SAVE AT THE PROJECT START

When starting a project, consider establishing a few initial views right away. The first one is usually a home view (one that you and others on your project will return to often) that you can create with the ViewCube® tool or as a saved viewpoint. Then think of a few others that may be useful and set them up as saved viewpoints. One approach is to create a viewpoint with a section cut for each level. That way, when you work on a project with multiple levels, you can easily click the viewpoint to automatically section the building to view the level in question. Completing this task at the start of the project can save you countless hours of trying to navigate back to your starting point in the model.

On many projects, it is essential to take the time to consider such important elements as orientation of project viewpoints, what items should be hidden (or not hidden), material overrides, and additional effects that should be added.

For a quick reference, you can set up your home view in the ViewCube by pressing Ctrl+Shift+Home to save your current view. You can also use the right-click method and set the home view directly from the ViewCube.

Saving Viewpoints

You can create viewpoints in various ways. The real work is not in saving the viewpoint but in setting up the elements beforehand: getting the orientation correct, items hidden, materials applied, and so forth. Once you've placed those elements in the scene, you can save the viewpoint. One easy way to do this is to select the Viewpoint tab on the Save, Load & Playback panel and click the camera icon, as shown in Figure 5.2.

FIGURE 5.2
Saving a viewpoint

There are a few additional options for saving viewpoints, which we'll describe in the following sections.

SAVING A VIEWPOINT FROM THE CONTEXT MENU

Another quick way to save a viewpoint, especially on the fly, is to use the in-scene context menu. This approach allows you save a viewpoint pretty much any time you need, as shown in Figure 5.3. Follow these steps:

1. Right-click in the scene (with or without an item selected).

2. Select Viewpoint ➤ Saved Viewpoints ➤ Save Viewpoint from the context menu.

3. The dialog box will disappear after adding a new Viewpoint. From there, you can rename the viewpoint as needed.

FIGURE 5.3
Saving a viewpoint from the in-scene context menu

RESTORING FROM THE CONTEXT MENU

Did you notice that while in the context menu, you have the option to quickly access already saved viewpoints? This way, you don't have to stop what you're doing and expand the Saved Viewpoints palette to restore an existing viewpoint. This approach has a few limitations, though: You cannot access viewpoints that are in folders, and it displays only the first 20 viewpoints listed.

SAVING A VIEWPOINT FROM CLASH DETECTIVE

Here's an added benefit of the Clash Detective tool (which you'll learn more about in Chapter 8, "Clash Detection"): You can create viewpoints as a result of running a clash report (see Figure 5.4). The viewpoints, once saved, are placed in a folder with the name of the clash you ran. Here's how that process breaks down:

1. After completing a clash, in the Results tab of the Clash Detective, locate Report Format.

2. Change the drop-down to As Viewpoints.

3. Select Write Report.

This process places the images from the clash in the Saved Viewpoints palette for later use. When creating the viewpoints, you can filter them by type. For example, suppose you want to create viewpoints only of active clashes. You select only the active clashes in Include Clash Types. When the viewpoints are created, only those types of clashes are sent to viewpoints. See Chapter 8 to learn more.

FIGURE 5.4

Viewpoints from Clash Detective report

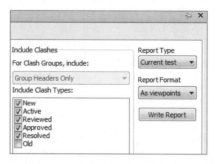

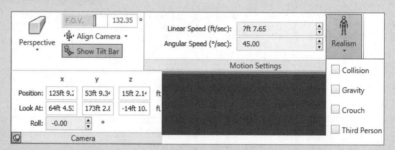

FINE-TUNING YOUR SCENE

With the Camera and Motion tools, you can further adjust the scene to improve the quality of your view before creating a viewpoint.

Using these tools to manually adjust your view before saving gives you the flexibility to set up a viewpoint exactly the way you need it to display. For example, you might use the field of view (FOV) to move farther away from an object, adjust the rollback to 0 degrees after flying around the model, or turn Third Person on, all before creating your viewpoint.

USING THE SAVED VIEWPOINTS PALETTE

The Saved Viewpoints palette acts as centralized storage for organizing viewpoints. It allows you to make changes to viewpoints, rename them, create animations, and create folders for them. Along with other tools explained later in this chapter, the Saved Viewpoints palette is generally located at the upper right of the screen (see Figure 5.5). Toggle the display by pressing Ctrl+F11, or select the Viewpoint tab in the Save, Load & Playback panel and click the small arrow at the end of the panel. To select a view from the Saved Viewpoints palette, left-click on the view, which activates it.

In addition, all of the views are available from the Current Viewpoint drop-down menu on the Viewpoint tab of the Save, Load & Playback panel. This drop-down menu provides quick access to viewpoints, but if you have several views, you'll have to scroll through a long list to find the one you need. In many cases, it can be easier to select the viewpoints from the Saved Viewpoints palette.

FIGURE 5.5
Saved Viewpoints
palette with a few
views already saved

ORTHOGRAPHIC AND PERSPECTIVE CAMERAS

As you work through viewpoints in Navisworks, there are two types of cameras to use: orthographic and perspective. An orthographic camera will display all edges of the model at the same distance from the camera. Perspective will show the model as it is calculated from the camera viewpoint, meaning the closer you are, the more distortion that can occur. In the real world, we view everything in perspective so it makes sense to default to perspective in Navisworks. However, there are some cases where you may need all of the edges parallel with each other, and it might make sense to work with an orthographic camera. Such instances might include seeing a plane view or elevation view.

You can tell whether a saved viewpoint is using an orthographic camera or a perspective camera by looking at the images beside the text. See the images in the viewpoint palette shown here for examples of the symbols.

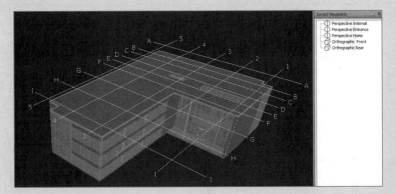

Also note that the grids will not display if the view is set to Orthographic. If you need the grids in your view, make sure to change it back to Perspective. To change the viewpoint, go to the Viewpoint panel ➤ Camera tab and change the view with the Perspective/Isometric drop-down menu.

There is another thing to consider when using Walk and Fly tools with the two cameras. If you have a camera set to Orthographic and you try to use the Walk and Fly tools, it will revert to a perspective camera. Walk and Fly tools can only work with the perspective camera.

If you switch to Perspective after being in an Orthographic view, sometimes the camera will zoom to a faraway location. To avoid a massive camera shift, before switching camera modes, click the Focus tool on the Navigation Bar and focus on an object in the view. Then switch camera modes.

Viewpoint Folders

Viewpoints can be divided into folders and even into subfolders, as shown in Figure 5.6, to help you organize the views contained in the Saved Viewpoints palette. It is often helpful to create folder names that make sense to everyone on the project. For example, you can create folders by date or by building element type (mechanical, structural) that you need to display in a unique way. To create a viewpoint folder, follow these steps:

1. Right-click in the open space of the Saved Viewpoints palette or select New Folder from the in-scene context menu (refer back to Figure 5.3).

2. Give the folder a unique name.

3. Drag and drop the needed views into the folder.

Once placed, views can be moved in and out of folders or to different folders as needed.

FIGURE 5.6
Example of view-
points in folders
within other folders

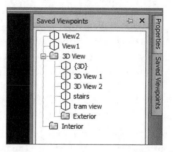

VIEWPOINTS IN FOLDERS NOT DISPLAYING IN CONTEXT MENU

While it may be practical to create viewpoints and place them in folders, one of the downsides is that viewpoints in folders do not show up in the context menu for easy access. If you need to select the viewpoints in folders, do so from the Saved Viewpoints palette.

Editing and Updating Viewpoints

Say you've worked out the initial view for your viewpoint and you need to make some further modifications to the already saved viewpoint. There are tools available to help you refine the viewpoint or make the needed changes without creating an entirely new viewpoint. Of course, there will be cases where it might make sense to create a new viewpoint—for instance, if the model changed or your viewpoint is no longer valid.

When you first create a viewpoint, it gives you the option to create a unique name; sometimes, the default name is chosen instead (ViewX). There may come a time later when you need to rename the viewpoint. You can do so in one of two ways:

◆ Select a viewpoint and press F2. Rename as needed.

◆ Left-click the viewpoint. Pause, then left-click the same viewpoint again (similar to what you'd do in Windows Explorer), and you can then rename the view.

Alternatively, you can use the context menu (Figure 5.7) in the Saved Viewpoints palette. This menu offers a wide variety of ways to modify an existing viewpoint. Let's look at some of these options:

FIGURE 5.7
The Saved
Viewpoints palette
context menu

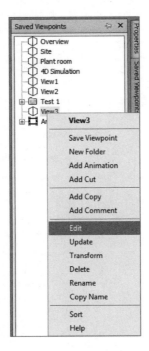

Add Copy (Copy Viewpoint)   The Add Copy feature creates an exact copy of the selected viewpoint, allowing you to make changes as needed. Multiple viewpoints can be copied at once by selecting them with the Ctrl key and then clicking Add Copy.

Add Comment   Opens the Add Comment dialog box (Figure 5.8), where you can add comments to a viewpoint. The status of the comment can also be set at this time.

FIGURE 5.8
Add Comment
dialog box showing
additional Status
options

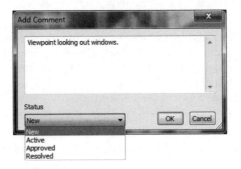

Comments are available in the Comments palette after they have been added, and you can edit or view them as needed.

Edit   The Edit Viewpoint command, also available from the Viewpoint tab in the Save, Load & Playback panel, gives you access to the Edit Viewpoint – Current View dialog box, which contains the following options for enhancing an existing viewpoint (Figure 5.9):

FIGURE 5.9
Edit Viewpoint –
Current View dialog
box

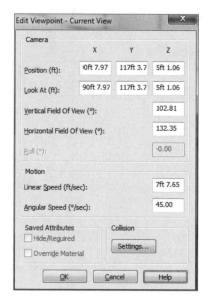

Camera   Similar to the Camera settings found on the Viewpoints tab and Camera panel, Camera allows you to change the existing viewpoint's Position, Look At, Vertical Field Of View, Horizontal Field Of View, and Roll settings. Look At allows you to quickly change the focal point of the camera, and Roll rotates the camera around an axis (great for helping you align yourself when using Fly). These settings can be useful for further refining the existing viewpoint. At times, you may find that the FOV is not accessible because the viewpoint was not saved in perspective mode. Revise the viewpoint and you should be able to access the FOV.

Motion   Similar to the Motion settings found on the Viewpoints tab and Motion panel, Motion allows you to change the existing viewpoint's Linear and Angular settings. These settings can be useful for further refining the existing viewpoint. As a good rule of thumb, a practical Linear speed could range from 10 to 25 feet/second (or 3 to 8 meters/second) and 45 degrees/second.

Saved Attributes   Hide/Required and Override Material apply to already saved viewpoints. These options allow you to save hidden/required markup information and material override information with the viewpoint. When a viewpoint is used again, the hidden/required and material override information that you saved is reapplied. Keep in mind that enabling these settings can sometimes greatly increase the file size for each viewpoint.

Collision   This option opens the Collision dialog box, where you can change the Collision, Gravity, Crouch, and Third Person settings for existing viewpoints. This dialog box is a useful place for changing or enabling/disabling settings for these features on previously created viewpoints.

Update   Using the Update feature will save the current scene as the selected viewpoint. This becomes useful when you need two similar viewpoints but from different perspectives. You could copy the viewpoint, move around, and use Update to save the new viewpoint. You can also adjust an existing viewpoint and select Update to save the changes.

MULTIPLE VIEWPOINT UPDATE

Sometimes, you need to update elements in your viewpoint. If you create a viewpoint folder and place the items you want to update in the folder, you can select the entire folder and make changes to common elements like Lighting and Render Mode. You can use Update to apply all the changes to all the viewpoints in the folder at the same time, saving you a lot of effort.

Transform   Opens the Transform dialog box (Figure 5.10), where you can adjust the camera orientation of the viewpoint. Move in X, Y, and Z directions with both positive and negative numbers.

FIGURE 5.10
Transform dialog box

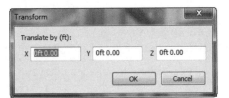

You will notice that while you are able to adjust the camera position by using Edit, the Transform tool starts at 0 and allows you to input a specific dimension. Edit uses the exact camera location, which means you can add or subtract numbers to move the camera the required distance.

Rename   Selecting Rename from the context menu highlights the current name and makes it editable. You can also select a viewpoint and press F2 and then rename as needed.

Copy Name   Copies the name of the viewpoint only. This gives you a quick way to copy a name and add additional information as needed.

Transform, Comment, and Update can be useful tools during a Navisworks session. With a little time and practice, you'll find that these tools can add efficiency to any project. They allow you to make minor adjustments to viewpoints or to create a duplicate, which provides a great foundation for creating a new viewpoint based on one already created.

Let's walk through an exercise where you'll use Transform, Comment, and Update to work with a viewpoint:

1. Launch Navisworks Simulate or Manage application (not Navisworks Freedom).

2. Open the file c05-viewpoint.nwd.

3. Open Saved Viewpoints and select the Office viewpoint, as shown in Figure 5.11. As you do so, take notice of the column in the immediate view.

FIGURE 5.11
Example viewpoint:
Office area

4. Use the Transform tool to move the camera to avoid the column right in front of the view. Move 14' (4.25 m) in the X and –2' (–.06 m) in the Y direction.

5. Add a comment about the change that you made to the viewpoint.

6. Create a copy of the Office viewpoint using Add Copy and rename the copy **Office 1**.

7. Using the Walk tools and with the newly copied viewpoint (Office 1) active, navigate around to change the orientation so that you are looking out the windows. Ensure that you have enabled Third Person, Gravity, and Collision (see Figure 5.12).

8. Use the Update tool to save the changes made to the viewpoint.

9. Create a comment for the Office 1 viewpoint that describes the changes made.

FIGURE 5.12
Updated viewpoint looking out the window with Third Person turned on

Exporting Viewpoints

At times, you may need to get the viewpoint information out of Navisworks. You may want to set up similar viewpoints in other sessions of Navisworks or share your comments and saved viewpoint images. Two methods of exporting viewpoints are explained next.

CREATING AN XML FILE OF ALL VIEWPOINTS

By selecting the Output tab and clicking Viewpoints on the Export Data panel, you can export all of the viewpoints into an XML file. This XML does not export the images as in the Clash Detective XML but exports a file with detailed information. The export contains all associated data, including camera positions, sections, hidden items and material overrides, redlines, comments, tags, lighting, rendering, and collision-detection settings.

Once exported, the XML file can be used in other applications or reimported into another Navisworks session. From there, you can set up camera viewpoints from the existing data. This method is preferred when multiple users have the same Navisworks file and wish to exchange information in a lightweight container.

CREATING VIEWPOINT REPORTS

By selecting the Output tab and clicking Viewpoints Report on the Export Data panel, you can create a report of all saved viewpoints. The report contains camera position, comments, and other associated data. If you have created an animation, the report will also include the animation frames as individual images as part of the report.

Exporting a viewpoint report (Figure 5.13) exports all viewpoints, including animations, in the Navisworks session. Navisworks exports two file types: a single HTML file that contains this information as well as all the associated image files. The advantage of this approach over exporting an XML file is that you get the images along with a bit of information, such as camera position. If viewpoints were created from a clash report, you'll get the subsequent clash information as well.

FIGURE 5.13
Viewing a viewpoint report in Internet Explorer with a comment shown

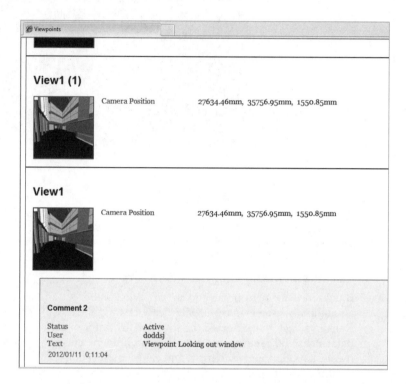

CREATING A FOLDER FOR THE VIEWPOINT REPORT

When creating a viewpoint report, you should create a folder to store the HTML file and accompanying image files. If possible, avoid saving them to your desktop, because you may end up with lots of image files scattered across your desktop. Placing them in a folder could save you a huge amount of frustration.

Creating Animations

Creating animations in Navisworks gives you the flexibility to record simulations, combine viewpoints into animations, and use the Navigation tools to move around while recording. Animations become essential in relaying information both inside and outside of Navisworks. Of course, it doesn't hurt to have a great foundation in viewpoints prior to using or creating animations, since it will make them a little easier to deal with.

Essentially, there are two ways to create an animation in Navisworks. First, you can use the Record feature to record your movements as you go along, creating frames of each movement. Second, you can create a series of viewpoints and place them inside an animation.

BEFORE RECORDING AN ANIMATION

One of the best pieces of animation advice we can offer is to plan what you want to record before actually recording, especially when adding tools like Walk, Fly, and Sections to your animations. By planning, you allow yourself the chance to give your animations a little something extra—and you may find that you save more time in the end.

Using Record to Make Quick Animations

Using Record (Figure 5.14) allows you to create quick animations on the fly as you navigate around your model (using tools like Walk and Fly).

FIGURE 5.14
The Record button is located on the Viewpoint tab

While creating your animations, you are able to add things like Section Plane slices (see "Using Sections" later in this chapter for more information) to the animation. To use Record, do the following:

1. On the Viewpoint tab of the Save, Load & Playback panel, click Record.

2. At the right corner of the Viewpoint tab is a Recording drop-down (Figure 5.15) that contains Pause and Stop controls. You can use the controls on the Playback panel as well.

FIGURE 5.15
Recording drop-down with Pause and Stop controls

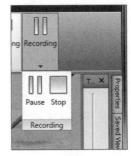

3. Use your Navigation tools (Walk and Fly) to move around your model.

4. Use Pause to stop and readjust as needed. Doing so will create a "cut" in the animation for the duration of the pause. See "Pause and Cut" later in this chapter.

5. Click Stop when you have completed your navigation.

After the animation has been created, it will be saved automatically in Saved Viewpoints under the `Animation` folder. Once recorded, the animation becomes the active animation in the Animations drop-down list located on the Playback panel of the Viewpoint tab.

Creating an Animation from Viewpoints

Another method for creating animations is by adding viewpoints to a blank animation. Using this method can sometimes be a little easier than using Record because you can define key locations that you wish the animation to show and have Navisworks interpolate the transitions between the viewpoints. You can set up your views in advance and then add them to the animations later. It may also cut down on the number of frames that it takes to create an animation. The downside is that using viewpoints to create a good animation can take a bit more planning and care than using Record. The main difference in using Record is that you can just set up Record and start navigating. Using Viewpoints for your animations might require a little more thought but provide some additional flexibility. Here's how to do it:

1. Go to the Saved Viewpoints palette and right-click (see Figure 5.16). Select Add Animation from the context menu to add a blank or empty animation. This is where you will later add your viewpoints.

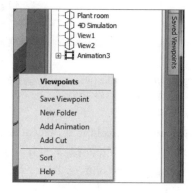

2. Navigate around your model as needed to create your viewpoints. While it does not matter in which order you create your viewpoints, it will matter in which order they are added to the animation. Feel free to use the Add Copy feature to reuse existing viewpoints.

3. Select your viewpoints to add to the animation. Use Ctrl+Shift to select multiple viewpoints. Drop them in the previously created blank animation.

4. Viewpoints will be added in the order in which they were dropped into the animation. To make changes or to change the order, drag and drop (Figure 5.17) the viewpoints within the animation folder.

FIGURE 5.17

Drag and drop
viewpoints within
the animation
folder

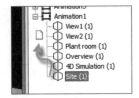

Something to keep in mind about using viewpoints is that they respect things like Third Person, hidden items, and item overrides (transparency, color, and transform), provided they are added to begin with. One of the benefits of using interpolated viewpoints over Record is that you can take advantage of the saved items in the viewpoints without having to stop and set up additional scene elements during your recording.

ADDING VIEWPOINTS TO EXISTING ANIMATIONS

Viewpoints can be added to existing or previously recorded animations. Simply drag and drop them into place between frames. Move around as needed.

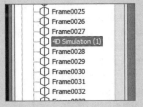

Any of the viewpoints that have been added can be edited the same way as any other viewpoint since animations are essentially a collection of viewpoints. Frames can also be moved out of the animation and into viewpoints.

Editing and Updating Animations

Animations are played by selecting them from the Saved Viewpoint drop-down located on the Viewpoint tab of the Save, Load & Playback panel. Click the drop-down and select the animation you want to play. Then use the controls to play, fast-forward, pause, and rewind as needed.

Once animations have been created, sometimes they need to be edited. With the edit tools, you are able to change duration of playback, add pauses, and use some of the viewpoint tools like Transform and Update to further refine the animation.

If you right-click the animation from Saved Viewpoints, you have access to the context menu. Here, you can select Edit, which opens the Edit Animation dialog box (Figure 5.18). Here are its options:

Duration This useful feature allows you to edit the duration of the animation sequence. For example, when you create an animation by using viewpoints, Navisworks determines the duration of the playback based on the viewpoints being added. Being able to edit the time allows for complete control of the sequence.

Loop Playback   Selecting this option will repeat the animation continuously until you tell it to stop. Loops become useful when you're setting up animations to run continuously for demonstration purposes.

Smoothing   The None value means that the camera will move from one frame to the next without any attempt to smooth out the corners.

Synchronize Angular/Linear Speeds will help smooth the differences between the speeds of each frame in the animation, resulting in an animation that is less irregular, or "jerky," on the screen.

PAUSE AND CUT

You can also insert pauses or delays in your animation. An animation cut is essentially a placed pause within the animation. They are created every time you use the Pause feature when creating a recorded animation. You can also manually add animation cuts by right-clicking the animation in the Saved Viewpoints palette and selecting Add Cut.

Once added, cuts can be moved around the animation by dragging and dropping them, allowing you to control the exact location of the pause.

You can specify the animation cut or pause duration by right-clicking the cut and selecting Edit. Doing so opens the Edit Animation Cut dialog box, where you can set the duration of the delay or pause.

ANIMATIONS ARE REALLY JUST VIEWPOINTS

Animations are essentially a collection of viewpoints saved in an animation folder, whether created using the Record tool or with viewpoints. The items in the animation folder allow you to use many of the basic viewpoint editing tools like Transform, Update, and Edit Current Viewpoint (to change camera position and motion speed).

Here is another quick piece of advice about animations and viewpoints to consider: If you have added viewpoints to the animation folder and decide to delete an animation, your viewpoints will be deleted as well. If you need the viewpoints in the animation folder, prior to deleting, you might want to make sure you move them out of the animation folder first or use Add Copy prior to adding them to your animation. The last thing you want to do is lose a valuable viewpoint. Please note that animations are not really folders but animations that have viewpoints attached as children objects. The term "folder" is used for clarity.

Exporting an Animation

What's the point of creating an animation if you cannot share it outside Navisworks? With the Export tools, you have the ability to disseminate animations outside Navisworks.

There are two ways to export an animation:

◆ In the Visual panel, choose Output ➤ Visual Panel ➤ Animation.

◆ Click the Application button and choose Export ➤ Export Animation.

Both methods open the Animation Export dialog box (Figure 5.19), where you can begin to adjust settings as needed. After clicking OK, you will be prompted for a save location. We'll discuss the various export settings next.

FIGURE 5.19
Animation Export
dialog box

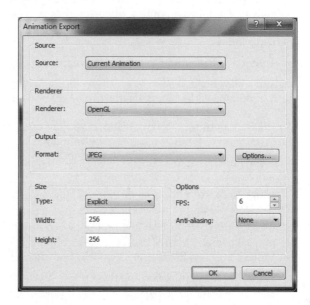

Real World Scenario

QUICK WALKTHROUGH ANIMATION

A great use of animations, and especially of viewpoints, is to create them for the purpose of a project walkthrough. This is an efficient way to communicate information and export the completed sequence out of Navisworks quickly. Oftentimes, a project walkthrough is one of the most common reasons to export an animation out of Navisworks.

Let's say you want to show your building owner certain aspects of a planned renovation. You've applied materials to parts of your project and you want to record an animation to further get a sense of the space. You could quickly save your viewpoints along the way, put them into a viewpoint animation, and then export the information out of Navisworks as needed. Think of a viewpoint animation like a folder or container to store your viewpoints.

Source Choose from three available options. Source selects the animations that Navisworks uses to create the export.

Current Animator Scene   The currently selected object animation

TimeLiner Simulation   The currently selected TimeLiner sequence

Current Animation   The currently selected viewpoint animation

Renderer   Renderer determines the render engine that Navisworks will use during the export.

Presenter   This option uses the highest-quality render settings and ensures materials as well as shadows are applied when you export. Note that this type of output can consume system resources and may take a while to complete. This property also does not support text overlays.

OpenGL   This option is for quickly rendering or previewing animations.

Output   Output allows you to select the format that will be used for the export. Each output format contains various options that can be changed through the associated file type.

JPEG   Choosing this option allows you to export a sequence of static images, which are taken from individual frames in the animation.

PNG   Choosing this option allows you to export a sequence of static images, taken from individual frames in the animation.

Windows AVI   Choosing this option allows you to export your animation as a commonly readable AVI file. There are many different codecs (located under Options) that can be used in video production that produce good results. For example, the top-level Intel IYUV may take longer than Microsoft Video 1 but has better quality, whereas using Microsoft Video 1 may produce better video than the often-choppy uncompressed option.

Windows Bitmap   Choosing this option allows you to export a sequence of static images, which are taken from individual frames in the animation.

Windows AVI is the only option that produces an actual video; the other three options produce static images based on the file type selected.

Also keep in mind that choosing a file location like your desktop will place the exported images for bitmap, PNG, and JPEG on the desktop. You may want to create a folder before exporting the static images.

Size   Size controls the width, height, and type size that Navisworks will use for the export. There are three different Type options:

Explicit   This option gives you full control of the width and height and is the most often used feature. 1280×720 is considered the best export size.

Use Aspect Ratio   This option enables you to specify the height. The width is automatically calculated from the aspect ratio of your current view.

Use View   This option uses the width and height of your current view. This setting typically produces the largest export. Exercise care when considering Use View.

Options   Options give you the ability to control a few additional features of the animation prior to exporting:

FPS   This option controls the number of frames per second (fps) that will be exported. The higher the number, the smoother the exported animation, but using this option will greatly increase rendering time. Generally, 10 fps is a good number to produce an acceptable AVI. For DVD quality, use 23 fps.

Anti-Aliasing   This option is used to smooth the edges when using the OpenGL renderer. The higher the number, the smoother the exported animation, but using this option will greatly increase rendering time. Generally, a 4X Anti-Aliasing setting will produce an acceptable AVI.

In some cases, you may wish you leave these settings at the default, especially when using OpenGL to preview an animation.

COMBINING ANIMATIONS

Once created, animations can be nested inside each other. This gives you the opportunity to link multiple animations to play together or to add a sequence to an existing animation.

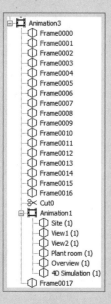

To combine animations, drag and drop one animation inside the other animation. Then, you can adjust the duration for each animation and location as needed. Don't forget to use Add Cut as needed to emphasize transitions.

A typical problem that you might run into is that you cannot add recorded frames to saved views and expect them to render correctly. So, keep that in mind when you plan to create your animations and decide how they will be used later.

Using Sections

Sections (Figure 5.20) in Navisworks enable you to create various cross-section views of your model. This becomes important as you work on a project so you can view various aspects of the model from different perspectives or slices.

FIGURE 5.20
Building with section planes for right and top enabled

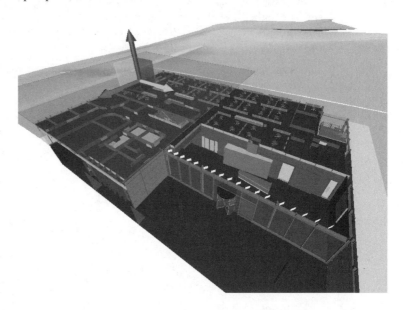

Sections in Navisworks can be combined with tools like Clash Detective, animations, the Navigation tools, and TimeLiner and saved as viewpoints. This allows you great flexibility in how and where you choose to use sections.

Section tools go beyond being able to simply section your model into individual views or sections. You have the ability to create multiple section planes that can be linked together. You can also choose to use the Box or Planes mode to control how to section your model. There are also individual controls to help with aligning with individual section planes.

The Section tool must first be enabled; to do so, select the Viewpoint tab, and in the Sectioning panel, click Enable Sectioning. This opens the Section tools panel (Figure 5.21). Enable Sectioning can also be accessed through the context menu by selecting Viewpoint ➢ Sectioning ➢ Enable Sectioning.

FIGURE 5.21
Section tools panel

> **TEMPORARY SECTION TAB**
>
> When the Section tool is enabled, it temporarily becomes an additional tab in Navisworks. When you disable the Section tool, the tab will disappear along with the active section planes.

Sectioning in Planes Mode

Planes mode allows you to make up to six sectional cuts in any plane while still being able to navigate around the scene. With Planes mode enabled, you have access to the Planes Settings panel, shown in Figure 5.22, where you have additional settings and controls to further enhance and link your sections.

From the Planes Settings panel, you can change which active section plane you want to have enabled (or enable multiple planes), specify the alignment, and then choose Link Section Planes. Let's take a closer look at each of these options:

FIGURE 5.22
Planes Settings panel

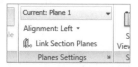

Active/Current Section Plane   This drop-down provides quick access to the six available section planes and allows you to set one as the active or current section plane. You also have the option to toggle section planes on/off with the light bulb toggle next to the plane.

Alignment   The Alignment drop-down allows you to choose from the nine alignment options you can assign to an active section plane. Top, Bottom, Front, Back, Left, and Right align the current plane to the respective side of the model. The remaining three options are discussed here:

Align To View   This option aligns the current plane to the current viewpoint camera.

Align To Surface   This option enables you to pick a surface and place the current plane on that surface at the point where you clicked.

Align To Line   This option enables you to pick a line and place the current plane on that line, at the point where you clicked.

To assign an alignment to a section plane, first set it as Active (by selecting the plane from the active section drop-down) and then set the alignment.

Link Section Planes   Linking section planes in Navisworks allows you to move the linked sections together as a single entity. You can link up to six sections together.

Using linked sections lets you set alignments and then begin to manipulate the model in several directions at the same time. For example, you could enable Plane 1 from Top and Plane 2 from Left and then link those section planes together. After they are linked and you move the section plane around or use Transform, you actually move the plane in both the Top and Left directions simultaneously. The Move tool is further explained later in this chapter. Be sure to click just to the left of the view plane in the Planes Settings window or in the active section drop-down to activate it—this can often be missed and is a source of frustration.

Open the Section Plane Settings dialog box (Figure 5.23) by clicking the arrow in the bottom-left corner of the Planes Settings panel. This dialog box, even when docked as a palette, is only available when sections are enabled. It lets you make many of the changes available from the Planes Settings drop-downs.

FIGURE 5.23
Section Plane
Settings dialog box

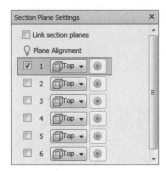

From this dialog box, you have access to all six section planes, can toggle them on/off, set the alignment, and toggle Link Section Planes. For some, this provides a more heads-up type of workflow, whereas others may prefer to utilize the Planes Settings drop-down menus.

Sectioning in Box Mode

Switching from Planes to Box mode does a couple of things. First, it disables access to the Planes Settings panel. Second, it allows you to create a specific size section "box" to work within.

Box mode gives you the opportunity to focus on or review specific areas of the model. While you do not have access to the number of section planes (Planes mode), you can change the size of the box.

ANOTHER ADVANTAGE OF SAVING VIEWPOINTS

If you save a viewpoint with a section enabled, it will respect the Section setting. For example, if you saved a viewpoint with Box mode active, it will create that viewpoint using those settings. The same goes for Planes mode. For example, if you saved a viewpoint with linked section planes (maybe Top and Left), then those settings will be saved.

The one thing that returning to your saved viewpoints does not do is enable sectioning for you. That is something that you will have to do yourself. However, you can edit the section plane as needed by using the settings saved with the viewpoint without having to enable sectioning. If necessary, use Update Viewpoint to resave the view (provided the options are set correctly).

Using the Gizmo

By now, you have noticed the gizmo, which has been redesigned and improved upon for Navisworks 2012 and continued on within the 2013 release (Figure 5.24). It appears as you move between Box and Planes modes as well as between Move, Rotate, and Scale. This feature in Navisworks allows you to dynamically interact with your model. You can select points on the gizmo to move around and see your changes update in real time. Depending on which Transform tool you have selected (Move, Rotate, or Scale), the shape of the gizmo will change, as you'll see in the next section.

FIGURE 5.24
Gizmo axes

Using the gizmo is Navisworks is rather easy. Notice the hand symbol in Figure 5.24. If you stop and hover over one of the axes, the hand will appear and allow you to begin to move the gizmo along that axis. Hold down the left mouse button and move as needed.

Change Transform mode to Move, Rotate, or Scale (Box mode only) to access different shapes and moves.

MOVE THE ENTIRE GIZMO AND NOT JUST AN AXIS

Notice that the gizmo has large, colored, square planes (if using Move) or arc planes (if using Rotate). Selecting these planes with the left mouse button will allow you to move the gizmo around.

Also note that moving the location of the gizmo affects the position for inactive planes. It does not affect the location of the gizmo in saved viewpoints. However, it is important to note that if the gizmo is active when saving viewpoints or creating animations, the gizmo will be shown.

Transforming Sections

The Transform tools (Figure 5.25)—Move, Rotate, Scale—along with Position, Rotate, and Size, help you further fine-tune the manipulation of the Section tool as well as provide an alternate way to move the plane and box (without having to use the gizmo) numerically. You can only use these tools if the gizmo is visible on the screen. Let's see what each of these tools does.

FIGURE 5.25
Transform tools
panel

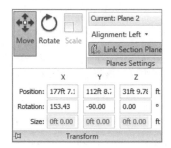

Move   Move (Figure 5.26) is the default tool when a section plane is selected. Move allows you to move the section plane or box around in the X, Y, and Z planes. You can only manipulate one plane at a time unless you have linked sections. Notice the shape of the gizmo; this is your indication that you are using Move.

FIGURE 5.26
Section plane
with Move gizmo
enabled

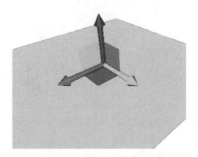

Rotate   Similar to Move, the Rotate (Figure 5.27) tool lets you revolve around the axes instead of move. This will create an angular slice of the model. You can manipulate only one plane at a time unless you have linked sections. Notice the shape of the gizmo; this is your indication that you are using Rotate.

FIGURE 5.27
Section plane
with Rotate gizmo
enabled

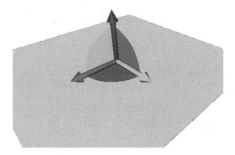

With Rotate, you can control the Position and Rotate settings numerically. Using the Rotate tool gives you the chance to slice your building at an angle, say 45. Position moves the entire plane or box around the X-, Y-, and Z-axes. Size is available only when Box mode is active.

Scale   When Box mode is active, you have access to the Scale (Figure 5.28) tool, which allows you to control the size and shape of the box. Using Scale, you can change the size of the box into a more concentrated entity by using the gizmo or by using the numeric features of Size.

Scale behaves a little differently than Move and Rotate, as follows:

- Using the axes (blue, green, and red arrows) to change the Scale will change the size only along that axis.

- Using the colored squares (planes) scales the box in two directions at the same time.

- Using the point at the centroid where the blue, green, and red lines meet scales the box equally in the X, Y, and Z directions at the same time.

FIGURE 5.28
Section box with
Scale gizmo
enabled

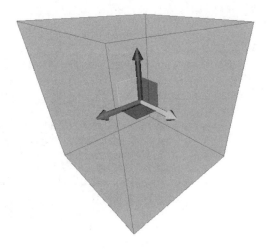

Sectioning a Project

Sectioning can become a powerful ally when you work on a project, create an animation or viewpoint, or need to further analyze a specific area of your project. At first, it can seem like a daunting tool to use, but you will quickly realize that this tool is easy to utilize and can provide a great deal of insight into a project. To practice sectioning, try the following procedure:

1. Launch the Navisworks Freedom, Simulate, or Manage application.

2. Open the file c05-sectioning.nwd.

3. Open Saved Viewpoints and select the Sectioning viewpoint.

4. Go to the Viewpoint tab and in the Sectioning panel, click Enable Sectioning.

5. Click the arrow in the Planes Settings panel to open the Plane Settings palette. Select Plane 1 as Active, and set it to align to Top.

6. Enable Plane 2 and set Alignment to Left.

7. Use the gizmo, set Position and Rotate to align the section plane as shown in Figure 5.29.

FIGURE 5.29
Transform informa-
tion for Position and
Rotate

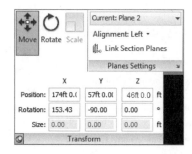

8. Rotate the scene as shown in Figure 5.30 and save a viewpoint.

FIGURE 5.30
Rotate the scene
and save the
viewpoint.

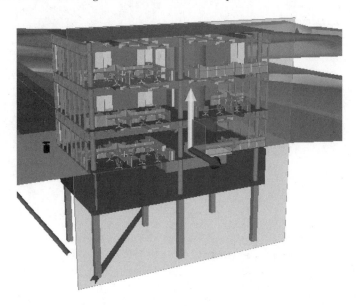

The Bottom Line

Create and save animations. Using real-world examples and adding realism to a project can give those involved a sense of depth and realism when participating in a project or when trying to get a point across. Animations combined with Navigation tools can be a great way to achieve success and clarity on a project.

Master It You're working on a project and need to create a quick animation of a flyover of a large site. What are the steps involved for using recording and animation with Fly?

Link sections. While creating sections is vital to a project, sometimes you need to section them in more than one direction at a time. Linking sections together allows you greater flexibility to slice your model in more than one direction simultaneously.

Master It How do you link top and left sections in Navisworks?

Save and edit viewpoints. Viewpoints have a lot of uses. Some are created on the spur of the moment to capture a quick view, whereas others are created to maintain visibility states of objects or to store comments.

Master It While working on a project, you have made changes (changed transparency, hidden items) to the scene, but before restoring the items to their original state, you want to save a viewpoint on the fly. How can you quickly save this viewpoint?

Part 2

Simulation and Clash Detection

Chapter 6

Documenting Your Project

As you've experienced so far, the Autodesk® Navisworks® 2013 product affords you the opportunity to display information in a variety of ways, from 3D model perspectives to orthographic plan views and sections. In each of these cases, the same model is driving these distinct views. Looking at some typical construction workflows and processes, you will occasionally need to embellish these views with user-defined data such as dimensions and redline markups. Furthermore, when appending models from different trades and applications, you may need to translate objects to align to a common origin. This section will further refine your skills with the Measure and Redline tools and help you understand when to use them with the model documentation process.

In this chapter, you'll learn to:

◆ Measure objects in the model

◆ Align models with unknown coordinates

◆ Use the Redline and Commenting tools

Using the Measure Tools

When you're working with 3D models in general, annotations, callouts, and other details are often limited to the 2D sheet views and thus not easily referenced in the model view. One way to reference these details is by using the Project Browser. This tool allows you to leverage and incorporate these details and easily switch between the 2D and 3D viewpoints when reviewing the model. The Measure tools in Navisworks provide a plethora of functions, including ways to dimension model objects and calculate area as well as transform objects in your scene. As we'll explore, these workflows allow you to query the model for accurate dimensions and save them for future reference or the design review/model coordination process. In this section, we'll introduce a scenario that mimics a real-world project from a typical model coordination perspective. For most of the exercises in this chapter, we'll be using the file c06_Meadowgate_Measure.nwd, which you can download from the book's web page at www.sybex.com/go/masteringnavisworks2013.

Here's the scenario: You have been advised by the manufacturer of one of the mechanical components in your project that due to unforeseen circumstances, they will not be able to deliver the equipment within the original agreed-to timeframe. To complicate matters, the owner has dictated in your contract that the project must be finished on time or you will be subject to liquidated damages for every day late. To keep the project on schedule, you decide to move ahead with installing the surrounding components and install the delayed piece of equipment out of sequence after it arrives. Because of the tight tolerances within the project, you need to be absolutely sure that the equipment will fit through the now-finished corridor and into the mechanical room on the ground floor. In the following sections, you'll explore the various Measure tools to establish if this scenario is feasible.

Working with the Dimension and Area Tools

Navisworks offers seven dimension and Measure tools for you to choose from. They provide the basis for capturing measurements from the multiple models in your scene. Prior to measuring any objects, you need to make sure the snap and pick settings are configured properly. Recall that all appended model data is stripped of any vector data and converted into a surface model when imported into Navisworks. This allows for easy navigation and small file sizes for collaboration. However, with this conversion, you lose the standard endpoint and midpoint object snapping that is available in most design software. To assist with object selection, Navisworks provides several cursor snapping properties. In the left side of the Options Editor, select Interface and then Snapping to access the options shown in Figure 6.1.

FIGURE 6.1

The Snapping page in the Options Editor

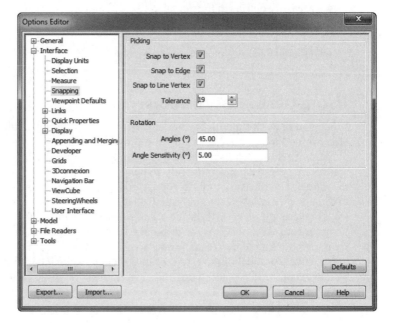

These options define the snap settings and tolerances for picking model objects. Let's explore these settings before diving into the Measure tools. In the first area of the Snapping page, you can configure the Picking settings:

Snap To Vertex   This setting is used to snap the cursor to the nearest vertex. To see exactly where the different vertices are located in the model, change your render style to either Wireframe or Hidden Line. In Figure 6.2, you see the hidden line view of one of the wall assemblies in our model. With this setting enabled, the cursor will snap to the corner point of any of the triangle surfaces in the model.

FIGURE 6.2
Wireframe view of
the model

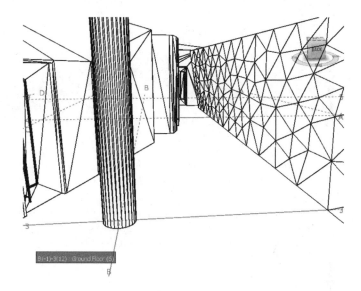

Snap To Edge   The Snap To Edge setting allows Navisworks to pick any point along the edge of the triangle surface. Depending on the model geometry and surface density, the snap points may be spread out. If you're working with DWG® or DGN files, you can modify the faceting factor to increase the number of polygons. This will allow for a tighter snap selection; however, it will also increase the file size. See Chapter 2, "Files and File Types," to learn more about configuring file readers.

Snap To Line Vertex   In addition to bringing in 3D surfaces, Navisworks reads lines, text, and points. This setting is used to snap the cursor to the nearest line end.

Tolerance   When you select one of the Picking settings, Navisworks will snap the cursor when you are in close proximity to a vertex, edge, or line element. The Tolerance setting allows you control how close you need to be to the object before the snap feature engages. The smaller the value, the closer you must be to the object.

IMPROVING THE ACCURACY OF MEASUREMENTS

If you're working with vector-based file formats such as DWG and DGN, there are several settings that will increase the accuracy of your measurements. When CAD/BIM files are opened or appended in Navisworks, the program converts the geometry into a surface made up of hundreds if not thousands of triangles.

As a result, the standard object-snapping techniques such as snap to endpoint or midpoint are no longer valid. In the following image, you see a standard pipe elbow that was created in the Autodesk® AutoCAD® platform.

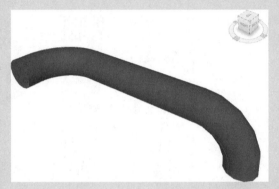

If you take that same DWG file and open it in Navisworks, the surface is converted to a series of triangles. Turning on the wireframe view, you can see that there are no midpoint or endpoint places to snap to. However, you can snap to the individual lines or the vertex where the points of adjacent triangles meet.

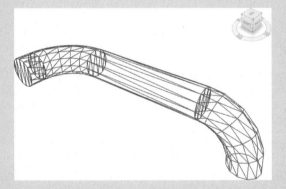

Since your snapping points are limited to these intersections, you can increase the facets of the DWG file to increase the number of areas to snap to. A word of caution: By increasing the Faceting Factor value, you are also increasing the file size. You can modify this setting by going to the appropriate file reader (e.g., DWG/DXF, DGN) and entering a value in the text box. By default, this is set to 1. Increasing the number will increase the density of the triangular mesh in your model.

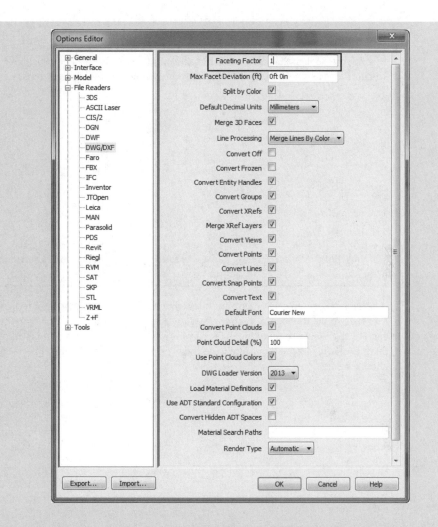

In the following close-up image, Faceting Factor is left at the default setting of 1. In the Scene Statistics, this translates to 1,352 triangles, lines, and points. The file size for this object is 13.2 KB.

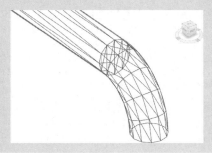

In the next image, Faceting Factor has been increased to 10. Notice how the triangular mesh is much denser. This provides additional snapping points to take measurements. However, it also provides a smoother look to the pipe elbow since the mesh is considerably tighter. In the Scene Statistics, this translates to 4,738 triangles, lines, and points. Also, the file size has more than doubled to 29.1 KB.

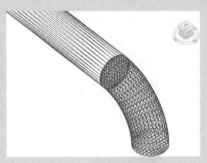

Increasing the Faceting Factor is one way to add additional snap points and increase the smoothness of round or curved objects, but it also increases the file size.

As a best practice, it's recommended that all snap settings be enabled. When you engage the Measure tools, the icon will change when you encounter either an edge or a vertex. By default, each of the Measure tools looks like a plus sign. When you hover near an object and engage the Snap tool, the icon will change for either vertex or edge snapping. The various snap cursors are shown here:

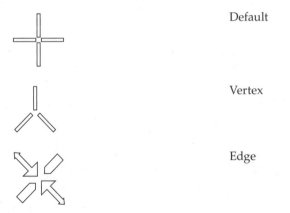

Default

Vertex

Edge

The last settings you need to configure are the measuring options. In the Options Editor, under Interface, choose Measure to open the page shown in Figure 6.3. As you can see, you can modify five additional settings:

Line Thickness   This setting controls the thickness of the measuring lines. By default, it is set to 1. Larger values equate to a thicker line.

Color   This option allows you to control the color of the measuring line in your scene.

In 3D   When working in 3D models, Navisworks will keep all dimension lines displayed in the model even if you navigate to occlude the original selections. If you check this box,

Navisworks will hide the dimension lines when you navigate around the model, thus keeping the model easier to view.

Show Measurement Values In Scene View   This setting controls the visibility of the text callout in the measurement. If you deselect this option, only the dimension lines are visible.

FIGURE 6.3
The Measure page in the Options Editor

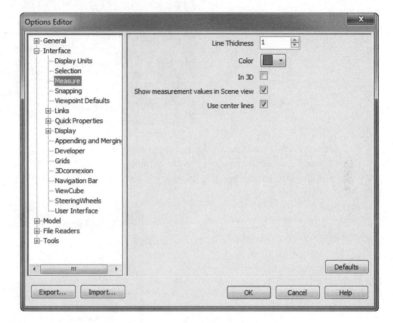

Use Center Lines   Occasionally, you want to measure from center to center of an object. This is especially useful in piping runs where spacing is based on the measurements between the centers of the pipes. When this option is checked, you can snap to the center of parametric objects. Selected objects will show the center line (CL) and snap to the center line, as shown in Figure 6.4.

FIGURE 6.4
Measurement showing snapping to center line

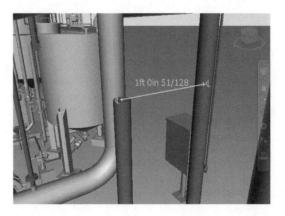

If Use Center Lines is left unchecked, the Measure tool will snap to the outside face of the object (Figure 6.5).

FIGURE 6.5
The Measure tool
will snap to the
outside face.

Once you have configured your snap and measure settings, you can now use the Measure tools much more effectively. Let's investigate these features in greater detail. In the Review tab of the ribbon, you can access the measure functions from the Measure drop-down menu (Figure 6.6).

FIGURE 6.6
The Measure drop-
down menu

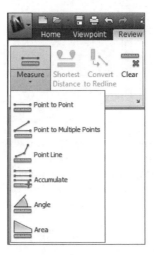

In addition, you can access these tools from the Measure Tools dockable window (Figure 6.7). This view also provides the X, Y, and Z coordinates of the start and endpoints along with any differences in these measurements between points. The Distance field shows the distance registered for all points in the measurement, including accumulations from the Point Line and Accumulate measure functions. To access this window, select the small arrow pointing to the lower right in the Measure panel of the Review tab.

FIGURE 6.7
The Measure Tools
window

POINT-TO-POINT MEASUREMENT

The Point To Point tool is most useful when you're identifying the distance between two objects in your Navisworks scene. Open the C06_Meadowgate_Measure.nwd file and let's go through some exercises, starting with these steps:

1. Using the Sectioning tools, section the model to show the first floor only. As an alternative, you can choose the Ground Level viewpoint, which has already been defined to show the ground-level section.

2. Select Point To Point from the Measure drop-down, and zoom into the area between the elevators and staircase.

3. Measure the distance between the elevator wall and stair railing, as shown in Figure 6.8.

4. If you get a different measurement than what is shown, practice taking additional measurements in the model, including the double doors in the model view, until you're comfortable with this feature. You may need to zoom in to the model to make sure you're selecting the edge of the objects.

5. For the scenario mentioned at the beginning of this chapter, the piece of equipment you need to bring on site is almost 5 feet (152 cm) wide. Using the Measure tools, identify which set of doors can accommodate the equipment, assuming it's already in the lobby (Figure 6.9).

6. Select Clear to remove the dimension from your model view.

FIGURE 6.8
Measuring the distance between the elevator wall and stair railing using Point To Point

FIGURE 6.9
Using Point To Point to measure and identify the larger door

MEASURING OBJECT ELEVATIONS

Using the Point To Point tool, you can easily measure object elevations with a single click. Instead of calculating the elevation by measuring the difference between the model base and a specific object, you can use the values displayed in the Measure Tools fly-out window to identify the object elevation. When you select the first point, Navisworks calculates the X, Y, and Z values of that point. Since the Z value is what you need for measuring the elevation, you can select any single point in the model to quickly see the value in the Z field of the Start area, as in the following image. Right-clicking unselects that object so that you can quickly check multiple objects. Doing so allows you to verify ceiling heights or other height-specific objects in quick succession.

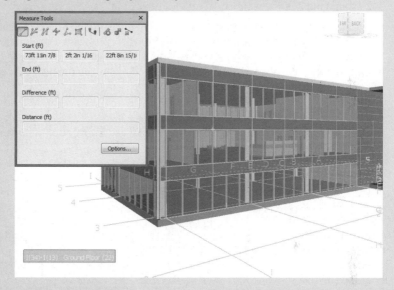

In addition, sometimes you wish to know the ceiling height in a room. If you use the regular Point To Point tool and only check the bottom of the ceiling, the Z value will not give you the information you are looking for because its value will display the absolute Z location. To find its height relative to the floor, you have to interpolate the data. After selecting the bottom of the ceiling, simply click the top of the floor as the second point. Look in the measuring fly out window and check the difference in Z value. This value represents the true elevation for the height of the floor.

MEASURING POINT TO MULTIPLE POINTS

The Point To Multiple Points feature allows you to register a series of points while maintaining the same starting point. Here's how:

1. Select Point To Multiple Points from the Measure drop-down menu.

2. Specify the bottom left of the larger doorframe and measure the horizontal distance to the other jamb.

3. Without deselecting the command, select the upper-left corner of the double doors. Notice how Navisworks keeps the original base point intact and allows you to select any number of secondary points.

4. Select Clear to remove the dimension from your model view.

CREATING MEASUREMENTS ALONG A POINT LINE

The Point Line measurement tool is used to measure the total distance along a series of points or a route. This tool becomes extremely useful when you want a running total of your measurements. Let's say you need to calculate the amount of trim around the door(s) in the model. Using the Point Line tool, we'll go through this example in detail using the file c06_Meadowgate_Measure.nwd.

1. Select the Lobby viewpoint or navigate to the double doors to the right of the stairs in the lobby of the ground floor.

2. Select the Point Line tool from the Measure drop-down or from the Measure Tools window.

3. In the model, select the outside of the lower-left doorjamb.

4. Select the upper-left, upper-right, and finally the outside of the lower-right jamb. The total distance is displayed on screen as well as the Distance field in the docked window (Figure 6.10).

FIGURE 6.10
Point Line
measurement

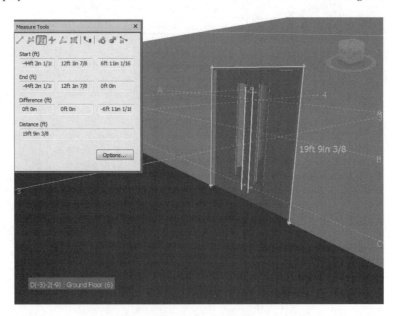

5. When you've finished, select Clear to remove the measurement from your model view.

ACCUMULATE

The Accumulate tool functions similarly to the Point Line tool, except it measures a series of point-to-point measurements. The advantage of this tool is that you can measure several objects that have different start points and maintain a running total of the lengths. Here are the steps you should follow:

1. Select Accumulate from the Measure drop-down menu or the Measure Tools window.

2. Select the lower-left doorjamb for your initial selection.

3. Finish by selecting the upper-left jamb.

4. Remember that this feature is an accumulation of point-to-point measurements, so you need to define a new start point. Select the upper-left doorjamb and continue across to the upper-right jamb.

5. Select the upper-right and finish up with the lower-right jamb.

6. Repeat this process on the remaining doors in the scene. Navisworks will keep a running total of these dimensions both on screen and in the Distance field in the Measure Tools window (Figure 6.11).

7. Select Clear to remove the dimensions when you've finished.

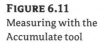

FIGURE 6.11
Measuring with the Accumulate tool

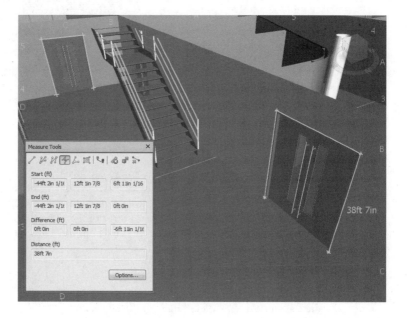

ANGLE

The Angle tool is used to calculate the angle between two lines. This tool requires a three-click operation. Let's look at this function in more detail:

1. Select the Angle tool from the Measure drop-down menu.

2. Choose the first point on your line that you wish to measure.

3. Select the second point on the line that represents the intersection of the second line.

4. Choose a point on your second line to calculate the angle (Figure 6.12).

5. Select Clear to remove the angle dimension from your model.

FIGURE 6.12
Measuring angles

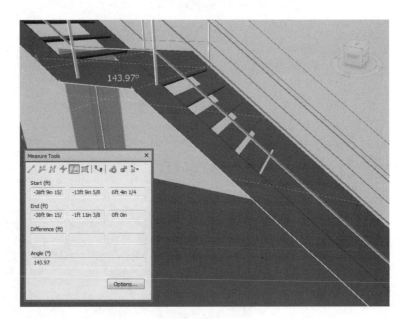

AREA

The Area tool is useful when you are looking to capture the area of a specific plane. This tool functions much like the Point Line tool by allowing you to select numerous points that make up the perimeter of the object you wish to measure. As you select points in the plane to measure, Navisworks will draw a dashed line to the start point and begin calculating the area of the outline. As more points are added, the area total will update. Let's try this out with the following steps:

1. Open the Saved Viewpoint Area Plan.

2. Using the Area tool, select the four corners of the room (Figure 6.13). You may need to reorient the model to get a good view of the edges and make sure you're snapping to the base. Remember, for the calculation to be accurate, all points need to be on the same plane.

3. Select Clear to remove the area calculation from your model.

FIGURE 6.13
Calculating areas

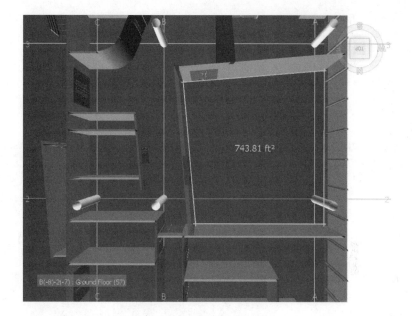

743.81 ft²

B(-8)-2(-7) : Ground Floor (57)

SHORTEST DISTANCE

Let's look back at our earlier scenario of determining if a piece of equipment will fit through the hallways of our model. You can use the standard Measure tools to identify and dimension specific surfaces, but the model may contain uneven surfaces and/or twists that make using the standard tools challenging. The Shortest Distance feature, as its name implies, will identify the shortest route between two selected objects and display the dimension. In the Meadowgate model, we have a curved wall opposite a wall with a twist architectural feature. Using the Shortest Distance feature, you can determine the narrowest portion of the hallway to determine if the equipment will fit:

1. Navigate to the curved wall opposite the office doors or select the viewpoint labeled Shortest Distance.

2. Select the curved wall on the left and, holding the Ctrl key, select the twisted wall on the right.

3. In the Measure panel of the Review tab, select the Shortest Distance command from the menu (Figure 6.14).

4. In your model window, you should have a dimension between the curved face of the wall and the twist (Figure 6.15). Select Clear to remove the shortest distance dimension from your model.

FIGURE 6.14
Select the Shortest
Distance tool in the
ribbon.

FIGURE 6.15
The shortest dis-
tance between the
two wall faces

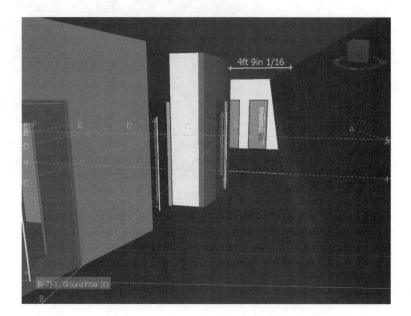

Translating Items

In Chapter 4, "Climbing the Selection Tree," we discussed using the Transform tools to translate the model to a new location by using the numerical override if the distance is known or by manually moving the model with the onscreen gizmo. In this chapter, we'll explore the workflows of using the Measure tools to translate objects of unknown distances. This process becomes useful when you're working with models that are designed in different coordinates. As a best practice, it's recommended that all models have a common origin so that they align properly when appended into Navisworks. If you are working with Autodesk® Revit® models using shared coordinates, be sure to check Shared Coordinates in the Export Options dialog box. Refer to Chapter 2 for more information. Keep in mind that even shared coordinates Revit models may pose alignment issues if their base origins are in different locations. The origin in Revit ultimately dictates where the model will display. Other CAD/BIM formats are typically based on a Cartesian coordinate system and display in Navisworks based on their saved location in the source file.

Conflicts arise when the models with different origins are appended into your Navisworks scene. The result is that the models don't align properly. Even being off by an inch or less can cause false results for clash detections and potentially ignore legitimate clashes. This section will cover the procedure for aligning models of different coordinates. For this exercise, you'll be using the files c06_Meadowgate_Arch.nwd and c06_Meadowgate_Struct.nwd, available from the book's web page.

1. Open the file `c06_Meadowgate_Arch.nwd` and zoom out to the extents of the model. You can use the Page Up key on the keyboard to accomplish this or use the Zoom All command in the Navigation Bar.

2. Use the Append function to add the file `c06_Meadowgate_Struct.nwd` to your scene.

3. Use the Zoom All command to display the full model.

4. You can use the Measure tools to determine the distance the models are apart and manually override their location to align, but the easier way is to snap the models together using a common point between both models.

5. Using the Point To Point tool, select a point that can be referenced in both models. Examples of this are column grid intersections or consistent geometry between both models. For this exercise, use the end of the grid line "H" before it connects to the circle indicator (Figure 6.16). Make sure you have the object snaps enabled. If you see a block over the gridline letters, disable solids by clicking the Surfaces tool on the Render Styles panel in the Viewpoint tab of the ribbon.

FIGURE 6.16
Snapping to the column grid

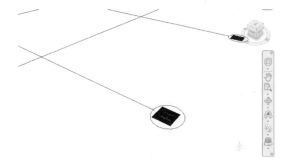

6. Change to Navigation mode and orient your model window to reference the same grid point in the Architectural model. Navisworks will remember the first point you selected while you reconfigure your view as long as you don't click Clear.

7. Select the Point To Point tool again and select the same grid intersection on the second model. You should have a measurement displayed between the two models on your screen (Figure 6.17). If you have the Measure Tools window open, it'll display the different X, Y, and Z values as well.

FIGURE 6.17
Moving path between the two models

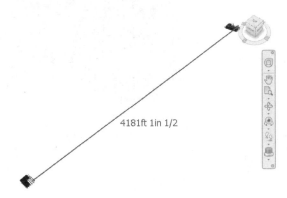

4181ft 1in 1/2

With this dimension line in place, you can tell Navisworks to move the model from the first selection point of the Structural model to the specified point in the Architectural model. When translating objects, the first point selected can be thought of as the point to translate "from" and the second point to translate "to." Since the first point you selected was on the Structural model, you need to specify this file in the selection tree to highlight all the objects you wish to translate.

8. In the Measure drop-down menu, select the Transform Selected Items command, as shown in Figure 6.18. If it's grayed out, you need to make sure you have the Structural model highlighted.

FIGURE 6.18
Selecting the Transform Selected Items command

Navisworks will translate the model to align with the common points between the two models.

9. When finished, close the file without saving.

In this exercise, you used the Measure tools to align models of unknown coordinates. While this is an easy fix, it's best to make sure all of the models in your scene are referenced to a common origin. Also, think about incorporating some type of common element in all of your models for reference if you need to move and align. In this case, you used a column grid that was consistent between all the models; other options include arrows or crosshairs, as shown in Figure 6.19.

FIGURE 6.19
Sample coordinate origin markers

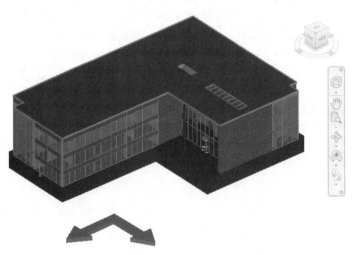

Working with Multiple Files from Revit

In the past, your options for working with Revit files were to export to another format such as the DWF® format or to use the add-on NWC exporter. In Navisworks 2013, you can now open Revit files natively without the need for exporting to a separate format. If your Revit file contains linked files, those will import as well, although they will be listed as children to the host file.

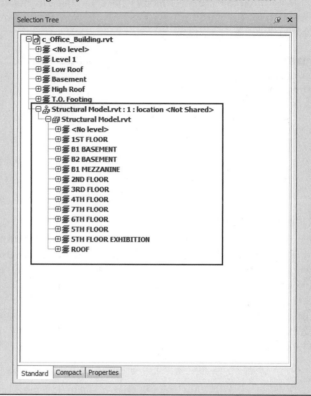

Marking Up with the Redline Tools

Besides capturing dimensions and onscreen measurements, Navisworks provides a whole suite of Redline tools that can be useful for marking up the models to include text notes, linework, and revision clouds. The benefit of this functionality is that these changes can be saved in the model views, which in turn can be shared among the project team members. Users don't need to reference a separate document to review the changes but can interact with the model and see exactly where the issues are situated. Also, users can add additional comments that are user/time/date stamped, so there is a historical record of any notes and annotations.

The Redline tools can be accessed under the Redline panel of the Review tab, as shown in Figure 6.20.

FIGURE 6.20
Redline panel

In addition to features to modify the color and line thickness, the Draw drop-down provides the full listing of Redline tools (Figure 6.21). Note that the thickness and color controls do not change redlines that are already drawn.

FIGURE 6.21
Draw tools available from the Draw drop-down menu

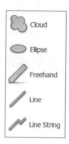

Using the Text Tools

One of the simplest markups to create is the basic text redline. It can be used to capture notes about changes or other modifications and saved to a viewpoint to be recalled a later date. When working with any of the Redline tools, keep in mind that they can only be saved to a viewpoint or clash result. Navisworks will generate an error message if you attempt to save without properly selecting a view. Think of the viewpoint as a Polaroid snapshot of the model that you can use a marker to write on. Without capturing the view first, there's nothing to write on.

For the exercises, let's use the file c06_Meadowgate_Redline.dwf and add a few redline markups, using the following steps:

1. Open the file and select the Project Browser [icon] icon in the lower-right screen.

2. Select the 3D View from the list, navigate to a view on the outside of the model, and create a viewpoint called **Exterior**.

3. Select the appropriate color for the text redlines from the Color drop-down. Redline text has a default size and weight that cannot be modified.

4. In the Redline menu, select Text. Your mouse pointer will change to a pencil icon. If you receive an error message, make sure you have a viewpoint currently selected.

5. Specify the area where you want to place the text markup and click onscreen.

6. A new dialog box will open. Enter the contents of the redline (e.g., **Verify wall panel clearances**) and click OK (Figure 6.22).

7. Your text will be displayed in the model according to the color specified in the Redline panel of the ribbon (Figure 6.23).

8. To add additional text, make sure you're still in the current viewpoint and repeat steps 3–6.

FIGURE 6.22
Enter Redline Text
dialog box

FIGURE 6.23
Model view with
added text

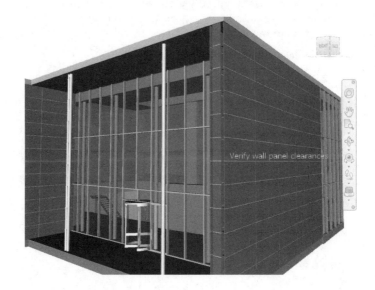

9. To make changes to text, right-click the text string and select Edit from the context menu. Update the text in the dialog box and click OK when complete.

10. To move the text box, right-click the text string and select Move. The mouse pointer will change to a crosshair. Navigate to a new location and press the left mouse button to confirm.

In addition to marking up the 3D model, you can introduce markups on the 2D sheets. Instead of creating section views of your floor plates, you can use the predefined 2D views to add text markups. Also, since there may be additional detail on these views that is absent in the model, it sometimes makes sense to reference both views in the design review process.

Using the Draw Tools

Similar to the Text tools in the Redline panel, the Draw tools allow you to add linework and revision clouds to your viewpoints. Occasionally, you need to highlight elements in the model, and the Draw tools allow you to identify specific regions. Used with the text markups discussed in the previous section, the Draw tools let you easily capture redline information to share with the extended project team.

In addition, you can also specify a unique color for these markups, as well as alter the line-weight to create thin or thick lines. In Chapter 4, we discussed best practices for color-coding the model based on disciplines. You can create a similar standard especially if you're working with multiple review sessions. Each discipline can be represented by a different color so it's easier to identify the text and redlines when they are being reviewed.

CLOUD

Navisworks creates revision clouds made up of a series of sequential arcs. This markup standard is common and typically used to designate changes in the model. The revision cloud is built up through a series of mouse clicks around the object(s) you wish to reference. Let's go through an example:

1. Select either the 3D or 2D view in the file.

2. Create a viewpoint and name it **Revision Cloud** or something similar.

3. With the viewpoint highlighted, select the Cloud tool from the Draw drop-down menu.

4. Specify the start point and left-click once.

5. Move away in a clockwise motion from the initial start point and left-click again. Navisworks will create an arc between the two points. The closer the points are, the smaller the arc, and vice versa.

6. Continue moving around the model and left-clicking to create the cloud (Figure 6.24).

7. Right-click to end the Cloud tool. This will also close the cloud to form a closed loop.

FIGURE 6.24
Revision cloud on
the 2D sheet

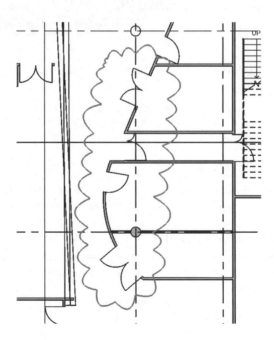

ELLIPSE

The Ellipse tool is useful for quickly marking up the drawing with a continuous line segment. When working with the Ellipse command, you can create anything from a perfect circle to a Lissajous curve or ellipse by specifying the size of the bounding box. Follow these steps:

1. Select the 3D model from the Project Browser and navigate to an exterior view of the entryway.

2. Create a viewpoint named **Entry** or something similar.

3. In the Draw drop-down menu, select the Ellipse tool.

4. In the model viewing window, specify the start point of the ellipse by left-clicking the mouse and drag the mouse away from the start point, keeping the left button pressed. As you move the mouse, you'll see a dotted line that represents the extents of the ellipse.

5. After you've encompassed the area to create the ellipse, let go of the left mouse button. Depending on the shape of the bounding box, you should see a continuous line segment that follows the approximate shape of the area you specified (Figure 6.25).

FIGURE 6.25
Ellipse markup on
the entryway

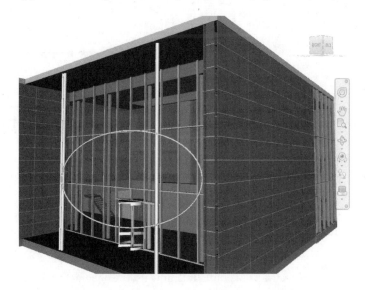

Go ahead and attempt several additional shapes using the Ellipse tool. Also, practice creating them on the 2D sheets as well.

FREEHAND

Occasionally, you may want to sketch a proposed solution or quickly mark out items in the model. The Freehand markup tool allows you complete flexibility to incorporate any type of geometry or hand-drawn text. Using a tablet computer or stylus/drawing pad will aid with the accuracy of the drawing, but the typical mouse will do fine for most redlines. Holding down the left mouse button and moving around the model will engage the pen; letting go will disable it. Let's try this out using these steps:

1. Select either the 3D or 2D view in the file.

2. Create a viewpoint and name it **Freehand** or something similar.

3. With the viewpoint highlighted, select the Freehand tool from the Draw drop-down menu.

4. Specify a start point and select the left mouse button.

5. As you drag the mouse around, you'll see the drawing update to include your redlines.

   Figure 6.26 shows how Freehand can be used in conjunction with the Text tool to quickly create simple yet informative redlines.

FIGURE 6.26
Simple Freehand
markups in 2D

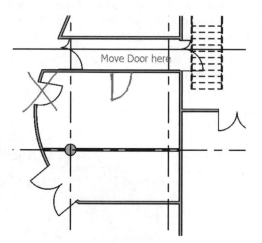

LINE

Similar to the Freehand tool, the Line tool is useful for creating linework in the markups. It can be useful for documenting recommendations and proposed solutions, and you'll have a straight line between two points. Let's work through this example:

1. Select either the 3D or 2D view in the file.

2. Create a viewpoint and name it **Line** or something similar.

3. With the viewpoint highlighted, select the Line tool from the Draw drop-down menu.

4. Specify a start point and click the left mouse button.

5. Navigate to the second point and click the left mouse button again. Navisworks will draw a solid line between the two points (Figure 6.27).

FIGURE 6.27
Simple Line markup

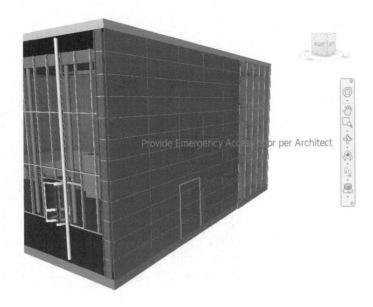

FIGURE 6.27
Simple Line markup

LINE STRING

The Line String tool allows you to create a multisegmented line without having to redefine the start point each time. This is identical to working with polylines in most CAD formats where you specify each point on the string. To end the string, simply right-click. Follow these steps:

1. Select either the 3D or 2D view in the file.

2. Create a viewpoint and name it **Line String** or something similar.

3. With the viewpoint highlighted, select the Line String tool from the Draw drop-down menu.

4. Specify a start point and click the left mouse button once and let go.

5. Navigate to the second point and click the left mouse button again. Navisworks will draw a solid line between the two points.

6. Select a third point to add another line.

7. Continue specifying additional points to create additional lines.

8. When complete, right click or press Esc to temporarily end the Line String command. You can now specify a new start point to create a new line segment (Figure 6.28).

FIGURE 6.28
Line String markup

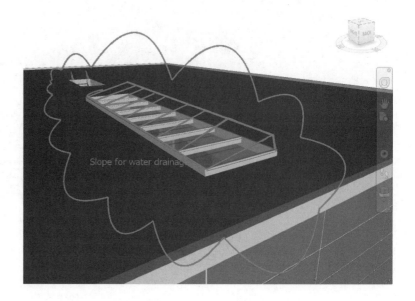

ERASE

Lastly, the Erase command allows you to remove both text and drawing redlines from your viewpoints. This tool functions similar to the Ellipse feature, but you specify a bounding box onscreen to reference the areas you wish to delete. You'll need to fully enclose the line, geometry, or text you want to delete. Individual line segments of a line string can be deleted but must be wholly selected. Let's try this:

1. Select a viewpoint with redline markups you want to delete.

2. With the viewpoint still selected, choose the Erase command from the Draw drop-down menu.

3. Select a start point and drag the mouse to create a bounding box that fully encompasses the redline you wish to delete.

4. Text redlines can also be deleted by right-clicking them and selecting Delete Redline.

5. When all modifications are complete, right-click the current viewpoint in the Saved Viewpoints window, and choose Update from the context menu.

   All changes to the viewpoint are now saved.

Adding Comments and Tags

In addition to text notes and redlines, Navisworks provides review tools such as tags and embedded comments to associate additional user data into the model. These tools become useful when there is a large amount of remarks you want to add to the model that would otherwise clutter up the viewpoint. It's important to note that while redlines and comments are annotations that are applied directly to viewpoints or clash results, comments can also be incorporated into animations, selection/search sets, and schedule tasks. Tags combine the best of both redlines and comments by creating an easy-to-use tool that incorporates redlining, creating viewpoints, and adding comments in one action. This section will focus on some of the project management workflows and is imperative to the mastery of Navisworks. If you take time to understand the concepts presented here and work through the exercises, you'll have a good grasp of the collaboration tools and workflows.

GENERATING COMMENTS

Comments are similar to text redlines, but they are not displayed in the model window; rather, they are listed in a separate dialog box that can accommodate considerably longer text strings. Comments can also be searched so that you can obtain information quickly. In addition, comments track the time/date, author, ID, status, and subject of each comment. The ID and status are important concepts that will be useful throughout the review process. Let's go through a few examples of adding comments to our model. For this exercise, we'll be using the c06_ Meadowgate_Comments.nwd file.

1. Open the Saved Viewpoints window and select the viewpoint labeled 4D Simulation.

2. Right-click the 4D Simulation viewpoint icon and select Add Comment.

3. A new dialog box will open, prompting you to enter the contents of your comment (Figure 6.29). Go ahead and enter **Need Site view added to this viewpoint**.

FIGURE 6.29
The Add Comment
dialog box

4. In addition to entering text, specify a status for this comment by selecting one of the following from the drop-down list:

   ◆ New

   ◆ Active

   ◆ Approved

   ◆ Resolved

5. When finished, click OK to accept.

6. Once a comment has been added, you can edit it by right-clicking the viewpoint icon and selecting Edit Comment or Delete Comment.

7. Try entering additional comments for areas such as search or selection sets and view-point animations. In subsequent chapters, you'll learn about schedule tasks and clash results, which can also have comments associated with them.

To view comments, open the Comments window by clicking the View Comments icon in the Comments panel of the Review tab (Figure 6.30).

FIGURE 6.30
Clicking View
Comments

The Comments window, like other windows in Navisworks, can be docked or viewed as a free-floating window. By default, this window is blank until you highlight a viewpoint, anima-tion, search or selection set, or so forth that contains comment data. Select the 4D Simulation icon in the Saved Viewpoints tab, and you should see the comment you previously entered (Figure 6.31). If you've added additional comments to other areas, select those and notice how the Comments window updates.

FIGURE 6.31
The Comments
window show-
ing viewpoint
comments

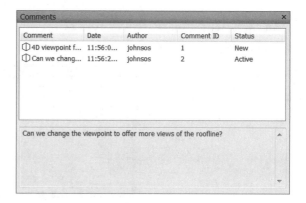

In addition to showing the comment text, you'll notice that Navisworks displays the time and date the comment was saved and the username (computer name) of the comment's author. The ID listed is a sequential numbering that increments with each new comment added. Finally, the status that was designated for each comment is also listed. To help with the various types of comments, Navisworks displays an icon showing what area the com-ment is associated with. For example, in our viewpoint comment, the perspective box icon to the left of the comment name indicates that the comment is associated with a viewpoint from a perspective camera. Practice with comments for search and selection sets and animations and notice how the icon changes. For additional information, refer to Table 6.1 for a description of the various comment icons. For further information on Clash Detective and TimeLiner, see Chapter 7, "4D Sequencing with TimeLiner" and Chapter 8, "Clash Detection."

TABLE 6.1: Comment Icons

ICON	DESCRIPTION
	Selection Set
	Search Set
	Clash Detective Result—New Clash
	Clash Detective Result—Approved Clash
	Clash Detective Result—Reviewed Clash
	Clash Detective Result—Resolved Clash
	Clash Detective Result—Active Clash
	Saved Viewpoints—Orthographic Camera
	Saved Viewpoints—Perspective Camera
	Saved Viewpoints—Animation
	Saved Viewpoints—Animation Cut
	Redline Tag
	TimeLiner Task—No Attached Items
	TimeLiner Task—With Attached Items
	TimeLiner Task—No Attached Items And Synchronized Link
	TimeLiner Task—No Attached Items And Old Or Broken Link
	TimeLiner Task—With Attached Items And Synchronized Link
	TimeLiner Task—With Attached Items And Old Or Broken Link

Take a moment to think about where comments would be useful in addition to the redlining tools. With redlining tools, you can add text to any viewpoint or clash result, but these are best served by using small sentences or fragments to quickly convey information efficiently. If you need to add a detailed description, a comment allows you to enter a lengthier text string without cluttering up the drawing. Also, by tracking dates, authors, and status, you can search through the model to locate specific comments, as covered in the next section. When creating comments, a best practice is to identify who owns any problems discovered so it's easy for that discipline to review all comments they are responsible for. For example, if the comment is referencing an issue the mechanical engineer needs to address, you might type **Mechanical to fix**. In the next section, you'll explore ways to search for comments with specific text. In this scenario, you could easily search through the model to identify all comments that are the responsibility of the mechanical engineer.

Also, comments become an important communication tool outside your Navisworks scene. When you export a viewpoint report, the comments are included in the HTML file in addition to the screen views of your model. See Chapter 5, "Model Snapshots: Viewpoints, Animations, and Sections," for more information on exporting viewpoints.

FINDING COMMENTS

Managing comments can be challenging, especially if others on your project team are referencing the model and adding their own; however, Navisworks makes it easy to track comments by allowing you to search by text, author, ID, or status (Figure 6.32). Open the Find Comments dialog box by clicking the Find Comments icon in the Comments panel of the Review tab.

FIGURE 6.32
Find Comments
dialog box

You can further filter down the query by specifying date ranges to search and which type of comments to search for (viewpoints, animations, search sets, etc.) by selecting either the Date Modified or Source tab (Figure 6.33 and Figure 6.34).

FIGURE 6.33
The Date Modified
tab in the Find
Comments
dialog box

Let's go through a few examples, beginning with the following steps using the file c06_
Meadowgate_Comments.nwd:

1. With the Find Comments dialog box open, leave all the fields blank and click the Find
   button in the upper-left corner. Navisworks will populate the selection table at the bottom of the window with all four of the comments currently saved in the model. Notice
   the different source of each of the comments identified by their icons. If you select the
   comment from the list, Navisworks will select the source of the comment. For example,
   if you select the Overview comment, the model view will update to reflect that current
   viewpoint. Coincidently, you can select the First Floor Columns Selection Set to highlight
   the columns in the model.

2. If the list is too long to manually navigate, use the comments filter to narrow your search.

3. In the Text field, enter the word **Verify** and click Find. You should receive an error indicating that no objects were found.

4. Since you're probably not going to remember the whole text string related to that particular comment, Navisworks allows you to use wildcard statements to help locate items.
   Clear the text field, enter **Verify***, and click Find.

   You should have one comment listed that is associated with the Plant Room viewpoint
   (Figure 6.35).

   You can also use the wildcard searches for locating specific authors.

FIGURE 6.34
The Source tab in
the Find Comments
dialog box

FIGURE 6.35
Search results in
the Find Comments
dialog box

5. To sort the columns, select the column head to alphabetize the display order.

Another option when you want to identify comments is to use the Quick Find Comments area. Just below the Find Comments button is a text box that allows you to enter text from the comment you're looking for (Figure 6.36). Similar to the Find Comments dialog box, you can use wildcard statements to identify partial values.

FIGURE 6.36
Quick Find
Comments

RENUMBERING COMMENT IDS

When you are working with comments, Navisworks assigns a unique ID to each comment. While this is an effective method for tracking the numerous comments in a typical Navisworks scene, problems arise when additional models are merged into the scene with identical comment IDs. Consider this typical review workflow. The master NWF is being reviewed by the various disciplines on the project. Each team is adding their own comments and redlines to their copy of the file. At the conclusion of the review period, all the files are merged into a single file. Recall that merging NWF files removes all duplicate geometry but keeps all unique views, redlines, tags, and comments intact. In such cases, you can renumber the IDs by selecting Renumber Comment IDs from the Comments drop-down menu (Figure 6.37). Doing so will remove all duplicate values and ensure that all IDs are unique to the scene once again.

FIGURE 6.37
Renumber
Comment IDs

USING TAGS

Tags are extremely useful because they combine numerous functionalities into one tool. Think of them as a one-stop shop for Navisworks, where you can mark an object in your model view but at the same time create a viewpoint and add a comment with a status. Unlike redlines and comments, which require that you have a saved viewpoint in place to mark up, tags can be used on any item regardless of what has been configured. This flexibility makes them excellent tools for use in your review sessions; you can easily tag items in the scene for follow-up. Furthermore, you can associate a comment with the tag, so not only do you have a visual mark on the model indicating the item, but also the accompanying text string provides additional details or suggestions. Consistent with the commenting process, you can also specify a status for each of these comments.

Another benefit of using a tag is that Navisworks will create a new viewpoint to display the tag markup and access to the comment data. Recall that all markup data is displayed only in viewpoints and not on the model itself. If you tag an item that is being displayed in a current saved viewpoint, the tag does not create a new viewpoint; instead, it updates the existing one to show the new mark.

In the following exercise, you'll use the file c06_Meadowgate_Tags.nwd:

1. Open the Saved Viewpoints window and select the Plant Room view.

2. Select the Add Tag tool from the Tags panel of the Review tab (Figure 6.38). Once this command is active, the mouse pointer will change to a pencil icon.

FIGURE 6.38
Redline tag in the
ribbon

3. Select the furnace or any other object in the scene. Navisworks will place a numbered tag and open the Add Comment dialog box.

4. Enter a comment in the dialog box and set the status as necessary. Click OK.

In this case, the tag becomes part of the Plant Room viewpoint. Experiment with adding tags to other items and views. When creating new tags and setting the comment status, think about how this technique can be useful in the review process. The reviewers create tags, add comments, and save the status as New. When the NWF file and all subsequent reference files are returned to the project coordinator for review, that person can easily search for all comments with a New status to quickly locate the items and review the comments. Once any design changes are executed and refreshed in the NWF, the status can be changed and additional text added to the comment. The NWF and accompanying files are then sent back to the project team for additional review iterations.

LOCATING TAGS

As part of the workflows between the project teams and their sharing of the NWF file(s), managing the abundance of redline tags can be perplexing. Since comments are an integral part of the tag, you'll use the Find Comments tool to identify any tags in the model. Akin to locating comments, you can use the search filters to identify portions of the text, author, ID, or status to limit what is shown in the selection table. Let's run through an example using these steps:

1. Open the Find Comments and Comments windows and dock them in the model or keep them easily accessible. It works best to have them located next to each other.

2. In the Find Comments window, select New from the Status drop-down and click Find to display the list of available comments.

3. From the selection table, choose Tag View 1:Tag1. Navisworks will populate the Comments box with the text specific to Tag 1 and update the view to reflect the saved viewpoint (Figure 6.39).

FIGURE 6.39
Navisworks
populates the
Comments box
with the text spe-
cific to Tag 1 and
updates the view
to reflect the saved
viewpoint.

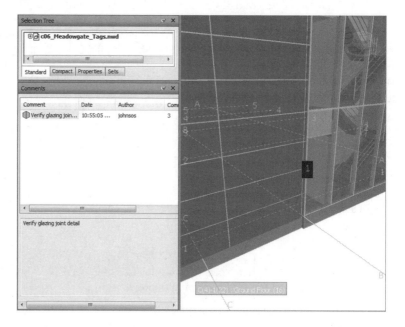

4. Practice cycling through the other comments/tags.

If you want to search for tags by their ID, you need to first understand how tags and comments are organized. If you go back and do a search for New status comments, you'll notice that the two tags listed, Tag 1 and Tag 2, have a comment ID that doesn't match up with the redline tag ID (Figure 6.40). Remember, Navisworks allows users to create comments that are independent of redline tags. Since all comment IDs are incremented with each new comment added, it's easy to tell which ones are newest. However, if a comment is deleted, that particular ID is no longer available. The next comment will be assigned the next unused ID. As a result, it's possible to encounter gaps in the comment IDs.

FIGURE 6.40

Tag IDs differ from comment IDs.

Name	Comment	Date	Author	Comment ID	Status
Overview	Can we chang...	10:50:...	johnsos	2	New
Tag View 1:Tag1	Verify glazing ...	10:55:...	johnsos	3	New
Tag View 2:Tag2	Relocate Door...	11:03:...	johnsos	4	New

Tags are numbered in a similar fashion, but since comments are also parts of the redline tag, the IDs may not always correspond to each other. Here's an example to consider. The project coordinator adds comments to a selection set and the saved viewpoint. These occupy comment ID numbers 1 and 2. Assuming you're working with the same file, another member of the project team decides to add a tag to an object in the model. While the redline tag is listed as number 1, the associated comment ID is listed as number 3.

To help manage this situation, it's a best practice to use the Find Comments and Comments windows together. When searching for redline tags, you can isolate them from the other search items by unchecking the other items in the Source tab of the Find Comments dialog box. Remember, the ID field in this dialog box will search for comment IDs only. Once your search yields the tag data, select the appropriate tag from the list. In the Comments window, the comment data associated with that tag is displayed. The model display is also updated to display the redline on screen showing the tag number.

If the tag ID is known, you can quickly activate the Tag view by using the Go To Tag tool in the Tags panel of the ribbon (Figure 6.41). Let's try this out using these steps:

FIGURE 6.41

Go To Tag tool

1. Enter the tag ID in the text field or use the up and down arrows to navigate to the proper ID.

2. Click the Go To Tag icon to the right of the text box.

   Navisworks will update the model display to show the redline tag. Also, the Comments window will update to show the text from the associated comment.

3. You can also use the four buttons under the Tag ID field to advance from tag to tag or jump to the first or last tag.

RENUMBERING TAGS

As mentioned, Navisworks assigns a unique ID to each redline tag. When multiple identical files are distributed for review and merged back into one single file, there is a potential to have duplicate tag IDs. Recall that merging NWF files removes all duplicate geometry but keeps all unique views, redlines, tags, and comments intact. In this case, you can renumber the IDs by selecting Renumber Tag IDs from the Tags drop-down menu (Figure 6.42). Doing so will remove all duplicate values and ensure that all IDs are unique to the scene once again.

FIGURE 6.42
Select Renumber Tag IDs from the Tags drop-down menu.

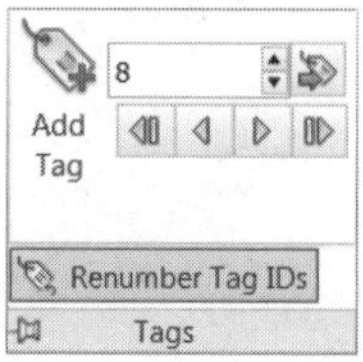

Saving in Viewpoints

Once you create your saved viewpoints, adding redlines and other markup is a straightforward process. With redlines, you simply add the different text, revision clouds, or other linework and right-click at the completion of each action. Doing so automatically adds the markup to the saved viewpoints. When comments or tags are added, they too are automatically updated in saved viewpoints when you click OK in the Comments window.

CONVERTING MEASUREMENTS TO REDLINES

Occasionally, you may want to capture specific measurements in the model to share as an issue for follow-up. Currently, the Measure tools provide temporary dimensions that are overwritten by subsequent measurements. To retain the measurements, you can convert them to a redline, which becomes part of a saved viewpoint. Let's try this using the c06_Meadowgate_Tags.nwd file:

1. Open the Save Viewpoints window and select the Plant Room viewpoint.

2. Using any of the Measure tools, take a dimension of the components in this view.

3. To capture this measurement as a redline, select the Convert To Redline tool in the Measure panel (Figure 6.43).

FIGURE 6.43
Clicking Convert To Redline

The measurement will be converted into a redline and updated as part of the Plant Room saved viewpoint.

When measuring objects that are not currently displayed in a saved viewpoint, Navisworks will create a new viewpoint labeled View1 and increment as necessary.

Real World Scenario

COMPARING CONSTRUCTION PROGRESS TO THE NAVISWORKS MODEL

One of the biggest benefits Navisworks offers is the large number of file formats that it can read. In addition to the major CAD and BIM formats, Navisworks reads a variety of laser scan files, or point clouds. These point clouds are extremely accurate representations of the field conditions. With this technology becoming cheaper, firms are adopting scanners to capture existing site conditions and compare the Navisworks model before any work commences.

Once work starts, scans are periodically taken and compared against the Navisworks model to ensure compliance with the approved design. Using the Measure and redlining tools, users can quickly compare the two models and document any discrepancies before too much work has been done. An example is shown here:

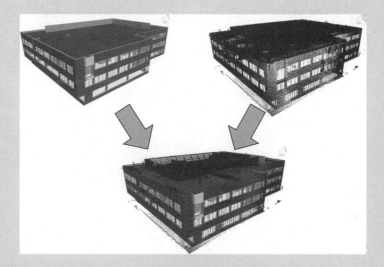

Some of the areas in which this workflow becomes useful include:

◆ Ensuring that the civil site grading is accurate and properly sloped for drainage

◆ Verifying that excavations are to the proper depth

◆ Developing safety plans based on accurate site conditions

◆ Ensuring that pedestrian ramps are properly sloped for Americans with Disabilities Act (ADA) compliance

◆ Corroborating actual progress against the model for percentage complete

The Bottom Line

Measure objects in the model.   Navisworks provides six Measure tools that allow for a variety of ways to calculate distances, areas, and angles.

Master It   Which tool allows you to measure multiple points and accrue the results?

Align models with unknown coordinates.   Occasionally, models are appended with different coordinate systems and do not align properly in the model.

Master It   What tools are available to correct misaligned models?

Use the Redline and Commenting tools.   Design reviews can easily be documented and communicated in Navisworks with the aid of the Redline and Commenting tools. These include any combination of text, linework, and tags.

Master It   What is the advantage of using the redline tag?

Chapter 7

4D Sequencing with TimeLiner

Up to this point, you've explored the basic features and functionalities within Autodesk® Navisworks® 2013. This chapter will draw on those concepts and introduce one of the major workflows: creating 4D sequences with the TimeLiner module. Using the TimeLiner feature, you'll better understand the construction sequence of your design. Furthermore, being able to virtually construct your design allows you to identify any potential scheduling conflicts before materials are delivered to the site, thus avoiding costly changes. In addition, the 4D model can be used to create and manage a dynamic construction site safety plan.

Since this topic is quite broad, you'll want to spend a fair amount of time becoming comfortable with the workflows and concepts mentioned in this chapter. Additionally, this is a *Mastering* book, so we'll be pulling in real-world ideas and situations that will help explain the principles of 4D. Finally, this chapter will rely heavily on the functions explained in earlier chapters. Make sure you're comfortable with topics such as search and selection sets, object properties, and object animations (covered in Chapter 10, "Animating Objects").

In this chapter, you'll learn to:

◆ Link your model to a project schedule

◆ Create a 4D sequence

◆ Automate schedule linking with rules

◆ Explore safety and site logistics planning

Introducing TimeLiner

TimeLiner allows you to connect your Navisworks model to a project schedule to create a 4D sequence that allows you to visualize the order of schedule tasks. Let's explore the concept of 4D in more detail. Instead of viewing the horizontal lines of the traditional Gantt chart or sometimes the dizzying array of network diagram connections (Figure 7.1), a 4D model acts as a visual interface between the Gantt chart and 3D model by displaying the associated model elements concurrently with the progression of construction activities over time. This allows you to quickly understand which areas of the model are being referenced by the schedule, but more importantly, you can start to understand the context of multiple activities and quickly see which areas are impacted. With 4D, there's no more conceptualizing the construction process and hypothesizing how it impacts the current design.

As a project manager or coordinator who needs to make informed decisions about alternatives to uncover the best manner to construct a particular design, you'll find that the traditional planning tools do not represent and communicate the complexities of the construction site such as the spatial and time (four-dimensional aspects). Succinctly, Navisworks bridges the inefficiencies of existing planning tools with a rich interactive model interface.

FIGURE 7.1
Typical scheduling network diagrams

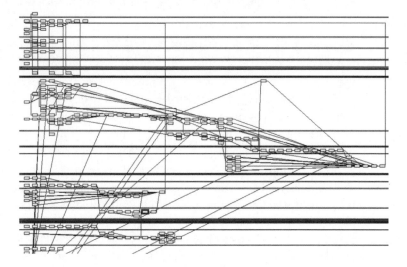

Navisworks retains the same file format–agnostic approach with TimeLiner by allowing users to link in multiple schedules from numerous sources to view the potential impacts by visualizing the entire construction process and identifying inefficiencies early in the coordination review. This strategy allows for making smart, informed choices on construction means and methods, site staffing, and safety planning. Also, this approach enables a greater number of project stakeholders to quickly understand the scope of the construction process. In short, the benefits of 4D are as follows:

◆ The ability to understand the full scope of the project

◆ Improved project execution strategy

◆ Enhanced communication and team building

◆ The ability to identify time and space conflicts

The TimeLiner area of Navisworks has been updated and retooled in the 2013 release to include a refined interface plus additional features to improve the 4D workflows. Some of these new features include the ability to simulate the cost of the project over time. This chapter will dive into a detailed overview of the 4D features of TimeLiner and also explain some best practices to incorporate in your projects.

TimeLiner Availability

TimeLiner is available with Navisworks Manage and Simulate; however, there is a playback-only version of TimeLiner included with Freedom.

Open the TimeLiner module by clicking the TimeLiner button in the Tools panel of the Home tab (Figure 7.2). Similar to other features, TimeLiner is a dockable window that can be placed anywhere in the Navisworks interface.

FIGURE 7.2
Click the TimeLiner button in the Tools panel.

Because of the size of this window, it's preferable to dock it at the bottom of the screen and encompass the full width of the monitor. If you're using dual monitors, you may want to drag this window to the second monitor to free up the model viewing area. In addition to the TimeLiner window, we'll be using the Properties, Search Sets, and Selection Tree windows. Take a few minutes to open and arrange these areas so they're easy to reference for the following exercises.

Let's focus again on the TimeLiner window. In the 2013 release, the development team redesigned the layout to remove some redundancy in the interface. When creating and configuring the 4D model, you'll be using all the tabs intermittently, so it's a good practice to become comfortable with the features. The process of creating a 4D sequence involves a few steps, but the workflows are streamlined and efficient. The flowchart shown in Figure 7.3 displays the typical scenario. Most users will leverage their existing master project, but it's also smart to save a separate NWF for the TimeLiner sequence. If you need to combine this file at a later date, you can merge the files.

There are four distinct stages to creating the 4D model. While there is no specific protocol for configuring the model, the order of steps presented here is considered a general best practice and will streamline the overall process. Referencing the flowchart in Figure 7.3 again, you'll notice there are several ways to add, link, and configure tasks. We'll cover these methods in the examples that follow. You'll quickly see how using some of the concepts covered in previous chapters such as search and selection sets will greatly expedite these processes and automate portions of the workflow.

Let's examine the TimeLiner interface.

FIGURE 7.3
Typical 4D model-
ing workflow

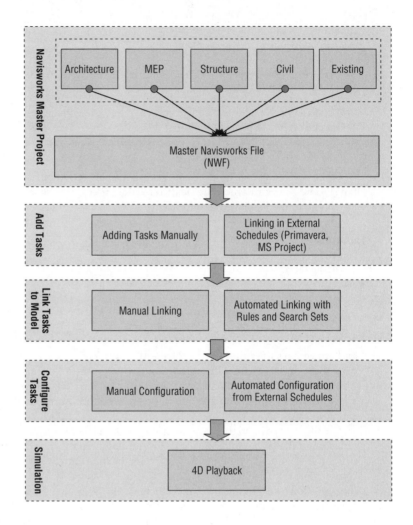

Exploring the Tasks Tab

The Tasks tab is the first of the tabs in the TimeLiner window, and you can think of it as the "home tab" when you're setting up your 4D model. By this, we mean that all the basic editing functions and views are based in this tab. Without a data model loaded, most of the functions are unavailable (grayed out). For this part of the chapter, we'll be using the file c07_Autodesk_Hospital.nwd from this book's web page at www.sybex.com/go/ masteringnavisworks2013. Open the NWD file; notice how the Tasks tab is divided into three basic areas (Figure 7.4).

The topmost commands control the creation of tasks, visibility of the columns, and ways to filter the various schedule tasks. The lower-left area displays the schedule task names, start and end dates, and task types. On the right side, you see the standard Gantt chart view.

FIGURE 7.4

TimeLiner interface showing the Tasks tab layout

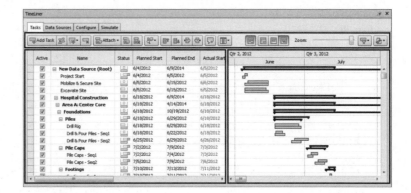

Refocusing back at the top, the Tasks subarea can be further broken down into several subgroups: the Tasks, Gantt Chart, and Filter/Export areas.

Let's look at the Tasks subarea in detail (Figure 7.5). This area contains functions that are used to:

◆ Add tasks

◆ Attach model items to schedule tasks

◆ Find/locate items

◆ Add comments

◆ Configure column layouts

FIGURE 7.5

Tasks tab subarea

The Gantt Chart area as shown in Figure 7.6 contains functions that are used to:

◆ Toggle on/off Gantt chart visibility

◆ Toggle views between actual and planned dates.

FIGURE 7.6

Gantt Chart tasks area

The Filter/Export area as shown in Figure 7.7 contains functions that allow you to:

◆ Filter schedule status

◆ Export TimeLiner data

FIGURE 7.7
Filter by Status and
TimeLiner Export
buttons

Let's expand on these commands by exploring the interface of the Tasks tab in detail. Table 7.1 lists the buttons and describes their function.

TABLE 7.1:   Task Button Descriptions

Button	Button Name	Description
Add Task	Add Task	The Add Task button adds a new task at the bottom of the task list.
	Insert Task	The Insert Task button inserts a new task above the one currently selected in the Task view.
	Auto-Add Tasks	The Auto-Add Tasks button automatically adds a task for every topmost layer, every topmost item, or every search and selection set.
	Delete Task	The Delete Task button deletes the tasks currently selected in the Task view.
Attach ▾	Attach	The Attach button enables you to: Attach Current Selection—attaches the currently selected items in the scene to the selected tasks. Attach Current Search—attaches all items selected by the current search to the selected tasks. Append Current Selection—appends the currently selected items in the scene to the items already attached to the selected tasks.
	Auto-Attach Using Rules	The Auto-Attach Using Rules button opens the TimeLiner Rules dialog box, where you can create, edit, and apply rules for automatically attaching model geometry to tasks.
	Clear Attachment	The Clear Attachment button detaches the model geometry from the selected tasks.
	Find Items	The Find Items button enables you to find items in a schedule based on the search criteria that you select from the drop-down list. This option can be turned on/off in the Options Editor (Tools ➢ TimeLiner ➢ Enable Find check box).
	Move Up	The Move Up button moves the selected tasks up the task list. Tasks can only move with their current level of hierarchy.

TABLE 7.1:   Task Button Descriptions *(CONTINUED)*

BUTTON	BUTTON NAME	DESCRIPTION
	Move Down	The Move Down button moves the selected tasks down the task list. Tasks can only move with their current level of hierarchy.
	Indent	The Indent button indents the selected tasks by one level in the task hierarchy.
	Outdent	The Outdent button outdents the selected tasks by one level in the task hierarchy.
	Add Comment	The Add Comment button adds a comment to the task.
	Columns	The Columns button enables you choose one of three predefined column sets to display in the Tasks view: Basic, Standard, or Extended. Alternatively, you can create a customized column set in the Choose TimeLiner Columns dialog box by clicking Choose Columns and then selecting Custom when you have set up your preferred column set.
	Show/Hide Gantt Chart	Click the Show/Hide Gantt Chart button to show or hide the Gantt chart.
	Show Planned Dates	Click the Show Planned Dates button to show Planned Dates in the Gantt chart.
	Show Actual Dates	Click the Show Actual Dates button to show Actual Dates in the Gantt chart.
	Show Planned vs. Actual Dates	Click the Show Planned vs. Actual Dates button to show Planned vs. Actual Dates in the Gantt chart.
Zoom:	Zoom Slide	The Zoom slider enables you to adjust the resolution of the displayed Gantt chart. The utmost left position selects the smallest available increment in the timeline (for example, days); the utmost right position selects the largest available increment in the timeline (for example, years).
	Filter By Status	The Filter By Status button enables you to filter tasks based on their status. Filtering a task temporarily hides the task from the Task and Gantt Chart views but does not make any changes to the underlying data structure.
	Export Schedule	The Export Schedule button enables you export a TimeLiner schedule as a CSV or Microsoft Project XML file.

In addition to these basic functions listed, several of the Taskbar buttons have drop-down menus that access more options.

Column Configuration   The Column Set drop-down menu 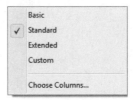 allows you to customize the columns displayed in the task view. Navisworks provides three predefined options for the grid layout, or you can customize your own layout (Figure 7.8).

FIGURE 7.8
Column Set
drop-down menu

Let's explore the options and what can be customized. Table 7.2 lists the differences among the three predefined versions and what other functions are available in the custom menu as well as a brief description of these features.

TABLE 7.2:   Column Set Options

BASIC BASIC	STANDARD	EXTENDED	CUSTOM	DESCRIPTION
Active	Active	Active	Active	Used to toggle the task on/off.
Name	Name	Name	Name	Task name.
Planned Start	Planned Start	Planned Start	Planned Start	Planned start date.
Planned End	Planned End	Planned End	Planned End	Planned end date.
Task Type	Task Type	Task Type	Task Type	Drop-down menu with defined options for 4D playback. See the Configure tab for more information.
Attached	Attached	Attached	Attached	List of model objects that are referenced by the schedule task.
–	Actual Start	Actual Start	Actual Start	Actual start date.
–	Actual End	Actual End	Actual End	Actual end date.
–	Status	Status	Status	Actual vs. planned status icons.

TABLE 7.2: Column Set Options *(CONTINUED)*

BASIC BASIC	STANDARD	EXTENDED	CUSTOM	DESCRIPTION
–	Total Cost	Total Cost	Total Cost	Total cost is the sum of all costs assigned to a particular task.
–	–	Material Cost	Material Cost	Cost of material for a specific task.
–	–	Labor Cost	Labor Cost	Cost of labor for a specific task
–	–	Equipment Cost	Equipment Cost	Cost of equipment for a specific task.
–	–	Subcontractor Cost	Subcontractor Cost	Cost of the subcontractor for a specific task.
–	–	Script	Script	Area to specify scripting for enhanced 4D playback.
–	–	Animation	Animation	Area to add predefined animation to the 4D playback.
–	–	Animation Behavior	Animation Behavior	Area to control the animation timing in 4D playback.
–	–	–	Data Source	Lists the name of the external schedule.
–	–		Display ID	Task IDs from external scheduling applications.
–	–	–	Comments	User-defined comments.
–	–	–	Provided Progress %	Area to manually update project status.
–	–	–	User 1–10 columns	Custom fields that can be used to link in additional data.

To change between the different column sets, specify Basic, Standard, Extended, or Custom from the Column Set drop-down. To customize the layout, click Choose Columns in the drop-down. A new window will display, allowing you to select which columns you want to include (Figure 7.9).

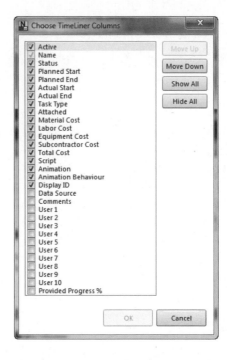

The second part of the Tasks subarea is centered on the display of the Gantt chart (Figure 7.10). This area provides several basic functions aimed at controlling the visibility of the Gantt chart and either planned or actual schedule data.

FIGURE 7.10

Gantt Chart
subarea

Show Gantt Chart   The Show Gantt Chart button is used to toggle the Gantt chart on/off at the lower-right side of the Tasks window.

Display Dates   One of the nice features in Navisworks is the ability to work with planned and actual schedule values. The Display Dates menu allows you to quickly select between Planned, Actual, or Planned vs. Actual dates (Figure 7.11).

FIGURE 7.11

Display Dates menu
selector

Similar to the status icon, Navisworks displays the planned values in the Gantt chart as light-gray bars. Actual values are displayed in light blue. When Planned vs. Actual is selected, the bars are stacked with the planned values displayed on the bottom (Figure 7.12).

In addition to the schedule value bars, Navisworks displays schedule milestones as diamond-shaped dots. In certain cases where there is a WBS hierarchy, Navisworks will display a summary bar (Figure 7.13).

FIGURE 7.12

Planned vs. Actual Gantt chart view

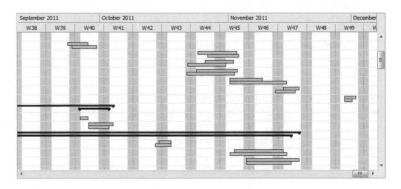

FIGURE 7.13

Schedule milestones and summary bars

ctive	Name	Status	Planned Start	Planned End	Actual Start	Actu	2011 Q1	Q2	Q3
✓	⊟ **Mechanical/Electri...**		11/26/2007	12/1/2011	11/26/2007	12/2/2C			
✓	Rough-In Phase Be...		9/24/2011	9/24/2011	9/24/2011	9/24/2C			◇
✓	Rough In Complete		11/29/2011	11/29/2011	11/29/2011	11/29/2			
✓	⊟ **HVAC**		4/9/2011	12/1/2011	4/9/2011	12/2/2C			
✓	Prepare and Solicit ...		4/9/2011	4/9/2011	4/9/2011	4/9/201	◇		
✓	Review Bids for He...		4/12/2011	4/12/2011	4/12/2011	4/12/2C	◇		
✓	Award Contract for...		4/16/2011	4/16/2011	4/16/2011	4/16/2C	◇		
✓	Fabricate and Deliv...		4/17/2011	4/17/2011	4/17/2011	4/17/2C	◇		
✓	Install HVAC Ducts		9/24/2011	9/30/2011	9/23/2011	9/28/2C			
✓	Insulate Ducts		10/27/2011	11/3/2011	10/24/2011	11/3/2C			
✓	Install HVAC Chiller		10/22/2011	10/31/2011	10/26/2011	11/2/2C			

Zoom The zoom slider is used to control the density of the Gantt chart. Depending on the zoom level, the two horizontal header bars in the Gantt chart will change. At full zoom, Navisworks will display the quarter, year, and abbreviated month. When you zoom in gradually, the timescale will expand to include additional detail down to hours and minutes. Figure 7.14 shows the timescale configurations.

FIGURE 7.14

Timescale zoom options

Qtr 1, 2011			Qtr 2, 2011		
February	March		April	May	June

February 2011				March 2011	
W6	W7	W8	W9	W10	W11

February 2011					
06	07	08	09	10	11	12

Wednesday February 02, 2011					Thursday
4 AM	8 AM	12 PM	4 PM	8 PM	12 AM

Wed Feb 02 '11, 11 AM				Wed Feb 02 '11, 12 PM		
0	15	30	45	0	15	30	45

Now that you're comfortable with the different Tasks window settings, let's focus on the Tasks and Gantt Chart areas. Depending on your column display settings, the Tasks window will vary. Figure 7.15 is showing the layout using the Standard setting.

In addition to configuring the column display, you can adjust the column placement by dragging the column header to a new location in the Tasks window. Grabbing the sides of the column header allows you to expand or shrink the size. You can sort the columns by clicking the header to sort ascending or descending.

The Gantt Chart area provides the typical bar chart view of the project schedule. Furthermore, to step through the zoom levels for the timescale, you can use the zoom slider or double-click the timescale to zoom in. Holding down the Shift key and double-clicking will zoom out.

FIGURE 7.15
Task area using
Standard column
display

Active	Name	Status	Planned Start	Planned End	Actual Start	Actual End	Task Type	Attached	Total Cost
☑	Fabricate and Deliv...		4/17/2011	4/17/2011	8/1/2011	8/1/2011			
☑	Install HVAC Ducts		9/24/2011	9/30/2011	9/23/2011	9/28/2011	Construct	Sets->MEP-...	
☑	Insulate Ducts		10/27/2011	11/3/2011	10/24/2011	11/3/2011	Construct	Sets->MEP-...	
☑	Install HVAC Chiller		10/22/2011	10/31/2011	10/26/2011	11/2/2011	Construct	Sets->MEP-...	
☑	Set Heat Pump		10/22/2011	11/2/2011	10/24/2011	11/3/2011			
☑	Startup and Test H...		11/1/2011	11/15/2011	11/1/2011	11/9/2011			
☑	Install AC Grills and...		11/12/2011	11/17/2011	11/14/2011	11/18/2011	Construct	Sets->MEP-...	
☑	Test and Balance H...		11/29/2011	12/1/2011	11/29/2011	12/2/2011			
☑	⊟ **Elevator**		9/26/2011	10/3/2011	1/26/2011	10/4/2011			
☑	Install Elevator Rail...		9/26/2011	9/28/2011	1/26/2011	1/28/2011			
☑	Install Elevator Ca...		9/28/2011	10/3/2011	9/28/2011	10/4/2011			
☑	⊟ **Plumbing and Ele...**		11/26/2007	11/16/2011	11/26/2007	11/18/2011			
☑	Set Mechanical and...		10/14/2011	10/18/2011	10/15/2011	10/18/2011	Construct	Sets->MEP-...	
☑	Rough-In Plumbing...		11/1/2011	11/15/2011	11/2/2011	11/14/2011	Construct	Sets->MEP-...	
☑	Install Wiring and C...		11/5/2011	11/16/2011	11/5/2011	11/18/2011			
☑			11/26/2007	11/26/2007	11/26/2007	11/26/2007			

USING THE CONTEXT MENU IN TIMELINER

In addition to using the buttons and keyboard shortcuts, most of the features in TimeLiner are
replicated in the context menu. Depending on where you right-click, the features list will vary.
Selecting the Task headers will yield sort settings.

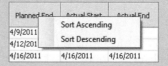

Selecting anywhere on either the Planned or Actual Dates listing will yield the full list of options.

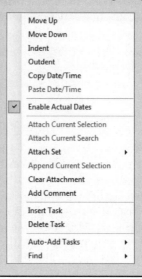

In addition to the Tasks tab buttons, let's explore some of the other features of the Tasks view window.

Filter By Status   When referencing schedule data, Navisworks handles both actual and planned dates. Depending on how the data is structured, each task will have an icon that represents actual against planned relationships. The status icon is composed of two horizontal bars. The topmost bar represents the actual dates, while the bottom bar represents the planned dates (Figure 7.16).

FIGURE 7.16

Actual vs. planned dates status icon layout

Actual Dates

Planned Dates

The Filter By Status button  allows you to modify the task display by choosing the Start and Finish values. By default, Navisworks will display all statuses. In the drop-down menu, you can choose between Start values of Early, On Time, Late, and After Planned Finish, and Finish values of Before Planned Start, Early, On Time, and Late (Figure 7.17).

FIGURE 7.17

Filter By Status drop-down menu

For variations between the actual and planned dates, the status icon in the task view will be displayed in red for late values and blue for early values. On-time values will be displayed in green and missing data will be displayed in dark gray. Table 7.3 lists the variations between actual and planned dates and the icon configurations.

TABLE 7.3:   Status Icon Variations

ICON	STATUS FILTER (START/FINISH)	DESCRIPTION
	On Time/On Time	Actual start and end dates equal the planned start and end dates.
	After Planned Finish	Actual start date after the planned end date.

TABLE 7.3: Status Icon Variations *(CONTINUED)*

ICON	STATUS FILTER (START/FINISH)	DESCRIPTION
	Early/Before Planned Start	Actual start date before the planned start date and the actual end date before the planned start date.
	Late/Early	Actual start date after the planned start date and the actual end date before the planned end date.
	Late/On Time	Actual start date after the planned start date and the actual end date equals the planned end date.
	On Time/Early	Actual start date equals the planned start date and actual end date before the planned end date.
	On Time/Late	Actual start date equals planned start date and actual end date after planned end date
	Early/On Time	Actual start date before the planned start date and the actual end date equals the planned end date.
	Late/Late	Actual start date after the planned start date and the actual end date after the planned end date.
	Early/Early	Actual start date before the planned start date and the actual end date before the planned end date.
	Early/Late	Actual start date before the planned start date and the actual end date after the planned end date.
	NA	No comparison.

SHOWING SCHEDULE HIERARCHIES

Most scheduling applications allow you to create a work breakdown structure (WBS) to define the discrete work elements within the total scope of work. Navisworks will read and display these hierarchies in the Tasks window. Working with this type of formatting allows you to quickly collapse groupings of tasks not being referenced. Clicking the plus or minus sign next to the task name expands or collapses the grouping.

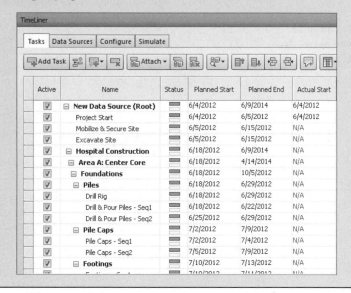

ADDING TASKS MANUALLY

Recall from the earlier flowchart that the first step toward building the 4D model is to add the schedule data (Figure 7.18). It's important to note that Navisworks allows you to create your own tasks one at a time, automatically from an object hierarchy or search and selection sets or by linking them from an outside scheduling program. There are several steps and best practices that we need to cover before you create your first 4D model.

Depending on the scenario you're trying to simulate, the project may have a few basic schedule milestones that you wish to sequence or several thousand schedule items in a complex scene. It's important to note that while Navisworks has some internal scheduling tools, it's not intended to replace the power and functionality of a true stand-alone scheduling application. Instead, Navisworks is a BIM simulation and analysis tool that teams up and augments existing scheduling applications. Most of the workflows mentioned will focus on this "team" environment, whether it's managing data internally or externally. TimeLiner is part of a suite of features inside Navisworks aimed at providing an easy-to-use yet powerful solution. Either way, adding tasks manually is an important skill to learn and will be useful for creating a new schedule from scratch or augmenting an existing one. Let's give it a try using these steps:

1. Open the file c07_Meadowgate_Manual_Tasks.nwd and open the TimeLiner window.

2. Open TimeLiner from the Home tab ➤ Tools Panel ➤ TimeLiner.

3. In the TimeLiner Tasks tab, select the Add Task button [Add Task] just below the Tasks tab (Figure 7.19). Navisworks will add a new task with blank dates.

FIGURE 7.18
Adding tasks in the 4D model

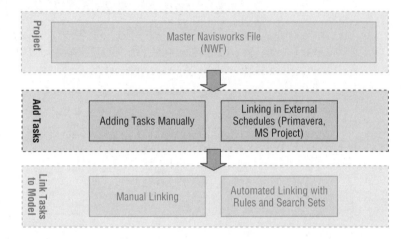

FIGURE 7.19
Adding a new task

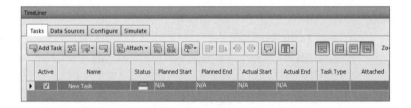

4. In the Name column, rename the activity to **Install Footings** or a typical schedule activity name.

5. Select the Planned Start column and adjust the dates to reflect the anticipated start date for this task.

6. Repeat this for the Planned End dates. Note that the Status column is still gray since you don't have any actual dates to compare against.

7. Select the Actual Start field and enter dates for both the Actual Start and End. Experiment with adjusting the dates to notice how the status icon changes.

SELECTING DATES IN THE TASKS TAB

When selecting dates in the Planned Start/End and Actual Start/End columns, Navisworks will by default display the current date and will reference that date on subsequent entries. Rather than cycle through the months by clicking the forward or backward arrow to get to the proper date, you can simply select the date at the top center of the calendar view (e.g., May 2012). Navisworks will back out from the current month view to show all months. Selecting the date again backs out to the years. Additional selections will list the different decades, as shown in the following graphic. Once you've backed out to the extents you need for selecting dates, picking any of the values will reverse the process and dive down all the way to the month view again. This is an extremely useful tool that is important for TimeLiner configuration.

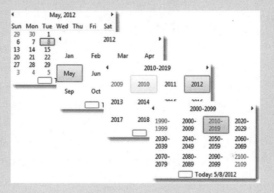

This exercise was aimed at adding a few tasks to the model to prepare for the simulation. However, let's assume that you have a model that already contains numerous tasks, but when configuring the model, you need to add additional tasks. This scenario arises quite often in the early 4D coordination efforts where the project schedule was created by a different department without much thought to the BIM process. To accurately depict the construction simulation, you need to add additional detail to the schedule. One option is to modify the original project schedule to add in the extra tasks. However, because most project schedules are legal instruments and part of the overall contract documents, modifying them may not be feasible. Using the Insert Tasks feature, you can manually augment the existing data to include the additional line items. We'll discuss linking in external schedules later in this chapter, but for now, open the file `c07_Meadowgate_Augmenting_Tasks.nwd`. Let's try this workflow using the following steps:

1. Open the file and then the TimeLiner window.

2. Select the Tasks tab and locate the Foundation WBS in the Tasks window. You need to add an additional task to reflect stripping the formwork, backfilling, and compacting the walls.

3. On the left side of the Tasks window, highlight the task Foundation Phase Complete.

4. Click the Insert Task button 🔲. An additional schedule item labeled New Task is added above the aforementioned task (Figure 7.20).

FIGURE 7.20
Foundation task listing

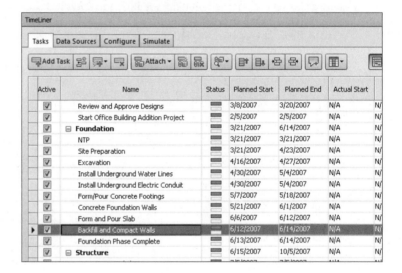

5. Rename the task **Backfill and Compact Walls**.

6. Modify the dates as needed.

7. To update the column sorting to reflect the new dates, click the Planned Start column heading to reorder the tasks.

In this exercise, you added a new task to part of the existing data hierarchy. As you become familiar with this workflow, think about other examples where this would be useful.

BUILDING SCHEDULE HIERARCHIES IN NAVISWORKS

New to Navisworks 2013 is the ability to create custom hierarchies in the task listing. In addition to adding blank tasks to a schedule, you can specify parent-child relationships by using the new Indent and Outdent features. When blank tasks are added, you can specify the placement of the task in the hierarchy using the following buttons:

Move Up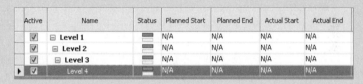

Move Down

Indent

Outdent

When working with the Indent feature, you can create parent tasks with up to three levels of subtasks.

Active	Name	Status	Planned Start	Planned End	Actual Start	Actual End
☑	⊟ **Level 1**		N/A	N/A	N/A	N/A
☑	⊟ **Level 2**		N/A	N/A	N/A	N/A
☑	⊟ **Level 3**		N/A	N/A	N/A	N/A
☑	Level 4		N/A	N/A	N/A	N/A

MODIFYING DATES WITH THE INTERACTIVE GANTT CHART

An exciting feature of Navisworks is the ability to modify actual and planned dates as well as percent complete directly inside the Gantt chart. In addition to changing the date value in the Tasks window, you can manipulate the dates by dragging the start and end dates of the horizontal taskbars.

When you hover your mouse over the taskbars, the mouse pointer will change to a crosshair and the date properties of the schedule will be displayed, as shown here:

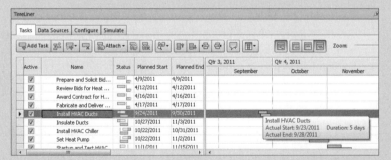

By selecting the taskbar near the middle, you can drag left or right to reposition that particular task. This method keeps the original schedule durations intact.

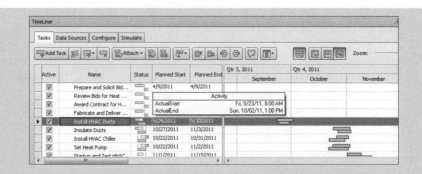

Selecting near the end of the taskbar will allow you to lengthen or shorten the task dates.

If you select near the start of a particular task, your mouse pointer will change to a right-facing arrow with a % sign. By dragging to the right, you can specify the percent complete on that particular task. In addition to the pop-up window listing the progress information, the bars in the Gantt chart are colored to show the approximate progress penetration.

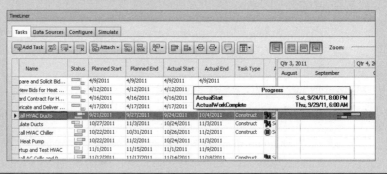

AUTO-ADDING TASKS

Another option when populating the Tasks window is to have Navisworks create the task names and add them for you automatically. These task names are based on layer, item, or selection set names and encompass all of the appended files in your scene. This workflow is useful if you don't have access to the project schedule but still want to create a 4D simulation without having to manually add the task names. In this case, you'll still need to define the dates, but this will expedite the process greatly. Follow these steps:

1. Open the file c07_Meadowgate_Automating_Tasks.nwd and open the TimeLiner window.

2. Select the Auto-Add Tasks button ![button] from the menu. In the drop-down menu, Navisworks provides you with three options to choose from (Figure 7.21). Let's explore them in greater detail:

FIGURE 7.21
Auto-Add Tasks
drop-down menu

For Every Topmost Layer This option creates tasks with the same names as the topmost layer in the selection tree.

For Every Topmost Item This option creates tasks with the same names as each topmost item in the selection tree.

For Every Set Selecting this option will create a separate task for every currently defined search and selection set utilizing the same naming convention.

3. Select the second option (For Every Topmost Item). Navisworks creates a separate task based on the names of the appended files in your scene. In addition, the model objects that make up that file are listed in the Attached column. We'll cover linking tasks to the model later in this chapter.

4. Delete the tasks by highlighting the entries and selecting the Delete Task button ⬛ to remove the previous entry.

5. Try this workflow again, this time using the third option (For Every Set) to attach the search and selection sets. You should see a new task for every defined search and selection set along with the named search and selection set listed under the Attached column.

6. Close the file without saving.

VERIFYING WHICH ITEMS ARE ATTACHED TO YOUR SCHEDULE

When you're working with the Auto-Add Tasks feature, model objects are automatically grouped and linked to the appropriate task. To quickly identify which items have been referenced, select either the Search and Selection Set name or Explicit Selection name in the Attached column. The referenced objects will highlight in the model. Using the standard visibility tools such as Hide Unselected, you can quickly isolate the highlighted objects. You can also right-click in the Attached column, hover over Find, and select Find Unattached/Uncontained Items.

LINKING IN EXTERNAL PROJECT SCHEDULES

The third method for adding tasks to the model is linking in data from external schedule applications. This process allows you to import large amounts of data without the manual effort mentioned earlier. In addition to importing activity names and dates, most scheduling applications support custom fields that can be used to supplement additional information in the model. Items such as discipline, critical path, and other planning information can be mapped to user-defined fields in the TimeLiner interface and are quite useful when you're sorting or filtering the tasks. Navisworks currently supports the following scheduling applications:

◆ Microsoft Project 2007–2010

◆ Microsoft MPX® format

◆ Primavera P6 (Web Services)

◆ Primavera P6v7 (Web Services)

◆ Primavera P6v8 (Web Services)

◆ Asta Powerproject versions 10–12

◆ CSV files

With the exception of the MPX and CSV formats, to leverage data from the other applications you need to have the core scheduling application installed prior to installing Navisworks. If you've recently added one of these programs, you need to repair or reinstall Navisworks to properly install the appropriate file reader. The topic of linking data from external scheduling applications will be thoroughly covered later in the section "Configuring the Data Sources Tab."

EXPORTING PROJECT SCHEDULES

After manually creating a schedule or augmenting an existing one, it's important to capture this effort for future reference. Navisworks allows you to export the schedule as a CSV or Microsoft XML file, which can be reused in future projects or modified and imported into most scheduling applications. Let's use the file c07_Autodesk_Hospital.nwd in the following steps:

1. With the file open, select the Tasks tab in TimeLiner.

2. Click the Export button on the right side of the screen.

3. In the Export drop-down menu, specify either CSV or MS Project XML (Figure 7.22).

FIGURE 7.22
Selecting the
Export options

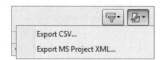

Navisworks will export the current schedule by creating a file with the embedded schedule data. Note that the data is exported in default order, without taking into account the column order or selection.

EXPORTING TIMELINER TO MICROSOFT PROJECT XML

Navisworks 2013 supports exporting to both CSV and XML formats. If you are exporting to Microsoft Project XML, there are additional options available on the Import/Export page that you can use to export task start dates and durations. Because different calendar types may be used in external project management software, it is recommended that you manage your task dates and durations either in Navisworks or by using external project management software, but not both.

In the Options Editor ➢ Tools ➢ TimeLiner ➢ Import/Export page, there are two options for XML files to consider.

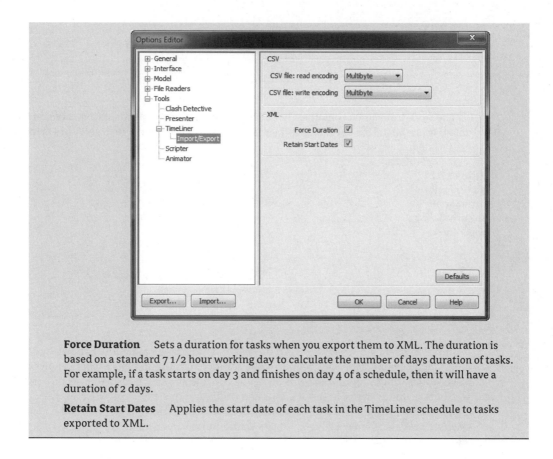

Force Duration   Sets a duration for tasks when you export them to XML. The duration is based on a standard 7 1/2 hour working day to calculate the number of days duration of tasks. For example, if a task starts on day 3 and finishes on day 4 of a schedule, then it will have a duration of 2 days.

Retain Start Dates   Applies the start date of each task in the TimeLiner schedule to tasks exported to XML.

Configuring the Data Sources Tab

The second tab shown in the TimeLiner module is used to connect to external scheduling applications. This tab was originally called Links, but the new name Data Sources is a more appropriate description since Links is commonly referred to as part of the hyperlinking functionality discussed in earlier chapters.

When external project schedules are initially linked in, Navisworks captures and stores a copy of the data and saves it to the project file. This is beneficial for users who have access to the project file but may not have access to the scheduling applications by allowing them to interact with the data. If the file is shared as an NWD, users who've downloaded the free viewer, Freedom, can also reference the linked-in schedule data when running simulations.

The Data Sources tab contains three buttons—Add, Delete, and Refresh (Figure 7.23)—and a window listing all successfully added schedules.

FIGURE 7.23
Data Sources command buttons

The Add drop-down contains a list of all the scheduling applications available for importing data (Figure 7.24). This list will display differently depending on which software is installed on your system.

FIGURE 7.24
Add drop-down listing available scheduling applications

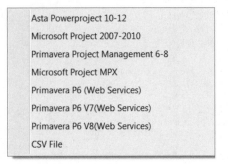

Importing data is a straightforward process and requires a modicum of knowledge for most of the applications listed; a few require some additional configurations to connect properly to Navisworks. Where appropriate, this book will provide as much information as possible to guide you, but due to variations in installations and configurations, this book will adopt a mainstream approach. Furthermore, with discrepancies between operating systems and product releases, the steps we provide assume a general system configuration and general computer knowledge.

ADDING DATA

When creating the 4D model, adding or linking disparate data is one of the benefits of Navisworks. Not only can project schedules from a variety of applications be linked, but also leveraging multiple schedule formats simultaneously aids in the overall construction planning and coordination process.

Here's an example. A typical construction project for a master campus plan might have construction activity taking place simultaneously in multiple locations. These distinct projects might be using a variety of trade disciplines and specialty contractors to fulfill the contract. Each of these construction sites uses its own project schedule that references data from the master plan but is completely isolated from the other construction activity. Add in site logistics planning and there is a chance that there could be numerous schedules to deal with. Figure 7.25 shows a breakdown of the various applications and where they might typically be used. Navisworks allows you to append multiformatted schedules the same way it handles model data by reading and aggregating a variety of formats.

Depending on the ultimate goal of your 4D simulation, having compatibility with the numerous scheduling applications allows you to create dynamic iterations for fully understanding the overall scope of the project. In this example, the numerous schedules and possibly thousands of individual activities would be hard to visualize and fully understand when working in a multidiscipline environment.

FIGURE 7.25
Multisite schedule
listing

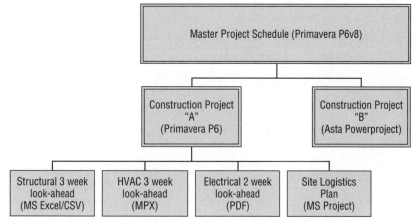

To assist with dissimilar nomenclatures from the various software vendors, Navisworks allows you to map the respective external data fields to the appropriate column in TimeLiner. This feature also allows you to create user-defined fields that can be populated with additional information. To help with this mapping process, Navisworks displays the Field Selector dialog box, which contains the TimeLiner columns (Figure 7.26). To the right of these is a series of drop-down menus that provide the available fields from that particular scheduling application. The options available are unique for each of the data sources. Depending on which data source is chosen, the columns displayed will vary.

FIGURE 7.26
Data sources Field
Selector dialog box

Table 7.4 lists the fields along with a description of their function.

TABLE 7.4: Field Selector Options

TIMELINER COLUMN	DESCRIPTION
Task Name	This field is required only for CSV files. Due to the variations in formatting, users need to specify which column contains the task names.
Task Type	Some scheduling applications define what type of activity the particular task represents, such as construction, demolition, or temporary items. This field is used to auto-populate the Task column in TimeLiner.
Synchronization ID	Each task activity needs to have a unique ID. This allows for synchronization between the external schedules regardless of whether major changes have taken place. When working with CSV files, you may need to manually specify this field.
Planned Start Date	Select the planned start date to permit working with planned versus actual comparisons.
Planned End Date	This field is used to specify the planned end date. This is useful for planned versus actual comparisons.
Actual Start Date	This is the actual start date value, but since some scheduling applications allow for multiple start dates, you can manually specify which dates you want to reference.
Actual End Date	Similar to the Start Date Import field, you want to specify an actual end date from the list of options if your scheduling application allows for multiple values.
Material Cost	This field maps over any cost data that is associated with materials to each imported task.
Labor Cost	This field is used to assign cost data that is associated with the labor on the project.
Equipment Cost	This field is used to assign equipment costs.
Subcontractor Cost	This field assigns any costs associated with the work of the subcontractor.
User-defined columns 1–10	Navisworks provides 10 user-defined fields that can be configured to link in data from the project source.

By default, Navisworks automatically imports the Task Name, Start, End, Planned Start, and Planned End values from most scheduling applications except the CSV format. To change these default settings, you can easily remap the fields by selecting a different value from the drop-down menu. As a best practice, it's a good idea to map these fields because nomenclatures are different among vendors. In addition to the standard columns, Navisworks provides 10 custom user-defined columns. Depending on the data source, the options available in the drop-down menus will vary, but typically, the custom columns are useful for tracking additional activity IDs, WBS IDs, and other planning-specific data. The next series of exercises will explore linking the scheduling applications to TimeLiner and importing the data. We'll cover adjusting dates and linking of model elements to the tasks and custom fields later in this chapter.

In earlier versions of Navisworks, there was a different configuration of the Actual and Planned Dates columns. In updating the semantics of the TimeLiner columns for Navisworks 2012 and 2013, these changes have reversed some of the features for existing users. For example, in earlier releases, most dates were primarily mapped to the Start and End columns unless explicitly configured for the Planned Start and Planned End columns. In the 2012 and 2013 releases, the Planned Start and Planned End are the primary sources for dates, with the secondary date tabs labeled Actual Start and Actual End. This tends to make sense because you need to have a planned or baseline date before you can conduct a comparison against the actual dates. This will affect some users who had populated models with the Planned Date columns in earlier versions.

CSV Files

The comma-separated value (CSV) file format is natively read in Navisworks without requiring an additional scheduling application. Since most users will have access to Microsoft Excel or other compatible spreadsheet applications, this format is extremely flexible and easily updated to reflect any changes. Using the file c07_Meadowgate_Data_Sources.nwd, let's go through the steps to load this file:

1. With the project file open, open TimeLiner.

2. Select the Data Sources tab and choose CSV File from the Add drop-down menu.

3. Specify the location of the CSV file (c07_Meadowgate_TimeLiner.csv).

4. Navisworks will display the Field Selector dialog box that will be used to map the external field names to the appropriate TimeLiner column (Figure 7.27). When working with the CSV format, the Field Selector dialog box contains a few additional import commands.

5. Since our CSV file contains row headings, make sure the Row 1 Contains Headings box is selected at the top of the Field Selector dialog box. If this is left unchecked, Navisworks will display the generic name of Column A, Column B, and so on instead of the actual header name in the External Field Name drop-down menu. Also, your heading can occupy only one row; otherwise, the file will return an error and not import properly.

FIGURE 7.27
CSV Field Selector
dialog box

6. Using the drop-downs under the External Field Name, map the fields to the appropriate columns (Figure 7.28), as shown in Table 7.5.

TABLE 7.5: CSV Field Mappings

COLUMN	EXTERNAL FIELD NAME
Task Name	Name
Display ID	
Task Type	Task Type
Synchronization ID	Unique ID
Planned Start Date	Planned Start
Planned End Date	Planned End
Actual Start Date	
Actual End Date	

FIGURE 7.28

Field Selector dialog box with mapped values

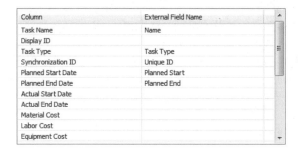

Column	External Field Name
Task Name	Name
Display ID	
Task Type	Task Type
Synchronization ID	Unique ID
Planned Start Date	Planned Start
Planned End Date	Planned End
Actual Start Date	
Actual End Date	
Material Cost	
Labor Cost	
Equipment Cost	

7. Click OK when finished. At this point, Navisworks has successfully connected to the data source. However, you still need to build the task hierarchy to copy the data over to Navisworks. The next section tackles synchronizing and rebuilding tasks.

8. Close the file without saving when finished.

Since CSV files can be formatted in a variety of ways, Navisworks will attempt to automatically detect the date and time format. You can also override these settings by specifying a specific date and time format by choosing the appropriate button at the top of the Field Selector dialog box.

Finally, a best practice when working with CSV files is to make sure your schedule contains a Unique ID field that is mapped to the Synchronization ID field when importing into TimeLiner. Failure to include such a field will prevent any changes made to the file at a later date from being synchronized properly. Also, be careful when editing the CSV file directly (e.g., not modifying Microsoft Project and exporting an updated CSV file but instead manually editing the file in a text editor); otherwise, it's easy to "break" the file.

MPX Files

The Microsoft Project Exchange (MPX) file format is advantageous in that it requires no installed third-party software such as Microsoft Project to link to TimeLiner. Also, this format is widely recognized and supported, so it serves as a generic container for data from many popular scheduling applications such as Primavera SureTrak. Using the same file from the previous exercises (c07_Meadowgate_Data_Sources.nwd) and the data file c07_Meadowgate_Planned .mpx, try another exercise:

1. Open TimeLiner and select the Data Sources tab.

2. Choose Microsoft Project MPX from the Add drop-down menu.

3. Browse for the c07_Meadowgate_Planned.mpx file.

4. In the Field Selector dialog box, specify the values (Figure 7.29) shown in Table 7.6.

TABLE 7.6:   MPX Field Mappings

COLUMN	EXTERNAL FIELD NAME
Task Type	
Synchronization ID	
Planned Start Date	start
Planned End Date	finish
Actual Start Date	actual start
Actual End Date	actual finish

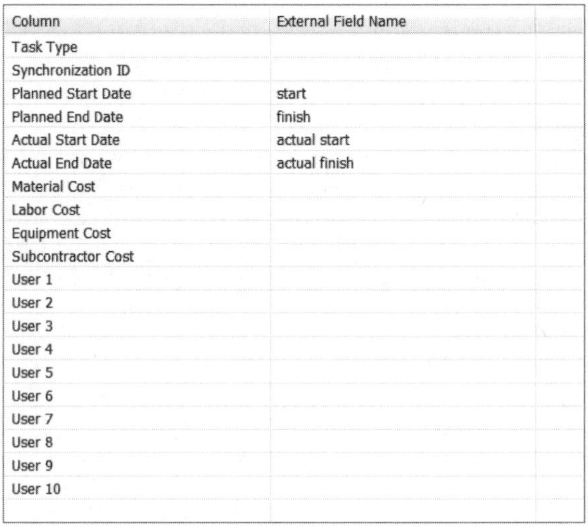

FIGURE 7.29
MPX field mapping

Column	External Field Name	
Task Type		
Synchronization ID		
Planned Start Date	start	
Planned End Date	finish	
Actual Start Date	actual start	
Actual End Date	actual finish	
Material Cost		
Labor Cost		
Equipment Cost		
Subcontractor Cost		
User 1		
User 2		
User 3		
User 4		
User 5		
User 6		
User 7		
User 8		
User 9		
User 10		

5. Click OK to connect to the external data source.

6. Close the file without saving when finished.

When you're working with Primavera SureTrak files, the unique ID is listed as the text10 field of the MPX file.

Microsoft Project Files

When working with Microsoft Project files (MPP), you need to have a copy of Microsoft Project installed on the same machine as Navisworks in order to load the data into TimeLiner. For users who have this application installed, you can access the files in the same manner as the MPX.

For this exercise, you'll be using the file c07_Meadowgate_Data_Sources.mpp along with the c07_Meadowgate_Data_Sources.nwd file:

1. Open TimeLiner and select the Data Sources tab.

2. Choose Microsoft Project 2007–2010 from the Add drop-down menu.

3. In the Field Selector dialog box, specify the values for the start and end dates as shown in Table 7.7.

4. Click OK to load the external data link.

5. Close the file without saving when complete.

TABLE 7.7:   Microsoft Project Field Mappings

COLUMN	EXTERNAL FIELD NAME
Task Type	
Synchronization ID	
Planned Start Date	Start
Planned End Date	Finish
Actual Start Date	Actual Start
Actual End Date	Actual Finish

Primavera Files

Primavera files utilize a variety of file formats and technology to connect to TimeLiner. In all instances, you must have the Primavera application installed on your machine to access the data. To explain the process more succinctly, we'll break them down into these three groups:

◆ Stand-alone (SureTrak)

◆ Software Development Kit Connections (P6v6–8)

◆ Web Services Connections (P6, P6v7, P6v8)

To access SureTrak data, use the MPX export listed earlier. The Software Development Kit (SDK) and Web Services connections require some additional configurations that extend beyond the scope of this book and will be covered briefly. We recommend that you consult the vendor's documentation for more information. Autodesk also provides additional information on these topics at their Construction Solutions Resource Center at www.autodesk.com/navisworksresources.

CONFIGURING PRIMAVERA SDK CONNECTIONS IN NAVISWORKS

All Primavera products with the exception of P3 and SureTrak are database driven and use either SQL or Oracle databases to host the data. The linkages to these applications are provided by an SDK or Web Services connection and require a number of additional components to be installed alongside Navisworks.

For connecting to Primavera via the SDK interface, you need to install the following:

◆ Primavera application (P6.2, P6v7, P6v8)

◆ ActiveX Data Objects (ADO) 2.1

◆ Primavera SDK (typically located on the installation media)

For configuring SDK connections when working with Primavera P6.2, you have the option of installing the database backend with either an Oracle 10g server or Microsoft SQL databases. If you upgrade to P7v7, you can maintain the SQL backend; however, if you're installing a fresh copy of Primavera P6v7 or newer, you must use the Oracle server backend. Following are the steps to install using the P6 with the SQL database.

1. Download and unzip Primavera P6 files to your local machine.

2. Open the unzipped folder `Client_Applications` and select Setup. When prompted, enter the Product Code and accept the License Agreement.

3. Make sure Primavera Stand Alone is selected. *Note: This will also install MS SQL Server/SQL Express Database*. This is recommended for most users since it will install all client applications, databases, and sample files.

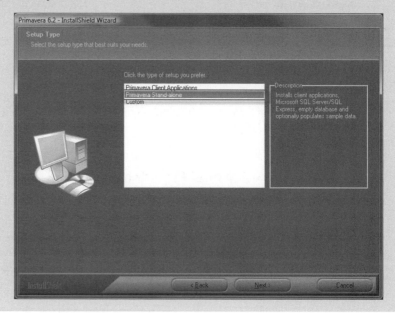

4. Select a destination for the install or click Next. Click through additional steps until the wizard asks for a license file. Browse out to the license TXT file that was sent to you earlier. Click Next to install.

5. Once the installation is complete, select Microsoft SQL Server/SQL Express from the drop-down list on the Database Configuration Wizard. Select Next.

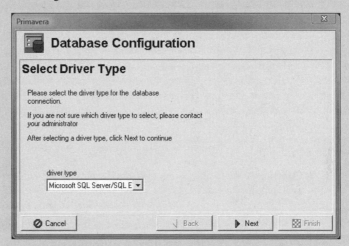

6. Specify a Host Name and Database Name. Note: this is typically your *Computer Name/PRIMAVERA* (e.g., Scott's-PC\PRIMAVERA) and the Database name is pmdb$primavera. Click Next when finished.

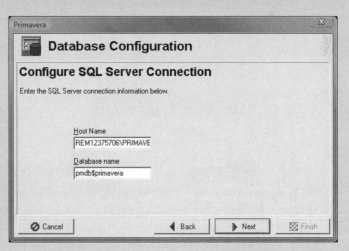

7. Enter the public login information. For SQL installations, you must use pubuser. For Oracle, you choose between the default users ADMPRM$PM, PRIVPRM$PM, or PUBPRM$PM. Keep the Public ID group set to 1. Enter the appropriate public login Information for your installation and click Next.

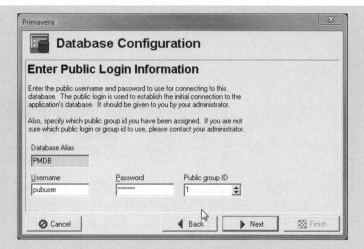

8. Click Next again to test the connection. If everything is configured properly, you should receive an acceptance message.

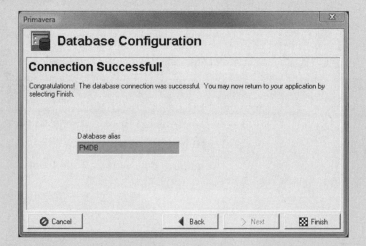

9. Click Finish to complete the Project Management installation.

10. Repeat the same steps for the MMDB (Methodology Management) configuration.

11. To link Primavera to NavisWorks, you need to install one additional item. Click Setup in the `Client_Applications` folder.

12. When prompted, select Modify and check Software Development Kit under Other Components. Do *not* uncheck Project Management or Methodology Management under Primavera Client Applications or you will uninstall these!

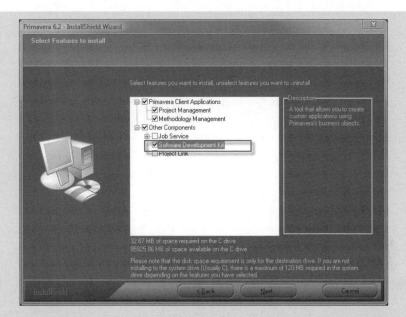

13. Continue through clicking Next until the install starts.

14. Once installation is complete, select Microsoft SQL Server/SQL Express from the drop-down on the Database Configuration Wizard. Click Next.

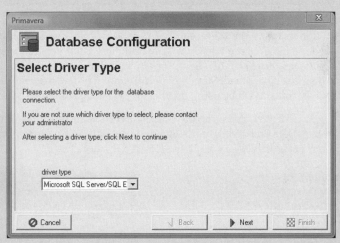

15. Enter Database settings from steps 5–9 again.

16. The last step is to define the mapping between the ODBC data source name and the Primavera database. Review the settings and click OK. The ODBC name listed (Primavera P6.2 SDK) is the name you will see when you select this data source in Navisworks. You can rename this field as you please.

Primavera Software Development Kit Setup

Define the mapping between the ODBC Data Source name (ODBC name) and the associated Database name.

ODBC Name: Primavera P6.2 SDK

Description:

Driver: Primavera Software Development Kit

Properties

If the alias specified below is not configured, press the button below to configure the alias.

Create database alias...

Property	Value
Database alias	PMSDK
Engine	Project Management
Filename for log messages	C:\temp\PMSDK.LOG
Options for logging messages	terse
Public group id for database alias	1
Public password for database alias	pubuser
Public username for database alias	pubuser

Remarks:

☐ SQL Describe Param Support

17. Click Finish to complete the install process.

Let's explore the steps required to connect Navisworks to the SDK interface. These steps and images are based on the P6.2 installation. Later versions may differ slightly. Ensure that Primavera has been installed properly and that you have a valid username and password. You must have *Admin Superuser* permission in order to connect to Primavera from inside Navisworks. We'll be using the file c07_Meadowgate_Data Sources.nwd for this exercise.

1. In TimeLiner, open the Data Sources tab and click the Add button. In the Primavera DSN Data Source Login dialog box, enter your login credentials for your Primavera account (Figure 7.30).

FIGURE 7.30
Primavera DSN
Data Source Login

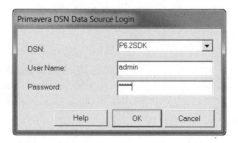

Primavera DSN Data Source Login

DSN: P6.2SDK

User Name: admin

Password: ******

Help   OK   Cancel

2. Once validated, you can select which project you wish to link to from the Select Primavera Project dialog box (Figure 7.31). Click OK.

FIGURE 7.31
List of Primavera
projects

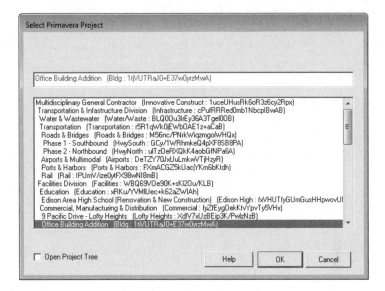

3. In the Field Selector dialog box, specify the appropriate values.

4. Click OK to load the external data link.

LINKING PRIMAVERA WEB SERVICES TO NAVISWORKS

For configuring Web Services connections, you need to install some additional components and configure a few system variables. Following are the steps to install web services using P6v7.

In addition to installing the main application, you'll need access to the Primavera Web Services application. This is usually included with the installation media.

Prior to installing P6v7 Web Services, you must install the services framework Apache CXF version 2.2.2. Download Apache CXF from the following website: `http://archive.apache.org/dist/cxf/2.2.2/`.

You must also install the Java Development Kit (JDK) version 1.6.x (update 15 or later is recommended) from this website: `http://java.sun.com/products/archive/j2se/6u15/index.html`.

P6v7 Web Services requires one of the following supported application servers:

◆ JBoss 5.0.1: `http://www.jboss.org/jbossas/downloads/`

◆ Oracle WebLogic Server 10g R3: `http://www.oracle.com/technetwork/middleware/ias/downloads/101310-085449.html`

◆ IBM WebSphere Application Server 7.0: `http://www-01.ibm.com/software/webservers/appserv/was/`

Download and install from the appropriate site. Note that JBoss application servers are not supported with P6v8.

1. Download and unzip Apache CXF and JDK files to your local machine.

2. Create a CXF_HOME environment variable. To set the variable, follow these steps:

   A. From the Start menu or Windows Explorer, right-click My Computer and then click Properties.

   B. Select the Advanced system settings icon on the left.

   C. In the System Properties dialog box, select the Advanced tab, and then click Environment Variables.

   D. In the Environment Variables dialog box, select New for the User Variable field and create a new variable called **CXF_HOME**. In the Variable Value field, type the location of Apache CXF on your local machine (i.e., `c:\apache-cxf-2.2.2`).

3. Set the JAVA_HOME environment variable in the same manner as described previously (i.e., `c:\Program Files\Java\jdk.1.6.0_15`).

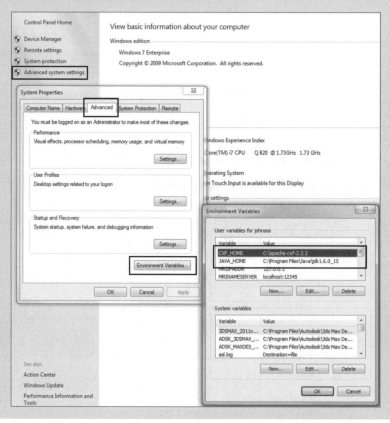

4. Install Primavera P6 Web Services from your install media. Note: don't confuse this with Web Access.

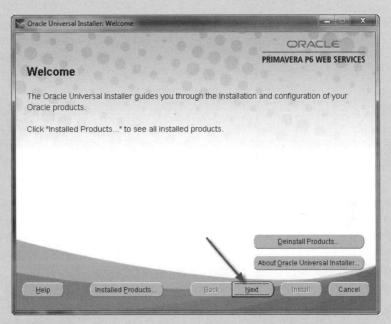

5. Select Typical installation.

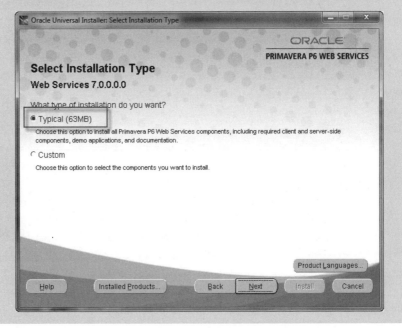

6. Continue through clicking Next until the install starts. Specify an install location for P6 Web Services (i.e., `c:\P6WS`).

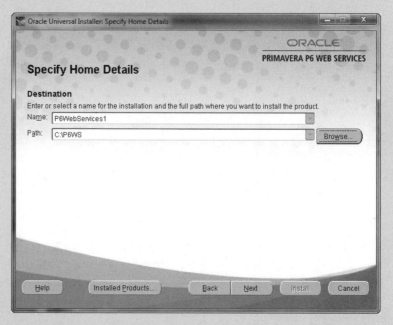

7. Specify the location for the Java Home install. In the next screen, specify the location of the Apache CXF installation.

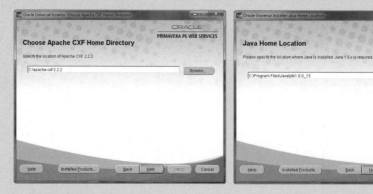

8. Specify the Authentication and Session Management protocol. Note: HTTP cookies for session management seem to work the best.

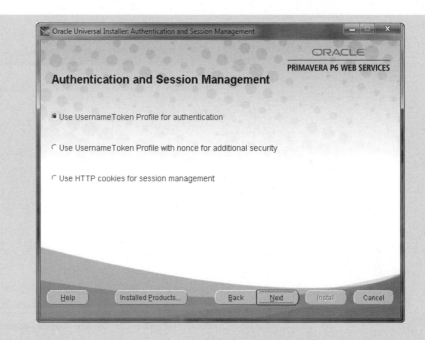

9. Click Next several times to finish the installation including the Configuration Assistants. Note: this will take several minutes to configure the databases.

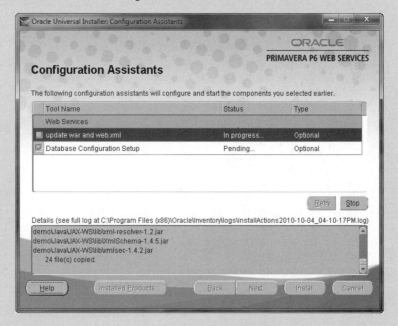

10. Specify the database to be configured.

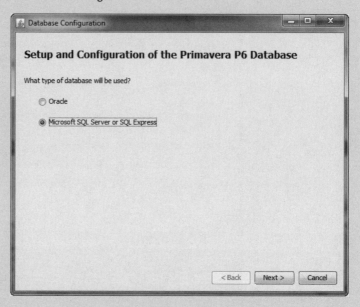

11A. Fill in the details for the database configuration for SQL installations. (For Oracle installations, go to step 11b.) These will be the default configurations for Primavera stand-alone installations for SQL databases.

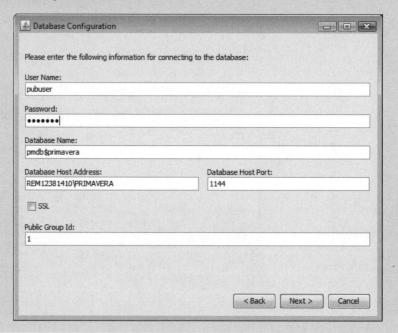

- User Name: **pubuser**

- Password: **pubuser**

- Database Name: **pmdb$primavera**

- Database Host Address is typically your *Computer Name\PRIMAVERA* (e.g., Scott-PC \ PRIMAVERA).

- Database Host Port can be located by going to the Start menu ➤ All Programs ➤ Microsoft SQL Server 2005 ➤ Configuration Tools ➤ SQL Server Configuration Manager. Select Protocols For PRIMAVERA from the drop-down under SQL Server 2005 Network Configuration (32 bit) and double-click the TCP/IP protocol name. Select the IP Addresses tab and scroll to the bottom. Under the area IP ALL is a listing for TCP Dynamic Ports. This is the Database Host Port for the Primavera database. Now, skip step 11b and continue with step 12.

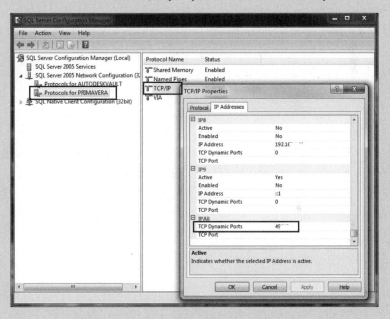

11B. Fill in the details for the database configuration for Oracle installations. These will be the default configurations for Primavera stand-alone installations for Oracle databases.

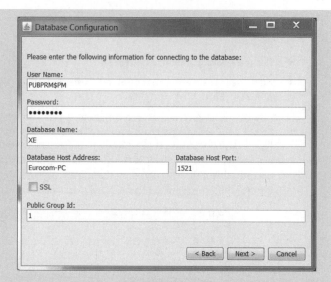

- ◆ User Name: **PUBPRM$PM**
- ◆ Password: <defined during Oracle installation>
- ◆ Database Name: **XE**
- ◆ Database Host Address is typically your Computer Name (e.g., Scott-PC).
- ◆ Database Host Port Default for Oracle is 1521.

12. If prompted for a server configuration, select Create A New Configuration.

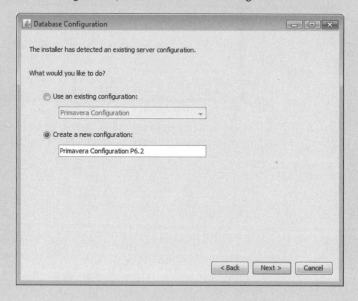

13. Click Next to finish the installation and configuration of the P6v7 Web Services component.

14. To deploy P6 Web Services, copy the p6ws.war file from `<P6 Web Services home>/server` folder to the following JBoss folder: `<JBOSS INSTALL LOCATION>/server/default/deploy`.

15. After placing the p6ws.war file in this folder, start the JBoss server by running the run.bat file located in `<JBOSS INSTALL LOCATION>/bin`. Note: you must leave the command window open while the server is running.

To configure Oracle WebLogic or IBM WebSphere application servers, please consult the Web Services admin guide that ships with Primavera for more information on installation and configuration.

Connecting to Primavera with Web Services requires creating environment variables and additional database configurations. Now that the database configuration is complete, let's look at the steps to link the schedule data into TimeLiner. Because of changes to the Primavera file format between the P6, P6v7, and P6v8 versions, there are three options for connecting to the Web Services. This is the basic process:

1. In the Add drop-down menu, select the option that matches your current version of Primavera.

2. In the login window, fill in the login connection details using your Primavera username and password.

3. The server address is typically the server name or IP address. For stand-alone users, this is typically localhost, or 127.0.01 (Figure 7.32). The default server port for localhost/127.0.0.1 SQL connections is 8080 and 7001 for Oracle installations.

4. Leave the Use SSL box unchecked and click Login.

FIGURE 7.32
Primavera Web
Services login

5. Navisworks supports multiple databases. Specify which database instance you want to connect with (Figure 7.33).

FIGURE 7.33
Selecting a Web
Services database

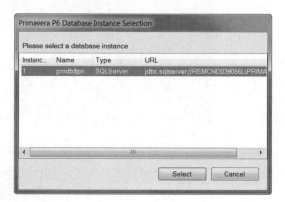

6. In the Project Selection dialog box, specify the Primavera project you want to link in (Figure 7.34).

FIGURE 7.34
P6 Web Services
project listing

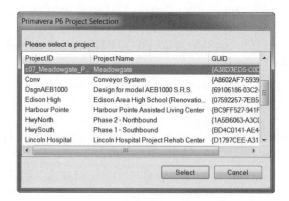

7. In the Field Selector dialog box, specify the appropriate values.

8. Click OK to load the external data link.

VERIFYING WEB SERVICES

When deploying P6 Web Services, you may experience an error message when attempting to connect. This can be for a number of reasons. To help troubleshoot where the issue is occurring, you can confirm that P6 Web Services is running by entering the following into a web browser:

```
http://localhost:port/p6ws/services
```

Note: you'll need to replace port with whatever port your web services instance is running on. If everything is configured properly, you should see a web page listing all of the available web services.

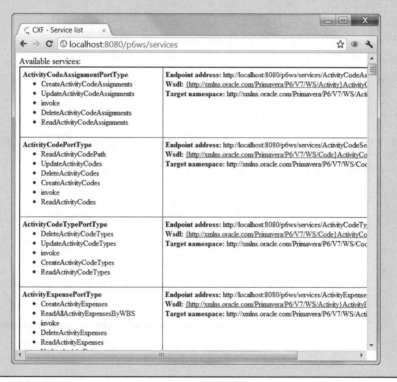

Asta Powerproject Files

Asta Powerproject is another stand-alone scheduling application that must be installed on the same machine as Navisworks to access the data. Here's how to do it:

1. Pin TimeLiner open and select the Data Sources tab.

2. Choose Asta Powerproject 10-12 from the Add drop-down menu.

3. In the Field Selector dialog box, specify the appropriate values.

4. Click OK to load the external data link.

SYNCHRONIZING AND REBUILDING TASKS

Once a project schedule has been loaded, it will display in the schedule window under the name New Data Source. You can easily rename it by selecting the name and typing in the new one. The fields to the right of the name list the type of file and the original file location.

To delete the file, highlight the name and click the Delete button. Doing so deletes the link to the external schedule only; the previously loaded tasks are still accessible in the Tasks window. The Refresh button serves two purposes: rebuild and synchronize. When you click Refresh, you'll be prompted to specify either a specific file or all the appended schedules (Figure 7.35). Note that Selected Data Sources is grayed out unless a data source is selected.

FIGURE 7.35
Choose either
Selected Data
Source or All Data
Sources.

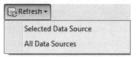

Once you've selected the appropriate files, a second dialog box will display asking you to select either Rebuild Task Hierarchy or Synchronize (Figure 7.36).

FIGURE 7.36
Choose Rebuild or
Synchronize.

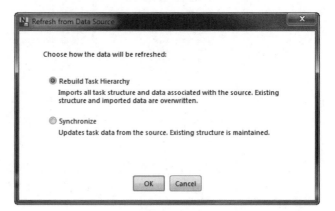

You select the Rebuild process to initially aggregate the schedule data into the Tasks window under the Tasks tab. Note that the Add button simply establishes the link to the external scheduling program. You need to rebuild the task hierarchy by clicking Rebuild. If changes are made to the original durations in the schedule or tasks are added, clicking Rebuild will update the changes in the Tasks window. However, if any additional tasks have been manually added to the task list, they will be removed and an exact copy of the original external schedule will overwrite any changes made. To preserve any manual changes made in the Tasks window, select the second option and synchronize to the external schedule. Doing so will update changes to schedule durations but preserve any manual changes.

Once the tasks have been added to TimeLiner, you need to move to the next step: linking the tasks to the model.

LINKING TASKS TO THE MODEL USING MANUAL SELECTIONS

To have Navisworks simulate the construction sequence accurately, first associate the schedule tasks with the appropriate model object(s). In other words, if you have a schedule task named *Install Footings*, you need to locate all the model elements that are represented by that task. Referencing our flowchart again, you'll notice there are two ways of linking the tasks to the model (Figure 7.37). The next section will cover both options and lay out the best practices for optimizing your performance.

FIGURE 7.37
Linking tasks to the model workflow

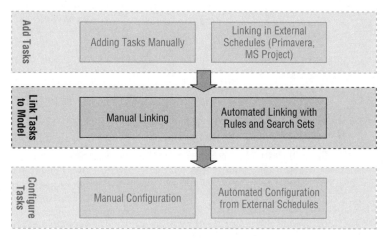

When you are working with manual selections, you have three ways of linking to the model: Attach Current Selection, Attach Current Search, and Attach Sets. The end result when working with these different groupings is the same, but the process is slightly different.

Attach Current Selection is the process of linking objects that have been highlighted in the model to a specific task in the Tasks window. This approach is useful when you need to add a one-off item or easily accessible items in the model. You should not use this option for linking numerous objects since the feasibility of this workflow is rendered useless by some of the other filtering tools in Navisworks. Let's step through an example of attaching the current selection to a task:

1. Open the file c07_Meadowgate_Linking_Tasks.nwd and open the TimeLiner window. Select the Tasks tab.

   For this exercise, you want to link the model objects that make up the civil site to the schedule task labeled A-Site.

2. Select the site objects by highlighting them in the model view window, or select the file Meadowgate - Civil.dwg from the selection tree.

3. Locate the task A-Site in the Tasks window in TimeLiner and highlight it.

4. Select the Attach button ![Attach] and choose Attach Current Selection from the dropdown menu. Navisworks will attach the grouping of objects to the task A-Site. You can also access this command by right-clicking the task A-Site (Figure 7.38).

FIGURE 7.38
Choose Attach
Current Selection
from the context
menu.

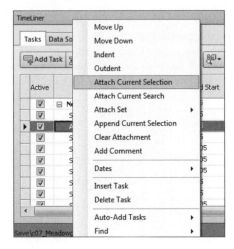

5. In the Attached column, note that the field now contains the words *Explicit Selection*. To verify which items this selection contains, press Esc to remove any previous selections and click the Explicit Selection text. All attached items will be highlighted in the model view window.

6. Delete the assignment by highlighting the task name A-Site and clicking the Clear Attachment button.

USING DRAG AND DROP WITH TIMELINER TASKS

In Navisworks 2013, you can link model elements to schedule tasks by simply dragging and dropping the following items:

Model elements from the scene view

Any entity from the selection tree

Any search/selection set

Once an item is initially selected, the mouse cursor will change to a circle with a slash through it. Keeping the left mouse button depressed, move your cursor over to the appropriate task in the TimeLiner window. Once you hover over a valid task, the mouse cursor will change back to a pointer. Let go and that model item is now assigned to that particular task.

In this example, you selected a grouping of objects by either highlighting them directly from the model or by accessing them from the selection tree hierarchy. Next, you'll be using the embedded object properties to define which model elements are selected for linking to the tasks. Here's how that works:

1. Using the same file, click the Find Items command located in the Select & Search area of the Home tab. You will need to keep the TimeLiner tab open as well, so spend a few minutes arranging the windows to allow for easy reference.

2. Conduct a model search for the following values:

   ◆ Category: Item

   ◆ Property: Name

   ◆ Condition: =

   ◆ Value: A-Door-G02

3. Keeping the results highlighted, navigate back to the Tasks tab in TimeLiner.

4. Locate the task A-Door-G02 and select Attach Current Search from the Attach button drop-down. You can also right-click the arrow next to this task and select Attach Current Search. Navisworks will add the results of the previous search to this task. In the Attached column, this will be listed as Custom Search.

5. Select the undo command or clear the attachment from the A-Door-G task.

The third option for linking is leveraging your existing search and selection sets. As you'll recall, these are defined groupings of objects that allow for easy highlighting and selection. Let's look at this workflow:

1. Using the same model as the previous exercises, locate the task name A-Door-G.

2. Right-click and select Attach Set from the context menu.

3. Navisworks will display a listing of all available search and selection sets in the model. Select the set External Doors (Figure 7.39).

The objects contained in the set External Doors will be attached to the A-Door-G task. However, instead of the objects listed under Explicit Selection, the set name is displayed in the Attached column. In addition to the right-click workflow, you can take advantage of new Navisworks 2013 functionality by simply selecting the External Doors selection set and using the drag-and-drop features to assign it to the A-Door-G task.

FIGURE 7.39
Select Attach Set from the context menu, and choose External Doors.

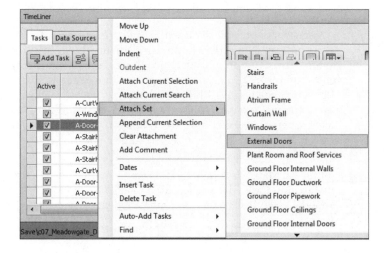

In the previous exercise, the search resulted in identifying elements from the selection tree that contained the same naming convention as the schedule tasks. This is no coincidence because one of the best practices is to consider using a common naming convention between tasks and your model elements and search sets. Another good practice to consider is using the unique ID name from your external schedule when defining the naming convention for your search and selection sets.

MAXIMIZING YOUR TIMELINER EFFICIENCY WITH RULES

Rules are one of the great features in Navisworks that allow you to automate the linking of schedule data to the model elements. Recall that a 4D model is a 3D model plus attached schedule data (Time). Attaching the schedule data to numerous model objects is time consuming and inefficient. Using rules, you can autolink the model elements to the appropriate schedule task by using search and selection sets or the internal properties. Clicking the Rules button opens the TimeLiner Rules Editor, where you can specify predefined rules or create your own.

AUTOMATING LINKING WITH RULES

The previous exercises explored linking model elements by manually selecting them from a predefined search or selection set, conducting an impromptu search, or tediously highlighting them from the model. This section will expose you to some of the automation inside Navisworks. Since we've expounded the concept of BIM, let's capture some of this potential by leveraging the embedded data in the models. Attaching tasks for a complex model can be time consuming and is an inefficient process. Using rules, you can instruct Navisworks to automatically connect selection tree layers, search and selection sets, or object property values to schedule tasks (assuming you've used a common naming convention). Not only does this greatly speed up the linking process, but by defining standards between the different departments (e.g., Scheduling, Design, Pre-Construction, etc.), you involve the entire project team early in the planning process. Having feedback from the different perspectives allows you to reap the knowledge of a larger group, which can be valuable when you're preparing the model.

Navisworks provides you with three predefined rules and an almost infinite number of customizable ones. The hallmark of them all involves using a standard naming convention to drive this automation. Once these rules have been defined, they can be saved and reused on future projects, so doing your due diligence up front and creating standards allows for even easier linking for your next project. Let's explore these rules in greater detail. In the Tasks tab in TimeLiner, click the Auto-Attach Using Rules button 🖼 in the Tasks subarea. A new dialog box will open with three predefined options and some buttons on the right that let you define or edit additional rules (Figure 7.40). The three predefined rules are as follows:

Rule #1: Map TimeLiner Tasks From Column Name To Items With The Same Name, Matching Case   This rule is used to identify and attach each geometry item from the model to the Tasks name assuming an identical name with matching case. To modify this rule, highlight it and click Edit. Doing so opens the Rules Editor dialog box (Figure 7.41). By default, this rule uses the Name column in TimeLiner's Tasks tab.

FIGURE 7.40
TimeLiner Rules
dialog box

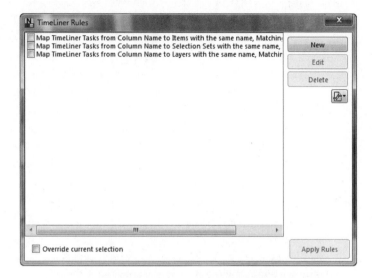

FIGURE 7.41
Rules Editor

To change the default value of any of the blue highlighted words to another column value, select the new value from the Name drop-down list (Figure 7.42).

FIGURE 7.42
Rules Editor's Name
drop-down list

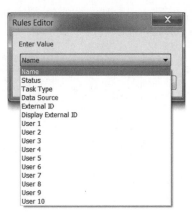

This list represents additional columns that can be configured for this rule. Selecting the Matching Case field allows you to change the rule to ignore case sensitivity.

Rule #2: Map TimeLiner Tasks From Column Name To Selection Sets With The Same Name, Matching Case   This rule is used to attach search and selection sets to each task name assuming an identical name. Modifying the rule is the same as for the first option. However, as you'll recall, when you set up your external scheduling links, Navisworks supports up to 10 user-defined columns. Think about what other data could be added to the schedule that would help define this rule and automate the linking. Instead of linking the task name to search and selection set names, try using the WBS or activity IDs as your standards. This allows you to keep the schedule activity names unchanged but institute a standard that is unique between your schedule and search and selection sets.

Rule #3: Map TimeLiner Tasks From Column Name To Layers With The Same Name, Matching Case   This rule is used to attach each layer in the model to each task name. When you are working with most CAD formats, the layer names are standardized and descriptive enough for you to easily identify the model objects.

Let's go through an example using rule #3 to automatically link model elements to our task list. In this exercise, the schedule task items replicate the layer names in our model. You'll use the file c07_Meadowgate_Using_Rules.nwd for this tutorial.

1. With the file open and TimeLiner open, select the Tasks tab.

2. Click the Rules button and in the TimeLiner Rules dialog box, check the last option: Map TimeLiner Tasks From Column Name To Layers With The Same Name, Matching Case.

3. Click Apply Rules in the lower-right corner.

4. Close the TimeLiner Rules dialog box.

In TimeLiner's Tasks tab, all the tasks should now have a selection of model elements associated with each task.

In addition to these predefined rules, you can create your own rule that references the object category and property values in the model. When you're working with data-rich models, this capability becomes useful because it allows you to skip the process of creating search and selection sets and link directly to the embedded object properties.

Custom rules function the same as the default ones, except you need to specify which object properties you're trying to link to. Let's go through an example using the file c07_Meadowgate_Custom_Rules.nwd and the schedule file c07_Custom_Rules.csv. In this exercise, you'll use one of the 10 user-defined columns. These columns can be linked to include supplemental data from the scheduling application such as construction IDs, WBS, and other descriptive data.

1. Open the file and then open the TimeLiner display.

2. Select the Data Sources tab and import the c07_Custom_Rules.csv file using the following settings (Figure 7.43) as shown in Table 7.8.

TABLE 7.8:   CSV Custom Rules Mappings

COLUMN	EXTERNAL FIELD NAME
Task Name	Name
Display ID	
Task Type	
Synchronization ID	Activity ID
Planned Start Date	Planned Start
Planned End Date	Planned End
Actual Start Date	
Actual End Date	
Material Cost	
Labor Cost	
Equipment Cost	
Subcontractor Cost	
User 1	User 1

FIGURE 7.43
CSV Field Selector
with defined values

3. Highlight the recently added data source in the Name field and click Refresh. Choose Selected Data Source and click Rebuild.

4. Click OK to add the task hierarchy to the model.

5. Select the Tasks tab and verify that the schedule tasks have been added.

6. Open the Auto-Attach Using Rules button and click New in the TimeLiner Rules dialog box. A new window labeled Rules Editor will open.

7. In the Rules Editor, select the second option: Attach Items To Tasks By Category/ Property.

8. In the Rule Description area, select the first underlined option and change the Column option from Name to User 1 using the drop-down.

9. In the second line, change the <Category> option to Element using the drop-down.

10. Finally, change the <Property> value to Construction ID using the Property Name drop-down.

11. Double-check your rule. It should look like Figure 7.44. Click OK to close the Rules Editor.

FIGURE 7.44
Completed rule
description

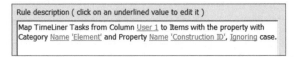

12. In the TimeLiner Rules area, you should see a new rule with the parameters we just specified. Check this rule and click Apply Rules.

13. Close the Rules Editor.

In the Tasks window, you should see Explicit Selections applied to a majority of the tasks. The remaining items in the Tasks window have been intentionally left out; however, you can easily attach them by dragging and dropping the selection sets in this file. When working with rules, you can optimize your performance by mixing default rules with custom ones as demonstrated here.

In this example, the user-defined tab contains a Construction ID number that matches an internal object property name. This was the result of embedding this information as a parameter in the Autodesk® Revit® model prior to exporting to Navisworks. Here is an example of leveraging the data in Building Information Models to automate the task-linking process. As data becomes more robust and incorporated into the project earlier in the design and coordination process, the linking process becomes far easier than manually linking the tasks. As a best practice, you should investigate what type of data is integrated in your data source files and look for opportunities to use rules to expedite the linking process.

CHECKING THE MODEL

After linking the model, you can easily double-check your work to make sure that all model objects have been associated to a specific task. One option is to hide the elements in your model after they have been linked. As you move through the task list, fewer objects will be visible in the model. At the end of your linking session, you'll see that any visible items in the model view have been orphaned and are not currently linked to any specific task.

The other option for checking your work is to use the built-in Find feature in Navisworks. This tool provides several checks that are useful when you're trying to determine what objects are not attached to any specific task or items that are referenced in multiple or overlapping tasks. In the following exercise, use the file c07_Meadowgate_Checking_Tasks.nwd:

1. With the file loaded and TimeLiner open, select the Tasks tab.

2. Select the Find Items button [icon].

3. Select Unattached / Uncontained Items (Figure 7.45) from the drop-down menu. Navisworks will highlight all objects that are not attached to or contained within a particular task.

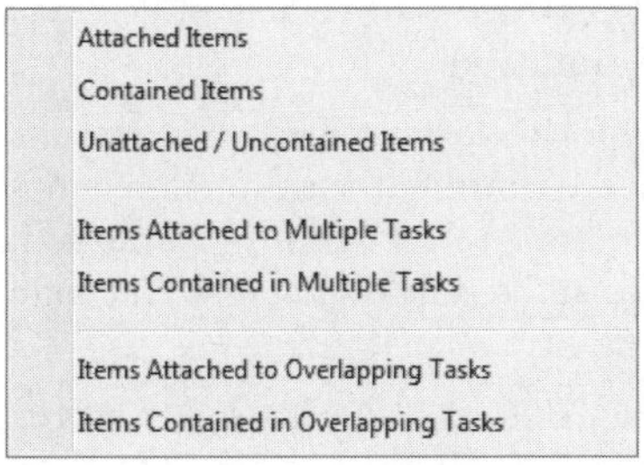

FIGURE 7.45
Context menu for
Find configurations

Attached Items

Contained Items

Unattached / Uncontained Items

Items Attached to Multiple Tasks

Items Contained in Multiple Tasks

Items Attached to Overlapping Tasks

Items Contained in Overlapping Tasks

4. Use the Hide Unselected command to isolate the selected objects.

5. Since you've hidden most of the components, the unattached objects can easily be selected. Note that most of the items in the selection tree are also grayed out, making it easy to highlight objects there as well.

6. If necessary, you can update your search and selection sets to incorporate these items, or right-click and select Append Current Selection to add the additional objects to the Explicit Selection.

ADDING COMMENTS

As discussed in Chapter 6, "Documenting Your Project," comments can be a useful tool to embed notes that contain additional information or directives for follow-up. In TimeLiner, comments can be added to individual tasks in the Tasks window:

1. With the Tasks window open in TimeLiner, highlight a task and select the Add Comment button 🗩.

2. In the Comment dialog box, enter any text and select a status for the comment.

3. Navisworks will display the number of comments in the Comments column 🗩 in the Tasks window. You may need to enable this from the Column Set drop-down.

4. To view the embedded comments, open the Comments window from the Review tab in the ribbon and highlight the specific task. All comments will be displayed, including Time/Date, Author, Comment ID, and Status.

For more information on working with comments, refer to Chapter 6.

DESIGNATING TASK TYPES

The final step in the 4D process is to specify a task from the Task Type column in the Tasks window. While this step is optional, it's a highly recommended best practice to consider since it will further enhance your project viewing and coordination efforts. When playing the TimeLiner simulation, Navisworks will display the linked model elements based on their schedule values, but you can further refine the simulation to color-code the various elements by specifying a task type to modify the view. This approach helps you easily distinguish between items represented by different trades or, more importantly, between temporary items and constructed elements. Similar to the other steps, there are a few options for configuring the tasks, as shown in Figure 7.46.

Navisworks provides three default task types that encompass the typical procedures in a construction simulation:

Construct This task type is used to represent items that are to be constructed. By default, when you are running the simulation, any objects attached to this task type are initially hidden from view. At the beginning of the simulation, the objects transition to a semitransparent green color at the start of that task and change to the model appearance at the conclusion of the task activity.

Demolish This task type is used to represent items that are to be demolished. When the simulation starts, all items attached to a task are fully visible. When the activity starts, they are shaded in a semitransparent red color at the start of the task activity. At the conclusion of the demolition activity, all items are hidden from view, thus emulating the demolition and removal process in the real world.

Temporary This task type is used to represent temporary items such as material, site logistics, equipment, and other nonpermanent objects that are used in the construction process.

These configurations can be accessed from the Task Type column drop-down in the Tasks window. In addition to the default task types, you can create your own or modify an existing one. In the next section, you'll have the opportunity to create custom tasks and examine some sample workflows for customizing the simulation process.

FIGURE 7.46
Configuring Tasks options

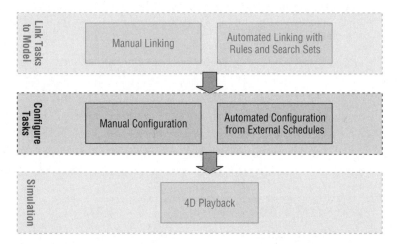

Using the Configure Tab

The Configure tab provides two basic functions: defining custom task types and creating appearance definitions. When simulating your 4D model, it's useful to know which elements are still under construction versus completed activities or which trades are currently working on portions of the site. Using task types allows you to modify the appearance of the model elements during the simulation by highlighting the objects in a different color or transparency to let you quickly identify specific procedures or disciplines. You can thus identify the various activities in real time without having to pause and investigate the model.

Let's explore the features of this tab in greater detail; we'll also create a few custom tasks for our 4D model.

DEFINING TASK TYPES

When defining task types, you need to consider what types of activities you wish to filter and modify. In addition to the three default task types, what action are you trying to show in your simulation? Here's a best practice to think about. Besides the default Construct task type, consider breaking this task out into separate tasks to define the different trades, such as Electrical, Plumbing, Painting, and so forth. If you're working in a tight area of the site, being able to identify the various trades quickly can highlight productivity and safety issues. Furthermore, your schedule may have multiple line items that all contribute to the completion of a multiprocess construction activity. Take floor slabs, for example. In addition to any excavation and site prep, there may be separate schedule line items for installing rebar, placing formwork, pouring concrete, and stripping the formwork. Concrete cure times are typically included in the schedule timeframe; however, this could be another task type if you want to display this portion of the simulation. If your model is detailed and includes some of these elements, it's useful to simulate these activities to get a better understanding of the various trades and their location on the site. Also, if you color-code items such as rebar, it's easy to see where additional safety protection may be required to avoid worker injuries.

Before you start customizing tasks, let's explore the set of visibility conditions that can be defined for each task. Open the file c07_Meadowgate_Defining_Tasks.nwd and navigate to the Configure tab in TimeLiner (Figure 7.47). In addition to the Name column, Navisworks provides five additional columns that can be configured to control the visibility of your task during the simulation.

FIGURE 7.47

Configure Tab showing Appearance options

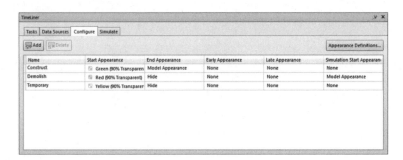

Start Appearance   This column defines how the task will appear when the simulation first starts. For example, the Construct task will initially appear as Green 90% Transparent.

End Appearance   This column defines how the task type will be displayed at the end of the scheduled finish for this activity. For the Construct task, this is currently defined as showing the Model Appearance. Thinking in the real world, this makes sense because items that are fully constructed will occupy that particular space. For the Demolish and Temporary items, these are shown as Hide. Once again, if you think about what happens on the site, with fully demolished items and temporary items removed, the site is free of those elements, so hiding them in our Navisworks scene re-creates that same visual.

Early Appearance   This column defines how activities that start before a planned time are displayed. When working with schedules that have both actual and planned dates, you can simulate these early appearance activities and have them shown in a different color to easily identify this status.

Late Appearance   This column defines how activities that start after a planned time are displayed. Using this setting is useful when working with both actual and planned dates.

Simulation Start Appearance   This column defines how the objects in the model are displayed at the start of the 4D simulation. When working with model elements that are permanent, you might want them to be displayed consistently throughout the simulation so it's clear that they're not part of any new construction. When working with items that are to be demolished, you also want to show these items as they appear in the model for the start of the simulation; however, when the demolition task begins, you may want to show that activity in another color and finally hide the element when the task is fully completed.

For our 4D simulation, you want to show the site model elements as permanent features of this project. Since you're not showing any demolition or temporary tasks, you could modify an existing task. However, if you decide to add in some site logistics or equipment at a later time, you'll need those tasks. For this exercise, we'll create a new task specifically for existing items. Using the same model, follow these steps:

1. In the Configure tab, click the Add button [Add]. A new task named New Task Type is added to the Name column.

2. Highlight the name and change it to **Existing** or something similar.

3. To change the appearance definition for a task type, double-click the Appearance field and select the definition from the drop-down (Figure 7.48).

FIGURE 7.48
Start Appearance drop-down menu

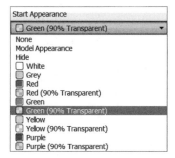

4. In the Appearance configuration columns, change All to None, except the Simulation Start Appearance, which will be changed to Model Appearance (Figure 7.49).

FIGURE 7.49
Configure tab appearance settings

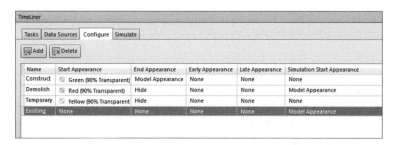

5. Continue to add additional task types as necessary to define all of the different activities you want to distinguish in your 4D simulation.

In this exercise, you created a new task type that is used to display existing model elements. Later in the chapter, when you get to simulate the entire construction process, these custom tasks will be useful in identifying portions of the model.

CREATING APPEARANCE DEFINITIONS

To create different definitions for the Appearance drop-downs, click the Appearance Definitions button on the right side of the Configure window. A new window with a listing of the current color definitions and transparencies is displayed (Figure 7.50). Let's create a custom definition for a new task using these steps.

FIGURE 7.50
Appearance
Definitions dialog
box

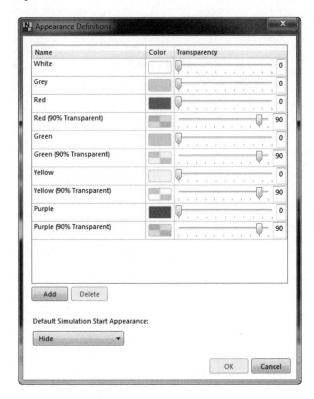

1. Click the Appearance Definition button to open the dialog box.

2. Click the Add button; a new definition named New Appearance is added to the Name column.

3. Highlight the name and change it to **Blue**.

4. In the Color column, double-click the color fill box and change it to a shade of blue. Remember, if your model has a large percentage of specific colors, you might want to define your appearances with a unique color scheme so it's easy to distinguish the different task types during playback.

5. To change the transparency, either drag the slider to the designated value or enter a number between 0 and 100. The color fill box will update to display the current value.

6. Click OK.

You can also edit existing color definitions by modifying their values in the Appearance Definitions dialog box. To define a standard Simulation Start Appearance, select the appropriate value from the Default Simulation Start Appearance drop-down (Figure 7.51).

FIGURE 7.51
Default Simulation
Appearance menu

Once you've defined the new appearance definition, you can create or modify existing task types by accessing the new definition from the Appearance drop-down list.

Using the Simulate Tab

After you've added schedule activities, defined tasks, and configured their appearance, the Simulate tab provides all the tools you need to finally execute your 4D simulation and create the animation that shows the sequence of construction activities. Besides the play and rewind buttons, the Simulate tab also incorporates additional settings that further define the display of the 4D simulation. This section will explore these features and further expand on the concept of 4D.

For the exercises in this section, you'll be using the file c07_Meadowgate_Simulation.nwd. When the Simulate tab is selected, the animation will queue up for the first date defined in our 4D simulation. In this mode, any object that is scheduled at a later date is currently hidden from view. Switching back to Tasks view or toggling off TimeLiner will restore the hidden items. The Simulate tab shares features similar to those on the Tasks tab and also consists of three distinct areas. The topmost area contains the basic playback controls and calendar view (Figure 7.52). In addition, there is a slider that can be used to quickly skip to a particular portion of the simulation.

FIGURE 7.52
Simulate tab play-
back buttons

The lower areas replicate the functionality of the Tasks area and Gantt chart in the Tasks tab; however, the fields are read-only and can't be overwritten. Furthermore, the columns are arranged slightly differently than the default view in the Tasks tab. To modify the layout, right-click in the column headers and select the Choose Columns menu. To change the timescale, zoom in to the Gantt chart area, and double-click either line of the timescale to zoom in. Hold down the Shift key while double-clicking the timescale to zoom out. During simulation, only the currently active tasks will display in the Tasks and Gantt chart areas.

PLAY, FAST-FORWARD, AND REWIND

The eight playback buttons are quite typical and allow for a variety of playback routines. Table 7.9 provides some additional information on their functionality.

TABLE 7.9:   Simulate Playback Options

BUTTON	NAME	DESCRIPTION
	Rewind	This button is used to rewind the simulation to the beginning of the simulation. This button remains grayed out until the simulation has advanced forward.
	Step Back	This button allows you to step backward one step at a time. For you to use this feature, the simulation must be paused. Step sizes are defined in the settings area.
	Reverse Play	This button plays the simulation in regular speed, albeit reversed.
	Pause	This button pauses the simulation at the current spot location. You must use this button in conjunction with the Step Back and Step Forward buttons.
	Stop	This button stops the simulation and automatically rewinds back to the beginning. To stop mid-simulation and resume, use the Pause button.
	Play	This button commences the simulation. If the simulation is paused, select the Play button to resume.
	Step Forward	This button allows you to step forward one step at a time.
	Forward	Use this button to fast-forward to the end of the simulation.

Let's work through a few exercises using the playback buttons and the other features of the Simulate tab using the following steps:

1. With the Simulate tab open, click the Play button. Navisworks will start the 4D simulation and add in additional model elements as the planned start dates advance.

2. Before the simulation reaches the end, click the Pause button to temporarily halt the simulation.

3. Select the Step Forward button to increment the simulation by one day at a time. You can also move backward using the Step Back button.

4. While still paused, use the slider on the top of the Simulate tab to advance or decrement the simulation.

5. Try using the Reverse Play button to simulate the project backward.

6. Click the Rewind button to return to the beginning. If the simulation is partway complete, the Stop button will also return you to the beginning.

In this example, you simulated a simple 4D model with an imported project schedule and a few task types. Try this exercise again, but this time, use the navigation tools to interact with the model while it's simulating. One of the nice features of Navisworks is the ability to move around the model while the 4D sequence is under way. Using the avatar figures, you can virtually walk the site like a superintendent does and identify potential issues that need to be addressed.

CREATING AN UNCLUTTERED VIEWING SPACE FOR SIMULATIONS

When simulating the project, it's useful to hide unused windows in the model to free up viewing space. Also, if you happen to have a dual-monitor setup, you can view the model view in the primary display and have all toolbars and windows located in the secondary.

1. Verify which monitor is the primary. Depending on your operating system, this information is usually located in the Control Panel under Display.

2. Make sure Navisworks is positioned in the secondary display area.

3. Hit F11 on your keyboard or click the Full Screen button in the Scene View panel of the View tab. This will place the model view in your primary view and leave the associated toolbars and dockable windows intact in your secondary display.

4. To return to a single display view, press F11 again or click the Full Screen button.

Let's look at another approach to using TimeLiner. Suppose you're the project coordinator who has been charged with helping assist with the pay application process for this project. The owner is having some concerns with the current pay schedule and is not very comfortable reading a Gantt chart. You can play back the simulation and pause along the way to highlight specific milestones. To further help, you decide to take snapshots along the way to submit with the pay apps that show the planned progress in addition to actual site photos. To accomplish this, you need to capture an in-progress image from your Navisworks model every month. Let's explore this option using these steps.

1. Instead of using the slider to locate the different dates, open the calendar view by selecting the right side of the calendar drop-down (Figure 7.53).

FIGURE 7.53
Expanded Calendar menu

2. Specify the date you want to take the progress snapshot by selecting the date in the calendar. The model will update to reflect that date along with any construction activity.

3. Keeping TimeLiner open, select the Output tab in the ribbon and choose the Image button from the Visuals panel.

4. In the Image Export dialog box, specify the format, image size, and any other options.

5. Specify a filename and location to save the image.

6. Repeat this process for future pay application periods. At the end of the simulation, you will have a series of images that reflect the planned work.

Depending on the complexity of your model, it may be useful to define several views of the model during the simulation. Using the Split View feature, you can create additional unique views of the model that will be useful by allowing you to view the simulation from different vantage points simultaneously. Let's try this out using these steps:

1. Select the View tab in the ribbon.

2. In the Scene View panel, click the Split View button and choose either Split Horizontal or Split Vertical from the drop-down list.

3. You should have two identical windows. When you select anywhere inside the view, that particular window becomes active. Using the navigation tools, including section tools, manipulate the view to define two different views. Practice adding additional windows to match Figure 7.54.

FIGURE 7.54
Split windows showing multiple TimeLiner views

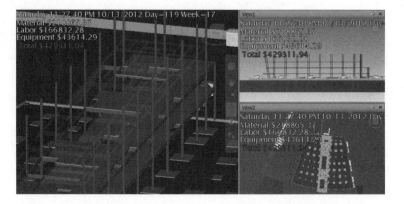

4. Start the 4D simulation and notice how the model is updated in both windows simultaneously.

5. You can drag the additional windows outside the Navisworks application to other displays or use the F11 key to spread the widows across multiple displays.

6. To remove the additional views, either click the X in the upper-right corner or minimize them for use later. Note that split-screen views do not export to video.

SIMULATION SETTINGS

In addition to using the playback buttons to step through the model, there are several settings that you can configure to modify the simulation. To access these configurations, click the Settings button in the Simulate tab. A new dialog box will open (Figure 7.55). The Simulation Settings dialog box contains six distinct areas that can be configured to add additional value to your 4D simulation.

FIGURE 7.55

Simulation Settings
dialog box

The topmost area, Start/End Dates, allows you to override the current start and end dates of the simulation. These options are useful when you're importing schedules that have additional tasks that aren't represented by any geometry in the model. Items such as design, procurement, permitting, or any other activities prior to the Notice To Proceed (NTP) typically have no model elements that can be represented by these tasks. During playback, items that have time allocated without any accompanying model elements will result in extended pauses before any construction tasks are represented. The Override Start/End Dates option lets you manually configure which dates Navisworks should simulate. Doing so allows you to skip over this dead time and have the simulation start when the construction activities are scheduled. These values are also used when exporting animations. Let's look at the steps to configure this option:

1. Check the Override Start/End Dates box.

2. Enter the appropriate values for the start and end dates. Navisworks will adjust the simulation start date to reference the new dates.

3. Uncheck the Override Start/End Dates box to disable this option.

The second area in the Simulation Settings dialog box is used to configure the interval size of the simulation (Figure 7.56). Depending on the type of simulation, you may want to represent the intervals as a percentage or as absolute dates. As you'll recall, these values are referenced when using the Step Back and Step Forward simulation buttons. Let's examine these settings in greater detail using the following steps:

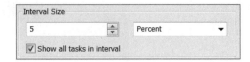

1. Use the up and down arrows on the number field to the left for entering the Interval step size. By default, Navisworks configures this value as 5 percent.

2. In the drop-down box (Figure 7.57), specify the Interval unit for your simulation. Most scheduling applications use Days as the unit of measurement.

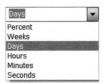

3. Select the Show All Tasks In Interval check box to highlight all tasks that are being represented by that specific interval in the simulation. For example, if the Interval Size is set to one week, all tasks being worked on during that week will be set to their Start Appearance in the Scene view, including those that begin and end within the bounds of the interval. Since the Weeks interval is based on calendar days and not business days, it's a best practice to work with the Days interval. However, in situations with tight schedules such as road closures or overnight work, you may find it prudent to use the Hours interval.

The Playback Duration (Seconds) option allows you to specify the time in seconds to complete the simulation from start to finish. This option is useful if the simulation is running too fast to easily recognize the activities or you wish to export the simulation to a specific timeframe. Values must be whole numbers only. By default, this value is set to 20 seconds.

The middle of the Simulation Settings dialog box contains the Overlay Text setting (Figure 7.58). With this setting, you can overlay the date information in the model view during the simulation. You'll want to do so if you plan to export the movie as an animation and wish to capture the time/date.

The drop-down menu on the right lets you configure where the text is placed in the model view: None, Top, or Bottom. The Edit button allows you to specify which data is included in the text overlay. By default, Day, Time, Date, Total Days, and Total Weeks are displayed. When you click the Edit button, the Overlay Text dialog box opens, where you can change the font, size, and color. You can also add additional fields to the text overlay such as currently active tasks or even custom notes (Figure 7.59). Since the task types are color-coded to reflect different activities, it's sometimes useful to create a legend that explains the color code.

FIGURE 7.59

Overlay Text dialog box

Let's create a custom legend for our 4D model using the three task types currently defined in our simulation:

1. In the Overlay Text dialog box, place the cursor at the beginning of the line and press Ctrl+Enter, or click the Extras button and select New Line.

2. Place your mouse cursor in the new line and type ****Construct****.

3. Create two additional blank lines by pressing Ctrl+Enter twice.

4. In the subsequent lines, enter ****Demolish**** and ****Temporary****.

5. To make this legend accurate, you need to color-code the legend names to reflect the task type colors. Select the first line and place your cursor at the beginning of that line.

6. Select Green from the Colors drop-down list.

7. Repeat this procedure for the Demolish name, but use Red for the color (Figure 7.60).

FIGURE 7.60

Assigning colors to task types

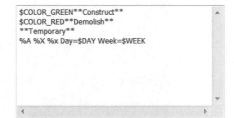

8. For the Temporary name, you need to use Yellow, but this color is not predefined in the drop-down list. This means you need to create a custom color using the RGB values.

9. Place the cursor at the beginning of the Temporary name and select RGB Color from the Colors drop-down list. Navisworks will place $RGB127,127,127$RGB in front of the legend name.

10. You'll need to modify the values between 0 and 255 in this field to create the yellow color. Knowing that yellow is composed of red and green, let's modify the RGB values to reflect **$RGB255,255,0$RGB**.

11. Let's add one last line to represent the currently active tasks in the text overlay. Add a new line and select Currently Active Tasks from the Extras drop-down list (Figure 7.61).

FIGURE 7.61
Overlay Text custom color settings

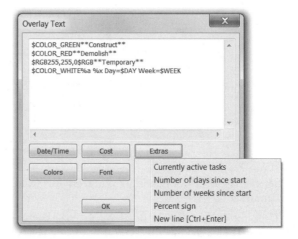

12. Click OK to close out of the dialog boxes. You should have a color-coded legend in the model view with three task types listed (Figure 7.62). If necessary, go back and modify the font and size. Remember, if you're saving your TimeLiner sequence as a video, you need to make sure the font sizes are legible for the audience to view.

FIGURE 7.62
TimeLiner window with custom text

When simulating the model, you can interact within the model and navigate around in real time. You can also link in a viewpoint and camera animations to create a simple flythrough while the model is being built up. Listed here are the steps to define this option:

1. In the Animation drop-down list, select Saved Viewpoints Animation (Figure 7.63).

FIGURE 7.63
Select Saved Viewpoints Animation from the Animation drop-down list.

2. In the model, open the Saved Viewpoints window and select the animation labeled Fly Around.

3. Back in the Simulate tab of TimeLiner, start the sequence.

   Not only will you see the construction activities, but also the camera will pan around the outside of the building during the simulation.

The View setting is used to configure the display of differences between actual versus planned dates (Figure 7.64). Navisworks can handle both of these sets of dates to create comparisons and easily identify early and late schedule activities.

FIGURE 7.64
TimeLiner View options

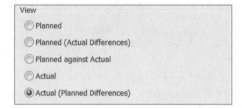

IMPORTING COSTS INTO TIMELINER

In the 2013 version of Navisworks, you can simulate cost data in your TimeLiner sequence. The costs can be broken down into the following categories:

◆ Materials

◆ Labor

◆ Equipment

◆ Subcontractor or Specialty trades

◆ Total cost

By having these categories loaded into your schedules, you can simulate how the project costs are accrued over the entire project duration, as well as take a snapshot of expected costs at any point in the project schedule. The cost information can then be displayed within your 4D simulation, creating a fifth dimension of data to simulate helping you better understand the impact certain tasks will have on project budgets at any given time.

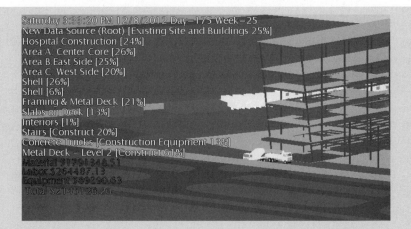

Costs can be added to your TimeLiner sequence by importing the data from a cost-loaded scheduling solution such as Primavera, or you can manually enter them in the appropriate cost column in TimeLiner. The Total Cost is the sum of the other costs assigned to a particular task and cannot be modified.

When you run a simulation, the cost data is displayed in the overlay text window; however, no cost data is displayed until that particular task is complete.

Also, it's important to note that costs are not based on any specific currency. Decimal places are rounded to two places for display purposes, but the underlying value remains as entered or imported, and it is the underlying value that is used during cost calculations.

When simulating your 4D model, Navisworks provides five options that let you control the visibility of the model using variations between the actual and planned dates. These options reference the task type appearance settings that are defined in the Configure tab. For example, items under construction are shown in a semitransparent green color; however, you can also configure a different color for Early Appearance or Late Appearance items (Figure 7.65).

FIGURE 7.65
Configure tab with Early and Late color settings

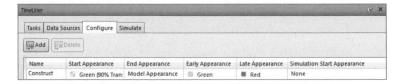

Planned   This setting is used to simulate the project with the planned start and planned end dates only. Early and Late Appearance colors are ignored in this simulation.

Planned (Actual Differences)   This setting is used to simulate the planned dates against the actual dates by highlighting the objects that are attached to a task within the planned start and planned end dates. For activities where the actual dates fall outside of the planned dates, either the Early Appearance or Late Appearance color definition will be applied to the portion of the activity that misaligns with the planned date.

Planned Against Actual   This setting is used to simulate the planned dates against the actual dates by highlighting the objects that are attached to a task that is represented by the planned and actual start and planned and actual end dates. For activities where the actual dates align with the planned dates, the Start Appearance task type will be displayed (i.e., semitransparent green). For activities where there is a variance between the actual and planned dates, either the Early Appearance or Late Appearance color definition will be applied to the portion of the activity that misaligns date overlap.

Actual   This setting is used to simulate the project with actual start and actual end dates only.

Actual (Planned Differences)   This setting is used to simulate the actual dates against the planned dates by highlighting the objects that are attached to a task within the actual start and actual end dates. For activities where the planned dates fall outside of the actual dates, either the Early Appearance or Late Appearance color definition will be applied to the portion of the activity that misaligns with the actual date.

After configuring the View settings, you'll be able to easily identify objects in the 4D simulation that are early or late by the color scheme identified in the task type configurations. Follow these steps:

1. Open the file c07_Meadowgate_Simulation.nwd.

2. In the Simulate tab, click the Settings button and choose Planned Against Actual in the View settings.

3. Run the TimeLiner simulation and note where the solid green and red instances are displayed.

4. Pause the animation and use either the Step Forward/Backward buttons or the time slider to locate the periods where the Early or Late Appearance definitions are displayed.

    The status icon in the Tasks area also provides this information, but since it is sometimes displayed rather abruptly during the simulation, having the model color-coded for any dates that fall outside the planned dates makes those dates easy to spot.

5. Run through additional simulations using the various View settings.

TRACKING CONSTRUCTION PROGRESS WITH FILTERS AND APPEARANCE SETTINGS

In construction project controls, the end result is to monitor and improve the predictability of:

◆ Cost

◆ Schedule

◆ Change management

In TimeLiner, you can track actual versus planned dates to understand where the schedule is slipping. In addition, with the integrated cost features, you can display the accrued cost to track project expenditures.

When projects fall behind schedule, there are usually several events that cause the schedule to slip and not just one event. In Navisworks, you can color-code the model to highlight late-finish activities. Using the Planned versus Actual simulations, this provides a quick and easy way to visualize where the delays are occurring and on what tasks. However, the color changes are quick and sometimes occluded by other objects in the scene.

An easier way is to filter the task list for all the late items; then use the visibility settings such as Hide Unselected to isolate these tasks. Recall that the Filter by Status feature allows you to screen out early and on-time events, leaving behind the late-finish tasks.

TIMELINER OPTIONS

Unlike the Simulation settings, which are file specific, the TimeLiner options configure the application and are reflected in all project files. These settings are useful if you need to override the date format, specify start and end times, and auto-select selections. Open the Options Editor by choosing Options ➢ Tools ➢ TimeLiner (Figure 7.66) to access the following options:

FIGURE 7.66
Open the TimeLiner
Options Editor.

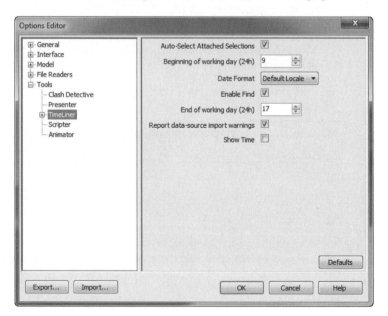

Auto-Select Attached Selections This option is useful if you need to quickly select all attached items in a particular task. While this functionality is already provided by clicking the link in the Attached column, enabling this feature highlights the model elements when you select anywhere in the task.

Beginning Of Working Day (24h) When working with dates that contain time units of measurement (i.e., hours, minutes), you can specify the default value for the beginning of the day. This setting is configured for 24-hour format.

Date Format This drop-down menu allows you to specify the format for the Date columns in TimeLiner.

Enable Find Enabling the Find command allows you to use the Find tools in the context menu in TimeLiner. The commands are useful when you're searching for unattached or uncontained objects and for verifying which items are orphaned from the schedule.

End Of Working Day (24h) Similar to Beginning Of Working Day, this option specifies the default working day end time.

Report Data-Source Import Warnings When selected, a warning message will display on issues pertaining to importing data in the Data Sources tab in TimeLiner.

Show Time This option enables the time display in the date columns.

Embedding Animations in 4D Simulations

In addition to simulating the construction sequence, it's sometimes useful to have object and camera animations add realism to the simulation to help define site movements and equipment paths. Object and camera animations provide more control and are created in the Animator module as keyframe-type animations. These types of animations are unique in that they can be assigned to a specific schedule task and triggered when the task is executed. Besides animating the camera view throughout the scene, you can animate individual objects to represent equipment arrangements, dynamic material laydown areas, worker traffic, and other site-related activities. Furthermore, besides animating object movements, you can animate scale changes, color, and transparency shifts to fully create realistic simulations of the construction process. This section will explain the procedure for embedding camera and object animations in TimeLiner. See Chapter 10 to learn more about creating keyframe animations.

In the Tasks tab in TimeLiner, you can assign animations to individual tasks by specifying the animation from the drop-down in the Animation column (Figure 7.67).

FIGURE 7.67
Animation drop-down in the Tasks window

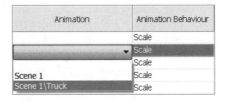

Embedding animations in TimeLiner requires a little more planning since the length of the animation must be taken into account when you're mapping to a specific task. For example, let's assume that you have a mobile crane that is lifting prefabricated wall assemblies on site. A schedule task in your TimeLiner sequence is created to represent the 7 days of time required for this activity. However, when you run the simulation, that particular task may only last for a few seconds in actual time. If you create an animation that is only 4–5 seconds long, it will appear to match up to the speed of the TimeLiner simulation, but that 5-second animation will technically last only 0.0000008 percent of the scheduled crane task activity. When animations are linked to the 4D model, the interval units in the animation must match the intervals in the TimeLiner simulation. If there are 7 days of activity for the crane activity, the animation must be created to represent 7 days of actual time. If you were to play the animation alone, it would take a whole week to complete the playback. However, when assigned to a task in TimeLiner, the animation is scaled to match the playback speed of the TimeLiner sequence. Navisworks provides three options that let you control the length of the animation when you're linking to a specific task. These options can be accessed via the Animation Behavior column in the Tasks window:

Scale   The length of the animation is matched to the duration of the task assuming the intervals are the same. This is the default setting for all embedded animations.

Match Start   This setting is used to start the animation when the schedule task starts. However, if the schedule has been adjusted to a shorter duration, the animation will continue to play until complete or the TimeLiner sequence finishes. For example, say the crane duration was shifted from 7 days to 6 days but the animation is queued up for all 7 days. When the crane task ends in TimeLiner, the crane animation will continue until all 7 days are animated.

Match End   This setting is similar to the Match Start animation option, except that it ensures that the animation will conclude at the same time the scheduled task completes. For example, suppose our 7-day crane activity has been pushed out to 9 days. If Match End is selected for the animation behavior, the crane animation of 7 days in length will start on day 3 and conclude at day 9 at the same time the schedule activity finishes.

In addition to using embedded animations, you can add life to the animations by including a script to sequence multiple animations or trigger different events. In the Tasks window, you can link a script to a specific task by selecting from the drop-down menu in the Scripts column. Scripting will be covered in detail in Chapter 11, "Giving Objects Life and Action with Scripter," along with additional information and exercises to illustrate this concept.

When using animations, consider what your goal is in animating the object. If you're creating a presentation for a potential owner and want to show the construction sequence, including equipment paths, deliveries, and so forth, then embedding animations is a quick way to add realism to your 4D simulation. For other uses, such as showing the swing of the tower crane, you'll find that using a static object is much more effective. In Figure 7.68, notice the tower crane was modeled with the extents of the horizontal jib and radii of the various lifting capacities as color-coded rings. Keeping a library of equipment models such as this tower crane handy for any project is a much quicker way to add information to the coordination and site logistics planning. While animations are extremely useful, sometimes the old adage that *less is more* holds true for object animations.

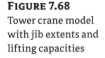

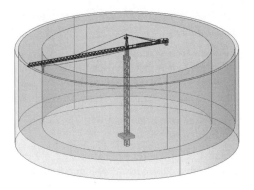

EXPORTING TIMELINER SIMULATIONS

In addition to the best practice of keeping your model files in the NWF format, saving a copy of your project file as an NWD allows you to share the TimeLiner sequence for users who may only have access to the Freedom viewer. To share your 4D simulation as a video (AVI only), you can easily export the model as either a shaded (viewport) or a fully rendered animation. Chapter 9, "Creating Visualizations," will cover using the materials and lighting to create more realistic renderings. When exporting to an AVI file, you can configure the following options:

Size   This setting is used to specify the output resolution of the AVI file. Generally, it is unnecessary to create high-resolution animations, and in most cases, standard screen resolutions, such as 640 × 480 or 800 × 600, are more than adequate.

Anti-Aliasing   This setting is used to smooth the edges in a model. Larger anti-aliasing values result in a smoother image but take longer to export because each frame must be generated that number of times. Therefore, if you set anti-aliasing to a value of 8x, the exporting process will take eight times as long. In most cases, an anti-aliasing value of 4x is sufficient. Note that this option is only available when exporting to a standard AVI file because anti-aliasing is an implicit part of generating rendered images.

FPS   This setting is used to specify the number of frames that will be shown per second of animation. A larger value results in a smoother animation but requires that more images be generated. For a professional video to be used on DVD/TV, you may require frame rates of 25 (PAL/SECAM) or 30 (NTSC). However, in most cases, a value of 15 is the bare minimum, with 25 being ideal for presentations.

Compression   One of the most complex choices when creating an animation is how you want to compress the video. Although this factor does not have a major effect on the time taken to create the output, it can have a huge effect on the picture quality and file size.

By default, exported AVI files are not compressed. To generate smaller AVI files, you need to have codec software, which compresses data, installed on your computer. The following is a list of the compression methods supported by Navisworks, along with an estimate of the file sizes likely to be generated with each method:

No Compression   This is the default output method. Each frame of the animation is stored as a full image. Since each frame is on average over 1 MB in size, even short animations will take up a large amount of disk space.

File size estimate: 1 GB with the following settings: 640 × 480, 24 bit, 15 fps, and 1 minute long

Lossless Compression The final AVI file retains the quality of the original output but the file size is much smaller. However, the final file will still be very large and difficult to distribute. Lossless compression is useful as an intermediate step to create an AVI file that can later be compressed using lossy compression.

File size estimate: 500 MB with the following settings: 640 × 480, 24 bit, 15 fps, and 1 minute long

Lossy Compression For demonstrations and distribution, a lossy compression method is your best choice because it generally offers small file sizes. The image quality will be reduced depending on the form of compression you use and the amount of movement in the animation. If you install an AVI codec on your computer such as DivX or Windows Media Encoder, you can select it in the Compression dialog box when generating an animation. You could also generate an AVI using no/lossless compression and then use video encoding software.

File size estimate: 20 MB with the following settings: 640 × 480, 24 bit, 15 fps, and 1 minute long

Here are the steps for exporting a TimeLiner simulation:

1. Open the Simulate tab in TimeLiner and select the Export Animation button [icon] on the far-right side of the screen.

2. In the Animation Export dialog box, select TimeLiner Simulation from the Source drop-down list (Figure 7.69).

FIGURE 7.69
Selecting TimeLiner
Simulation
from the Source
drop-down

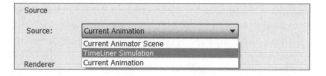

3. In the Renderer area, choose from the following options:

Presenter This setting allows you to render the animation with applied materials and lights. When exporting with this option, you'll find that rendering times are considerably longer. Also, text overlay is not supported in this mode.

Viewport This setting allows you to export the model with the basic shaded display. The quality of standard AVI video resembles the image quality displayed in the main Navisworks navigation window. All text overlays are supported in the export.

Autodesk This setting allows you to render the animation with Autodesk materials. Autodesk rendering is useful if your models contain Consistent Materials (e.g., exported to FBX® from Revit). As with the Presenter setting, rendering times take longer to process.

4. Specify the output. For videos, you want to select AVI from the list; otherwise, Navisworks will generate hundreds if not thousands of individual images.

5. In the Options box, specify the appropriate video compressor and compressor quality settings (Figure 7.70). Note that the codecs listed are not part of the Navisworks install,

but rather separate installs from specific vendors. When installing codes, make sure you correctly specify either 32 or 64 bit.

FIGURE 7.70
Animation Video Compression drop-down menu

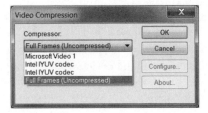

6. In the Size area, specify the export size for the animation. You can also use the predefined options in the Type drop-down.

7. Specify the FPS setting. A higher FPS will yield a smoother animation but will take longer to render.

8. Click OK and specify the filename and the location where you want to save the video.

Real World Scenario

COMPARING CONSTRUCTION METHODS IN TIMELINER

In the construction industry, there's a question that has been unanswered for many years: Is concrete or steel the better building material? Both products have numerous benefits, but in certain situations, one may be a better fit. This study isn't meant to sway decisions on which product to use but to show how TimeLiner can be another tool to help you determine which product is best suited to the job. Arguably, steel is more expensive than concrete; however, its price volatility is even more dramatic, as shown in this chart from the Bureau of Labor Statistics.

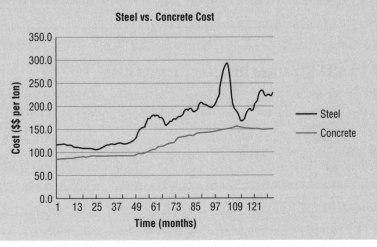

The argument of using steel versus concrete boils down to safety, the ability to obtain material, construction scheduling, design possibilities, and cost. While TimeLiner can't address all of these points, it can provide an intuitive way to display the differences in scheduling and a look at safety in relation to the various construction methods. The results of the simulation can then help you understand the cost impact.

Since concrete and steel 3D models have numerous differences in design and material applications, you shouldn't use the same model for both simulations. Instead, consider having two different models appended into Navisworks. To simulate the different models, create two separate schedules, one for concrete and one for steel, and import them into TimeLiner. Make sure they both start on the same date; otherwise, the simulation won't be a true comparison. With the new Navisworks 2013 cost features, you can also simulate how costs are accrued over the project duration for each material.

Once all tasks have been mapped, split the screen to show both models side by side. Start the simulation to display the differences between the two construction methods, as shown here. Adding in site logistics equipment such as a pumper for the concrete model and a tower crane for the steel model will allow you to fully grasp the scope of the project.

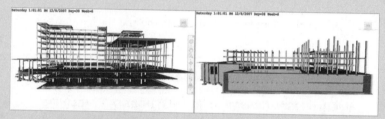

The example TimeLiner simulation frame shows steel construction on the left and concrete on the right. This example shows that while steel is more expensive than concrete, it can be prefabricated into common sizes and shapes and ultimately erected more quickly, thus yielding a finished product much sooner. Concrete, on the other hand, takes longer because you need to install formwork and rebar prior to each pour, but its cheaper cost and durability make it a contender for some projects. TimeLiner can help you identify where the strengths of each of these materials can best be utilized in the project.

4D Simulation Best Practices

A question we often encounter is "Why do I need 4D?" or "What do I do now that I have a 4D model?" In addition to a nice animation of the construction activities, 4D has a multitude of practical applications. This section will explore some of these workflows as well as lay out the best practices for implementing 4D into your project workflows. To paraphrase the definition of 4D given earlier in this chapter, a 4D model represents the various activities of a construction project constrained to a project schedule (time). This allows you to visualize the sequence of activities in an interactive environment where you can easily view the model from various angles and sections.

When addressing why 4D is useful, let's examine a typical construction project. Creating requests for information (RFIs) is a time-consuming process in which additional information is needed typically once the project has started. This can be due to ambiguity or contradiction in the design drawings or differing site conditions that need to be further evaluated. The costs associated with RFIs vary, but as a result of the administrative costs to prepare and document, along with any potential downtime while waiting on an answer, costs of several hundreds of dollars are not uncommon. If the answer to the RFI involves changing the design or reconfiguring work already in place, then the cost rises even more. Multiply the number of RFIs on a typical project by this cost and you'll get an idea of the amount of waste.

A 4D model provides visual clarity to the modeling process by creating a whole project visualization that is easy to understand by all stakeholders. For architects and engineers, a 4D model allows them to understand the interaction of the construction teams and evaluate the overall process. By providing a common "language" between the owner, designer, and contractor, a 4D model acts as a collaboration bridge that ensures all parties understand the full scope of the project. These efforts result in reduced errors and omissions in the design and eliminate scheduling conflicts that lead to delays and cost overruns. For the construction team, a 4D model decreases the efforts associated with conceptualizing a 2D plan into three dimensions by displaying the individual building components correct spatially in addition to addressing the typical site logistics challenges such as material laydown areas, crane siting, and site access.

Showing Context in the Model

Using a 4D model allows you to incorporate contextual elements that show how the project impacts safety, security, site access, neighborhood traffic, and other variables.

When developing your 4D model, consider what type of environment the project is being constructed in. A dense urban environment poses many more challenges beyond the site fence than a typical greenfield rural setting. Your 4D simulation should take into account such items as delivery access and material laydown areas in addition to emergency access and egress (Figure 7.71). Having these items as part of your model ensures that proper planning efforts are conducted prior to the start of construction. Any conflicts detected in the coordination phase can easily be redesigned or alternatives proposed without the cost associated with developing a workaround once construction has begun.

FIGURE 7.71
4D model showing site logistics and equipment

Too often, safety is an afterthought to the coordination efforts of the construction process. Typical site logistics plans are 2D paper-based drawings that are difficult to visualize and hard to update, and they provide limited communication. Using a 4D model to help with safety planning gives you unlimited site views of the entire project. If the schedule changes, you can easily identify potential risks such as excavations, fall/drop-off areas, crane reach and lifting radii, temporary structures, and exposed rebar by taking corrective action to ensure that all protections are in place (Figure 7.72).

FIGURE 7.72
Safety modeling in the 4D simulation

Recall that creating task types for the various trades allows you to easily create unique appearances of these activities in your simulation. If, for example, the concrete pours were delayed, you could identify the exposed rebar by quickly scanning the model for a specific colored task. Additional protections such as installing rebar caps or barricading the areas would allow work to continue without the risk of impalement or other injuries (Figure 7.73).

FIGURE 7.73
Color-coded rebar showing schedule status

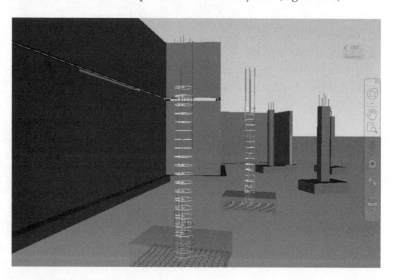

Creating Reusable Equipment Libraries

When simulating the construction process, it's helpful to have representations of the equipment that will be used on site for the various activities. Considering the flexibility of Navisworks when you append numerous file formats, it's a straightforward way to include the machinery in your site logistics plan from a variety of sources such as Trimble SketchUp, Autodesk® 3ds Max®, and other applications (Figure 7.74). Since these objects are temporary and strictly used to represent the space the equipment will occupy during construction, they do not need to have considerable object property data.

FIGURE 7.74
Typical site logistics components

In the past, site logistics planning was sometimes limited to tracing scale templates on an old site plan. While this gave an initial view of where equipment needed to be placed, the locations were static and didn't update with the construction progress. Instead of tracing the outlines of this equipment on a 2D sheet, you can append these objects into your Navisworks model. More important, you can save these objects and have a virtual library of equipment on hand for future projects. When planning and coordinating upcoming work, you'll be able to simply drop the objects in your scene and evaluate which equipment is the best choice for the work (Figure 7.75).

FIGURE 7.75
Reusable construction library

Tying these objects to your 4D simulation allows you to make smart choices on mobilizing and decommissioning. If road closures or other disruptions are required to bring large items on site, you can simulate when these disruptions would need to take place and work with the local jurisdiction early in the process to get approval. For owners, this is especially important since projects may be a multiphased construction with partial occupation occurring during the project. Being aware of equipment placement, risk zones, and transitions allows you to create safety plans that avoid the active areas of the site.

Simulating Trades and Equipment Paths

When you're working with numerous trades on site, safety and productivity issues may arise when too many workers are assigned to a small area. Even if early coordination efforts planned to have a buffer between the workers' areas, occasional schedule changes can modify your initial plans and have various disciplines working in tight spaces. To avoid trade-stacking issues and prevent safety problems, you can simulate the various trades by representing the footprint of their active work area and assigning a specific task so the area is easy to identify when running your 4D simulation. Depending on how the model is constructed, you may be able to use a common element in the existing model to reference, such as the floor for a specific area. After the initial floor is constructed, it can be additionally referenced as the work area for the framing crew, then electricians, HVAC, painters, and so forth. The other option is to model a generic volume or mass that represents the footprint of that particular trade and append it to the main model (Figure 7.76).

FIGURE 7.76
You can assign colors to volumes to identify work areas.

Once referenced in your 4D simulation, any schedule slippage will be easy to detect because the different color codes of your task type will identify when the new trades are supposed to begin their work in that area. You can also use the Clash Detective feature in Navisworks to quickly pinpoint when these various work packages will overlap. Chapter 8, "Clash Detection," will cover this functionality in greater detail.

To enable the simulation of the different trades, you need to manually add the appropriate schedule tasks or import the data from an external application. As a best practice when working with numerous trades and organizations, keep the different data sources intact. In other words, don't try to merge all the data into one schedule. Navisworks will read a variety of schedule formats, and keeping them separate makes it easy to update; in addition, you maintain the legal separation that some jurisdictions require. You can append in multiple schedules for the different tasks; for example:

- Master Project Schedule (Primavera P6)
- 3-Week Look-Ahead (Excel/CSV)
- Site Logistics Schedule (Microsoft Project)

Using Multiple Task Types for Schedule Analysis

Simulating the 4D model provides a task-by-task representation of the schedule. By using a common color code and multiple task types, you'll find it easy to identify not only the different trades and disciplines on the site but also (if you're working with actual versus planned dates) any variations that may result in late appearances. This information is crucial; you can quickly verify if the delayed items are on the critical path and make recommendations and changes to correct the schedule slippage.

Creating Focused 4D Simulations

Most of the examples we've used have referenced the model from a "macro" perspective, where you examine the project at or beyond the extents of the construction site. Another area where Navisworks is useful is when you are looking at smaller portions of the project in greater detail. This concept allows you to focus on a specific trade or element of the building, such as a curtain wall, by simulating all the steps necessary to construct and install. For example, with our 4D timeline, you can capture when the materials are delivered to the site, when the scaffolding is installed, and finally, when the components are installed. By keeping the work area small, you can manage these additional details much more successfully. This concept of working with "bite-sized" pieces from the model is a consistent best practice that is addressed when we define search and selection sets and sectioning and will be covered in depth in Chapter 8.

Automatically Mapping the Model to the Schedule

When working with BIM authoring tools, you can embed additional data in the model to create rules that map the project to the schedule. This practice allows you to increase efficiency in the 4D process by automating portions of the linkage.

For this example, we'll use the design application Autodesk Revit Architecture and create a project parameter named Construction ID (or something similar) and apply it to all elements that will be part of the 4D simulation. This parameter can be grouped in the Phasing area of the Properties palette (Figure 7.77). The goal is to create a parameter that can be populated in the early design and coordination efforts and drive the linking of model elements to the schedule. Take time to develop a naming convention that is consistent with your scheduling practices.

This is important because the nomenclature between the model and schedule must be the same for the linkage to work properly.

FIGURE 7.77
Construction ID
parameter in Revit

In your project schedule, create a user-defined field and populate the data using the same conventions. For example, in my Revit model, the Construction ID is A102 for the forming and pouring of the footings of this building. You want to make sure the task in the schedule for Form/Pour Concrete Footings also contains this value (Figure 7.78). In some scheduling programs such as Primavera P6, you can use the Global Change settings and user-defined columns to automate the creation of these codes. Another option is to use the more common Activity ID in scheduling applications and use that value as the Construction ID in Revit.

FIGURE 7.78
Schedule with a
Construction ID
column

Layout: Classic WBS Layout w/ 3 line timescale   Filter: All Activities

Activity ID	Activity Name	Construction ID	Original Duration	Remaining Duration	Schedule % Complete	Start
Foundation			66	13	63.31%	18-Apr-07 A
LH555	Foundation		64	13	82.81%	18-Apr-07 A
Excavation			20	0	100%	18-Apr-07 A
LH630	Begin Building Construction		0	0	100%	18-Apr-07 A
LH650	Excavation	E101	10	0	100%	02-May-07
Form Work			10	0	100%	09-May-07
LH660	Install Underground Water Lines	B114	5	0	100%	09-May-07
LH670	Install Storm water lines	B115	10	0	100%	09-May-07
Concrete			66	13	96.66%	18-Apr-07 A
LH640	Site Preparation		10	0	100%	18-Apr-07 A
LH680	Form/Pour Concrete Footings	A102	10	0	100%	23-May-07
LH681	Concrete Foundation Walls	A103	14	0	100%	06-Jun-07 A
LH690	Form and Pour Slab	A104	10	8	40%	26-Jun-07 A
LH700	Backfill and Compact Walls	A105	5	5	0%	12-Jul-07
LH701	Foundation Phase Complete		0	0	0%	

Load the Revit model into Navisworks. Link in the project schedule with the matching user-defined data; create a rule that links the user-defined field of your schedule with the Project Parameter name in Revit (Construction ID). Navisworks will identify all objects in the project scene and map them to the schedule task with the same name. In addition to creating a custom parameter in Revit to link the schedule, consider using other properties such as the Omnicodes and Phasing fields to automate the schedule linkage.

Besides mapping over the model objects to the task name, experiment with automating the linking of task types. You can create a naming convention for activity IDs or other custom fields where the first letter represents the different task types in your 4D model (such as C = construct, D = demolish, and so on). Using the Global Change options in Primavera, create a user-defined field that is automatically populated with this data. When the schedule is linked into Navisworks, you can specify this field from the Task Type drop-down. When working with intelligent models, use the embedded object properties to your advantage to speed up the coordination and linking process.

These best practices are meant to advance your use of Navisworks by challenging you to look for new opportunities and workflows outside the standard recommendations. As you develop these skills that lead to mastery of Navisworks, remember that the efficiency of this application resides in pulling in all the different workflows and functionalities mentioned in this book. Creating 4D models with TimeLiner is one of the concepts where it makes sense to reference topics covered in earlier chapters. Chapter 8 will introduce you to concept of clash detection and help you further develop your skills and competence.

The Bottom Line

Link your model to a project schedule.   Navisworks links to common scheduling applications as a means to add schedule data to TimeLiner.

> **Master It**   What formats don't require an installed scheduling application to view their data?

Create a 4D sequence.   Navisworks creates 4D models by linking in schedule data to generate models that address the time and spatial aspects of a construction site.

> **Master It**   What is the benefit of using a 4D model compared to traditional coordination efforts?

Automate schedule linking with rules.   Rules allow you to automate the time-consuming portion of connecting schedule tasks to specific objects in your Navisworks scene. When working with models that contain embedded object properties, you can further leverage this data to assist with the linking.

> **Master It**   How do you attach objects to schedule tasks by using the object properties?

Explore safety and site logistics planning.   Moving beyond static paper safety plans, a 4D model can identify potential safety issues and aid in the site logistics planning efforts.

> **Master It**   How can site logistics be better coordinated with a 4D model?

Chapter 8

Clash Detection

Clash detection demonstrates some of the most robust Autodesk® Navisworks® 2013 features. It allows you to explore your project further than you thought possible. With the Clash Detective feature, you can save time and money by finding errors and omissions in your project virtually. Clash Detective offers the ability to work with coordination teams to help you identify where changes need to occur so that you can respond accordingly. Clash Detective goes beyond the act of simply clashing objects together. With this tool, you can create reports, set up predefined clash tests (saved clashes), set rules, and group your clashes into groups.

In this chapter, you'll learn to:

- ◆ Create rules to examine various clash outcomes
- ◆ Select objects and geometry for clash detection
- ◆ Interpret and use clash reports

Starting Clash Detection

Clash Detective, which was originally an add-on module in the JetStream days (back before the Autodesk acquisition), is now part of Navisworks Manage (Clash Detective is the one module not available in Navisworks Simulate).

The Test panel (Figure 8.1) is essentially the starting point for clash detection. It gives you a place to keep track of your saved clashes, or tests. From the Test panel, you are able to see your project's clashes and learn when items have been updated and how many active items remain.

You can also import or export clash items from project to project, allowing you to create a standard set of clash options.

Test Panel Explained

Let's take a look at each item on the Test panel:

Name   Each new test item is added here with the default name of Test 1. You can quickly rename the individual items by pressing F2 or double-clicking the item you want to rename.

FIGURE 8.1

Test panel with a few clash items added

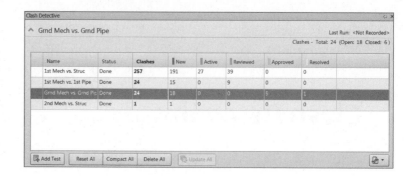

Status   Displays one of four available statuses of the listed clash tests and will change as clash tests are updated or run from the Select tab:

> **New**   Refers to a clash test that has not been run with the current model.
>
> **Done**   Refers to a clash analysis that has been completed successfully.
>
> **Old**   Indicates that the clash analysis may be out-of-date and is not the latest version or that it has modified in some way, including changing a setting or option of the selection.
>
> **Partial**   Typically indicates that a clash analysis was interrupted during execution. Results will typically be available up to the point of interruption.

Clashes   Shows the total number of clashes in the test minus the clashes that have been grouped into folders.

Clash Status   There are five types of status that can be displayed in the Test panel. They will change depending on how items and settings are adjusted in the Results tab (possibly during a coordination meeting). When you're in the Results tab you will notice that each of the statuses is denoted by a certain color as well.

> **New**   Denotes that a clash has been found for the first time in the current run of the clash; denoted as red.
>
> **Active**   Refers to a clash found in a previous run of the test and that has not yet been resolved; denoted as orange.
>
> **Reviewed**   Indicates that a clash was previously found and marked as reviewed; denoted as light blue.

Approved   Indicates that a clash was previously found and marked as approved; denoted as green.

Resolved   A clash found in the previous clash run but not in the current run. It is then usually assumed that the clash has been resolved; denoted as yellow.

Adding to and Maintaining Test Items

Test items are fairly easy to add and maintain; the real control comes from understanding the other tabs and what role they play in clash detection:

Add Test   Adds a new clash to the test sets. Once the test is added, its settings can be modified in the other tabs.

Reset All   Resets all the clashes back to New, as if you had never run a clash before. You can use Update to rerun the clashes again; however, all your organization will be lost. If you click Clean, it will remove all redlines and markups you have placed on clashes and reset all of your folder organization. You can undo this operation.

Compact All   Removes the resolved clashes and shortens the number of clash items available in the results. One rule about this function is that it will only remove resolved clashes that are not grouped in folders unless the entire folder has a Resolved status. If you wish to archive special items you have resolved, you can place them in folders to keep for the duration of the project and compact all the other clashes. You can undo this operation.

Delete All   Removes any selected clash test. There is no way to select more than one clash test at a time for deleting. You can undo this operation.

Update All   Updates all the clashes with the current settings. If new models have been loaded, new clashes will be performed in the background. On large projects with multiple clashes, the Update command may take a few minutes to complete its task.

Context Menu   When you need to update a clash test individually, you can use the context menu to change individual information (see Figure 8.2).

FIGURE 8.2
Context menu of
Test panel

Importing and Exporting Clash Tests

You have the capability to import and export your clash tests, as shown in Figure 8.3. This becomes important if you find yourself "clashing" similar items across multiple projects and with some of the same settings.

FIGURE 8.3
Importing clash
tests, located on
the Clash Detective
palette

Having a few XML files set aside that contain these settings, names, and possibly selected items could potentially save some time across projects. In order to properly export a clash test, the clash test must be defined by search sets. A unique property of this is that if you set up your clashes correctly, importing the clash test XML file will not only set up your Clash Detective but also will create all the different search sets you need to be successful in your project. If you export a clash test and it does not import into another project, this is because you did not define the clash between two or more search sets.

TEST WARNING

You may notice that the ⚠ exclamation mark icon appears at times. This occurs when the clash test has been altered in any way. To get rid of it, simply rerun the clash test and the items will update.

Working with Rules in Clash Detective

Clash detection rules are useful in that they give you parameters to run against your clash. You can use the rules to ignore certain types of geometry or certain items contained within the same file. Rules can also be created and modified as needed to give you flexibility on your projects; see Figure 8.4.

FIGURE 8.4
Clash detection
rules

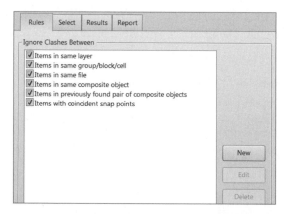

Enabling rules when running a clash can help reduce or filter the number of clashes that you might have on a given run. This brings you closer to the desired results for your project.

Creating New Rules

If you have ever used or created a rule in email programs like Microsoft Outlook, then you should be able to navigate the Rules feature in Clash Detective fairly easily since the concepts are similar.

Notice at the top of the Rules tab in the Clash Detective that you can see the total number of clash tests as well as the number of open or closed clashes. Selecting the check box next to a rule name enables that rule; unchecking the box disables that rule. Click New to open the Rules Editor (Figure 8.5), where you can select parameters from the existing rules templates.

FIGURE 8.5
Rules Editor dialog box

Once you have selected one of the templates, you can edit the information in the Rule Description field. This is where you fill in information that pertains to your selected template.

For example, if you want to ignore a particular selection set, you can specify that particular selection set in the template and then enable the rule. Now, that selection set will be ignored when running a clash detection.

You can also enter a name other than the default that is entered for you when you select a rule from the template. You'll find this ability useful when you have similar rules that differ only by a few small features, like the items selected in the selection set.

As a new rule is created, it will be available in Navisworks until it is deleted, even if the session is closed. Rules are also captured in XML files and will be imported into a project when the clash XML file is loaded.

Rules Templates

There are 10 predefined rules templates that you can use. The first 6 are default rules, and the remaining 4 are customizable rules templates where you can indicate your own information, such as selection sets or specific properties.

The default rules, which are already listed in the Rules tab (hence the name *default* rules), are not customizable or selectable options. The actions and the items that they ignore are already defined by the template and cannot be changed (although you can add and delete them as needed). They include the following:

◆ Items In Same Layer

◆ Items In Same Group/Block/Cell

◆ Items In Same File

- Items In Same Composite Object
- Items In Previously Found Pair Of Composite Objects
- Items With Coincident Snap Points

The 4 customizable rules templates allow you to select and add your own items to Navisworks:

- Insulation Thickness (used mainly for Clearance Clash)
- Same Property Value
- Specified Selection Sets
- Specified Properties With The Same Value (useful for ignoring clashes between two items)

You can edit a rule by clicking the Edit button at the bottom of the Rules tab (you can also double-click a rule to open the editor). Once you have the Rules Editor open, you will notice that it appears the same as when you add a new rule. Editing an existing rule and creating a new rule are essentially the same.

When you need to remove a rule, click Delete at the bottom of the Rules tab. You will not be prompted to verify that you want to delete the rule; Navisworks will just delete it. There is no way to undo a rule deletion, but you can always use New to add the rule back if needed.

As a good time-saver or a way to filter the number of clash results, a rule can be a valuable asset on a project. Here's how to create one:

1. Launch the Navisworks Manage application (not Navisworks Freedom or Simulate).

2. Open the file c08-rules.nwd.

3. Open Clash Detective and select the Test panel. Locate 1st Mech vs. Struc and select it (you can click Clean if you would like to start with a clean slate and reset all the clashes back to New).

4. Select the Rules tab and click New.

5. Select Specified Selection Set as your rules template.

6. From the <set> selection, choose First Floor Ductwork and Second Floor Slab. Doing so allows you to filter out the slabs from the clash tests and to control your results.

7. Name the rule **Ignore Duct and Slab**.

8. Click the check box next to the newly created rule.

9. Choose the Select tab and select Start to apply the new rule. Do not make any other changes.

10. Notice that the number of clash results is reduced to 1. The number of new clashes is now 1, but there are still 256 active clashes. This is because you filtered out slabs and you have only the columns to interfere with the ductwork.

Clashing Objects

You've now learned about some of the tools and functions that make Clash Detective operate. Now, let's get into clashing objects and taking full advantage of the power behind the Clash Detective engine (Figure 8.6).

FIGURE 8.6
Clash Detective
showing the
Select tab

FIGURE 8.6
Clash Detective
showing the
Select tab

When clashing objects, remember that you have multiple variables to take into consideration: what objects to clash against each other, the type of clash, how you want to select your objects, and what parameters you want to use.

One of the things that you might notice is that the Select tab may be a little small and hard to view. You can increase its size by collapsing the Test panel. There is a small arrow at the top of the Test panel to toggle expand and collapse.

Clash Object Selection

Notice the panes labeled Selection A and Selection B in Clash Detective's Select tab. Essentially, the Selection A and Selection B panes are windows into the Navisworks selection tree. If you take a moment to look at how the Select tab breaks down objects, you will notice how similar it is to the selection tree.

The Selection A and Selection B panes allow you to select the items you want to clash in Navisworks. Both panes do exactly the same thing. Imagine you have your left and right hands in front of you and you clap your hands together. Essentially, that is how we would describe the Selection A and Selection B panes.

It's pretty easy to get started with selecting your objects. Let's take a look:

1. Launch the Navisworks Manage application (not Navisworks Freedom or Simulate).

2. Open the file `c08-rules.nwd`.

3. Open Clash Detective and choose the Select tab.

4. Make sure the Standard tab in the lower section of each pane is selected for both the Selection A and Selection B panes.

5. Expand the c08-rules.nwd file and select Meadowgate - Services - First Floor Ductwork.dwg in the Selection A pane and Meadowgate - Structure.dwg in the Selection B pane. You have now selected your objects and are ready for clashing.

In this exercise, you chose Standard from the options at the bottom of the Selection A and Selection B panes. Standard is one of four additional options for controlling the state of selection (Figure 8.7). These options mimic the hierarchy available on the selection tree and can help you to save time in setting up your clash items:

Standard The default tree view, as shown in Figure 8.8, displays all the model information down to the geometry that can be used for clash detection.

Compact This option simplifies the standard tree view (Figure 8.9).

Properties This option shows Object Properties (Figure 8.10) and allows you to select specific properties to clash against.

Sets Displays the defined items on the Sets tab, as shown in Figure 8.11, and allows you to use them as items to clash; works for both search and selection sets.

FIGURE 8.7
State selection controls

FIGURE 8.8
Standard state tree view

FIGURE 8.9
Compact state tree view

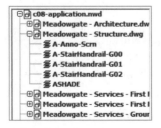

FIGURE 8.10
Properties state
tree view

FIGURE 8.11
Selection sets state
tree view

SETS: A GREAT WAY TO CLASH

Oftentimes, using selection or search sets for clashing can help save you a great deal of time on your project. This is repeatable way to standardize a way project clashes are performed as well. Sets are created by object, area, and/or floor and give you ways to break projects down further than just using the other tree view options such as Standard, Properties, or Compact.

Using selection sets may also be a good way to build and control clash rules on a project as well. You might find that it's easier to keep up with your clash items and quickly relate them back to your rules with just a glance.

Geometry Type and Self Intersect

Using the geometry type buttons (Figure 8.12) included with Navisworks lets you change how you clash your objects against each other. For example, say you have laser scan data (point clouds) that you have brought into Navisworks and want to clash that data against some existing structure. You would use the Points geometry type so that Navisworks would be able to recognize the data.

FIGURE 8.12
Geometry type
buttons

Each geometry type button is shown and explained next, along with the Self Intersect option, which allows you to clash geometry against itself:

Surfaces This is the first icon shown in the graphic. The default clash option, Surfaces clashes only the surface or 3D face of the selected objects.

 Lines This is the second icon shown in the graphic. This geometry type clashes items with center lines, usually used in conjunction with pipes.

 Points This is the third icon shown in the graphic. This geometry type allows you to clash points, usually when clashing point cloud data from laser scans.

 Self Intersect Self intersect provides a unique opportunity to clash selected geometry against itself as well as against the other selected geometry. For example, suppose you have selected Structure and Self Intersect in the Selection A pane and Ductwork in the Selection B pane. The clash test would clash Structure against the Ductwork as well as against itself (Self Intersect). Self Intersect can be performed for both the Selection A and Selection B panes at the same time.

USING CURRENT SELECTION

Using Current Selection (Figure 8.13) gives you the chance to use the selection tree, sets, or objects within the canvas as the objects to add to the A or B Selection pane. This gives you an alternate workflow to selecting and using objects for clash detection. Here's how it works:

FIGURE 8.13
Current Selection

1. Select your objects; they can be in the selection tree or selection sets, or you can select them from the canvas (don't forget that you can use the Ctrl key to add multiple objects to your selection).

2. Open Clash Detective to the Select tab.

3. Determine if they will be your A or B Selection pane objects.

4. Click Current Selection and your objects will be added to the pane.

USING THE CONTEXT MENU

In the Select tab of Clash Detective, to activate the context menu, just right-click in the A or B Selection pane and then choose one of the two available options:

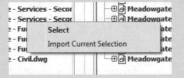

Select Clicking Select will choose the objects already selected in the Clash Detective pane (Selection A or Selection B) and then locate those objects in the canvas. You can use Hide Unselected to isolate the selected objects in the canvas, should you need to find them quickly.

Import Current Selection This tool works the same as using the Select Current button. It merely saves you the step of having to stop and click the button at the bottom of the tab.

Run Panel

The Run panel of Clash Detective (see Figure 8.14) tells Navisworks how you want to clash (Hard or Clearance), if you want to link to TimeLiner for time-based clashing, and where you can start your clash test. You also have additional functions such as Tolerance located here as well.

FIGURE 8.14
Run panel of Clash Detective

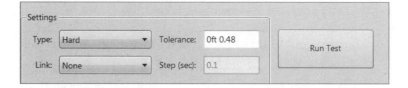

Hard Clash A hard clash is where two physical planes intersect with each other.

Hard (Conservative) Hard (Conservative) gives you an additional clash option in which the geometry intersections are clashed in more of a theoretical intersecting clash. In Navisworks terms, the two objects are treated as intersecting even though the geometry may not be. You will notice that using this option will net you a far greater number of results. So keep that in mind when using this feature.

By default, Hard (Conservative) is not enabled. If you want to enable it (you may never actually need it, but just in case), open the Application drop-down and select Options ➤ Interface ➤ Developer, and in the resulting dialog box, select the Show Internal Properties check box.

If you want to understand how the Hard (Conservative) clash type can affect your results in a little more detail, follow these steps:

1. Launch the Navisworks Manage application (not Navisworks Freedom or Simulate).

2. Open the file c08-application.nwd.

3. Open Clash Detective, click the Test panel, and select 1st Mech vs. 1st Pipe.

4. Note the number of clash results you have currently. Click the Select tab and change the clash type from Hard to Hard (Conservative). If Hard (Conservative) is not available, follow the steps described earlier to enable it.

5. Click Start at the bottom of the tab and notice that the results have increased greatly. Feel free to explore the differences, but do not save the file when you exit.

Clearance Clash Clearance Clash (Figure 8.15) gives the intersecting objects a specified distance that they must remain apart from each other.

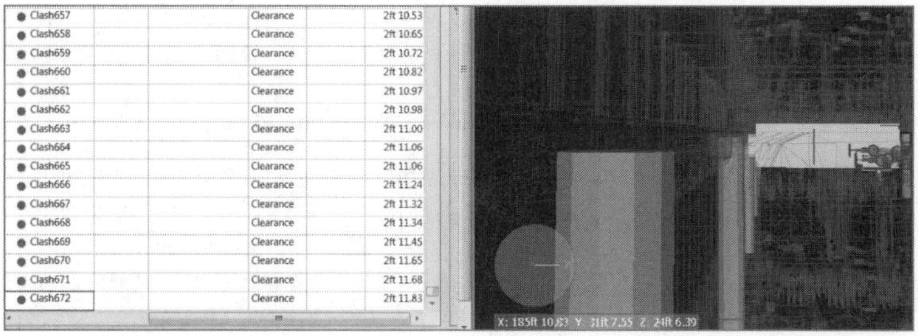

FIGURE 8.15
Clearance Clash, Ductwork vs. Structure

A good example is when insulation is applied to an object (pipe or ductwork, for example) and you need to remain a specific distance away from those objects.

Duplicate Clash   Duplicate Clash helps you to find intersecting objects of identical position and type (the objects have to have both type and position to be considered duplicate).

Often, the entire model may be clashed against itself to find duplicate clashes, but be warned that this could take some time to complete.

WORKING TOGETHER: DUPLICATE CLASH AND MODEL-BASED ESTIMATING

With the introduction of model-based estimating tools such as Autodesk Quantity Takeoff, Duplicate Clash is a powerful tool for bringing in a model (such as 3D DWF™) and verifying the integrity of a model before doing a takeoff.

Once you have loaded the 3D model that you plan to use, you could perform a Duplicate Clash on the entire model, make note of any clash report items, notify the extended team if needed, and be aware of these items when it comes time for the actual Quantity Takeoff operation.

Tolerance   Tolerance controls the severity of the clashes and lets you filter out what could be considered minor (fixed in the field) clashes. Tolerance is used for all types of clashes (Hard, Clearance, Duplicate). Be aware, however, that some materials such as ductwork created in CAD MEP might have a thickness of .001 and a pipe going through that duct will only clash .001. The most conservative tolerance is 0.

Link   Link allows you to link your clash test to a TimeLiner schedule or Animator scene.

Time Step   Time Step controls the time interval used when looking for clashes during a simulation.

Start Clash Detection   Start Clash Detection runs the clash test with the specified parameters and rules, if any were applied.

Found   Found displays the total number of clashes found in the clash test.

 Real World Scenario

CLASH DETECTION PROJECT CASE STUDY WITH C.W. DRIVER

C.W. Driver and Bohlin Cywinski Jackson Architects took an integrated design/build approach to the Newport Beach Civic Center and Park project. This $128M facility includes a 98,000 SF office building, parking structure, city council chambers building, and library addition. The 16-acre park features an enclosed dog park, civic lawn for outdoor events, places for art, wetlands, and 1.23 miles of walking trails. The 17,000 SF, two-story expansion of the Newport Beach Central Library will effectively link the library and Civic Center. A 440-space parking structure will provide 340 spaces to serve the city office building and 100 spaces dedicated for the library patrons. From the beginning of design on this project, BIM was integrated to share information and ensure quality.

The design team's efforts early on using 3D BIM proved to not only assist with visualization and documentation during design, but also assist in constructability reviews. Before the 100 percent construction document set was released, the design team took on the remarkable effort of reviewing different issues that were discovered through the use of Navisworks Clash Detective.

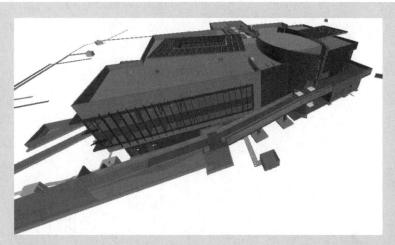

by Pixelcraft, Inc.

A unique aspect of the design coordination in Navisworks was the placement of the models. The design team located the models with Civil 3D coordinates in some models but in different coordinate planes in other models. Using the units and transforms in Navisworks, the team was able to combine all the models in the same space for analysis. Once all the models were in the same coordinate system, 3D coordination was performed in Navisworks.

After the design coordination was finished and construction documents were released, the construction coordination began. Before any modeling took place, a BIM coordination schedule was put together. This schedule matched the construction schedule in determining the order in which the different buildings were to be constructed. Creating and following this schedule was critical to ensure that the coordination effort was successful.

The first area to be coordinated was the underground. Although it might be thought of as unimportant, the underground civil coordination efforts proved essential throughout the rest of the building's coordination effort. The electrical subcontractor realized from the beginning of the project that the most efficient routing for much of the electrical systems would be underground. The electrical subcontractor not only modeled all the underground duct banks, but also modeled all the clearances necessary for the duct banks to be installed. This allowed the electrical components to be properly reviewed in Navisworks.

This project demonstrated during its underground coordination the importance of modeling zones of influences. All footings and piles in this project were required to have the area of influence modeled around them. Because of these areas that were modeled, Navisworks was able to detect all the structural problems associated between the MEPF disciplines and areas of influence from footings and piles.

A crucial area that had to be coordinated was between the Civic Center and the library expansion. This one area had a tremendous change in civil utilities as the project progressed, as shown in the following figure. One reason the coordination process was a success in this area was because of quick response times by the players involved. The plumbing systems more than doubled in this area, and Pan Pacific Plumbing within a day modeled all the proper locations of the pipes and included their new information to be clashed in Navisworks. Using search sets instead of hard selections provided the team with better ability to append all the new files and rerun all clashes without having to worry about ensuring all of a trade's files were actually clashed.

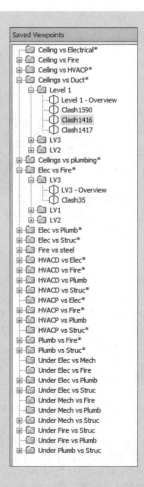

In tandem with the underground coordination was the coordination for the basement. This effort led to a number of innovative solutions. In one area of the basement, there was limited space and nearly an unlimited number of mechanical and plumbing lines that needed to be installed. To compound the problem, the team identified early on the importance of making sure all the pieces of equipment were serviceable to the facilities team down the line, so clearance zones were modeled to allow for special coordination. Navisworks Clash Detective used these clearance zones along with the model geometry gathered by the team to analyze all the relationships between the systems. As the results came in, it was apparent that a lot of engineering was required to make the situation work. The design team eagerly accepted weekly invitations to meet with the project team to coordinate the tight space. In order to best use their time, the project team first reviewed all the constructability issues and created suggestions for the design team to review. When the design team came on board, viewpoints were already established and possible solutions were created. This saved time for the designers and allowed for a synergistic environment. The results are shown in the following image.

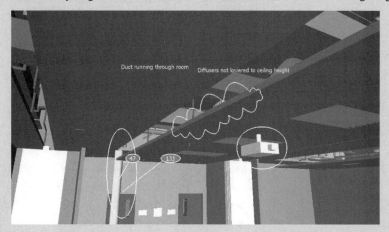

Careful documentation of the constructability reviews was done throughout the coordination process. Using Navisworks redline tools, all constructability issues were identified before any meeting was called. All duplicate clashes were removed using the Select and Filter tools in Clash Detective. This was essential because the whole team knew what issues were going to be reviewed during the meeting, and each member of the team knew their time was being used efficiently. When all constructability issues are identified and all duplicate clashes are removed, the coordination meetings become very effective.

During the meeting, the team kept the meeting minutes through tags. Each clash result was assigned to a member of the project team, and a date was set for the task to be complete. Reports were then generated in both an NWD format and the Excel format.

During the course of coordination, a number of structural issues came to light. Almost all the components on this project were designed to be prefabricated, and the steel was no exception. The structural engineering consultant did an amazing job meeting with the team in coordinating structural penetrations. Over 150 different penetrations were coordinated and updated in the steel model. These penetrations were then prefabricated, and the MEP systems were successfully installed in the field.

In addition to MEPF coordination, Navisworks was used during lean planning sessions. During each lean scheduling meeting, the Navisworks model was used to determine order of installation. Colors were used to map out sequences, and all parties were able to clearly see relationships between installations.

C.W. Driver
BUILDERS SINCE 1919

Clash Report

Clash Test	Folder Name	Clash Name	Comments	X Grid	Y Grid	X Dir	Y Dir
Ceiling vs Fire	LV1	Clash337	Fire detail to be added	D	Y1	Right	North
Ceiling vs Fire	LV1	Clash343		4	A	Left	North
Ceiling vs Fire	LV2	Clash266	Fire to move up	3	G	Right	North
Ceiling vs HVACP*	Level 3	Clash623	arch to cut ceiling back	2	K	Right	North
Ceilings vs Duct*	Level 1	Clash1590	Mech to move vav boxes down	2	A	Right	North
Ceilings vs Duct*	Level 1	Clash1416	Mech to move expresso exhaust to correct elevation	X2	XF	Left	South
Ceilings vs Duct*	Level 1	Clash1417	Mech move tap up on the plenum	2	F	Right	North
Ceilings vs Duct*	LV3	Clash1077	Mech to raise duct	1	F	Left	South
Ceilings vs Duct*	LV2	Clash908	Mech to move return	1	H	Left	South
Ceilings vs Duct*	LV2	Clash909	Mech to move return	1	G	Right	South
Ceilings vs plumbing*	Level 2	Clash35	Plumbing place water lines in the wall	2	E	Right	North
Ceilings vs plumbing*	Level 2	Clash86	Plumbing to raise above ceiling	E	Y1	Left	South
Ceilings vs plumbing*	Level 2	Clash61	Plumbing Place pipe in wall	1	E	Left	South
Ceilings vs plumbing*	Level 1	Clash154	Arch to move ceiling	4	G	Right	South
Ceilings vs plumbing*		Clash169	Plumb to move in wall	1	E	Left	South
Elec vs Fire*	LV3	Clash35	Fire to move	8	G	Right	North
Elec vs Fire*	LV1	Clash84	Fire to move	2	D	Right	South
Elec vs Fire*	LV1	Clash85	Fire to move	8	H	Left	North
Elec vs Fire*	LV1	Clash89	Fire to avoid conduit	2	L	Right	North
Elec vs Fire*	LV1	Clash92	Fire to move	7	H	Right	South
Elec vs Fire*	LV2	Clash86	Fire to move	2	D	Right	South
Elec vs Plumb*	LV2	Clash52	Plumb fixed hanger, review	5	E	Left	North
Elec vs Plumb*	LV2	Clash54	Elec to move hanger	1	L	Left	South
Elec vs Plumb*	LV2	Clash55	Elect to move ground pipe	4	B	Right	North
Elec vs Plumb*	LV1	Clash56	Plumb to move east	4	B	Right	North
Elec vs Struc*	Level 1	Clash554	Elect to move	4	B	Left	North
Fire vs steel	Level 1	Clash593		X2	XE	Left	North
Fire vs steel	Level 1	Clash595		A	Y1	Right	South
Fire vs steel	Level 1	Clash598		A	Y1	Right	North
Fire vs steel	Level 1	Clash568	Arch to review with struct for footing change	1	L	Right	South
Fire vs steel	Level 3	Clash578	Fire to fix	5	A	Right	South

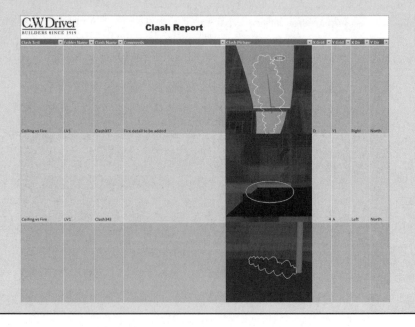

C.W. Driver
BUILDERS SINCE 1919

Clash Report

Clash Test	Folder Name	Clash Name	Comments	Clash Picture	X Grid	Y Grid	X Dir	Y Dir
Ceiling vs Fire	LV1	Clash337	Fire detail to be added		D	Y1	Right	North
Ceiling vs Fire	LV1	Clash343			4 A		Left	North

Understanding Clash Results

This is where things start to get interesting and where Clash Detective begins to shine (see Figure 8.16). You have spent plenty of time setting things up and understanding what the operations do, but now, you get to see the actual clash results come to fruition.

Of course, it's never that simple, and there is more to consider than just looking at the results of the clash. You have to take into account how you want to display your clash items and what to do with your information: grouping similar items into folders, assigning items, or maybe just using the SwitchBack tool to extend the power of the Results tab. Read on to understand more.

The Results area gives you a myriad of options and a wealth of information to consider when exploring the results of the clash test you just performed:

Name   Displays the name of the clash, which you can change as needed. The default numbering system is to simply count the clashes found and number them accordingly.

Status   Each clash has a status associated with it (Figure 8.17). Each status can be set by clicking the drop-down associated with it. Notice the colors of the objects change as you change the status.

FIGURE 8.16
Clash Detective
results

FIGURE 8.17
Clash statuses

New   Denotes that a clash has been found for the first time in the current run of the clash; denoted as red.

Active   Refers to a clash found in a previous run of the test that has not yet been resolved; denoted as orange.

Reviewed   Indicates that a clash was previously found and marked as reviewed; denoted as light blue.

Approved   Indicates that a clash was previously found and marked as approved; denoted as green. When a clash has a status of Approved and a clash test is run again, the status will remain as Approved.

Resolved   Indicates that a clash was found in the previous clash run but not in the current run. It is then usually assumed that the clash has been resolved; denoted as yellow. The resolved status will only change if the clash was manually set to Resolved.

NAVIGATION DURING CLASH DETECTION

Don't forget that you can use all your Navigation tools (Orbit, Look Around, Walk, and Fly) to further explore your clashes as you click through them. You can save viewpoints as you navigate around as well.

Level and Grid Intersection   When you're using a Revit file, the grids and levels will show up in the clash results.

Found   Lists the date and time the clash was most recently found.

Approved and Approved By   When the status of a clash is changed to Approved, the username of the system is added here, along with the date and time it was set to Approved.

Description   Lists the type of clash found: Hard, Hard (Conservative), Clearance, or Duplicate.

Assigned To   You can assign clash results to specific team members for resolution. You also can add notes directly in the Assign Clash dialog box as needed. You access the Assign Clash dialog box, shown in Figure 8.18, by using the context menu.

FIGURE 8.18
Assign Clash
dialog box

Distance   Displays the distance or depth of the actual clash.

CLASH RESULTS CONTEXT MENU

Right-clicking in the Results area gives you a context menu with a few tools to help speed things along:

Copy/Paste Name Allows you to copy and paste clash names.

Rename Allows you to rename the clash.

Assign/Unassign Opens the Assign dialog box or removes someone already assigned by using Unassign.

Add Comment Adds a comment to the clash that also shows up in reports.

Group Creates a folder of the selected clashes. Group will only appear on the context menu when you have multiple items selected.

Quick Filter By Allows you to filter the clash list by different criteria. Use the Clear Quick Filter located at the top of the Results panel to reset the clash list.

Sort By Proximity Sorts clash results by the distance to the selected clash.

Clash Groups

Clash groups give you the chance to divide and group clashes in a manner that makes sense to you on a project. Maybe you need to group all the clashes of a particular piping subcontractor into a folder so they can easily find the information they need. Another use could be to divide between Resolved or Approved clashes in a folder.

One good feature about folders is that when you change the status of the folder—say from New to Resolved—all the items contained in the folder will update as well. Comments and assignments can also be added to the folder level, saving you the time of having to add that information to each item in the container. You can still edit the individual items as well; you may see Varies in some columns since information differs.

Folders can be created in a couple of ways. You can highlight the clashes you want, right-click, and select New Group, and they will be placed in a folder. You can use the New Group button, as shown in Figure 8.19, at the bottom of the Results area. You can even create all of your folders first using the New Group button and apply the drag-and-drop method for adding your clashes manually.

FIGURE 8.19
Clash groups

The Explode Group button will remove the folder and return the items back to the results area without deleting the clash results. Explode Group is also available on the context menu.

You can create as many folders as needed, but folders cannot be combined with each other to create subfolders.

Display Settings

Using the clash Display Settings, as shown in Figure 8.20, you can take advantage of additional efficient ways to review your selected clashes. With these tools and options, you can change how Navisworks displays the clash items with Transparent Dimming or Hide Other, take advantage of Animate Transitions, or use Save Changes in the Viewpoints section to save the change you might make to the clash view. Let's explore each of these tools a little further.

FIGURE 8.20
Options in the clash
Display Settings
area

Highlighting (Item 1 and Item 2) Selecting either Item 1 or Item 2 will allow you to override the color of the items that are being clashed. This helps with display and to provide an additional way to distinguish between items.

Highlight All Clashes Highlights all the clashes found in the current scene for the selected clash test (see Figure 8.21).

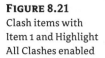

FIGURE 8.21
Clash items with
Item 1 and Highlight
All Clashes enabled

X: 129ft 7.46 Y: 66ft 9.32 Z: 26ft 4.41

Isolation Dropdown   Contains options for controlling the display of the canvas.

   Dim Other   Use Dim Other to turn all other objects to gray, making the selected clash results stand out.

   Hide Other   Hides all other objects in the scene except for the select clash results.

Transparent Dimming   Transparent Dimming, which must be used in conjunction with Dim Other, adds a transparency level (the default is 85 percent) to the objects in the scene. Your objects will appear as gray. To change the default transparency level, from the Application button ➢ Options ➢ Tools ➢ Clash Detective modify the Dimming Transparency slider.

Auto Reveal   Temporarily hides any items that might obstruct the view of the clash items so that you are able to clearly see the clash without having to pan or zoom.

Auto Zoom   Automatically zooms to show all items involved in the selected clash or clash group. When Auto Zoom is unchecked, you can click through the results without moving your main viewpoint.

Animate Transitions   Using Animate Transitions simply animates the view change between selecting clash results. When Animate Transitions is disabled, you will not see any animation when selecting your next clash, much like selecting between viewpoints.

When using Animate Transitions, you will want to have Auto Zoom enabled as well. The duration for the transitions can be controlled in Options.

Save Changes Saves changes made to the current viewpoint of the clash. This is really useful when you are adding comments or markups or you have changed the perspective to better view the clash.

Focus On Clash This tool is useful to help you restore your viewpoint if you have navigated away from the clash or view. You can use Focus On Clash to restore your view to the last-saved clash viewpoint.

Simulation Simulation is used in conjunction with time-based clashing. Checking this box gives you access to the time slider in TimeLiner so you are able to further explore the clash timeline and the events occurring immediately before or after the clash.

For clash items contained in a clash group or folder, the time slider is moved to a "center" clash among the clashes.

COMMON CLASH DETECTION DISPLAY SETTINGS

We're often asked about the optimum display settings. Of course, a lot of factors go into that, like your needs, computer performance, audience, and so forth. But here are the settings that should as a rule stay checked all the time:

◆ Auto Reveal

◆ Auto Zoom

◆ Save Changes in the Viewpoint section

◆ Dim Other

◆ Transparent Dimming

◆ Highlight All Clashes

As for the rest, you should experiment with your own settings and find the optimum performance for your individual project and computer.

View In Context The View In Context drop-down allows you to temporarily change your Zoom reference, giving you a point of context. This should help you to understand where you are in the model and possibly gain perspective or reference to the individual clash. You have three options to choose from. The zoom lasts only a few seconds and returns to clash results when complete. The timing of View In Context can be changed in Options ➤ Tools ➤ Clash Detective ➤ View In Context Zoom Duration.

All Zooms out to show all the elements in the scene, much like the Zoom All tool.

File Zooms out to make visible the extents of the files containing the items involved in the selected clash.

Home Home view takes you to the previously saved home view, as defined by the ViewCube® software; it's used more often than the other two since it can be customized.

Item 1 and 2 Panes

These panes, Item 1 and Item 2, contain data on the items being clashed. As you select each item in the Results area, the information in the Item panes will update as needed. From here, you can manipulate some of the information. You can choose if you should highlight the selected entity or speed the folder grouping process along just by right-clicking in Item 1 or 2; see Figure 8.22.

FIGURE 8.22

Item 1 and Item 2 with the context menu open

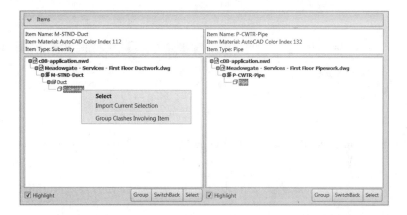

Highlight   Using Highlight (enabled by default) will override the color of the item in the scene with the color of the result status. Otherwise, the selection will usually appear as green or whatever base color you are using as the default color selection setting for Navisworks.

Disabling Highlight may make it difficult to locate the clash results, and you may find it easier to leave this box checked.

Group Clashes Involving Item   Available from the context menu, Group Clashes Involving Item creates a new clash group containing all clashes involved with the item or items that you have right-clicked on.

When creating a clash group, you may receive the following error message (Figure 8.23) if an item or groups of items have already been assigned to a group. Navisworks will not allow you to have items assigned to more than one folder or group and will prompt you to move them.

FIGURE 8.23

Clash group error message

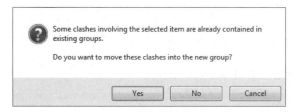

Select   Using the Select button or Select from the context menu will select the item in the scene as well as in the selection tree. If Highlight is enabled, the item will be highlighted as well.

SwitchBack

SwitchBack is a powerful tool that can aid in coordination meetings and design reviews or help you return to a specific view in the native file. Essentially, SwitchBack allows you to select an item from the Item 1 or 2 pane and switch back to the software program (and corresponding view) that it was created with. Alternatively, you do not have to be in a clash to use SwitchBack. If you select an item, the Item Tools panel appears, where you can select SwitchBack (see Figure 8.24).

FIGURE 8.24

Choosing SwitchBack from the Item Tools panel

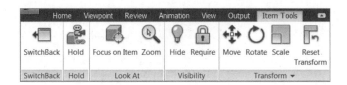

SwitchBack is available with Autodesk® AutoCAD®, AutoCAD® Civil 3D®, AutoCAD Architecture, AutoCAD MEP, and MicroStation-based applications as well as Autodesk® Revit® 2013 and 2012 software.

Note that when you select multiple objects from the selection tree, SwitchBack will not be available.

Using SwitchBack is essentially the same in all three programs: locate your items, activate SwitchBack in the corresponding software, and select SwitchBack in Navisworks. The key difference is the command used to activate SwitchBack in each program. Let's explore the processes a little closer.

SWITCHBACK IN REVIT

Revit will need to be installed on the same computer as Navisworks in order for SwitchBack to work properly. Revit will open a corresponding sheet or view to assist in locating the selected item.

As we mentioned, SwitchBack works for Revit 2013 and 2012. Here's how to access it:

1. Open Revit and the corresponding model.

2. Locate and select SwitchBack from Add-Ins ➤ External Tools ➤ Navisworks SwitchBack.

3. Return to Navisworks and select your item.

4. From the Item Tools panel, select SwitchBack.

You can also access SwitchBack from Clash Detective.

SWITCHBACK IN AutoCAD

AutoCAD or an AutoCAD-based program will need to be installed on the same computer as Navisworks in order for SwitchBack to work properly. SwitchBack works for AutoCAD version 2004 and later. To use it, do the following:

1. Open your AutoCAD or an AutoCAD-based program as well as the corresponding file.

2. In AutoCAD, type **NWLOAD**.

3. Return to Navisworks and select your item.

4. From the Item Tools panel, select SwitchBack.

You can also use SwitchBack from Clash Detective.

SWITCHBACK IN MICROSTATION

MicroStation or a MicroStation-based program will need to be installed on the same computer as Navisworks in order for SwitchBack to work properly. SwitchBack works for MicroStation versions J and v8. To use it, follow these steps:

1. Open your MicroStation or a MicroStation-based program as well as the corresponding file.

2. In MicroStation, select Utilities ➢ Key In and type **mdl load nwexport9** in the dialog box.

3. Return to Navisworks and select your item.

4. From the Item Tools panel, select SwitchBack.

You can also use SwitchBack from Clash Detective.

Time-Based Clash Detection

Combining TimeLiner with the Clash Detective gives you the unique opportunity to monitor your project on a timely basis. You can take into account logistical items like cranes, bulldozers, materials, or equipment that usually impact a schedule because they are moved around a site (or installed on the project). Since these objects are often scheduled as temporary, demolished, or other schedule types (even construct), you can link them to Clash Detective to make sure they do not interfere with the project as they are moved around the jobsite.

In the next example, you'll install the MEP services for the first floor and examine the structure:

1. Launch the Navisworks Manage application (not Navisworks Freedom or Simulate).

2. Open the file c08-link.nwd.

3. Open TimeLiner, located on the Tools panel of the Home tab.

4. On the Tasks tab, look at the Planned Start dates for the First Floor Ductwork and First Floor Pipework.

5. Open Clash Detective and select 1st MEP vs. Struc on the Test panel.

6. Select the Rules tab and make sure all the default boxes are checked.

7. Next, click the Select tab and select First Floor Ductwork And Pipework in Selection A and Structure in Selection B.

8. In the Link drop-down, select TimeLiner; this will establish the link between TimeLiner and Clash Detective.

9. Click Start to begin the clash test. It may take a few moments for the sequence to complete since it's running against the actual TimeLiner simulation (you should see a pop-up alerting you to this fact).

10. Move over to the Results tab and scroll to the right to observe the Start, End, and Event that the clash is now linked to (this information can also be exported to a report).

11. Make sure that the Simulation box is also checked in the Display section of the Results tab. If the Simulation box is not checked, you will not be able to access the slider in TimeLiner.

12. Explore TimeLiner's Simulate tab and use the slider to determine the potential impact in the schedule. Don't forget to use your navigation tools as well.

One of the great things about linking your clash items to TimeLiner is that as you locate them in the clash results and have TimeLiner open to the Simulate tab, you can see the Simulate slider right where you are in TimeLiner. Then, you can select a different clash result and move the Simulate slider around to see how these results are affected before and after the clash. Having the knowledge that a clash could occur based on more than just static data could mean the difference between success and failure on a project.

Clash Detection Redlines, Markups, and Comments

It's essential when you're working on a project to be able to communicate intent across a wider scale. Navisworks allows for communication beyond Clash Detective and TimeLiner. As you learned in Chapter 6, "Documenting Your Project," tools are available for commenting and marking up clash items, and those tools can be applied to clash results (see Figure 8.25).

FIGURE 8.25
Clash with comments and tags

Redlines, dimensions, text, revision clouds, tags, and other review information can be added to clash results at any time, helping you to communicate your intent.

When you're using the Review tools, make sure the Save Viewpoints box is checked; otherwise, your additions will be lost as soon as you click to the next clash result.

 **Real World Scenario**

NAVISWORKS MODEL COMPARISON

Scenario Virtual Design and Construction Services (Scenario) and their client working on a hospital project in California leveraged BIM throughout the design process to manage changes while producing shop drawings. Key to this process was the powerful clash-detection and model-comparison tools in Navisworks Manage. The design team was producing the construction documentation using a combination of the three Autodesk Revit products (Architecture, Structure, and MEP), and the trade contractors were using a combination of Autodesk AutoCAD–based products to produce the shop drawings. The Navisworks compare models function was then used to provide context for the Scenario Virtual Project Delivery (VPD) change management engine and to inform the team of changes made from one version to the next. Navisworks made visualizing the movement of a wall or the change of a door size easily apparent by colorizing the deltas.

Models were distributed and shared on a biweekly basis with the construction team for constructability and scope input. The latest Architectural, Structural, and MEP model elements were cross-referenced against the previous versions to identify potential scope increases and constructability issues for discussion with the entire team. The ability to use Navisworks to reduce to overall review time from 2 weeks to 2 days has resulted in a more complete and coordinated plan set for the Office of Statewide Health Planning and Development (OSHPD) back check (a review process), which will likely result in fewer change orders.

Scenario and their client started with a discovery process where high-impact change items such as soffit and shaft locations were discussed along with a schedule of deliverables. The team decided to use Navisworks in conjunction with VPD to compare models on a biweekly basis until OSHPD submittal.

Using the NWC export in Revit, the teams were able to share their lightweight models through Scenario's managed filesystem that automated file versioning. The models were compiled into Navisworks and compared to the previous versions in an NWF file. Geometry that changed between versions was automatically highlighted and viewed in Navisworks Manage, and the team was able to use the colorization in the model to discuss the impact of the changes. Because the files were exported as NWC files from Revit, they were able to be automatically tracked back to the Revit model using the SwitchBack function for further discussion with the design team.

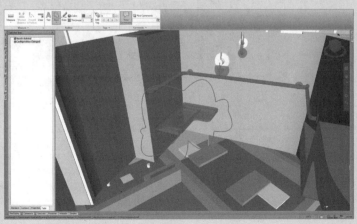

During the meetings, changes were identified and communicated quickly and confidently without ambiguity. Changes were highlighted in red and superimposed over the previous NWC version. The team was able to assess the impacts on a global scale and discuss and mitigate any ADA or clearance issues before the design went to OSHPD back check. The results were delivered to each team member using NWF files. By using Navisworks, the changes were given context, and the team was able to greatly reduce the review cycle time by letting the BIM inform their constructability review.

Once the design team was finished, the trade contractor team used Navisworks to combine all the trade models into a federated model on a weekly basis. The models were divided by floor to reduce the overall file size and improve performance. After the models were combined by floor, the team used search sets (a function in Navisworks that allows users to build custom queries to interrogate and filter the model into discrete pieces) to logically separate coordination issues into systems such as Medical Gas and Heating, Ventilation, and Air Conditioning using clash tests.

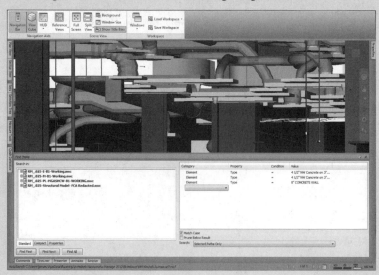

The individual clashes of each clash test were then aggregated into issues using the grouping function of Navisworks. Specific issues were discussed and assigned within Navisworks to the party most capable of resolving the issue with the least impact. The Comment tool was used to record how each issue was to be rectified. After all issues were assigned, the results were exported to a tabular HTML file from the Reports tab of Clash Detective, where they could be tracked on an issue-by-issue basis and distributed to each team member.

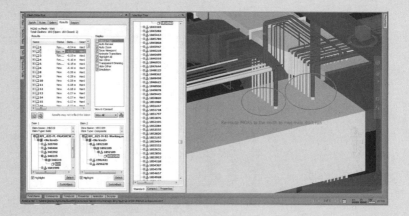

At subsequent meetings, the trade contractor files were replaced with files of the same name and the clashes were run again. Navisworks automatically changed the status of clashes that had been moved successfully to Resolved, and the color of the clash was changed to yellow to provide visual cues on the overall status of the model. The clashes that were not resolved were then reviewed again by the team and reissued. Once the clashes were either resolved or an acceptable solution was agreed upon, an NWD file was issued as a signoff model and then shop drawings were issued.

Clash Reports

Creating a report (Figure 8.26) outside of Navisworks gives you the opportunity to explore details of your clash results or to share that data with others. You can even save viewpoints of the clashes inside Navisworks for use later. Reports are somewhat customizable, at least in terms of the type and details available for exporting.

Once the report has been exported, its possible uses become almost infinite and will depend on the needs of the organization. You could keep it as simple as sharing the report with your team in a USB drive, creating a website with the HTML export to share the report, importing the XML export into your own customized database, or coming up with something new that fits the needs of the project.

FIGURE 8.26
Report tab

Report Contents

Having the ability to control what information is contained in each report is essential. This section covers the available options:

Contents Gives you the option to control which items are included (or not included) in the clash report. Check or uncheck the various boxes as needed. The more boxes selected, the more detailed your report will be.

Include Clashes: For Clash Groups, Include This option will only be available if you have created clash groups. It allows you to control how to display your clash groups in your reports. Choose from the following:

Group Headers Only Reports will only include summaries of the clash group folders.

Individual Clashes Only Reports will only include individual clash results.

Everything Reports will contain both summaries and individual clash results for the clash groups.

Include These Statuses This option allows you to select which clash status to include in your report.

Output Settings

Just as it's important to be able to select the content, it's equally important to have other options available for your report's type and output format. Having access to different formats such as XML or viewpoints gives you greater flexibility.

Report Type   Three choices are available in the Report Type drop-down:

Current Test   Creates a single report of the current clash test.

All Tests (Combined)   Creates a single report of all the clash tests (combined into one file).

All Tests (Separate)   Creates separate reports of all the clash tests (multiple files).

Report Format   There are five different types of reports, each having a purpose inside and outside of Navisworks. Navisworks 2013 includes the HTML (Tabular) report, which can be opened in programs like Microsoft Excel. The five types are as follows:

XML   Creates an XML file complete with images. The XML can then be imported into other databases, such as Autodesk® Constructware® databases.

HTML   Creates an HTML file complete with images. If you click an image, you will be able to see an enlarged version of the image.

HTML (Tabular)   Creates an HTML file (see Figure 8.27) complete with images and in a table format. The HTML (Tabular) option can then be opened in programs like Excel. If you click an image, you will be able to see an enlarged version of that image.

FIGURE 8.27
HTML (Tabular) report opened in Excel

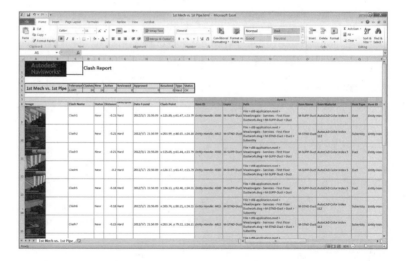

Text   Creates a text file complete with images.

As Viewpoints   Creates a folder of all the clashes in viewpoints, named according to which clash test is selected. The clashes will be listed as they were named in the Results tab.

When exporting viewpoints with clash groups, you will want to make sure you take full advantage of the For Clash Groups drop-down. Selecting a different option (Everything, for example) can greatly enhance your viewpoints experience.

REPORT CONSIDERATIONS

When you're creating a report, here are a few things to keep in mind that could save you from banging your head against the wall:

◆ Navisworks makes every attempt to create images with the reports (XML, HTML, and even text). But if you find that your images are not being created, check that you have the Image box selected in the Contents area. Also take a look at your Include Clash Type check boxes. Sometimes, an unselected check box can be the reason for images not showing up.

◆ When picking a save location for your report, avoid your desktop, unless you will be saving to a folder on your desktop. Remember that the report is creating images and another associated file, and it could be a great deal of information to manage, especially if you export several reports.

Group Headers Only   Exports only the clash group Overview image—not always the most useful of images (Figure 8.28).

FIGURE 8.28
Clash group
viewpoints

Individual Clashes Only   Creates viewpoints as if they were not in clash groups. Effective if you do not need to maintain your clash group folders (Figure 8.29).

FIGURE 8.29
Individual clashes

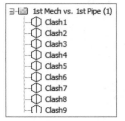

Everything   Creates viewpoints based on how they were created in the Results tab. This is usually the best option for working with clash groups and viewpoints (Figure 8.30).

FIGURE 8.30
Everything

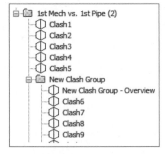

Write Report Creates the selected report or creates viewpoints. A report may take a few minutes to complete. Remember that it is exporting images out of Navisworks, and the more images you have, the longer it will take to create the report. The report pictures will use the same settings specified on the Results tab. If you have Dim Other on, all of your viewpoints will save as Dim Other; if you have Hide Other on, all of the viewpoints will show only the clash.

Writing a Report

Let's explore how to create an HTML (Tabular) report:

1. Launch the Navisworks Manage application (not Navisworks Freedom or Simulate).

2. Open the file c08-application.nwd.

3. Open Clash Detective and select 1st MEP Vs. 1st Pipe in the Test panel.

4. Select the Reports tab, and change any of the contents that you would like. But make sure that Report Type is set to Current Test and Report Format is set to HTML (Tabular).

5. Select Write Report and choose a location to save your report.

6. Open Excel.

7. Select File ➢ Open and change File Type to HTML. Browse to the location where you saved your file.

You should now have your clash report open to do with as you choose.

 Real World Scenario

USING VIEWPOINTS WITH CLASH DETECTION

The Viewpoint tool was an integral part of the construction process for a new office building at DreamWorks Animation's campus in Glendale, California. Gensler designed the building using Autodesk's Revit Architecture as the design and documentation tool. At the time the project began, only the architectural model was developed using BIM software. Structural and MEP consultants documented using 2D CAD software. Construction began and the general contractor (GC) for the project decided to use the Architectural Revit model as a tool for coordinating HVAC, plumbing, electrical, and data systems. This was a new process for Gensler, but the team decided it was a worthwhile experience and there was value to using a fully developed 3D model.

Navisworks Manage was chosen by Gensler and the GC as the coordination tool to bring together subcontractor models with the Gensler design model. While the project team provided a Revit model, it was unrealistic to require subcontractors to provide Revit-compatible models. Instead, the project team required that subcontractors have the capability to provide a Navisworks-compatible 3D model for coordination purposes.

The GC organized a kickoff meeting where subcontractors, the design team, and the GC gathered for the first time. This meeting outlined the process and discussed main points of the project and areas of congestion that the project team needed to focus on. Due to the time constraints and known congestion of systems above the ceilings, the GC and subcontractors agreed to meet on a biweekly basis. The design team was required to attend only critical meetings and milestone meetings, as needed.

Results		
Start	End	Event
11:00:00 AM 8/12/2009	11:00:00 AM 9/30/2009	First Floor Ductwork
11:00:00 AM 8/12/2009	11:00:00 AM 9/30/2009	First Floor Ductwork
11:00:00 AM 8/12/2009	11:00:00 AM 9/30/2009	First Floor Ductwork
11:00:00 AM 8/12/2009	11:00:00 AM 9/30/2009	First Floor Ductwork
11:00:00 AM 8/12/2009	11:00:00 AM 9/30/2009	First Floor Ductwork
11:00:00 AM 8/12/2009	11:00:00 AM 9/30/2009	First Floor Ductwork
11:00:00 AM 8/12/2009	11:00:00 AM 9/30/2009	First Floor Ductwork
11:00:00 AM 8/12/2009	11:00:00 AM 9/30/2009	First Floor Ductwork
11:00:00 AM 8/12/2009	11:00:00 AM 9/30/2009	First Floor Ductwork
11:00:00 AM 8/12/2009	11:00:00 AM 9/30/2009	First Floor Ductwork
11:00:00 AM 8/12/2009	11:00:00 AM 9/30/2009	First Floor Ductwork

Subcontractors developed their models one level at a time, and a few weeks later, clash detections were run and problems were found that needed solutions. Gensler and the design team received requests for information (RFIs) addressing these conflicts. The RFIs generated from these meetings were always accompanied by a brightly colored 3D image, or viewpoint, taken directly from the model. Some viewpoints were self-explanatory, with visible clashes; some had transparencies set to show hidden elements; some clouded specific clashes or contained notes on the image. All of this made the RFIs easy to understand, and the issues to be resolved were clear.

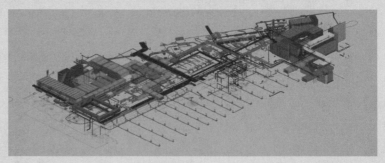

When attending one early coordination meeting, the GC would bring up one preset viewpoint at a time, with redlines on screen and a list of comments and dates attached to each item the team discussed. Once clashes in a viewpoint were discussed, the project team would move to the next viewpoint and discuss the next set of issues. The preset viewpoints allowed the meetings to be focused and organized, maximizing the design team's time at the meetings.

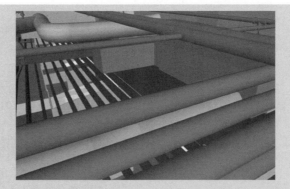

All of these methods made the review process much quicker for the design team. The project team was able to see what the conflict was, and with the tags, a form of redlining inside the viewpoint, the project team could tell what the GC and subcontractors were specifically focused on. The whole process allowed the contractor and design team to resolve the conflicts before issuing final shop drawings. After performing clash detection through Navisworks, the shop drawing review process was faster and resubmittals were less frequent, which helped speed up the construction administration for the design team and avoid delays for the contractor.

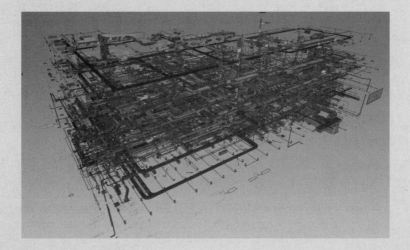

The coordination process using Navisworks allowed the team to resolve conflicts in a virtual environment that the design team and contractor could sign off on before fabrication and installation. It is always easier, faster, and cheaper to fix conflicts before they are built. On this project, the design and contractor teams were confident that the project team resolved conflicts in the model and that the fabricated elements would all fit together, even in areas of congestion. The project team experienced very few changes in the field, which can be costly and can stop work for days at a time. This process helped the contractor deliver the project to the client ahead of schedule—which was a success for the contractor, the design team, and the client.

The Bottom Line

Create rules to examine various clash outcomes. Rules for clashes can be a great asset and affect the outcome of a clash. Rules can help you filter specific objects, like items contained in a selection set, so that you're clashing only the specific elements needed.

    Master It Rules are divided into two types: default and rules templates. What is the key difference between default rules and rules templates?

Select objects and geometry for clash detection. Navisworks provides the ability to import over 40 types of files, which means there could be all types of geometry for Clash Detective to try to clash. Therefore, you have the ability to change the geometry type to suit your needs.

    Master It What are the three types of geometry that you can choose to clash against?

Interpret and use clash reports. Clash reports come in various shapes and sizes and can be saved internally to Navisworks as well as externally. These reports have various uses: They can be imported into other software programs or databases, used with Microsoft Excel, or included as images inside Navisworks. Reports can also contain a great deal of customizable information that you can easily control.

    Master It Let's look at a specific aspect of creating a report. You have created an HTML report, but the images do not appear to be exporting. What could be a possible solution for your problem?

Part 3

Advanced Navisworks Tools

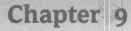

Chapter 9

Creating Visualizations

The Autodesk® Navisworks® 2013 product has a unique presentation and rendering tool called Presenter, which lets you add materials, lighting, and effects to bring your models to life. We have spent plenty of time in this book laboring on our projects, learning how to complete tasks associated with clash detection and scheduling and some of the navigation features. Now, it's time to focus on the visualization tools within Navisworks, because with Presenter, you can go way beyond clash detection and scheduling.

In this chapter, you'll learn to:

◆ Add RPC objects to your model

◆ Determine which of the two graphics systems better suits your purpose

◆ Use the rendering engine inside Navisworks

Presenter Overview

Before we get too deep into creating visualization with Navisworks, let's take a few minutes to explore Presenter (Figure 9.1), see how it works at the conceptual level, and preview a few of the options.

Archive and Palette

Presenter is divided into two major components: the archive (Figure 9.2) on the left and the palette on the right. In principle, the defined items, such as lighting and materials, are contained in the archive. When one of the archive items is added to the scene, it will be displayed on the palette.

Three predefined archives are installed with Presenter and can be found on the Materials, Lighting, RPC, and Effects tabs: Recommended, Standard, and Templates. Note that these predefined archives cannot be renamed, added to, or deleted.

Recommended   Used for interactive navigation in Presenter, Recommended contains items for materials, lighting, effects, and rendering (but not RPC, or Rich Photorealistic Content). These items can also be fully rendered and will appear best when rendered with one of the photorealistic settings.

Standard   Standard contains items for materials, lighting, effects, rendering, and RPC. The items in this archive cannot be seen properly during interactive navigation but will appear when rendered with one of the photorealistic settings.

Templates   Any material, lighting, effect, RPC, or rendering may be used as a template, but the Templates archive has been provided with each type of item to give you a starting point.

FIGURE 9.1
Presenter interface

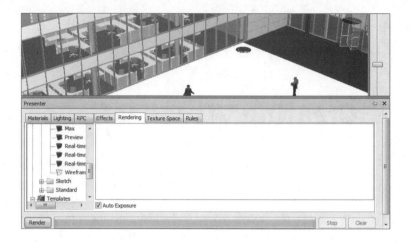

FIGURE 9.2
Presenter archive
(left) and palette
(right)

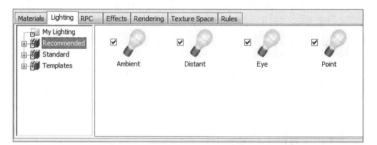

As you select your items (materials, lighting, effects, RPC, rendering) from the archives, you'll see them appear in the palette. You can select items by double-clicking, by using drag and drop, or by right-clicking the item and choosing Edit from the context menu. Since you cannot edit anything in the archive, as soon as you select Edit from the context menu, the item will appear in the palette so you can begin editing.

USER-DEFINED ARCHIVES

You'll notice a My Materials or other aptly named user-defined archive under each of the tabs for materials, lighting, RPC, and effects. This gives you a place to store user-defined or edited items. Once an item has been added to the palette and modified, you can use the user-defined archive to store your information. Simply drag and drop the item to the user-defined archive.

When you exit Navisworks, you'll be prompted as to whether you want to save your user archive, as shown here:

Clicking Yes will save your items so they are available in the next session of Navisworks.

Interface Options

The Interface options (choose Application ➤ Options ➤ Interface ➤ Display) give you several options to enhance your Navisworks and Presenter experience. You may want to use some of these settings to enhance performance or change settings based on your level of experience.

DISPLAY

The Display options, as shown in Figure 9.3, allow you to adjust the Navisworks display performance.

FIGURE 9.3
Display options

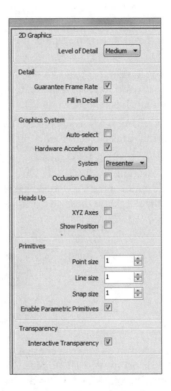

2D Graphics   With these options, you can adjust settings that will allow you to choose performance over fidelity—and by fidelity, we mean adherence to 2D detail:

Low   Low 2D fidelity but better rendering performance

Medium   Medium 2D fidelity and medium rendering performance (default option)

High   High 2D fidelity but low rendering performance

Detail   These two options can greatly affect the performance of Navisworks during navigation; by default, both options are checked:

Guarantee Frame Rate   Guarantees the frame rate specified, even if items have to be dropped from the scene. If this box is unchecked, the complete model will always be drawn no matter how long it takes (the frame rate may not be respected).

Fill In Detail   Fills in discarded details when navigation has stopped.

Graphics System   Navisworks supports two graphics systems: Presenter and Autodesk. These settings permit you to specify which graphics system you want to use as well as a few other key settings:

Auto-Select   To enable the System drop-down, you will have to clear this check box, which is checked by default. Navisworks will choose which graphics system to use based on your video card.

Hardware Acceleration   Select this check box to take advantage of OpenGL hardware acceleration on your video card, provided it is supported.

If you find that Navisworks becomes sluggish with this box checked, it may be that your video card does not support OpenGL hardware acceleration and you will need to deselect the check box.

System   The System drop-down allows you to choose between the default Presenter graphic system and its associated materials or the Autodesk graphics system and its associated materials (and options).

Occlusion Culling   Allows Navisworks to draw only visible objects and ignores objects located behind other objects. Selecting this check box can help improve performance.

Heads Up   Allows for an additional location to enable or disable the XYZ Axes or Position Readout (Show Position) display, as shown in Figure 9.4. You can also access this option from the Navigation Aids panel of the View tab; click HUD (Heads-Up Display). One of the new features for 2013 is that the toggle for the Grid Locations display is also located in the HUD dropdown.

FIGURE 9.4
The XYZ Axes
display

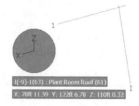

Primitives   In Primitives, you can change the size of Point, Line, and Snap as well as enable or disable parametric primitives. The Enable Parametric Primitives check box allows Navisworks to choose whether to render primitives during navigation. If the box is checked, they will be rendered and the level of detail will change as you change distance from the primitives.

Transparency   Transparency controls your interaction with transparent items during navigation. When this option is checked, transparent items will render along with everything else during navigation. When it is not checked, transparent items will only render after navigation has stopped. By default, this feature is enabled. Be careful with this option because it can greatly affect video card performance if your video card is not configured to handle transparent rendering. If you need transparent items to render during navigation, then select this check box, but otherwise, it's best to leave it unchecked.

DRIVERS

The Available Drivers area (Figure 9.5) lists all drivers that Navisworks can support. Deselecting any of the boxes will disable the driver and cause Navisworks to ignore it. By default, all drivers are selected.

Autodesk (DirectX 9), (DirectX 10), and (DirectX 11)   Supports the Autodesk graphics system and works with 2D and 3D geometry.

Autodesk (OpenGL)   Supports the Autodesk graphics system and works with 2D and 3D geometry.

Autodesk (DirectX 11 Software)   Supports the Autodesk graphics system and works with 2D and 3D geometry.

Autodesk (DirectX 10 Software)   Supports the Autodesk graphics system and works with 2D and 3D geometry.

Presenter (OpenGL)   Supports the Presenter graphics system and works only with 3D geometry.

Presenter (OpenGL Software)   Supports the Presenter graphics system and works only with 3D geometry. The is the default driver and it cannot be disabled.

FIGURE 9.5
Available drivers

AUTODESK

When using the Autodesk graphics system, use these settings to make adjustments to effects and materials:

GRAPHICS SYSTEMS: PRESENTER VS. AUTODESK

The Presenter materials are only available when using the graphics system in Presenter mode (using Presenter materials from the Presenter palette). Also, while in Presenter mode, you have access to many materials in real time, meaning that you can see a representation of them once they are applied. When using the Autodesk graphics system, you'll have to create a quick preview rendering to see the applied materials. Real-time navigation is supported by both graphics systems.

One reason to choose the Autodesk graphics system involves importing FBX® files. The consistent materials brought over from the FBX plug-in will utilize the Autodesk graphics system instead of the Presenter graphics system. This will help you to deliver a better rendering of an FBX file that has predefined Autodesk materials.

In addition, if you are using the new project browser and 2D sheets, they'll also use the Autodesk graphics system for 2D display.

In many cases, using Auto-Select will meet your needs and help Navisworks to determine which graphics system is best to use.

Autodesk Effects   Autodesk Effects defines three options:

Basic Materials   Default option; materials appear similar to how they would in the real world.

Gooch   Materials appear warm or cool instead of dark or light; they may be difficult to see in a shadowed or realistic display.

Phong   Materials appear smoother and more realistic when lighting is applied.

Autodesk Materials   These settings allow you to make decisions as to what level of texture resolution to use, the size of the texture dimensions, whether to enable highlighting or reflecting, and other settings that may improve the performance of your video card.

Multi Sample Anti Aliasing (MSAA)   Antialiasing is used to smooth the edges of geometry. The higher the number, the smoother the geometry but the longer your rendering will take. Also, if your video card does not support MSAA, you'll want to use a lower MSAA value.

Stereo   The stereo options allow you to toggle on and off stereoscopic viewing. This means that a model can be viewed in 3D if the proper glasses are worn. This option is only available if your graphics card has Quad Buffer stereo support. Many graphics cards have a setting to enable this feature. Stereoscopic viewing can only be enabled when the perspective mode is active. When navigating the model with stereo enabled, point-based navigation modes (such as orbit) will project items close to the focal point of the screen. Other navigation modes (walk/fly) project items between you and the camera in front of the screen.

PRESENTER PROFILES

In Chapter 1, "Getting to Know Navisworks," we talked about Presenter having different profiles that give you flexibility to control the complexity of how Presenter is used based on your knowledge.

For the most part, Basic, the default setting, will work well. However, if you find that you need to increase your level of complexity, choose Application ➢ Options ➢ Tools ➢ Presenter, and from the Profiles drop-down list, select the Standard or Advanced profile.

Standard provides more Presenter features than Basic, such as greater access to menu items for materials, lights, and render styles.

Advanced gives you access to the advanced Presenter features, such as extra materials, lights, and render styles.

Applying Materials

Materials are the first step in giving color and texture to your models in Navisworks. As you most likely noticed, most models come into Navisworks with some sort of color or material already applied. This is because some materials transfer from the native application (such as the Autodesk® AutoCAD® or MicroStation® applications). But the materials may not appear as desired for rendering or even presentation purposes.

Adding Materials to the Scene

It's not terribly hard to add materials to items. Essentially, there are two methods for assigning materials to your items: dragging and dropping or using the context menu. No matter which method suits your style, the first step is to add materials to your Materials palette, as shown in Figure 9.6.

FIGURE 9.6
Adding to the Materials palette

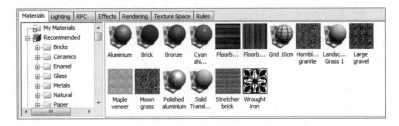

Drag and Drop

Selecting your materials from the palette and then using drag and drop, you can add materials to your items in the three following ways:

- Items directly in the scene (individually selected items)

- Items in the selection tree (individually or group selections)

- Items in search or selection sets (individually or group selections)

As you grab the materials and move toward your item, notice the + symbol that appears, as shown in Figure 9.7, when using drag and drop.

FIGURE 9.7
Material being dragged and dropped directly in the scene

This indicates where the material is being added. Once you release the mouse, the material will be added, as you can see in Figure 9.8.

FIGURE 9.8
Grid material added
to curtain wall

Assigning Materials from the Context Menu

Another method for assigning materials is to right-click an item or group, either from the Presenter palette or directly in the scene (although many users find this method less expedient) and then apply the material.

To use this method, you must have selected an item or group of items and the material, as shown in Figure 9.9. You then right-click and have the option to apply the material to the selected items only or to all instances of the selection.

FIGURE 9.9
Context menu for
assigning materials

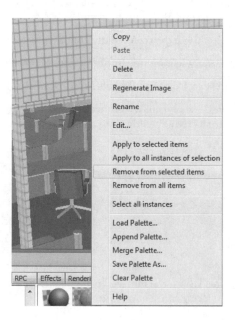

Removing Materials

To remove a material from an item, locate the item in the selection tree or, in the scene, right-click and choose Presenter ➢ Remove Material, as shown in Figure 9.10.

FIGURE 9.10
Choose Presenter ➢
Remove Material.

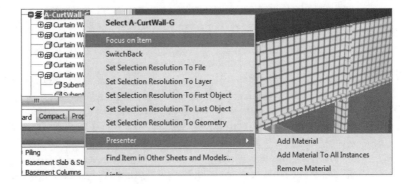

While in concept removing a material may seem easy, that may not always be the case. Removing a material may depend on where in the model the material was applied and how you are selecting the material to remove it.

For example, say you remove a material at the top level but notice there is another material applied at the subentity level, as shown in Figure 9.11. This could be because the material was added later, it's a different material, or for many other reasons. The point is that the material was not removed because it was added at a different level in the tree and will have to be removed using the context menu.

FIGURE 9.11
Example of
subentity material
that remained
after top tree-
level material was
removed

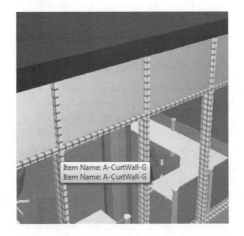

There may come a time when you simply need to remove a material from all items instead of trying to find where it might exist in the scene. If you right-click a material in the Materials palette, you'll find a few useful tools:

- Remove From All Items

- Select All Instances

- Remove From Selected items

If no material is applied, none of these tools will be available.

 **Real World Scenario**

CLEAR PALETTE

Be careful of the Clear Palette tool. Selecting Clear Palette from the context menu can sometimes do more harm than good. If you use it, it will remove all materials from the palette as well as any that have been applied to the model. If this is what you're after, then great, but if you were only trying to make a clean slate on the palette (removing all materials from the palette and keeping them assigned), you might want to reconsider.

We have seen many projects derailed because of the Clear Palette command. For example, recently, one of our colleagues spent a great deal of time applying materials to a project in preparation for a rendering and then used Clear Palette, thinking, incorrectly, that it would help clean up the unused materials. Before he knew it, all the materials were gone. Out of frustration, he closed the model for the day since all of his hours of effort were apparently lost. He also saved his changes along the way. Oops.

If you happen to use Clear Palette unintentionally, then quickly use the Undo function (Ctrl+Z) to return all materials back to your palette, provided you have not closed your Navisworks file right after using Clear Palette (in that case, it might be too late to save yourself).

The Undo function will also reapply your lost materials. Everything will be right in the model again.

If you find yourself having saved the model after you made a terrible error, don't panic. All is not lost. Navisworks still has its Auto-Save file. You can access these Auto-Saves from the Autosave directory. To find the directory, select Application ➤ Options ➤ General ➤ Auto-Save. The directory is listed. Simply open the directory, grab the most recent Auto-Save, and resume your work.

On large models with many materials applied, it may first take a while to remove the materials and then even longer to reapply those materials. Here's a quick example of when Clear Palette, intentionally used, sped a project along. Recently, one of the authors received a large project with tons of materials that were applied at the subobject level (more than two item levels deep). He needed to remove a few of the materials to clean up the project and add a few new ones to complete a new rendering. Once he got started, he decided that it would be much easier to remove all the materials and apply them from the start. So, he used Clear Palette to remove all the materials from the palette as well as from the items. Doing so saved a huge amount of time in removal and the reapplication was quick, too.

Clear Palette may not be something that you use often, but being aware of its uses and pitfalls could save your project.

SEARCH SETS TO THE RESCUE

If you see common sublevel items and you want to remove the Presenter materials from them, you can use search sets to find them all. One of the unique properties of search sets is that they capture the items at the geometry level. Because of this, even when items have Presenter materials attached at different levels, search sets can be used to remove them from all levels when the context menu is used in the scene view or the selection tree. This is not true of materials applied to a search set itself.

Editing Materials

Materials cannot be edited in the archives. You must add them to the palette or to the My Materials folder.

For the most part, editing materials is a matter of personal and project preference. To access the editor, shown in Figure 9.12, you can right-click any material and select Edit, or double-click and the editor will open. From there, you can begin to make changes as needed by using the sliders or manual inputs.

Edited materials are saved with the NWF or NWD file or in the Navisworks palette file (NWP). NWD files will only contain material information if you use the Publish tool and select the Materials check box.

With materials that have access to image files, you can change the path to your own image file so that you can further customize the material to suit your needs.

FIGURE 9.12
Material Editor

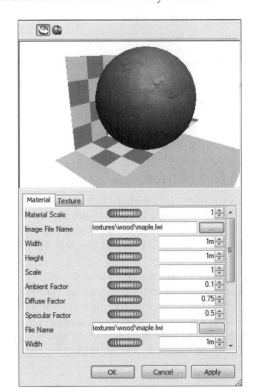

The NWP file allows you to save your list of materials into an external file. Any changes or modifications that you made to the materials in the palette are saved with the NWP file. This gives you the chance to create a palette that you can share with other team members or experiment with certain colors or standards. To save an NWP file, right-click the palette and select Save Palette As from the context menu (see Figure 9.13).

FIGURE 9.13
Select Save Palette
As from the context
menu.

Let's practice adding materials, using the following example:

1. Launch the Navisworks Manage application or Navisworks Simulate (but not Freedom).

2. Open the file c09-materials.nwd.

3. Open Presenter.

4. Click the Materials tab.

5. From the Recommended archive, add materials to the palette for the following:

    ◆ Glass: Window Glass

    ◆ Metals: Aluminum

6. Add the Aluminum material to the Curtain Wall selection set.

7. Add the Window Glass material to the External Doors and Windows selection sets. You can do this by dragging and dropping the item to the selection set. You can also accomplish this action by selecting the selection set, clicking the Standards tab of the selection tree, right-clicking one of the highlighted items, hovering over Presenter in the context menu, and clicking Add To All Instances.

Lighting the Model

Lighting in Navisworks is essential to give you control over the feel of your model. The last thing you want is a dark and uncomfortable model. With lighting, you are able to add elements such as Ambient or Eye lighting to help bring warmth to the model or specific scene. Without even the simplest lighting elements added, your model could be left in the dark, literally (see Figure 9.14).

As with the other categories in Presenter, Lighting has several components. Recommended, Standard, and Templates each contain useful information.

You are able to use the same processes that you've learned: dragging and dropping from the archives to the palette or double-clicking an item to move it into the palette. One key difference between materials and lighting is that materials are applied to objects and lighting is controlled by simply turning it on and off from the palette. That's the purpose of the check box that appears next to added lighting elements.

FIGURE 9.14
Model with no
lighting applied

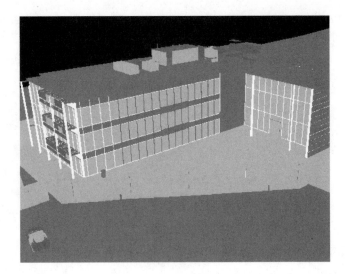

FIGURE 9.14
Model with no
lighting applied

Lighting Types

Navisworks has six types of lighting that you can select from that will appear in both interactive and photorealistic rendering:

Ambient   Applies a general background light.

Distant   Applies a distant directional light—you can choose a location.

Eye   Located at the individual viewpoint level.

Point   Individual point lights—you can specify locations. This light will shine in all directions. A standard light bulb would be a point light.

Spot   Directional light, similar to Point, but you can control the direction. A flood light is an example of a spot light.

Sun   Simulates the light from the sun. You can add information to include position for Presenter for calculate azimuth (arc of the horizon) and altitude for you. Having access to these settings will help you to produce a more realistic Sun setting.

Three additional types of lighting are only visible after a photorealistic rendering has been completed. The following lights, when added, can increase rendering times:

Projector   Allows you to select a file to "project" onto surfaces.

Sky   Helps you to simulate settings for the sky (Figure 9.15). You can add information to include a position for Presenter to calculate the azimuth (arc of the horizon) and altitude for you. Having access to these settings will help you to produce a more realistic Sky setting.

Goniometric   Allows you to use industry-standard file types such as CIE, IES, CIB, and LDT in Presenter.

FIGURE 9.15
Model lit by
Accurate Sky And
Sun

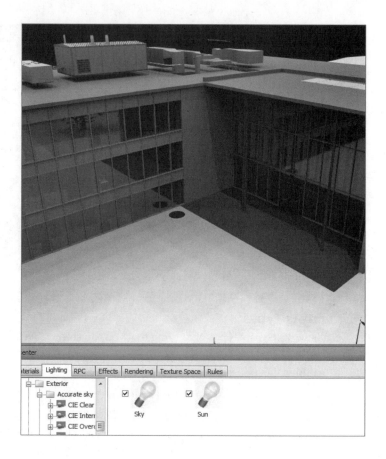

Adding Lights to the Model

Now that you have a basic understanding of the lighting types, you can use them in the model. Ambient, Distant, and Eye provide a fair amount of easy lighting right from the start.

From there, you have the option to explore other lights and see how they affect the environment. It comes down to what you need to accomplish your rendering goals. And sometimes, it's just plain fun to play around with the effects that various lights have to offer.

When adding your lights to the model, you should keep in mind a few factors. For example, you might want to control color, intensity, and possibly location (Point, Distant, Projector, and Spot all have location settings), along with some of the other options for lights (see Figure 9.16).

The Color and Intensity options can be used in combination to create custom lighting for scenes. There are already a few preset combinations that take advantage of intensity and color, as shown in Figure 9.17.

Using a light's Location tool can help you hone in on and enhance a scene. Suppose you want to use the Spot light to shine on a specific place, like the back of a desk, as shown in Figure 9.18.

FIGURE 9.16
Light Editor for
Distant with
Presenter in
Standard mode

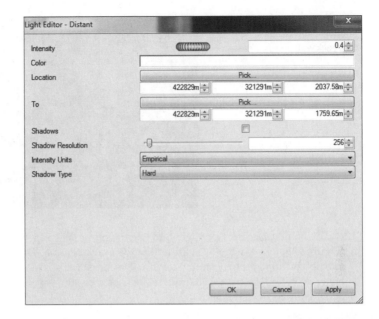

FIGURE 9.16
Light Editor for
Distant with
Presenter in
Standard mode

FIGURE 9.17
Red With Green
Spot lighting
applied to the
model

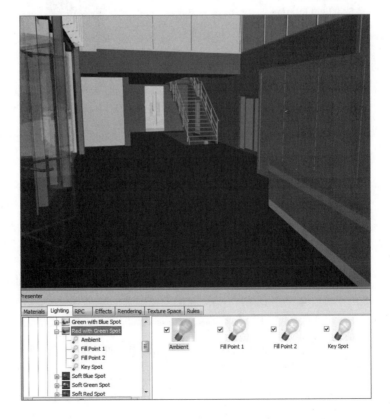

FIGURE 9.18
Spot light shining
on a back wall

FIGURE 9.18
Spot light shining
on a back wall

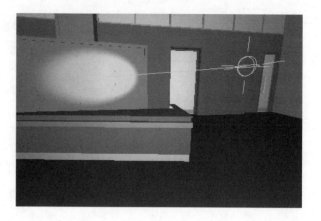

You could place the Spot light and use the numerical adjustments or the physical gizmo (Figure 9.19) to move the light around to the exact location. The gizmo gives you a hand icon to help you adjust the location. You can also adjust the cone size to change the size of the light being projected. Being able to update the cone size allows you to control the size of the light being emitted from the Spot light.

FIGURE 9.19
Spot light location
adjustment gizmo

In general, lighting can be added by individual components (Spot, Distant, Eye, and so on). Or you could use Standard Light Studio, which has all of the default lights. It can also be a faster way to add predefined lights to the scene.

Let's explore lighting a little further by trying out the following example:

1. Launch the Navisworks Manage application or Navisworks Simulate (but not Freedom).

2. Open the file c09-lighting.nwd.

3. Open Presenter. Make sure you are using the Presenter display and not the Autodesk display.

4. Click the Lighting tab. Notice that your model is very dark. That's because you need to add a few new lights to complete the lighting for the exterior color scheme.

5. From the Recommended archive, add lighting to the palette for the following:

    ◆ Ambient

    ◆ Eye

As an alternative, you could add the Standard Light Studio.

6. Now change your viewpoint to the Plant Room.

7. Add a Point light to the room and edit the lighting settings to use the color Red. Notice how the scene changes.

LIGHTING COMBINATIONS

As you're working through the various types of lights, keep in mind that you can put them together to form unique combinations to help you achieve your desired lighting results. A lighting combination may already exist in the archives; you only need to take the time to look through them and use a few of the lighting permutations to see how they fit your needs.

Advanced Lighting Techniques

There are a few additional things to consider, such as shadows and HDRIs, for those times when you need to get more out of your lighting tools.

SHADOWS

Lighting types for Point, Distant, Spot, Sky, Sun, Projector, and Goniometric lights can have shadow settings applied to them.

Consider very carefully whether you should use shadows for all lights. If you aren't careful, you may end up with too many lights and objects in shadow. Also, your rendering may take too long to produce. We have found that using shadows is best for smaller models, small scenes, or strategically placed lights.

You will have to be in Standard or Advanced mode in Presenter to edit the shadows for these lighting types.

In addition to choosing whether to apply shadows at the lighting level, you can also control lighting at the item level. In some cases, this can grant you great flexibility and reduce confusion in the model when you have enabled shadows. Let's take a quick look at how to change the settings for shadows at the item level:

1. Select an item or group of items.

2. Right-click and select Presenter ➤ Shadows from the context menu.

3. Make your selection to control the shadows, as shown in Figure 9.20. Choose from one of three options:

   ◆ On: Enables shadows.

   ◆ Off: Disables shadows.

   ◆ Inherit: Allows the object to inherit its shadow option from the parent object (directly above) in the selection tree. This means if the object above is set to On and the object below is set to Inherit, then it will also be turned On because of the parent object.

FIGURE 9.20
Selecting shadows
in the context menu

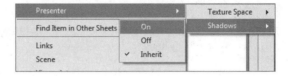

HIGH DYNAMIC RANGE IMAGES

As you work through lighting, you may have noticed that some of the materials and scene lighting might not appear as realistic as you would want them to. Take, for example, the image in Figure 9.21. It was rendered using the basic lighting modes, which in most applications will suit most renderings and model applications just fine.

FIGURE 9.21
Rendering using
normal lighting

But there comes a time when you need to get more out of a scene. When you need materials to appear with more realistic lighting, Point lighting needs to have proper shadows and the image should appear to wrap the scene to provide an overall more natural feel.

That's where using the high dynamic range image (HDRI), sometimes referred to as image-based lighting, can be your ally. See Figure 9.22. HDRI allows materials to reflect light and images onto other materials. The model is put into a sphere with all light being directed toward it, allowing the light to bounce. Only the environment lighting is HDRI. Also keep in mind that using an HDRI environment will remove any previous lighting added to the scene. You can add it back as needed.

To use HDRI, select Environment Light Studio from the Recommended archive. You will sacrifice rendering time for quality, but in many cases, this can be worth the time and effort.

You can also add other predefined HDRI lighting schemes from Standard ➤ Environment ➤ Empirical. This gives you more options to create variations in your renderings. You can also customize these by double-clicking the environment from the palette and then clicking Edit. This gives you the chance to change the image that the HDRI is using.

FIGURE 9.22
Rendering using
HDRI

Enhancing Scenes with RPC

Rich Photorealistic Content, or RPC (Figure 9.23), enables the addition of 2D or 3D geometry for the purpose of enhancing a scene for rendering. The geometry could be things like furniture, cars, people, equipment, or other elements to help enhance the scene. They usually do not have much purpose beyond helping to enhance the scene.

Although only a few default items come with Navisworks, a number of third-party manufacturers specialize in making RPC content to add to models.

FIGURE 9.23
RPC elements added
to the model

It's easy to add RPCs to a model, and they quickly provide an added effect.

Adding RPCs

Your first step in getting an RPC into the model is to add it to the palette using the double-click or drag-and-drop method. Once you have your instance added to the palette, you can add that element in places where it's needed. There are two ways to add RPCs to the model:

◆ To drag and drop, select the RPC from the palette and drag and drop it into the scene. Wherever you release the cursor is where the RPC will be placed.

◆ Right-click the palette and select Add Instance; then select a point where the RPC will be placed.

Notice that as you add multiple RPCs of the same element, only one instance exists in the palette. In most cases, this will be okay. But if you have to make changes to this RPC to properties like Rotation or Scale, those changes will apply to all the occurrences in the model. Keep that in mind as you are adding your RPC items in the future. If you only see a man in a circle in your RPC palette, you will have to search for the RPC image. The default location for users of Windows Vista and Windows 7 is C:/Program Files/Autodesk/Navisworks Manage 2013/ presenter/lads/layla_data/textures/RPC.

Deleting, Moving, and Editing RPCs

You may have noticed that once you place an RPC, you cannot select it as you would a normal item in Navisworks. Clicking the RPC only highlights it in the RPC tab of Presenter. You might also have noticed that you cannot use the Delete key to remove an RPC element if you placed too many or put one in the wrong spot and just want to remove it. In addition to using the Undo function, you have three options for deleting or removing the RPC:

Remove   If you select the RPC and right-click it, you will notice a Remove option in the context menu. Select this option if you wish to remove only this one RPC.

Remove All Instances   If you right-click the RPC in the palette, you'll see on the context menu the option Remove All Instances Of The RPC. Selecting this option will remove all of the selected RPCs from the model. The RPC will remain on the palette for you to use again as needed.

Delete   Also available on the palette's context menu is Delete, which removes all instances of the RPC and removes the RPC from the palette.

There is no expedient way to remove all of the RPCs from the model other than removing them from the model one RPC at a time. Materials and Lighting have a Clear Palette tool, but RPC does not. Keep that in mind as you are adding RPC items.

Just as deleting was not as straightforward as it appeared, moving may not be either. Right-click the RPC and select Pick Position, as shown in Figure 9.24.

FIGURE 9.24
Using Pick Position
to move an RPC

After you select Pick Position, the curser will change to a target, allowing you to select a new position for the RPC. Continue the right-click and Pick Position operations to move the RPC around until you have the correct placement.

You may have noticed on the context menu for the RPC palette that there is no Edit option. Does that mean that you cannot edit your RPC elements? No, you just need to double-click them to open the RPC Editor (Figure 9.25), where you can make changes.

FIGURE 9.25
RPC Editor

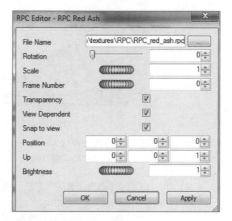

The RPC Editor is especially useful when the path for the File Name field needs to be changed or you need to customize settings like Rotation or Scale.

CREATING NWD FILES WITH RPC CONTENT

When you're using the Publish To NWD dialog box, RPC content is not saved with the file. This is due to copyright constraints with many of the types of RPC content that are used within Navisworks. The default Navisworks content will publish, but any other RPC content won't.

RPC content can enhance a scene. In this brief exercise, we'll explore adding RPC elements to the scene and manipulating them:

1. Launch the Navisworks Manage application or Navisworks Simulate (but not Freedom).

2. Open the file c09-rpc.nwd.

3. Open Presenter.

4. Open Saved Viewpoints and open Plant Room.

5. Select the RPC tab. From the archives, choose Standard ➢ 3D People and add RPC C1 Tony to the palette.

6. Add Tony RPC to the scene in a location similar to the one shown in Figure 9.26.

FIGURE 9.26
Default position for
Tony RPC

7. Double-click Tony RPC in the palette to edit his rotation so that he is looking at his equipment. Change the rotation setting to 240 degrees; see Figure 9.27.

FIGURE 9.27
Tony RPC looking at
equipment

Completing the Scene with Effects

Effects in Navisworks are essential to completing any good scene or rendering. You can apply background images or scene views to enhance your rendering or use foregrounds to add effects like fog or snow to the rendering (see Figure 9.28).

FIGURE 9.28
Example of a background applied

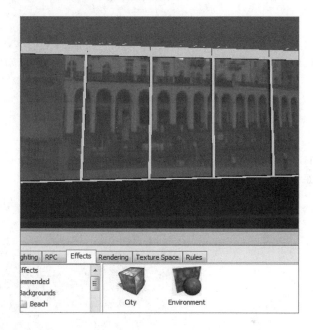

Backgrounds, foregrounds, and environments give you quick and easy access to effects that you can use in combination with each other or independently. As with everything else in the archives, you can double-click or drag and drop to move an effect from the archive to the palette. Explore and understand what each effect does, and then customize an effect so that it suits the needs of your project.

Backgrounds and Foregrounds

Background effects are used to change or enhance the background in Navisworks (see Figure 9.29). You can have only one background added to the palette at a time. Because some files associated with backgrounds can be rather large, Navisworks can sometimes take a while to process the addition or removal of a background from the palette.

Foreground effects are used to enhance the rendering in the foreground, as shown in Figure 9.30. You will not be able to see your foreground effects until you render your project. You can have only one foreground added to the palette at a time.

FIGURE 9.29
Twilight Overcast
background

FIGURE 9.30
Scene with Twilight
Overcast back-
ground and Snow
foreground

Environments

Environments give you a way to use predefined image mappings—a single image or a group of images—to link a scene together in order to build an environment. Figure 9.31 shows the Sky environment.

When you first add an environment to the palette, you might notice that it does not show up in the scene. That is because environments are essentially an extension of backgrounds. Therefore, you need to add the environment from the Backgrounds folder when using one of the predefined environments. These elements are codependent on each other, and there are settings in backgrounds that help environments to function.

FIGURE 9.31
Sky environment

Let's take a quick look at how to create the Sky environment used in Figure 9.31:

1. In the Effects archive, locate Recommended and select Environment Effect from the Backgrounds folder. Add it to the palette either by double-clicking or using drag and drop. It will replace any existing background you might have already added.

2. Move down to the Environments folder under Recommended. Expand Panorama and add Sky to the palette by double-clicking or using drag and drop.

3. Sky should now appear in the Presenter display as the environment in the background.

You can use foreground effects in combination with environments as well.

So far in this chapter, you have learned about materials, lighting, and RPC elements. Now, let's look at the whole scene to add a few effects to the overall model:

1. Launch the Navisworks Manage application or Navisworks Simulate (but not Freedom).

2. Open the file c09-effects.nwd.

3. Open Presenter.

4. Select the Effects tab. From Standard, click the + for Backgrounds, and then select Exterior, Horizon to add Hazy to the palette.

5. From Standard, click the + for Foreground, select Nature, and then select Snow to add Snow to the palette.

6. You will have to render your project to see your final results, so select Render at the bottom of Presenter to see your results. A render style has already been defined for you; all you have to do is click Render and wait for it to complete. Your final results should look like Figure 9.32.

FIGURE 9.32
Rendered image
with Hazy and
Snow applied

Rendering

Navisworks contains its own rendering tools that let you create realistic images directly from the model. These images can be exported as animations or image files and used for a variety of applications. Within Navisworks, you have access to several render styles. See Figure 9.33 and Figure 9.34 for examples.

FIGURE 9.33
Exterior high-
quality render with
materials and light-
ing applied

Consider this your chance to take advantage of all the work you have put in with materials, lighting, and effects. It all culminates with using the render styles within Navisworks to complete the rendering of your scene. Whether you want to create an animation for exporting or simply create some rendered images, now you're ready.

Render Styles

Navisworks comes with several predefined render styles. You can also create your own and add them to My Render Styles or modify them once you have added the render style to the palette.

You can have only one render style on the palette at a time. When you add another, it will replace the one you previously had. So, keep that in mind if you've made changes on the palette. You might want to add your style to My Render Styles before adding a new one to the palette.

We encourage you to explore and get to know each of the render styles in order to form your personal preference.

RECOMMENDED

Recommended contains only three render styles. These do a great job and you will probably find yourself using them most of the time:

Low Quality   Very low quality; uses no reflections or transparencies and completes in a short time. Good for trying to see a preview of lighting, effects, and materials. Not recommended for a final rendering.

Medium Quality   Gives you a first glimpse into reflections and transparencies. Works well as a prefinal preview.

High Quality   Takes the longest amount of time to complete but includes all materials, reflections, effects, lighting, and items.

If no render style is on the palette, Navisworks defaults to High Quality.

STANDARD

Many Standard styles come with Navisworks (see Figure 9.35). These include Cartoon Sketch, Oil Paint, and Mosaic Pattern. For the most part, the render styles in Standard do not produce photorealistic renderings and are a combination of shaded or vector-based render styles (see the next section, "Templates").

Completing a render when using a Standard style may require multiple passes and increased rendering time.

TEMPLATES

The Templates archive contains five types of render styles that you can use as a basis to create your own styles, as shown in Figure 9.36.

FIGURE 9.36
The Templates archive render styles

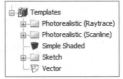

◆ Photorealistic (Raytrace): Use for photorealistic where much of the scene or model is obscured; think of an interior rendering.

◆ Photorealistic (Scanline): Use for photorealistic where much of the scene or model is visible; think of an exterior site rendering.

◆ Simple Shaded: Simple rendering style where shading is needed and textures and transparencies are not required.

◆ Sketch: Base for basic Sketch style of rendering and may require multiple passes to complete a rendering.

◆ Vector: Renders in wireframe.

RENDERING TIME

When choosing your render style, pay careful consideration to the trade-off between time and quality. Some render styles are better suited only to small models or scenes, like many of the Standard styles, whereas others work fine just about everywhere. In many applications, just using the Recommended render styles will get you what you need.

But if you do decide to create a render that is going to take some time to create, especially when exporting a long animation sequence where each frame needs to be rendered, you may want to consider using a second computer, if it's available. Having access to a second computer allows you to optimize the system resources so you can maximize your video card and RAM for rendering and still continue on with your day-to-day activities on your primary computer.

Click the Auto Exposure check box, located at the bottom of the palette, to automatically balance brightness and contrast when creating a rendering. The Auto Exposure check box becomes necessary when using settings for Sun, Sky, and HDRI rendering. If Navisworks detects Sun and Sky in your model and Auto Exposure is not enabled, you will be prompted to turn it on. Auto Exposure can increase your rendering time.

Final Rendering

Finally, it's time to take what you've learned in this chapter and put together a complete rendering:

1. Launch the Navisworks Manage application or Navisworks Simulate (but not Freedom).

2. Open the file c09-presenter.nwd.

3. Open Presenter and select the Rendering tab.

4. The model with all the materials, lighting, and effects has been set for you to render this view. Select Render. Wait for the render to complete.

5. Let's render a second view. Go to Saved Viewpoints and select Reception 2.

6. You will have to enable the proper lighting set for this viewpoint. Select the Lighting tab and check the Reception Light option.

7. Since you're doing an interior scene, go to the Effects tab and delete Snow.

8. Return to the Render tab and change Render Style to Medium Quality and check the Auto Exposure option.

9. After the render is complete, change Render Style back to High Quality and deselect the Auto Exposure option.

10. Now export your rendered image. From Output ➢ Visuals, select Rendered Image.

11. Use JPEG as your image type and set the remaining settings as you like (Use View for Size works well). Save your image and take a look at your creation.

Additional Presenter Tools

There are a couple of additional tools in Presenter that help enhance the rendering abilities within Navisworks: Texture Space and Rules. While not overly complex to learn, these additional elements will help you fine-tune your renderings.

Texture Space

Texture Space is essential when you need to fine-tune or map a material or texture to an object. For example, say you have applied a texture or material to a wall and the material is not lining up the way you need. You can use Texture Space to further refine the shape of the texture to better align with the object.

Navisworks works with the following Texture Space parameters:

◆ Box (the default)

◆ Plane

◆ Cylinder

◆ Sphere

◆ Explicit

However, if you are not achieving your desired results by simply changing Texture Space, you can further edit each item to refine the shape.

Take, for example, the piping shown in Figure 9.37. The material (not that you would ever use grid on a pipe—this is just for illustration purposes) was applied with Texture Space set to Box. Notice that the material is not able to wrap around the piping.

If you change Texture Space to Cylinder, the material is able to wrap around the piping, as shown in Figure 9.38.

FIGURE 9.37
Grid material
applied with
Texture Space set
to Box

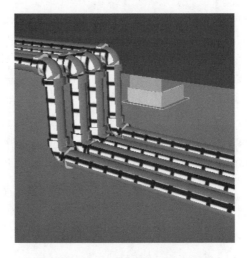

FIGURE 9.38
Grid material
applied with
Texture Space set to
Cylinder

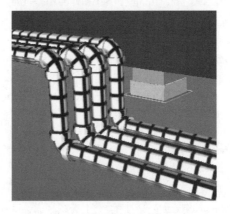

While you can change the Texture Space setting of several objects at once, you cannot edit multiple items at the same time. They have to be edited individually.

To change the Texture Space setting of objects, select them individually or in groups from the selection tree or sets. Once you've selected the objects, you have two options for applying or changing the Texture Space setting. The most obvious is to select your objects and use the Texture Space tab in Presenter.

The second and sometimes more efficient method is to use the right-click method when selecting objects. The Texture Space command on the context menu lets you make your changes without having to open Presenter (see Figure 9.39). The only tool missing is Edit; you still have to use Presenter if you need to edit your individual items.

FIGURE 9.39
Changing Texture
Space with the con-
text menu

Editing items begins with changing them from Box to one of the other settings. Edit is not available while an item is still set to Box. First, select a single item, and choose Edit from the Texture Space tab. Doing so opens the Texture Space Editor dialog box, as shown in Figure 9.40.

If you get too far out of alignment, you can always use Reset to bring the texture or material back to the original starting point.

FIGURE 9.40

Texture Space Editor dialog box

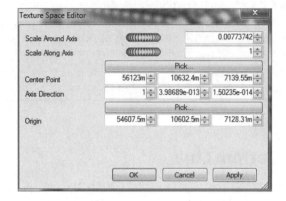

Rules

The Rules tab (Figure 9.41) of Presenter aids you in applying materials. You can set up defined categories and search through the model to apply materials instead of having to drag and drop materials to individual components. This also saves time when you update a model because you only need to reapply the rules instead of reapplying the materials.

FIGURE 9.41

Presenter's Rules tab

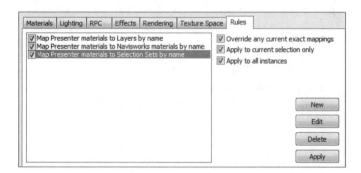

You can create custom rules as well as save the NWP file for future use on other projects.

You can rename materials in the palette to match items in selection sets and then use one of the rules to apply materials. This approach is especially efficient if you use similar selection sets on several projects.

DOWNLOAD ARCHIVE

You may notice as you work through the various tabs in Presenter that there is an option when you right-click to download an archive for materials, lighting, RPCs, effects, and rendering.

When you select Download Archive, you will be taken to an external website, where you can access various items to enhance your renderings. Some items are free of charge, whereas others have a fee. (This site is not a part of Navisworks but the company Lightworks has been a partner with Autodesk for years.)

In many cases with the materials, HDRI environments, RPC elements, textures, and other items, you can enhance your Navisworks renderings in additional ways.

Once the archives are downloaded, you can add them to My Materials, My Lighting, My RPC, My Effects, and My Render Styles for future access.

The Bottom Line

Add RPC objects to your model.   With RPC objects, you have a chance to improve the visual appeal of your model or scene for rendering. You can add furniture, trees, people, vehicles, equipment, or other items as needed. When rendered, they usually appear visually appealing and help augment a scene.

> **Master It**   Adding RPCs can be quick and easy. What are the two ways that you can add an RPC to your model?

Determine which of the two graphics systems better suits your purpose.   Navisworks utilizes two distinctly different graphics systems, the Navisworks graphics system (Presenter) and the Autodesk graphics system. Each one has its own advantages and disadvantages; Presenter is the default system.

> **Master It**   Explain the key difference between the Navisworks graphics system and the Autodesk graphics system.

Use the rendering engine inside Navisworks.   Navisworks contains its own rendering tools, which you can use to create realistic images directly from the model. These images can be exported as animations or image files and used for a variety of applications. Within Navisworks, you have access to several render styles.

> **Master It**   How many render styles can be combined in the palette to produce an accurate rendering?

Chapter 10

Animating Objects

In Chapter 5, "Model Snapshots: Viewpoints, Animations, and Sections" you created simple animations by stitching viewpoints together or by recording your navigations through the model. This chapter introduces you to animating objects and cameras in your Autodesk® Navisworks® 2013 model by using the Animator module. With Animator, you can bring your model to life by creating animations that allow you to further interact and better understand sequences and object movements. For example, you can animate the heavy machinery on a construction site to visualize the path and identify any obstacles in the way. For tall structures, you can animate the concrete slipforms or even the "jump" of a tower crane. In a tight site condition, you can animate the material delivery to ensure that your laydown areas are properly located and within easy reach of the equipment. With Animator, there are enormous opportunities to expand and improve the impact of your model.

In addition to interacting with objects, you can animate cameras throughout your model to create custom view sequences. You can use this approach to create fly-through animations that fully capture the project scope or depict the path of the user on the site. Furthermore, by using the sectioning tools, you can animate the section planes to show a progressive cut through the model. This allows you to create exciting animations that can add impact and provide a better understanding of your model presentation.

To enhance the overall experience, you can render the animations with materials and lights to create Audio Video Interleave (AVI) movies that can be used for marketing or training purposes. These and other best practices are showcased in this chapter and are meant to advance your use of Navisworks by challenging you to look for new opportunities and workflows outside the standard recommendations. As you continue to build and develop these skills that lead to mastery of Navisworks, remember that the optimum efficiency of this application lies in leveraging all the various workflows and functionalities described in this book.

In this chapter, you'll learn to:

◆ Create a simple animation

◆ Manipulate geometry

◆ Export animations

Animator Overview

Animator allows you to create detailed animations by defining the movement of individual objects or cameras within your Navisworks scene. Creating camera animations is similar to the viewpoint animation process discussed in Chapter 5. However, with the Animator tools, you have a larger degree of control and can combine other animations to create more compelling sequences. For object manipulation, the movements can be simple translations of objects to a different position; changes in rotation or object scale, transparency, and color shifts; or a combination of all. In Chapter 11, "Giving Objects Life and Action with Scripter," we'll explore how to add even more realism and interaction by scripting animations together and triggering them from a variety of activities.

The Animator module behaves similarly to other modules in Navisworks: It's a dockable window that you can arrange in multiple configurations. To open the Animator window, click the Animator icon on the Tools panel of the Home tab. We recommend that you dock the window at the bottom of your screen for easy access. In addition to the Animator window, a typical workflow requires the use of the selection tree and the Selection Sets window. Take a few minutes to organize your desktop so that all windows can easily be accessed. In this chapter, we'll be referencing the file c10_Meadowgate_Animator.nwd.

With the Animator window open, let's explore the layout in greater detail (Figure 10.1). You'll notice that it's divided into two panes. The left pane contains the scene view and scene controls. The right pane contains the timeline view. Spread across the top of both panes is the Animator toolbar.

FIGURE 10.1
Animator module

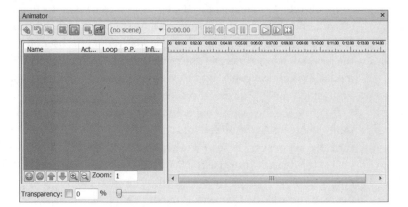

As you define your animation, the animator tree view will list the components of a typical animation. This includes the sets of objects to be animated, any camera viewpoints, and the section plane views. In addition, the animator tree view provides a hierarchy for easily creating and organizing animations. At the bottom of the animator tree view are controls used to add, delete, reorder, and modify the timescale zoom. Using the existing file, let's examine the scene view in greater detail by following these steps:

1. In the Animator window, click the Add icon 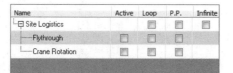 and choose Add Scene from the context menu. A new object named Scene 1 is displayed in the scene view.

2. Double-click the scene name and replace it with **Flythrough**.

3. Using the same procedure from step 1, create a second scene and rename it **Crane Rotation**.

4. To help categorize these scenes, create a scene folder by selecting the Add Scene Folder option from the Add pop-up menu. Rename this folder `Site Logistics`.

5. To associate the Flythrough scene to this new folder, select the scene and drag and drop it into the `Site Logistics` folder. Do the same for the Crane Rotation object. You should have a folder with two scenes (Figure 10.2).

FIGURE 10.2
Scene folder structure

Name	Active	Loop	P.P.	Infinite
Site Logistics		☐	☐	☐
Flythrough	☐	☐	☐	
Crane Rotation	☐	☐	☐	

6. To finish the scene, you need to add the appropriate view component, such as a camera for a viewpoint animation, an animation set for an object animation, or a section plane. Right-click the scene Flythrough and choose Add Camera ➤ Blank Camera from the context menu. Note that this step is for setting up a camera animation. To animate objects, see the sidebar "Exploring the Differences with Animator Scenes."

7. To delete an animation set from the scene view, right-click the animation set and select Delete from the context menu or click the Delete icon ⊗.

8. To move objects up or down in the hierarchy, highlight the object and use the up and down arrows ⬆⬇.

In addition to the scene view hierarchies, you can configure additional options for each scene component. These options are used to adjust the playback of the individual scene components.

EXPLORING THE DIFFERENCES WITH ANIMATOR SCENES

The Animator module in Navisworks is a powerful tool that can simulate both camera and object animations. Camera animations are created in the animator tree by simply right-clicking any scene and choosing Add Camera ➢ Blank Camera. Note that you can have only one camera animation per scene.

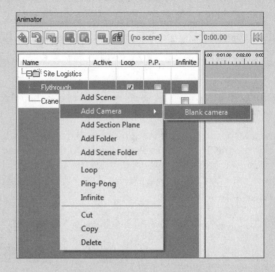

To animate objects, you need to first select the objects. This can be accomplished several ways. If you're animating a single object, the simplest way is to highlight the object in your model. When you right-click the scene, there is now an additional option. You can choose Add Animation Set ➢ From Current Selection to create an object animation for the scene.

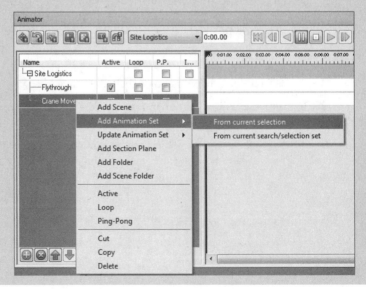

A better way to specify which objects you want to animate is to use Add Animation Set ➤ From Current Search/Selection Set. This option is extremely useful because as changes are made to the model, any updates to the search/selection sets are incorporated into your animations. Also, unlike with camera animations, you can have multiple animation sets per scene.

Active   When working with multiple scenes in the animator tree, you can toggle their visibility on/off by using the Active check box. By default, all newly added views are set to display. Only scenes that have the Active check box selected will play.

Loop   The Loop option allows you to create an animation in loop mode. When the animation reaches the end, it will reset to the beginning and start again. This option is useful if you have a repetitive animation. Let's use the example of a seesaw or teeter-totter. Rather than animate the back and forth of each side repetitively, you can animate one full iteration and then use the Loop option to create a continuous animation.

P.P. (Ping-Pong)   This option will play an animation to its end and then play the same animation back from its end to the beginning. The animation will play in this fashion only one time unless you have selected the Loop option.

Infinite   This option will allow the entire scene to play indefinitely until the animation is manually stopped. By default, this option is unchecked, allowing the animation to conclude when the endpoint is reached.

The right pane of the Animator window contains the timeline view. This view shows the timeline for each animation set, camera view, or section plane. Similar to a Gantt chart, it displays the length of the animation components over time in a bar chart format. Each timeline has a colored animation bar that represents the various view components, as follows:

Animation Set: Blue

Camera Set: Green

Section Plane: Red

In addition to the colors, the timeline view displays keyframes, or snapshots, of the model (Figure 10.3). Keyframes are displayed as black diamonds in the timeline. The duration of each can be edited by dragging the keyframe to the appropriate location in the timeline. Keyframes will be covered in detail in the next section.

FIGURE 10.3
Timeline showing colors and keyframes

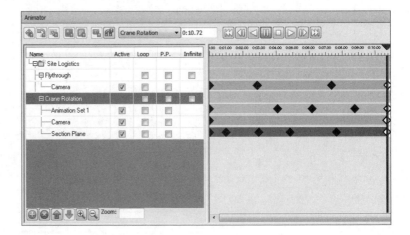

Just above the timeline view is the timescale bar. This tool displays the overall animation time starting at 0:00 and extending to the final length of your animation. By default, all values are shown in seconds. To modify the units on the timescale bar, use the Zoom buttons at the bottom of the scene view.

The time slider is the black vertical bar that represents the current position within your animation (Figure 10.4). When the animation is played, the slider will track along to indicate the current position. Also, you can adjust the position by dragging the slider left or right. The end slider is the vertical red line that represents the end of the animation.

FIGURE 10.4
Timescale bar with end slider

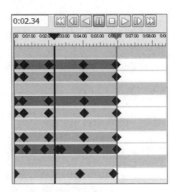

At the very top of both panes is the Animator toolbar. This area contains the controls that let you create, edit, and play animations. Table 10.1 provides an overview of the functions of the Animator toolbar.

TABLE 10.1:   Animator toolbar

ICON	FUNCTION NAME	DESCRIPTION
	Translate animation set	This function is used to modify the position of an object in your model.
	Rotate animation set	This function is used to modify the rotation of an object in your model.
	Scale animation set	This function is used to modify the scale of an object in your model.
	Change Color Of animation set	This function is used to modify the color of an object in your model.
	Change Transparency Of animation set	This function is used to modify the transparency of an object in your model.
	Capture Key Frame	Use this icon to create a keyframe, or snapshot, of your model. A new keyframe will appear in your timeline view.
	Toggle Snapping	This feature is used to snap the selected geometry to a relevant point in the animation, such as center or corner.
Scene 1 ▼	Scene Picker	The Scene Picker displays all available scenes in your overall animation and allows you to specify which one to make active.
0:00.00	Time Position	This field displays the current position or time in your animation. You can use the timeline slider to adjust the position or type in the new value.
	Rewind	This action rewinds the animation back to the beginning.
	Step Back	This action steps the animation backward one keyframe at a time.
	Reverse Play	This action plays the animation backward.

TABLE 10.1: Animator toolbar *(CONTINUED)*

ICON	FUNCTION NAME	DESCRIPTION
❚❚	Pause	This action pauses the current animation. Selecting it again resumes the animation.
▢	Stop	This action stops the animation and automatically rewinds the animation to the beginning. Use the Pause command to start and stop without rewinding to the beginning.
▷	Play	This action starts the animation.
❚▷	Step Forward	This action steps the animation forward to the next keyframe.
▷❘	Fast Forward	This action fast-forwards the animation to the end.

Animating with Keyframes

Unlike composing traditional animations, where every frame is painstakingly drawn out to create the proper simulation, Navisworks uses the concept of keyframes to expedite this process. With keyframes, you define the start point and endpoint of the animation by moving either the camera or the object to the desired location. Since doing so may entail defining keyframes over the span of a few seconds or longer, the end result is choppy simulation jumps to each view that don't create the simulation of movement. To rectify this, Navisworks, by default, interpolates the frames between the start and end so that when the animation is played back, the result is a smooth transition. Creating the *in-betweens*, a process commonly referred to as *tweening*, not only gives the animation a smooth evolution between the keyframes but also greatly speeds up the animation process for the user.

Let's create a basic animation using keyframes. For this series of exercises, you'll be using the file c10_Meadowgate_Keyframes.nwd.

1. With the file open, open Animator and pin it at the bottom of the screen.

2. Select Animation View from the saved viewpoints.

   For this simple animation, you'll animate the dozer in the foreground to move from the left side of the screen to the right. Because you're only moving this object in a straight path, you'll use just a few keyframes.

3. Add a new scene in Animator by clicking the green + icon or by right-clicking in the animator tree and selecting Add Scene. Rename the scene **Dozer**.

4. Select the dozer by highlighting the model CAT Bulldozer.skp from the selection tree.

5. Right-click the scene named Dozer to open the view components. Select Add Animation Set ➤ From Current Selection. Doing so adds a new view component to your scene. If this option is missing, make sure that you have the Dozer object selected.

6. Keeping the object selected, toggle on the Translate Animation Set icon. Doing so activates the Move gizmo for the selected object (Figure 10.5).

FIGURE 10.5
Highlighted
animation object

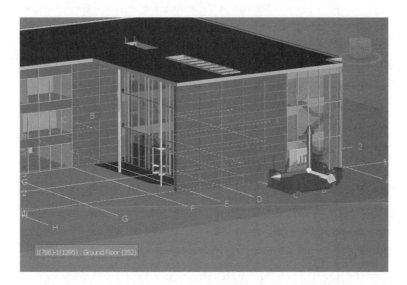

7. Before you attempt to move or animate the object, you need to capture the current position of this object. Click the Capture Key Frame icon in the Animator toolbar. An open diamond is shown to denote that this position has been captured.

8. Drag the timescale slider out to 0:10, or enter this value in the Time Position field.

Hover over the green handle on the gizmo. It will change color when you're locked on. By dragging the object with one of these handles, you can move the object in the X, Y, and Z directions. To move the object on a combination of these axes, grab the 2D plane that spans between each handle (see Figure 10.6). For example, to move an object across the surface of the model, select the purple plane to move in a combination of the XY axes. Selecting the other planes will allow you to drag the gizmo in the XZ and YZ directions. If you do not see the gizmo in your scene, zoom out in the model until it appears.

FIGURE 10.6
Translate animation
set's gizmo

9. Drag the dozer to the right using the gizmo.

10. To capture this position, click the Capture Key Frame icon again. You should see a light blue line spanning from start to finish in the timescale bar and a black diamond indicating the position has been captured.

11. Toggle off the Translate Object icon and click the Stop icon. Always disable the animation option at the end of the animation session; otherwise, the gizmo will remain in view during playback and even when you're exporting to a movie.

12. Click the Play icon to display your animation. If you don't see the dozer in your animation, try making the dozer a required object. Highlight the CAT Bulldozer.skp file in the selection tree and select the Require icon in the Visibility area of the Home tab. This will force Navisworks to prioritize what objects are displayed first.

13. To modify the playback time, simply drag the keyframe to the left or right to extend or shorten the animation playback.

In this exercise, you created a simple animation by creating two keyframes that define the start and stop positions of the object. Using the timescale slider, you can define the length of the animation. When this animation is played back, Navisworks automatically creates the in-between frames to ensure a smooth playback. Take a few minutes to practice this process with other objects in the scene.

ANIMATION TOOLS VS. ITEM TOOLS

When creating animations, the onscreen gizmos for the animation tools are exactly the same as the transform tools in the Item Tools contextual menu. Make sure you are selecting the Transform, Rotate, and Scale animation set tools from the Animator window.

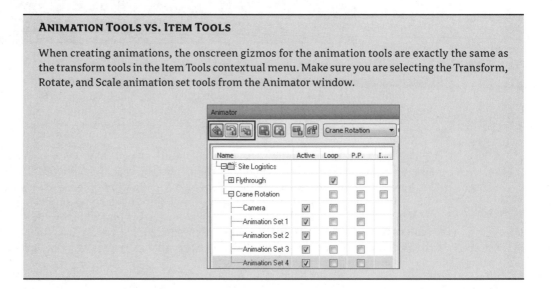

These best practices are meant to advance your use of Navisworks by challenging you to look for new opportunities and workflows outside the standard recommendations.

CREATING ANIMATIONS FOR TIMELINER

In addition to simulating a 4D construction sequence in TimeLiner, you may find it useful to have object and camera animations to add realism to the simulation and help define site movements and equipment paths. Object and camera animations provide more control and are easily created in the Animator tool.

When creating animations for use in 4D TimeLiner simulations, you need to take into account the length of the animation compared to the TimeLiner schedule task. In other words, when animations are linked to the 4D model, the interval units in the animation *must match* the intervals in the TimeLiner simulation.

To assist with creating animations that span several days, use the Zoom command to rescale the timescale or manually enter the time in the Time Position box. For example, say you have a schedule task that is 7 days long. When specifying the time position, you can enter days and hours. To create the keyframe for this value, type **7d 0h 0:00.00** in the Time Position box to represent a position of 7 days. If you want to use the slider, use the Zoom icon to extend the timescale to show this larger timeframe.

Setting Up Cameras and Viewpoints

In addition to animating objects, you can animate cameras as keyframes. This process is useful if you wish to create a fly-through of your model or move the user to a specific point in your animation. Furthermore, you can leverage your existing saved viewpoints animations as keyframes.

Recall that a camera animation contains a series of viewpoints—or in this case, keyframes—that define how the scene will play back. If no keyframes are defined, the animation will show a static view, but if you specify several different locations and save them as multiple keyframes, Navisworks will animate the camera as a smooth transformation between the keyframes. In the next set of exercises, you'll create an animation from a blank camera. Then, you'll copy an existing viewpoint animation to the camera animation.

For this set of exercises, you'll be using the file c10_Meadowgate_Camera_Animations.nwd. Here are the steps:

1. With the file open, open the Animator window and pin it at the bottom of your screen.

2. Add a new scene and name it **Flythrough**.

3. Right-click in the scene name and select Add Camera ➢ Blank Camera from the context menu.

4. Select the Camera object and navigate to the desired view in your model.

5. Click the Capture Key Frame icon to capture your starting position. Note that it may take some time for the Capture Key Frame icon to become active after you select your Camera object.

6. Adjust the timescale by dragging to the right to define the next camera keyframe.

7. Modify the view in your model to represent the path endpoint of your initial animation.

8. Click the Capture Key Frame icon to capture the next position.

Using these steps, you can continue to add keyframes to represent various camera views. Remember that Navisworks will interpolate and create the difference between the keyframes. If your goal is to have a fly-through animation that encircles the outside of the building and then finishes up in the inside, you'll need to make sure that you have a series of keyframes that capture multiple external views before capturing the inside views. When Navisworks creates the in-betweens, it animates the shortest path between the keyframes. The more keyframes you have, the more accurate your camera path will animate.

For the second part of this exercise, let's add a camera from an existing viewpoint animation. You'll be using the Saved Viewpoints window, so it's a good idea to have that open and easy to access.

1. Add a new scene and name it **Existing Viewpoints**.

2. In the Saved Viewpoints window, highlight the animation labeled Flythrough.

3. Back in the Animator window, right-click the scene name and select Add Camera ➢ From Current Viewpoint Animation. Navisworks will create keyframes from the separate saved viewpoints.

4. Click the Play icon to display the animation.

5. To modify the duration of the animation, drag the keyframes to shorten or extend.

6. To add keyframes to this animation, drag the time slider to the right.

7. Adjust the camera view in the model and click the Capture Key Frame icon. A new keyframe will be added to your existing animation.

In this exercise, you created a camera animation from an existing saved viewpoint animation. In addition to being able to reuse these viewpoints, you can easily modify the playback duration or add keyframes to expand the scope of the animation. Practice creating various camera animations using the skills you gained from the previous exercises. Note that you'll need to set up a separate scene for each object you intend to animate, because although each scene can have numerous animation sets, it can contain only one camera and section plane. Later in the chapter, we'll cover other object animation options.

Manipulating Geometry

When it comes to animating objects, Navisworks provides five tools to manipulate the geometry. They can be used individually or in combination to fully animate the objects. As you'll recall from the earlier exercise, you used the Translate animation set to animate an object from one point to another. In addition to the basic translation function, Navisworks provides tools to rotate, scale, and change color or transparency. In the next series of exercises, you'll use these manipulation controls to modify objects in the model and capture those changes as keyframes.

Before working with the various geometry manipulation tools, you need to define the objects as animation sets. You must be able to quickly select the model objects for use in your animation. You can achieve this by manually selecting the objects either from the model view or the selection tree. The other option, and best practice, is to use search or selection sets to define the objects. Not only can you easily select multiple objects with the click of a button, but if your animation set is based on search or selection sets, the contents of the animation set can be easily updated if the contents of the source search or selection set are modified.

Translating

The Translation gizmo is used to move an object by a linear movement. This could be represented by a vehicle or equipment moving across the site or by something more detailed such as material distributed to different areas. Whatever the intended outcome, Navisworks allows you to animate the objects smoothly from one location to another using the keyframe technique. For this example, you'll use the file c10_Meadowgate_Object_Animations.nwd:

1. With the file open, open Animator and create a new scene named **Crane Movement**.

2. Select the saved view Object Animation from the Saved Viewpoints window.

3. In the Sets window, select the crawler crane in the foreground by selecting the Crawler Crane selection set.

4. Right-click the scene name and select Add Animation Set ➤ From Current Search/ Selection Set.

5. Make sure the scene and objects remain highlighted. Click the Translate Animation Set icon on the Animator toolbar.

6. The Translation gizmo will appear in the approximate center of the object. To move the gizmo, hold down the Ctrl key and select the vertex of the X-, Y-, and Z-axes. Keeping the Ctrl key pressed, drag the gizmo to the new location (see Figure 10.7). If Toggle Snapping is enabled, the gizmo will gravitate toward any relevant snap points in the object.

FIGURE 10.7
Relocated
Translation gizmo

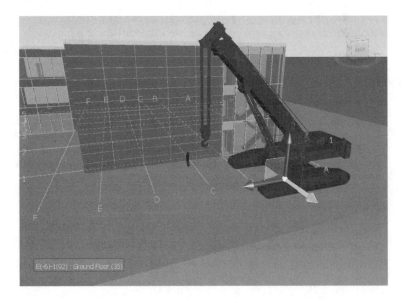

7. To capture the starting point of the animation, click the Capture Keyframe icon. In the timescale view, a black diamond will appear at 0:00.

8. Drag the time slider to the right to set the time for the first keyframe (in this example, **0:15**).

9. Grab one of the axes to move along a straight path or the various 2D squares to move along two axes.

   To move the object along a point-to-point translation, hold down the Ctrl key while dragging the gizmo vertex to the start point. Remember to use the snapping tools to help snap to a specific location. Once the start point is located, release the Ctrl key and drag the gizmo and snap to the endpoint. This workflow is useful if you want to animate an object a specific distance.

10. After you've finished moving the object, click the Capture Key Frame icon to save the current keyframe.

11. Add additional keyframes using steps 7–10 to finish the animation.

12. When the animation is complete, click the Translate Animation Set icon again to deselect it and click the Stop icon.

13. Click the Play icon to display the animation. You can also play the animations by selecting the appropriate scene from the Playback area of the Animation tab in the ribbon (see Figure 10.8).

FIGURE 10.8
Playback area of the
Animation tab

In this exercise, you created a simple animation to move a crawler crane around the site. What other types of objects could you animate using this feature?

Rotating

Occasionally, you want to display an object rotating in your scene. This is useful if you want to show the horizontal jib swing of a tower crane or other equipment in your model. Typically, this feature is used in conjunction with the previous command, Translation. Doing so allows you to fully animate objects in your model to show realistic equipment movement. Using the same file from the previous exercise, try this example where you left off:

1. Highlight the Crawler Crane search set.

2. In the scene view, select the previously defined animation set.

3. Click the Capture Key Frame icon to save the current position as a keyframe.

4. Drag the time slider to a new value. Note that if you recently played the animation, the time slider will be docked at the beginning of the animation.

5. Click the Rotation icon. The Rotation gizmo will appear in the model.

Similar to the Translation gizmo, the Rotation gizmo can be snapped to a different location on the object. This is especially useful if you want to rotate an object along a specific axis. In this exercise, you want to rotate the crawler crane to create a realistic turning movement. When working with items such as tower cranes, create a separate search or selection set for the top portion of the object that rotates (such as the cab or jib). That way, you can use the unselected hidden command to hide the bottom portion of the crane and easily snap your Rotation gizmo to the central axis.

6. Move the gizmo so that it's centered above the crawler tracks (Figure 10.9).

FIGURE 10.9
Centered Rotation gizmo

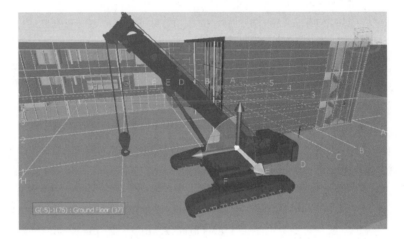

7. Once the gizmo is positioned correctly, select the purple colored curve between the X- and Y-axes. Drag the gizmo to the correct position. The crane will rotate along the new axis.

8. Click the Capture Key Frame icon to save the keyframe.

9. Deselect the Rotation icon and click the Stop icon.

10. Click the Play icon to display the animation.

11. To re-record, right-click the keyframe and choose Delete from the context menu.

This exercise illustrated the importance of the pivot point. You must position the Rotation gizmo in the location you wish your object to pivot on. This pivot location can change from keyframe to keyframe, though generally, you will want the center position to stay in the same place on the object for each keyframe.

AUTOMATING PLAYBACK WITH THE LOOP AND PING-PONG OPTIONS

When animating objects using the Rotate animation set, you can easily automate portions of the animation using the Scene View options. For example, suppose that you want to animate the horizontal jib of a tower crane to show the swing to ensure that it won't hit any nearby buildings.

Instead of capturing numerous keyframes to define the back-and-forth rotation of the jib, simply capture the beginning and end frames. Select the P.P. (Ping-Pong) option in the animation playback. When the animation reaches the end, it will run backward until it reaches the start. To keep the animation running nonstop, select the Loop option. The animation will run until you click the Stop or Pause icon.

Scaling

The Scale animation set is used to scale up or down an object in size. Using the onscreen gizmo, you can scale any object along a specific axis or a combination of them. In addition, you can manually specify the exact scale in the scale field area in the Animator module. As with all the tools, it's important to note that this scaling feature is used only to scale an object in an animation and should not be confused with the Scale command in the Item Tools context menu.

The Scale animation set is useful for showing items such as excavations. During the construction process, the spoils are sometimes left in large piles and slowly hauled away. Using the Scale command, you can animate the excavated material slowly being removed from the site. When coordinating trades, equipment, and deliveries, you'll find it useful to have a realistic view of the site logistics. Let's go through an example of the Scale command. You'll be using the file c10_Meadowgate_Object_Scaling.nwd for this exercise:

1. With the file open, open Animator and create a new scene named **Excavation**.

2. Select the saved view Object Scaling from the Saved Viewpoints window.

3. Select the excavated pile in the foreground of the model by selecting the Excavation selection set.

4. Right-click in the scene name and select Add Animation Set ➢ From Current Search/Selection Set.

5. Click the Scale Animation Set icon on the Animator toolbar. The Scale gizmo will appear in the approximate center of the object.

6. To capture the starting point of the animation, click the Capture Key Frame icon. In the timescale view, a black diamond will appear at 0:00.

7. Drag the time slider to the right to set the time for the first keyframe.

8. Grab one of the axes to scale up or down in a specific coordinate (X, Y, Z), or grab one of the triangular planes to scale across two axes (XY, XA, YZ). To scale all axes uniformly, drag the vertex of the three axes. Alternatively, you can manually type in the value in the Scale field at the bottom of the Animator module (Figure 10.10).

FIGURE 10.10

Scale field in the scene view

9. After you finish scaling the object, click the Capture Key Frame icon to save the current keyframe.

10. Deselect the Scale Animation Set icon and click the Stop icon.

11. Click the Play icon to display the animation.

Changing Color

Another object manipulation tool that is used in animations is the Change Color animation set. In this case, no geometry is moved or scaled—just the object colors are modified. This function is used when you want to visually change a static object. For example, you might have some cast-in-place concrete items that can't be disturbed during the curing process. Creating a color animation will allow you to change to a color that signals when the curing is complete. Note that when animating color shifts, they do not interpolate or gradually shift between hues; rather, they instantly update to the new assigned color. Let's go through an example using the file c10_Meadowgate_Color_Animations.nwd:

1. With the file open, open Animator and create a new scene named **Concrete**.

2. Select the saved view Color Animation from the Saved Viewpoints window.

3. Select the floor slabs in the model by selecting the Floors search set.

4. Right-click in the scene name and select Add Animation Set ➤ From Current Search/Selection Set.

5. Click the Change Color Animation Set icon on the Animator toolbar.

   There is no gizmo since you're not moving or scaling any geometry, but there is a field at the bottom of the Animator module for entering the RGB values. Also, you can select the color from the drop-down menu (Figure 10.11).

FIGURE 10.11

Color field

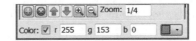

6. To capture the starting point of the animation, click the Capture Key Frame icon. In the timescale view, a black diamond will appear at 0:00.

7. Drag the time slider to the right to set the time for the first keyframe.

8. Enter the new color value.

9. After you've finished modifying the color of the object, click the Capture Key Frame icon to save the current keyframe.

10. Deselect the Change Color Animation Set icon and click the Stop icon.

11. Click the Play icon to display the animation.

Changing Transparency

In addition to modifying the color of the objects in your model, it's sometimes useful to turn certain objects transparent to be able to peer inside. Similar to the color change animations, the transparency shifts do not change gradually. Let's go through an example of this using the same file from the previous steps:

1. With the file open, open Animator and create a new scene named **Transparency**.

2. Select the saved view Transparency Animation from the Saved Viewpoints window.

3. Select the front façade in the model by selecting the Curtain Panel search set.

4. Right-click the scene name and select Add Animation Set ➤ From Current Search/ Selection Set.

5. Click the Change Transparency Animation Set icon on the Animator toolbar.

6. To capture the starting point of the animation, click the Capture Key Frame icon. In the timescale view, a black diamond will appear at 0:00.

7. Drag the time slider to the right to set the time for the first keyframe.

8. Enter the new Transparency value.

9. After you've finished modifying the transparency of the object, click the Capture Key Frame icon to save the current keyframe.

10. Deselect the Change Transparency Animation Set icon and click the Stop icon.

11. Click the Play icon to display the animation.

In these exercises, you used several object manipulation tools to modify the objects during animation. To expand your mastery of Navisworks, try using more than one tool. For example, animate a camera view that encircles the building while the crane is moving around the front of the building with a shifting wall color or transparency. Remember that each scene can have only one camera view; however, you can incorporate as many animation sets as necessary.

Animating Section Planes

Similar to the object animations discussed in the previous section, Navisworks can animate sectioned views using section planes. This feature allows for a quick and robust way to create compelling animations that not only provide interior views of your model but can also be used to create accurate cutaways of site utilities and underground components. Using the standard object animations, you can create impressive fly-through animations that you can use to inform all project stakeholders of the project's scope.

For these exercises, you'll be using the sectioning tools that were originally discussed in Chapter 5. Make sure you're comfortable with using these tools. Let's use the file c10_Meadowgate_Section_Animations.nwd for the following steps:

1. With the file open, open Animator and create a new scene named **Sections**.

2. Right-click the scene name and select Add Section Set. A new view component will be added to your scene.

3. In the ribbon, activate the section tools and specify which cutting plane you wish to animate (see Figure 10.12). Adjust the plane if necessary for your starting view. You can animate only one plane at a time; however, you can easily switch to a different plane mid-animation to encompass a top section cut followed by a section cut to the front of the building.

FIGURE 10.12
Section Tools menu

4. Capture the starting point of the animation by clicking the Capture Key Frame icon.

5. Drag the time slider to the right to set the time for the first keyframe.

6. Move the Section gizmo to cull the model as necessary. Depending on what section plane you're going to manipulate, you can simply enter the value in the Transform drop-down menu (see Figure 10.13).

FIGURE 10.13
Transform drop-down menu

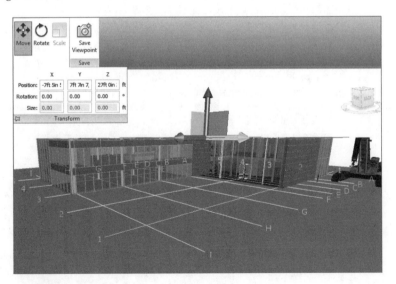

7. Click the Capture Key Frame icon to save the keyframe.

8. Click the Stop icon when the animation is complete or repeat the previous steps to add more keyframes.

9. Click the Play icon to display the section animation.

Real World Scenario

SITE COORDINATION WITH ANIMATOR

Along with TimeLiner and clash detection, animations are useful in the model and site coordination process. For example, heavy equipment on a construction site can be animated to show the path and reach. Any potential safety issues can be documented and a mitigation plan enacted to address them. A recent U.S. Bureau of Labor Statistics study reveals that approximately 40 percent of occupational deaths occur on construction sites.

Manner in which fatal work occurred

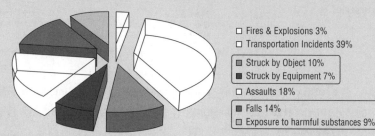

☐ Fires & Explosions 3%
☐ Transportation Incidents 39%

■ Struck by Object 10%
■ Struck by Equipment 7%

☐ Assaults 18%

■ Falls 14%
☐ Exposure to harmful substances 9%

**Typical accidents that occur
on construction sites = 40%
of total occupational deaths**

SOURCE: U.S. Bureau of Labor Statistics, 2010

With the Animator tools in Navisworks, you easily visualize equipment paths and the flow of materials on a construction site. In the following image, the HVAC rooftop unit was animated to better grasp what the hoisting process would look like. The project coordinator was able to fully coordinate the lift by simulating the entire process and visualizing every aspect of the procedure. Once this animation was complete, the project team had a very clear process in place. The site crew knew exactly where to stage the HVAC unit for the pick. Also, the other trades working on the site were aware of the impending lift and made provisions to have their work scheduled away the lifting zone.

In addition to the HVAC unit lift, the following items were taken into consideration in additional animations to ensure better visualization and mitigate any risks:

◆ Proper safety measures

◆ Site logistics

   ◆ Site and Surroundings

   ◆ Adjacent Buildings

   ◆ Equipment and Temporary lay down areas

   ◆ Transportation areas

   ◆ Crane reach and lift capacities

◆ Temporary Items

   ◆ Excavations

   ◆ Fall Protection

When working with the Animator tools, this extra effort quickly highlights inefficiencies. You can also use the animation to inform all the stakeholders and site personnel of the current layout. As the BLS study shows, 17 percent of deaths occur from being struck by an object or equipment. From a model and site coordination perspective, you can start to better plan material laydown and staging areas. If your project has multiple segments with phased turnovers, you can once again animate the various site components to ensure that they won't pose any safety concerns or interfere with the finished areas.

On another project, the contractor needed to replace an aging vessel inside a hospital mechanical room. One option for removing the vessel was to cut it into smaller pieces for removal; however, that would require asbestos remediation and delay the replacement process. Instead, the project team used the standard navigation tools and clash detection in Navisworks to determine that it was feasible to move out the old unit intact on a series of dollies through the utility doors.

Before they could move forward with this plan, they needed to convince the hospital staff that this was attainable and wouldn't disrupt the daily activities of the medical staff. Using the Animator tool, the project team was able to create an animation that showed the movement of the vessel through these tight spaces. By visualizing the whole process, the team was able to convince the staff and identify any risks in the process.

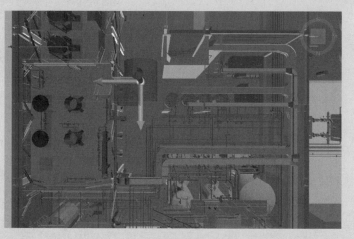

In all of these examples, the Animator tool was used in conjunction with the other tools and features in this program to create a solution that allowed the contractor in addition to the other stakeholders on the project to visualize the workflow and procedures. The strength of Navisworks rests on these compound workflows where features like clash detection, TimeLiner, Search/Selection Sets, and other modules combine to create a ubiquitous platform.

Exporting Animations

Animations are saved in your project file and, when played back, will reflect any model changes (such as deleted or added elements). Occasionally, you may want to capture periodic snapshots of the current model or save the animation as a separate AVI video file for viewing outside Navisworks. In addition to the best practice of keeping your model files in the NWF format, saving a copy of your project file as an NWD allows you to share your animations with users who may only have access to the Navisworks Freedom viewer. Note that you should make sure that all animation sets are deselected before exporting; otherwise, the gizmo may show up in your movie!

Listed here are the steps for exporting an animation:

1. Select the Animation tab and click the Export Animation icon. You can also access this feature in the Output tab of the ribbon in the Visuals area.

2. In the Animation Export dialog box, select Current Animator Scene from the Source drop-down menu (see Figure 10.14).

FIGURE 10.14

Selecting Current
Animator Scene
from the Source
drop-down

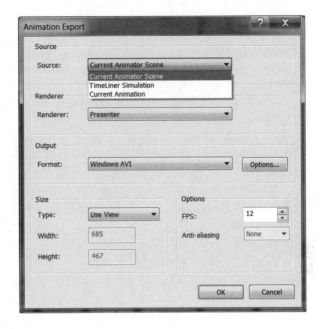

3. In the Renderer area, choose from the following options:

Presenter   This setting allows you to render the animation with applied materials and lights. When you export with this option, rendering times are considerably longer. Also, text overlay is not supported in this mode.

Open GL   This setting allows you to export the model with the basic shaded display. The quality of standard AVI video resembles the image quality displayed in the main Navisworks navigation window. All text overlays are supported in the export.

4. Specify the output. For videos, you want to select AVI from the list. The other option is to export as hundreds of individual frames (JPEG, PNG, or BMP), which can then be assembled in an external video editor to create the animation.

5. In the Options box, specify the appropriate Video Compressor and Compressor Quality settings.

6. In the Size area, specify the export size for the animation. You can also use the predefined options in the Type drop-down list.

7. Specify the FPS setting. A higher fps will yield a smoother animation but increase the render time. A frame rate of 24 is the standard rate for DVDs.

8. Specify an Anti-Aliasing value. Anti-aliasing allows you to smooth out actions in the movie. If this option is used, it will increase the time it takes to render the animation. This setting is only available when you're exporting with OpenGL.

9. Click OK and specify the filename and location where you wish to save the video.

The Bottom Line

Create a simple animation. Navisworks can create both camera view and object animations or a combination of both. These animations can be created from scratch or leverage existing saved viewpoints.

Master It When working with object animations, what is keyframe animation and what is its advantage?

Manipulate geometry. Animating objects in Navisworks greatly enhances the realism of your model, but more importantly, it can be used to uncover potential coordination issues and act as a tool to keep all stakeholders up-to-date on the project.

Master It Name the five types of object animation manipulation.

Export animations. Navisworks can export animations for use in marketing, education, and other areas.

Master It What are the two types of animation renderings that can be saved? What is the primary difference between the two?

Chapter 11

Giving Objects Life and Action with Scripter

Up until now, the model has been used in a static environment. Now that you have learned about animations and how to export images and movies, let's look at creating animations that act in real time with the model. This chapter will cover Scripter, a unique Autodesk® Navisworks® 2013 tool that allows you to connect custom animations to objects that react to user inputs. These inputs include mouse clicks, keystrokes, time, and collisions.

In this chapter, you'll learn to:

- ◆ Manage scripts
- ◆ Create events
- ◆ Create actions
- ◆ Interact with the model

Introducing Scripter

Scripter gives you the ability to bring life to the objects in the model. Bringing objects to life is important because it provides owners with a better understanding of how their future project will interact with real people. Scripter is made up of three tools: the script, events, and actions. Scripter works by connecting an event to an action in a container called a script.

The script itself is a container of rules. The script houses the event rules and the action rules. The event rules define the conditions a user has to meet in order to trigger the action rules to begin. The action rules define how the model will connect with a user. The ability to define both event rules and action rules in any configuration allows you to create unique interactive environments that can be explored while in the model.

Creating and Managing Scripts

A script is the compilation of a condition and an action. To understand scripts, you must have the Scripter window open. On the Tools panel of the Home tab, click the Scripter button ▤ Scripter. You can also open the Scripter window by clicking the Scripter button ▤ on the Script panel of the Animation tab. Once opened, the Scripter window can be docked just like any other window in Navisworks.

Because of the size of the Scripter window, we advise you to dock it on the bottom of your screen. If you are using dual monitors, consider opening Scripter on a different screen to maximize your model real estate. We also suggest that the viewpoint window be open as well to allow you to easily select animations and viewpoints.

The Scripter window consists of four main areas: Scripts, Events, Actions, and Properties, as shown in Figure 11.1. The first area is the Scripts view. In this workspace, you can create a script, organize scripts into folders, and toggle on and off active scripts.

FIGURE 11.1
Scripter window showing the Scripts, Events, Actions, and Properties areas

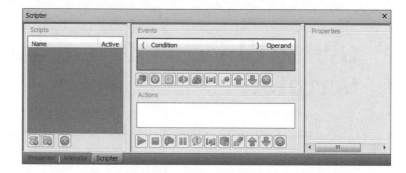

To create a new script, right-click in the Scripts section of the Scripter window and select Create New Script. You can also click the Add New Script icon ![icon]. You can assign a new name to the script by right-clicking the script and selecting Rename Item. You can also rename a script by left-clicking it and pressing F2 or by double-clicking the name.

Because many scripts tend to be similar, it is advantageous to group them into folders. Scripter even allows folders to be grouped into other folders. To create a folder, start by right-clicking in the Scripts window and selecting Add New Folder. You can also click the Folder icon in the bottom window ![icon].

To create a subfolder, select an existing folder, right-click the folder, and select Add New Folder. This can also be accomplished by selecting a folder and clicking the Folder icon. Scripter also supports the dragging and dropping of items. If you want to move a folder into another folder, left-click the folder you wish to move and drag it into the folder you want to host it in. While dragging, you should see an up arrow appear. Hover (or pause) the dragging arrow over the folder you wish to drop the folder into and then release the mouse button. Scripts can be moved in a similar fashion. Multiple objects cannot be moved at the same time.

If you move a script to a folder and later wish to remove it, select the script and drag it out of the folder and onto another script that's not in a folder. If you have no scripts out of a folder, you will have to create a new script in order to remove the original script from the folder.

Let's try out managing scripts by following these steps:

1. Open the file c11_Meadowgate_Grouping_Scripts.nwd.

2. Open the Scripter window by clicking the Scripter button on the Tools panel of the Home tab, and ensure Enable Scripts is not activated.

3. In the Scripts tab, locate the 2nd Floor Door and the 2nd Floor Door 2 scripts, as shown in Figure 11.2.

FIGURE 11.2
Door scripts

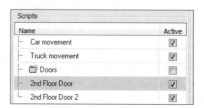

4. Left-click the 2nd Floor Door script and move it into the `Doors` folder.

5. Do the same thing for the 2nd Floor Door 2 script.

6. Create a new folder by clicking the Folder icon on the bottom of the Scripts window.

7. Name the folder **Traffic**.

8. Move the Car Movement and Truck Movement scripts into `Traffic`.

9. Create a new script by clicking the Add New Script icon at the bottom of the screen and name it **Pedestrians**.

10. Move Pedestrians into the `Traffic` folder.

For large projects, you can create all the folders and subfolders in advance to remind you what your end goal is in the project. Often, it is advantageous to create a written storyboard of what you want the model to do and then set up all the folders and subfolders to hold the actions you wish to take place.

Enabling and Disabling Scripts

Scripter allows you to quickly customize which scripts are enabled and which are disabled. This is an important feature of Scripter because you may want to demonstrate some scripts to one group of users that are not appropriate for another group of users. Scripter gives you the power to quickly toggle scripts on and off.

To disable all scripts, click the Enable Scripts icon, which you'll find on the Script panel of the Animation tab. To enable active scripts, you click this same icon.

To enable specific scripts, simply select the check box in the Scripts view in the Scripter window. If your scripts are grouped together in folders, you can enable or disable all the scripts in the folder by selecting the check box next to the folder. If you have some values in a folder checked and some unchecked, the folder's check box will have a solid view box representing a mixed-use folder.

Scripter has the ability to bring your model to life and simulate real-world experiences for users wanting to understand your project better. The tools give you nearly limitless possibilities to create an interactive world in your model.

Using Events and Actions

Now that you have learned how to create scripts, it's time to define what the scripts do. Before a script can become active, the user must trigger an event. Events are rules that define triggers. These events include clicking, tapping a mouse, collision detection, and more. Because of the wide array of available events, you can set up real-life situations for users walking the halls of the model.

Events are found in the Scripter window, as shown in Figure 11.3. To create an event, select any of the icons at the bottom of the Events view. We will go into detail specifically about what each event does later in this chapter. When an icon is selected, a condition row is created. Navisworks allows you to create more than one event in a script.

FIGURE 11.3
Events window

When multiple events have been selected, a condition is created and the Operand column becomes available, as shown in Figure 11.4. There are two options in the Operand column: AND and OR.

The AND operand signifies that a user will have to meet both event requirements in order for the script to start. Here's an example: The user must click a door and be within a certain distance of the door in order for the action to open the door.

The OR operand signifies that the user must meet one of the event requirements for an action to be taken. For example, a user must click a door or be within a certain distance of the door in order for the door to open. When the events are created and controlled with operands, conditions are formed to simulate real-life experiences.

FIGURE 11.4

Condition operands

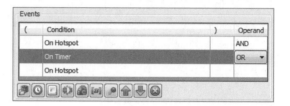

Consider the possibilities you can create in the model. When you are showing your Navisworks model to an owner, you can create a dynamic world with conditions.

 Real World Scenario

CONDITIONS IN INTERVIEWS

Scripter is useful not just for creating fun interactive environments but also for creating environments that demonstrate real events. These events can then be used to explain how situations will be handled.

There are great benefits to using Scripter conditions in the model to help explain the construction story to owners during interviews. When an RFP is sent out, the team assesses the project and then storyboards the proposed solutions.

The team first reviews all the construction documents and creates models of the systems they wish to highlight. The team then starts to design the scripts necessary to convey the messages they wish to speak to.

In the specific case of clients with strong facilities management departments, you could customize the model to allow the facilities management professionals to walk through the model with doors opening both on click and on proximity. The model is customized with links that are displayed on a site plan that take the owner to key locations in the model. When a key location is selected, the screen zooms in to the selected area and events unfold live. Highlights include areas of high traffic to show how an active site will have little impact from construction activities. Events where lanes of traffic are impeded are also shown with moving construction equipment and moving cars.

Using this process allows you to show the client exactly how construction will unfold and the impacts it will have. It allows critical areas to be highlighted with possible solutions displayed.

Types of Events

Events are represented by the icons in the Events window. There are seven events: On Start, On Timer, On Key Press, On Collision, On Hotspot, On Variable, and On Animation. Each event has useful characteristics that can be used to define when the script starts. When multiple events are used to define an action, a condition is formed. Let's take a look at the different events that you can use.

ON START EVENT

On Start is the first icon ![icon] in the Events window. This event starts the action as soon as Scripter is turned on. The On Start type is most often used to set the stage for the user experience by defining views and variables. An example of how it is used would be to start the user off in a predefined place. We will look more closely at variables later in the "On Variable Event" section.

Let's see how the On Start event works by following these steps:

1. Open the file c11_Meadowgate_OnStart.nwd.

2. Open Scripter and ensure Enable Scripts is not activated.

3. Select the Beginning script.

4. Create the On Start event by clicking the On Start icon.

5. Activate scripts by clicking the Enable Scripts icon in the Script panel of the Animation tab.

If you have trouble creating or editing a script, make sure that the Enable Scripts icon is not selected. When it is selected, you cannot edit scripts or animations.

ON TIMER EVENT

The On Timer event is the second icon ![icon] in the Events window. This event starts an action after a specified time interval. The On Timer event has two properties that must be defined, as shown in Figure 11.5:

FIGURE 11.5
On Timer
properties

Interval   The Interval property defines the amount of time you wish to pass in seconds before an action will happen. This is useful when you wish to draw the user's attention to an action that happens in time. For instance, you may want the user to explore the office area shown in the On Start event example above, but after 20 seconds, you wish to move the user to the parking lot to show them a traffic pattern. The On Timer event is perfect for this situation.

Regularity   The Regularity property defines the frequency with which the action will take place. You have two choices:

Once After   This property means that the action will happen only once after the time interval defined. This is the choice to use in our example of drawing the user's attention to the car in the parking lot after 20 seconds.

Continuous Choice   This means that the action will occur over and over with pauses between each occurrence based on the time interval specified. This option is useful to set on machines or other recurring events. For example, you could specify a crane boom moving and dropping its load to take place every 5 minutes.

See how the On Timer event works by doing the following exercise:

1. Open the file c11_Meadowgate_OnTimer.nwd.

2. Open the Scripter module and ensure Enable Scripts is not activated.

3. Select the On Timer script.

4. Create the On Timer event by clicking the On Timer icon.

5. Set Interval to 5 seconds.

6. Set Regularity to Once After.

7. Activate scripts by clicking the Enable Scripts icon on the Script panel of the Animation tab.

USING THE ON TIMER EVENT

In addition to allowing key elements to occur after a specified time, consider using the On Timer event to help guide the experience in the model. For instance, perhaps you wish to display a number of critical issues in the model but the locations are difficult to navigate to. You can use the On Timer event to coordinate the time from one area to the other.

You can allow users 3 minutes in one area before they are automatically taken to another area. In this manner, you can easily highlight all the information you wish to display.

ON KEY PRESS EVENT

The On Key Press event is the third event icon in the Scripter's Events window. This event triggers an action when a user interacts by pressing a button on the keyboard. The On Key Press event has two main properties, as shown in Figure 11.6:

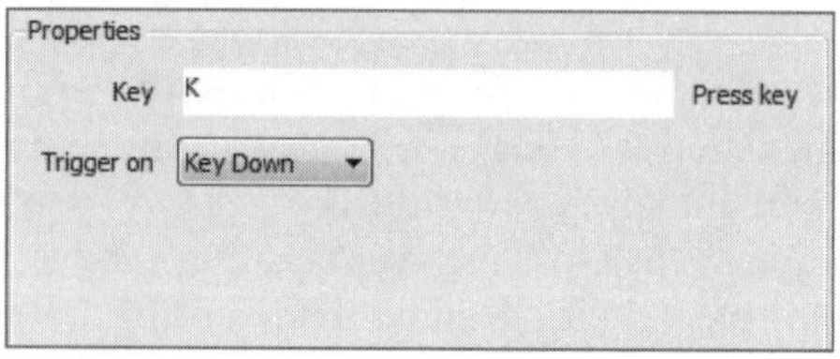

FIGURE 11.6
On Key Press
properties

Press Key The Press Key property defines which key triggers the event. The text box shown is an active box that records your keyboard strokes. Select this box and press any key to set the property. This property can contain only one keyboard stroke. The choice will show up after you have pressed any button on the keyboard. If you wish to change your selection, simply click in the Press Key box again and press the button on the keyboard that you wish to activate the action.

Trigger On This property defines how the trigger from the keyboard will be started. The choices in this drop-down list are as follows:

Key Up This property triggers the action when the user lets go of the key selected in the Press Key box. This means that if the key selected in the Press Key box is K, the action defined will not start until the user presses the K key and releases it. The action starts after the key is released.

Key Down This property triggers an action when the key in the Press Key box is pressed. If the letter K selected in the Press Key box, as soon as a user presses the letter K, an action will take place.

Key Pressed This property triggers an action while the key in the Press Key box is pressed down. This option is beneficial when you create conditions; we'll discuss this topic later in the "Conditions" section.

Let's see how the On Key Press event works by performing these steps:

1. Open the file c11_Meadowgate_OnKeyPress.nwd.

2. Open the Scripter module and ensure Enable Scripts is not activated.

3. Select the On Key Press script.

4. Create the On Key event by clicking the On Key Press icon.

5. Set Press Key to **K**.

6. Set Trigger On to Key Up.

7. Activate scripts by clicking the Enable Scripts icon in the Script panel of the Animation tab.

8. Press the letter K. If you are not automatically taken to the roof, navigate anywhere in the model and press K again.

Some events require an active scene in order to initiate. In the previous example, you have to activate all the scripts starting out. As soon as the view changes, the scripts become active.

ON COLLISION EVENT

The On Collision event is the fourth icon in the Events window. This event starts an action when the user collides with a selection set. For this event to be used, Collision must be selected while navigating the model. A third person does not need to be activated, nor does gravity. This event has three properties: Set, Show Part(s), and Include The Effects Of Gravity, as shown in Figure 11.7.

FIGURE 11.7
On Collision
properties

Set   This property is a drop-down box with three options:

Clear   This option removes all previously set objects. It will remove both objects selected with the Selection tool and objects selected by selection sets or search sets.

Set From Current Selection   This option allows you to select any number of objects in the model and attach the selected objects to this property.

Set From Current Selection Set   This option allows you to attach any search set or selection set to this property. When a search set or selection set is attached, the objects attached will change as the search set or selection set is updated. In this way, you maintain control over your objects without having to reset this property.

Show Part(s)   This property is a button that you click to show all the different objects selected in the current set. This can be very useful if you forget what objects are attached to the set property. Additionally, you can easily add or subtract items from the current set.

If you attached a selection set to the Set property, it will not highlight in the Manage Sets window, but all the objects in the set will highlight. Additionally, if you update a selection set, the update will not show up when you click Show Parts until you click out of the current script.

Include The Effects Of Gravity   This property is a check box that defines whether or not the effects of gravity will trigger a collision. When this box is checked, any objects that collide with the user because of gravity will also trigger an action. When this box is unchecked, the collisions caused by gravity will have no effect.

This property allows you to be extremely creative. For instance, with this property, you can define a door to open when you step onto a door mat or a roller coaster to start when you get to the waiting gates. The power of collision is only limited by your imagination.

Let's see how the On Collision event works:

1.   Open the file c11_Meadowgate_OnCollision.nwd.

2.   Open Scripter and ensure Enable Scripts is not activated.

3.   Select the On Collision script.

4.   Create the On Collision event by clicking the On Collision icon.

5.   Select Revolving Door from the Selection Sets window.

6.   Click the Set button and choose the Set From Current Selection Set option.

7.   Activate scripts by clicking the Enable Scripts icon in the Script panel of the Animation tab.

8.   Enable Collision and walk toward the revolving door.

The On Collision event especially can be useful to simulate an action a real person would perform on the building. For instance, you can simulate ADA compliance by showing an avatar roll up the building and enter the elevator. When the avatar touches the elevator wall, the elevator doors open to allow the avatar to navigate seamlessly through the model.

ON HOTSPOT EVENT

The On Hotspot event is the fifth icon ![icon] in the Events window. This event starts when the user nears a specified area called a hotspot. This event is useful when you want actions to take place when a user nears the hotspot. An example is to have a door open when a user is within 10 feet of it. The On Hotspot event has four properties, as shown in Figure 11.8:

FIGURE 11.8
On Hotspot
properties

Hotspot   The Hotspot property is a drop-down list with the choices Sphere and Sphere On Selection. The selection you make here will determine whether the third property of this event is Pick Position or Set Selection, respectively.

> **Sphere**   The Sphere option will create a perfect sphere around the hotspot with the radius you define. This option is useful for static objects because you must specify a point in space that cannot move. A perfect use for this option is to trigger any event that has a fixed position, such as a door and a floor.

> **Sphere On Selection**   This option will create a perfect sphere around a hotspot defined by a selection with a radius you define. This option is useful to trigger actions on moving objects—for example, when you want an action to occur when the user is following a truck and gets too close.

Trigger When   The Trigger When property is also a drop-down list containing the following options:

> **Entering**   This option starts an action when a user enters the defined sphere. This option is commonly used to open doors.

> **Leaving**   This option starts an action when a user leaves the defined sphere. This option is commonly used to close doors.

> **In Range**   This option starts an action any time a user is within the range. This property is most often used in combination with other events to form a condition.

Pick Position (or Set Selection)   The third property will change depending on whether you chose Sphere or Sphere On Selection earlier:

> **Pick Position**   This property is available if you selected Sphere as your Hotspot property. The Pick icon allows you to click on any object to place an invisible 3D point. The coordinates show up in the X, Y, Z axis Position boxes. You can manually enter these points or just use the Pick button to define the location of the hotspot.

Set Selection This property is available if you selected Sphere On Selection as your Hotspot property. The Set Selection property works the same way Set does in the On Collision event. The Set command creates the hotspot on whatever object you have set.

Radius Radius defines the distance from the hotpot that the sphere will be. As a general rule, you should make this at least 5 feet away. Otherwise, you are more likely to want to use collision to trigger an action.

Let's see how the On Hotspot event works:

1. Open the file `c11_Meadowgate_OnHotSpot.nwd`.

2. Open Scripter and ensure Enable Scripts is not activated.

3. Select the Create Hotspot script.

4. Create the On Hotspot event by clicking the On Hotspot icon.

5. Set Sphere as your Hotspot property.

6. Click the Pick button and select any point near you.

7. Make the radius **10′ (3.05m)**.

8. Activate scripts by clicking the Enable Scripts icon and walk toward your hotspot.

ON VARIABLE EVENT

The On Variable event is the sixth icon in the Events window. This unique event triggers an action when a variable meets defined criteria. On Variable has three properties, as shown in Figure 11.9:

FIGURE 11.9
On Variable properties

Variable This property is a text box that lets you define the name of your variable. You can use alphanumeric characters as well as wildcard characters (*!@#$%^&) to name your variable. Spaces are also allowed. We advise you, however, to use only one-word variables to allow for easier debugging.

Value This property defines what value has to be met before an action will take place. You have five option types:

Number Type This option is defined by numeric character only. If you define the value as 22, for example, the type would be Number. The Number type does not support any decimals.

Float Type This option is similar to Number but allows decimals. An example of Float is 3.98. Please note that Float does not need a decimal number, but it can utilize them.

String Type   This option is defined by an alphanumeric character wedged between double or single quotation marks. An example of a string is "Mastering Navisworks".

Variable Type   This option is defined by alphanumeric characters not wedged between double or single quotation marks. This value will compare the variable you defined in the first property to the variable you type in this box.

Boolean Type   This option is defined by true or false without any double or single quotes. In Navisworks, true = 1 and false = 0.

Evaluation   This property uses an operator to check the status of the variable and compares it with the value you defined in the Value property. There are six operators in this drop-down: Equal To, Not Equal To, Greater Than, Less Than, Greater Than Or Equal To, and Less Than Or Equal To.

If you are comparing string variables, your choices are limited to Equal To or Not Equal To. The other operators will still appear in the drop-down list but will not evaluate your variable.

Let's see how the On Variable event works:

1. Open the file c11_Meadowgate_OnVariable.nwd.

2. Open Scripter and ensure Enable Scripts is not activated.

3. Select the script On Variable and add the On Variable event.

4. Set the Variable property as BoilerGauge.

5. Set Value to **3**.

6. Set Evaluation to Equal To.

7. Activate scripts by clicking the Enable Scripts icon.

8. Press K three times on your keyboard.

9. If you are not moved to the correct location, try navigating the model and pressing K again.

The Variable property is very useful for gaining an understanding of how a person navigating the model is interacting with the current scripts. For large projects with numerous scripts, it can be a challenge to discover which scripts were activated, which scripts had errors, and which scripts were not used. The Variable property allows you to check all of these events quickly and efficiently when combined with the message action (which will be described later in this chapter).

On Animation Event

The On Animation event is the seventh icon in the Events window. This event triggers an action when a specific animation starts or stops. The On Animation event has two properties, as shown in Figure 11.10:

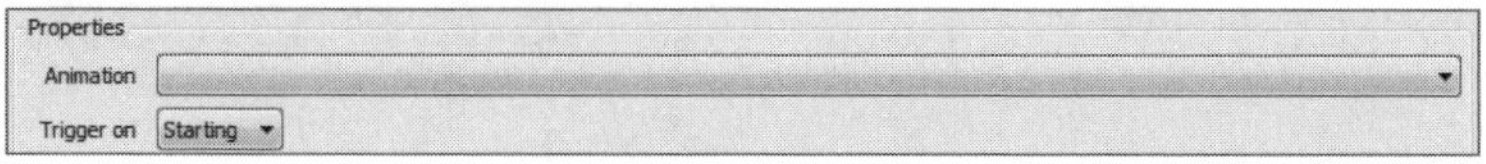

FIGURE 11.10
On Animation
properties

Animation   This property allows you to select which animation will trigger the event. For instance, if you wish a variable to be set after a door opens, you would set the door animation in this property.

Trigger On   This property defines when the action will happen. You have two choices in this drop-down box:

> **Starting**   The Starting command will start the action defined as soon as the animation selected in the first property starts. For example, you would use this command to set a room variable as soon as a user activates a door animation.

> **Ending**   The Ending command will start the action defined as soon as an animation ends. This property can be useful if you wish the user to be moved to a viewpoint after an animation has played.

Let's see how the On Animation event works:

1. Open the file c11_Meadowgate_OnAnimation.nwd.

2. Open Scripter and ensure Enable Scripts is not activated.

3. Select the On Animation script.

4. Add the On Animation event by clicking the On Animation icon.

5. Select Scene2 ➢ Truck from the drop-down list for the Animation property.

6. Select Ending for the Trigger On property.

7. Activate scripts by clicking the Enable Scripts icon.

The On Animation event can be very useful to arrange a sequence of events from beginning to end. For instance, when an animation to open the elevator door ends, there should be a natural pause until the door closes. After the door closes, the elevator should move and then the door should open again. For this whole sequence to be played out, the On Animation event can be used to chain the sequence together.

Conditions

A condition is formed when more than one event is selected to start a script. When more than one event is selected, the Operand column on the Events area populates with a drop-down list with two operands: AND and OR. Figure 11.11 shows the AND operand. You can have as many events as you desire in this window and can use the parentheses and the two operands.

FIGURE 11.11
Events view
showing conditions

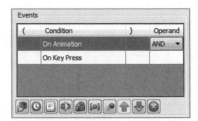

The parentheses will break the conditions into groups to be evaluated. Once grouped, the triggers in the group are evaluated first. If the group meets the conditions inside the brackets, it is evaluated against other groups as defined by the operands AND and OR.

When multiple events are selected, the AND operand will require that all events' triggers be activated before the script will start. When the OR operand is selected, if either of the events' triggers is activated, the script will start.

The AND operand is a valuable tool. You can use it to control the model by forcing the user to meet more than one trigger requirement. Perhaps you wish to lead the user down the halls of your project on a guided tour. You could easily have Collision turned on and only allow doors to open when the user is within a certain distance from the door and the previous door has already opened. In this way, you are given the freedom to direct traffic in the way you wish the users to travel.

The OR operand is a useful tool as well because you can use it to give the user a number of ways to start a script. The OR command can be used to start a car animation if the user collides with the car or if the user presses the O key. This condition provides the user with more choices to interact with the model scripts.

To manage events in conditions, use the last three icons ⬆️⬇️❌ in the Events window. The arrow icons move events up or down the Events window. The red circle with an X through it is the Delete command, which you use to remove unwanted events.

Let's see how conditions work by doing the following exercise:

1. Open the file c11_Meadowgate_Conditions.nwd.

2. Open Scripter and ensure Enable Scripts is not activated.

3. Select the Conditions script.

4. Add the On Timer event.

5. Set On Timer to **3** seconds.

6. Set Regularity to Once After.

7. Add the On Hotspot event.

8. For the operand, select OR.

9. Set the hotspot to Sphere On Selection.

10. Select Trigger When Entering.

11. Select the Door Condition selection set.

12. Click the Set button and choose Select From Current Selection Set.

13. Set the radius to **20′ (6.1**m).

14. Activate scripts by clicking the Enable Scripts icon.

15. Navigate toward the red door. If you still have the door selected, the door will be colored by your selection.

In this section, we examined what events are and how to use each of the seven events to trigger a script. We also explored how to make conditions in order to create user-interactive models.

These key principles of Scripter allow the interaction needed to start the actions the script will carry out.

Actions

Actions are the reaction the model has to the triggers set by events. As you may have noticed, the model reacted to the events you set. These actions were predefined to allow you to know you completed the exercise successfully. Likewise, actions will let you guide users in your model and help them see the features you wish them to see by reacting to their navigation.

Scripter has no limit to the number of actions you can set to any event or condition. When multiple actions are added to an event, they are listed from top to bottom in the Actions panel, as shown in Figure 11.12. After the event conditions are met, the actions will start from top to bottom; however, the actions do not wait for their predecessor to finish before starting.

FIGURE 11.12
Actions panel

Scripter has eight different action types. You will learn about each next.

PLAY ANIMATION ACTION

The Play Animation action ▷ will play a selected animation after an event is triggered. This action is very useful because it allows the user to see moving objects in Navisworks and creates a real-life situation. This action has four properties, as shown in Figure 11.13.

FIGURE 11.13
Play Animation
properties

Animation   This property allows you to define which animation you wish to play by selecting the animation from a drop-down list.

Pause At End   When this check box is unchecked, the object with the animation will return to its original position after the animation is completed. If this check box is checked, the object will not return to its original position but will stay at its last position in the animation. An example is when you want a door to stay open after you walk through it rather than appearing shut right after it is done opening.

Starting At   This property defines the starting position of the animation playback. Starting At has the following options:

Start   This option will play the animation from beginning to end.

End   This option will play the animation backward from the end.

Current Position   This option will resume play from a paused animation. If the animation was not paused, the animation will be played from beginning to end.

Specific Time   This option allows you to customize which part of an animation sequence you will play. When this option is selected, the Specific Start Time input becomes editable. The value of Specific Start Time sets the point in the animation playback that the animation will start.

Ending At   This property defines the ending position of the animation playback. Ending At has the following options:

Start   This option will end the animation at the beginning of the animation sequence.

End   This option will end the animation at the end of the animation sequence.

Specific Time   This option allows you to customize which part of an animation sequence you will play. When this option is selected, the Specific End Time input becomes editable. The value of Specific End Time sets the point in the animation playback that the animation will end.

Let's see how the Play Animation action works by doing the following exercise:

1. Open the file `c11_Meadowgate_Actions.nwd`.

2. Open Scripter.

3. Select the Action script.

4. Select the Play Animation action.

5. Set the animation to 2nd Floor Doors ➢ Door.

6. Select the check box Pause At End.

7. Set Starting At to Start and Ending At to End.

8. Activate scripts by clicking the Enable Scripts icon.

PLAYING ANIMATIONS

With all of the possible animations that you can create in your model, it is worth spending the time early on to storyboard the experience that you are trying to create. It is important to structure the creation and scripting of animations long before you actually start creating them.

The early planning will save you time and allow you to display the simulation that you envision. Don't forget that the Play Animation action along with all the other actions can be combined with multiple different events triggering them.

STOP ANIMATION ACTION

The Stop Animation action  will stop a specified animation. This action is useful if you have an animation that is repeated, such as a conveyer belt, and you wish to stop it when a user enters a control room. The Stop Animation action has two properties, as shown in Figure 11.14:

FIGURE 11.14
Stop Animation properties

Animation   This property specifies which animation sequence you wish to stop.

Reset To   This property is a drop-down box with two options:

Default Position   This option will return objects in the stopped animation back to their original position.

Current Position   This option will stop objects in the animation and freeze them in their current location.

Let's see how the Stop Animation action works:

1. Open the file c11_Meadowgate_StopAction.nwd.

2. Open Scripter and ensure Enable Scripts is not activated.

3. Select the Actions script.

4. Add the Stop Animation action.

5. Set Animation to Scene2 ➢ Truck.

6. Set Reset to Current Position.

7. Activate scripts by clicking the Enable Scripts icon and walk toward the moving truck. When the truck stops, you have completed the exercise. If the truck continues through the trees, try the exercise again.

You may have noticed that the truck does not stop right in front of you because it is not rendering seamlessly. If your video card has trouble rendering the animation as it plays, your script may not play as you originally intended. Consider this when creating your events.

SHOW VIEWPOINT ACTION

The Show Viewpoint action  will set the current view to a saved viewpoint. This action has many uses, including moving a user around the model. The Show Viewpoint action has one property: Viewpoint. Viewpoint is a drop-down box showing all the saved viewpoints in the project. To set this value, select any viewpoint in the drop-down box.

Let's see how the Show Viewpoint action works:

1. Open the file c11_Meadowgate_Actions.nwd.

2. Open Scripter and ensure Enable Scripts is not activated.

3. Select the Actions script.

4. Select the Show Viewpoint action.

5. Choose any viewpoint in the Viewpoint property.

6. Activate scripts by clicking the Enable Scripts icon.

PAUSE SCRIPT ACTION

The Pause Script action ▓ will delay the actions in the script queue for a specified amount of time. Since actions are executed one right after another with no pauses, this action can be used to create those pauses. You configure the sequence so that the first action in the queue is followed by the pause option. In this manner, the actions are broken up, allowing you to create a whole set of actions that will start when you let them start. The Pause Script action has one property: Delay. Delay is a text box that defines the number of seconds that must pass for an action to take place.

Let's see how the Pause Script action works by trying the following steps:

1. Open the file c11_Meadowgate_Actions.nwd.

2. Open Scripter and ensure Enable Scripts is not activated.

3. Select the Actions script.

4. Create your first action as Show Viewpoint.

5. Set the view to be Outside.

6. Create the second action as Play Animation.

7. Set the animation to select Scene2 ➤ Truck and ensure Pause On End is checked.

8. Create your third action as Pause.

9. Set the Pause Delay property to **10** seconds.

10. Create the fourth action as Play Animation.

11. Set the animation to select Scene2 ➤ Car.

12. Activate scripts by clicking the Enable Scripts icon.

SEND MESSAGE ACTION

The Send Message action ▓ creates a text file with a specified message. This message can be used to check on variable values while you are working on scripts.

The script file sends a message to the location defined in the Options Editor when this action is triggered. The path to the message file by default is blank. To set this value, choose Options Editor ➤ Tools ➤ Scripter. Browse to the folder you wish to send messages to and name your file something like **CheckVariable.txt**, as shown in Figure 11.15. Make sure you include the extension .txt with the filename; otherwise, the created file will not be recognized by text-editing software.

FIGURE 11.15
Send Message
Options Editor

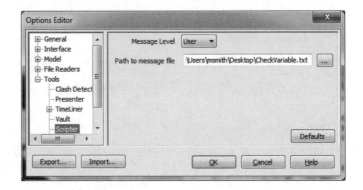

The only property you can assign to the Send Message action is Message. The Message property is a text box that defines a message to be sent to the text file defined in the options. Type any value in this box to have it displayed in your text file. Variables cannot be set here—only text will be sent to the text file.

The other option in the Options Editor is Message Level. There are two properties you can choose from:

User This option sends a message to the text file containing only information sent from message actions. When this property is selected, the text file will only contain information you send it through the Send Message action.

Debug This option sends a message to the text file with information sent from Send Message actions as well as Debug messages. The Debug messages describe exactly what scripter has done. This information includes the sequence of actions that the user has activated as well as any variables that have been defined with their respective values. The Debug option gives you the information you need to ensure your script files are performing exactly the way you want them to.

The Send Message action has the ability to record all the information that happens in the model when Scripter is activated. Using this tool, you can quickly debug your scripts and pinpoint errors. Make sure that you clean out the text file before you debug because the text file will not create breaks between different sessions of Scripter. Without clear breaks, it is difficult to follow the true actions that took place in the model. Try using Send Message by following these steps:

1. Open the file c11_Meadowgate_SendMessage.nwd.

2. Deactivate scripts by clicking the Enable Scripts button.

3. Set the Get Message file path in your options as described earlier.

4. Set Message Level in the options to Debug.

5. Select the Actions script.

6. Create the Send Message action.

7. Activate scripts by clicking the Enable Scripts button.

8. Navigate the model.

9. Open the text file and explore what happened during your navigation.

SET VARIABLE ACTION

The Set Variable action ![icon] allows you to introduce variables into your user interface. Previously, we defined events that were triggered based on the criteria of a variable. These variables are created by the Set Variable action. Variables can play a huge role in conditions by ensuring that new events are triggered only when old events have happened. This control is facilitated by the use of variables.

This action allows you to create a variable, assign a value to a variable, increase an existing variable value, or decrease an existing variable value. This action has three properties, as shown in Figure 11.16:

FIGURE 11.16
Set Variable
properties

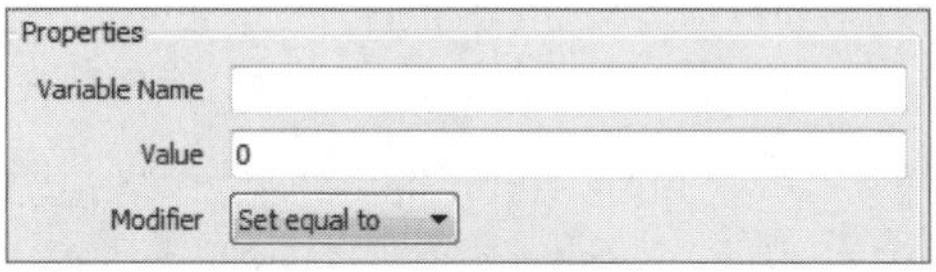

Variable Name   This property is a text box that defines the name of your variable. You can use alphanumeric characters as well as wildcard characters (*!@#$%^&) to name your variable. Spaces are also allowed. We advise you, however, to use only one-word variables to allow for easier debugging.

Value   This property assigns the variable a value. The value you can assign can be a number, an alphanumeric string, or a Boolean. For details on the definitions of these values, see the Event On variable.

Modifier   This property defines the operator for your variable. In this drop-down, you have three options: Set Equal To, Increment By, and Decrement By. The Set Equal To option will make the value of the variable equal to the value in the Value property. The Increment By option will increment the variable by the amount set in the Value column. The Decrement By option will decrease the value by the amount set in the Value column.

When creating the Set Variable action, keep in mind that strings can only be set to the operand Set Equal To. You cannot increment strings or decrement them.

Let's see how the Set Variable action works:

1. Open the file c11_Meadowgate_Actions.nwd.

2. Open Scripter and ensure Enable Scripts is not activated.

3. Select the Actions script.

4. Create your first action as Set Variable.

5. Set the Variable Name property to Scripter Started.

6. Create the second action as Send Message.

7. Ensure the Debug option is set for the Message Level setting in the Options Editor. (See the Send Message action for more details.)

8. Run the script.

9. Check the text file to see if your variable was defined.

STORE PROPERTY ACTION

The Store Property action  allows you to save an object property to a variable. This variable can be used later just like any other variable. Store Property will update its variable as the object it is connected to updates. When multiple objects are selected and attached to this variable, only the first root node will be considered. For example, if you select a group called door that has two subgroups, you may only store the properties listed in the original root door. The Store Property action has four properties: Set, Variable To Set, Category, and Property, as shown in Figure 11.17.

FIGURE 11.17
Store Property
properties

Set   This property is a drop-down box with three options:

Clear   This option removes all previously set objects. This will remove both objects selected with the Selection tool and objects selected by selection sets or search sets.

Set From Current Selection   This option allows you to select any number of objects in the model and attach the selected objects to this property.

Set From Current Selection Set   This option allows you to attach any selection set or search set to this property. When a selection set or search set is attached, the objects attached will change as the selection set or search set is updated. In this way, you maintain control over your objects without having to reset this property.

Variable To Set   This property is a text box that defines the name of your variable. You can use alphanumeric characters as well as wildcard characters (*!@#$%^&) to name your variable. Spaces are also allowed. We advise you, however, to use only one-word variables to allow for easier debugging.

Category   This property is a drop-down box that is filled dynamically depending on the object selected. To learn what the values of an object are, see Chapter 4, "Climbing the Selection Tree."

Property   This property is a drop-down box that is filled dynamically depending on the category.

Let's see how the Store Property action works:

1. Open the file `c11_Meadowgate_Actions.nwd`.

2. Open Scripter and ensure Enable Scripts is not activated.

3. Select the Actions script.

4. Create your first action as Store Property.

5. Select Windows Selection Set from the Sets window.

6. Choose Set From Current Selection from the Set drop-down.

7. Set the Variable Name property to Object_Property.

8. Set Category to Item.

9. Set Property to Name.

10. Create the second action as Send Message.

11. Ensure that the Debug option is set for the Message Level setting in the Options Editor. (See the Send Message action for more details.)

12. Run the script.

13. Check the text file to see if your property was saved.

LOAD MODEL ACTION

The Load Model action allows you to close the current model and open a new model. This action can be used to switch between similar projects to show clients different scopes of work. Additionally, it can be used to switch between large files that cannot be merged together without affecting the computer's performance. The Load Model action has one property: File To Load. File To Load defines the path of the file you wish to open. To set this path, select the Browse button next to the text box and browse to your file.

Let's see how the Load Model action works:

1. Open the file `c11_Meadowgate_Actions.nwd`.

2. Deactivate Scripts by clicking Enable Scripts.

3. Select the Actions script.

4. Create your first action as Load Model.

5. Set File To Load to **`c11_Meadowgate_OnStart.nwd`**.

6. Activate scripts by clicking the Enable Scripts icon.

Experiment with different triggers and actions to create real-life simulations. You can use Scripter to simulate how one event can have many different actions, such as clicking a button to start a conveyor belt that moves items across the screen. Be creative in your design, keeping in mind the end goal of simulating the story you wish to tell through scripts.

The Bottom Line

Manage scripts.   Scripter gives you the power to quickly toggle on and off scripts. This ability allows you to have a single model with many scripts that can easily be configured for any group.

Master It   How can you enable all scripts in a group?

Create events.   Events are rules that define special triggers. Users set off events by meeting the conditions set by the rules of the event.

Master It   Which event would you use to open a door when you near it?

Create actions.   Actions are the reaction the model has to the triggers defined by event(s). These actions allow you to control what the model will do in reaction to triggers you set.

Master It   How can you lead a user to a special viewpoint in your project and start an animation in that scene?

Interact with the model.   Interacting with the model brings to life real-world experiences in the model.

Master It   How could you create a scenario where a door opens as you near it and human avatars exit the door as soon as the door finishes opening?

Chapter 12

Collaborating outside of Navisworks

Up to this point, you've explored the numerous Autodesk® Navisworks® functionalities. Through examples and case studies, you've seen how Navisworks provides an interactive environment that can be used to validate design and construction workflows. This chapter will highlight additional features and workflows, but we'll be leveraging the model *outside* of Navisworks.

We'll also explore how to automate repetitive functions by using simple directives with command-line switches or by adding commands with the application programming interface (API). Looking at external applications such as Microsoft PowerPoint and the Autodesk® AutoCAD®–based platform, we'll explore how Navisworks not only integrates with these solutions, but also drives more efficient workflows.

In this chapter, you'll learn to:

♦ Interact with Navisworks Freedom

♦ Configure NWNavigator

♦ Export to third-party applications

Exploring the NWD File

As mentioned in earlier chapters, an NWD file is a snapshot of the model that can be packaged and forwarded to users without the need for the original source files to display properly. The benefit of this format extends beyond the core Navisworks application, because this file can also be viewed in several free viewers. That way, users can interact with the model and reference additional information such as comments, object properties, or even saved viewpoints and animations.

Using Navisworks Freedom

Navisworks Freedom is a free viewer that allows you to view NWD and DWF/DWFx/W2D files. While this application is strictly a read-only viewer, there are plenty of useful tools besides general navigation that make this an important part of the BIM workflow. Users can download Freedom at no charge from www.autodesk.com/navisworksfreedom. Follow the onscreen instructions to access and install the software.

Freedom provides many of the same tools found in the principal applications Navisworks Manage and Simulate, including the following:

♦ Full model navigation tools, including Third Person avatars

♦ The ability to view model hierarchy, including the 2D/3D project browser

◆ Embedded object properties and hyperlinks

◆ Embedded review data, including viewpoints, redlines, and comments

◆ Interactive measurement tools

◆ Model Sectioning tools (new to the 2013 release!)

◆ Saved animations and TimeLiner sequences

With Navisworks Freedom, you can get the whole-project view by using the interactive navigation tools and by viewing saved viewpoints with clash data, comments, and other review information. Since Freedom can read published NWD files, you can rest assured that data sent outside your organization will remain secure with features such as password protection and time-expiration settings. Table 12.1 provides a comparison of the features found in the core Navisworks versions and the Freedom viewer.

TABLE 12.1: Navisworks Product Comparison

FEATURE	NAVISWORKS MANAGE	NAVISWORKS SIMULATE	NAVISWORKS FREEDOM
Project Viewing			
Real-Time 3D and 2D visualization and navigation	X	X	X
Whole team review	X	X	X
Project Review			
File & Data Aggregation	X	X	
Review Toolkit	X	X	
NWD & 3D DWF Export	X	X	
Collaboration Toolkit	X	X	
Simulation & Analysis			
Photorealistic Visualization	X	X	
Object Animation	X	X	
4D Scheduling	X	X	
Coordination			
Clash & Interference Detection	X		
Substance Procedural Textures	X		
Clash	X		

MANAGING NWD VERSIONS

When using Navisworks Freedom, make note that the NWD file version must match up to the current application release. In other words, if you simply save or publish an NWD from Navisworks Manage 2013 without downgrading it, this file will not open properly in Navisworks Freedom 2012 or lower. If you're working with an older version, you can save back up to two release cycles (e.g., Navisworks Manage 2011); however, you lose some of the new functionality in the current release. For example, the new Grids and Levels functionality and the Selection Inspector are only available in the 2013 release and will not be displayed in earlier releases. Because Navisworks Freedom is available at no charge, users should upgrade to the most current version to maintain access to the newer functionality. Published NWD files cannot be saved back.

Viewing Navisworks Files on the Web

In addition to Navisworks Freedom, you can create a web portal to view NWD files over the Web using the ActiveX viewer, which comes as part of the initial installation. (Note that as of this writing, ActiveX is supported in Microsoft Internet Explorer only.) This viewer provides many of the same navigation tools as the core applications, but since the viewer can be embedded in HTML and modified with a CSS, you can easily modify the appearance of the viewer to customize the interface for specific projects or to embed into corporate locations. The benefit of using the web portal is that you can share the model with a larger audience without requiring that Navisworks Freedom or the primary applications be downloaded. Also, because the model file is only referenced over the Web, you don't have to worry about users viewing older or outdated model files.

To work effectively with the ActiveX controls, you should have a good understanding of HTML programming and web-based interaction. These functions go beyond the scope of this book and are covered in light detail only. When working with these controls, note that there are two versions of the ActiveX controls available for Navisworks. One is free (redistributable control) and the other requires a licensed copy of Navisworks to be installed alongside the ActiveX control (integrated control).

REDISTRIBUTABLE ACTIVEX CONTROL

The file `lcodieDX.dll` is the redistributable control that is free to any user. Depending on which operating system Navisworks is installed with, you will find either the 32-bit or the 64-bit installers for the ActiveX components here:

◆ `Program Files (x86)\Autodesk\Navisworks Manage 2013\api\COM\bin`

◆ `Program Files\Autodesk\Navisworks Manage 2013\api\COM\bin`

This control is supplied in a self-installing CAB file (`nw_ax_lite.cab`) and in a Windows Installer merge module (`ActiveX_redistributable.msm`). Multiple instances of the control may be used within the same process. This version offers functionality such as the following:

◆ The ability to open files using a Windows file path (NWD only)

◆ Model navigation

◆ The ability to view saved viewpoints, animations, and redlines

However, restrictions exist as well:

- ◆ You can't display presenter materials.

- ◆ You can't access object properties.

- ◆ Changes to the model can't be saved.

An example of the redistributable control implemented within a web interface can be found here: `www.aec-area.co.uk/NW/NW-Demo.htm`. In this setting, users can fully interact with the model and display saved viewpoints or animations (Figure 12.1). At the bottom of this web page is a link to download the ActiveX components if you don't have Navisworks installed on your machine. You can also use the ActiveX sample code located in the Navisworks install folder, `Program Files\Autodesk\Navisworks Manage 2013\api\COM\examples\ACTX_01`.

FIGURE 12.1
ActiveX viewer

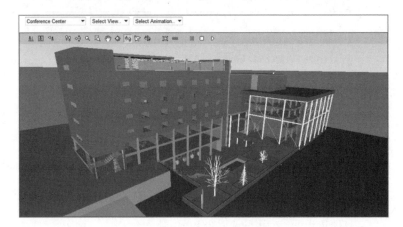

INTEGRATED ACTIVEX CONTROL

If you want to add controls for manipulating color or transparency for the model, leveraging object properties, viewing additional file formats (such as NWC or CAD formats), and displaying presenter materials, you'll need to use `lcodieD.dll`, the integrated control.

This component is installed as part of the Navisworks Manage and Simulate core products and can be located in the `API` folder in the install directory. In addition, this component offers comprehensive functionality and is available inside the ActiveX control as long as the main product is licensed.

Automating with Command-Line Switches

In addition to the easy-to-use interface, Navisworks allows some functions to be executed through the command-line interface for specific startup routines. You can use command-line switches to specify several options when you start the program. For example, you can run Navisworks in another language, perform additional memory checks, load and append files, and output error reports. With command-line switches, you can also set up several program icons, each with different startup options.

Think of command-line switches as parameters you can add to the `roamer.exe` command line associated with your Navisworks shortcut icon. Or you can use them independently in the Windows Run dialog box. You can include several switches within a single command line.

Table 12.2 lists the various switches available.

TABLE 12.2: Command-line Switch Options

COMMAND-LINE SWITCH	SWITCH ARGUMENT	DESCRIPTION
-dump	[file_name.dmp]	This switch is used to save an error report. You must provide the filename and path within quotation marks.
-lang	en-US = English de-DE = German es-ES = Spanish fr-FR = French it-IT = Italian ja-JP = Japanese ko-KR = Korean pt-BR = Brazilian ru-RU = Russian zh-CN = Chinese	This switch is used to launch Navisworks in the specified language. To fully support a different language, you need to make sure you have the appropriate language packs installed.
-log	[filename.txt]	This switch creates a log file to the specified file. You must provide the full filename and path in quotation marks.
-memcheck		This switch is useful if you're encountering memory errors. When you run Navisworks with this switch, additional checks for memory errors are conducted.
-nwc	[inputfile]	Use this switch if you want to convert an input file (DWG™, FBX®, DWF, and similar files) into an NWC file. You must provide the full filename and path in quotation marks.
-nwd	[outputfile.nwd] [inputfile]	This switch converts an input file into an NWD and places the file in a specific directory. You must provide the full filename and path in quotation marks.
-options	[filename.xml]	When working with global options files (XML), you can use this switch to load the various options on startup. You must provide the full filename and path in quotation marks.
-regserver		This switch is used to register the roamer .exe with the COM API.

The syntax for using command-line switches is as follows:

```
"drive:pathname\roamer.exe" [switches] ["file1"] ["file2"] ["fileN"]
```

where [*switches*] are the valid command-line switches listed in Table 12.2, and ["*file1*"]...
["*fileN*"] are the files to be loaded and appended together, if required. You must provide the
full file paths within quotation marks.

Let's examine this workflow in detail with the following scenario. Suppose you work with
both metric and imperial datasets and need to change global options profiles (XML) regularly.
Rather than manually load the various XML files every time you need to access one of the profiles, you can create a few desktop icons that, when clicked, will start Navisworks with the correct global option profile. (Saving and managing global option profiles will be covered in greater
detail in Appendix B, "Additional Resources and Tips.") Follow these steps:

1. Open the Global Options Editor and click the Export icon in the lower-left corner to
   save your options file. In the Select Options To Export window, click Display Units
   (Figure 12.2). When you click OK, Navisworks will save an XML file with all of your
   current settings.

FIGURE 12.2
Select Options To
Export window

2. Save the file as **Options Imperial.xml**.

3. Make changes to your display options (metric) and save the additional options profile as
   Options Metric.xml.

4. Move the options files to a designated folder on your machine (such as C:\Global
   Options).

5. Create two new Navisworks desktop shortcuts.

6. Label the shortcuts **Navisworks Metric** and **Navisworks Imperial** (Figure 12.3).

FIGURE 12.3

Desktop shortcuts
with different
options

Navisworks   Navisworks
Imperial   Metric

7. Right-click the Navisworks Metric icon and select Properties from the context menu. In the Shortcut tab, modify the Target field to read:

```
"C:\Program Files\Autodesk\Navisworks Manage 2013\roamer.exe" -options ↵
```

```
"C:\Global Options\Options Metric.xml"
```

Depending on your installation, you may need to modify the drive and path (Figure 12.4). Also, pay attention to the quotation marks and spacing; otherwise, you'll receive an error message.

FIGURE 12.4

Desktop shortcut
properties

8. Modify the properties for the Navisworks Imperial icon, but change the syntax to point to the `Options Imperial.xml` file.

Depending on which icon you select, the appropriate global options will be loaded upon startup.

Command-Line Batch Utility Options

In addition to the basic command-line switches previously discussed, you can use command-line switches to reference the Batch utility options to accomplish such tasks as automating the conversion of files. For more information on the Batch utility, see Chapter 2, "Files and File Types."

When working with command-line switches for the Batch utility, it's best to start by making a list of files you want to process. Create a text file (UTF-8 encoded) containing the file paths, with one file path per line. Here's an example:

```
C:\My Documents\Navisworks\Meadowgate\First Floor Ductwork.dwg
C:\My Documents\Navisworks\Meadowgate\Services-Plantroom.dwg
C:\My Documents\Navisworks\Meadowgate\Civil.nwc
```

The syntax for command-line switches is slightly different from the standard command-line options. Instead of using roamer.exe, you use FileToolsTaskRunner.exe. Here's the basic format:

```
FileToolsTaskRunner.exe /i <input file> [/of <output file>|/od <folder>|↵
/osd] [/view] [/over|/inc] [/log <log file>] [/append] [/lang <language>]
```

See Table 12.3 for an overview of these options.

TABLE 12.3:   Supported Command-line Switches

COMMAND-LINE SWITCH	DESCRIPTION
/i	Dictates that the next argument is the input file. All filenames and paths must be in quotation marks.
/of	Designates the output of a single Navisworks file; must be an NWD or an NWF. All filenames and paths must be in quotation marks. Example: "C:\Autodesk\Meadowgate.nwd".
/od	Use this command to output multiple NWD files into a specific folder. The path should appear within quotation marks.
/osd	This command outputs multiple NWD files into the same folder as the original source data files.
/view	Use this command if you wish to view the file after it's been created.
/over	This command is used to overwrite the output files.
/inc	This command increments the output filenames.
/log	Use this command if you wish to create a log file of your outputs. All filenames and paths must be in quotation marks.
/appnlog	This command switch captures new events and appends them to the bottom of the existing log file.

TABLE 12.3:   Supported Command-line Switches   *(CONTINUED)*

COMMAND-LINE SWITCH	DESCRIPTION
/lang	Available languages for use with the logging commands:
	en-US = English
	de-DE = German
	es-ES = Spanish
	fr-FR = French
	it-IT = Italian
	ja-JP = Japanese
	ko-KR = Korean
	pt-BR = Brazilian Portuguese
	ru-RU = Russian
	zh-CN = Chinese

Automating the Batch Utility with the Command Line

For our example, we want to append three DWG files into a single file named Meadowgate.nwd. You'll also create a log file of these actions. Follow these steps:

1. Create an empty folder in your C: drive and name it **Meadowgate**.

2. Download the following files and place them in the newly created Meadowgate folder (C:/Meadowgate):

   ◆ c12_Meadowgate_Architecture.dwg

   ◆ c12_Meadowgate_Civil.dwg

   ◆ c12_Meadowgate_Structure.dwg

3. Create a blank text file named filetools.txt and place it in the Meadowgate folder.

4. Edit the text file and list the filename and path to the three DWG files:

   ```
   C:\Meadowgate\c12_Meadowgate_Architecture.dwg
   C:\Meadowgate\c12_Meadowgate_Civil.dwg
   C:\Meadowgate\c12_Meadowgate_Structure.dwg
   ```

5. Open the Windows Run dialog box and enter the following (Figure 12.5):

   ```
   "C:\Program Files\Autodesk\Navisworks Manage 2013\ ↵
   FileToolsTaskRunner.exe" /i
   "C:\Meadowgate\filetools.txt" /of "C:\Meadowgate\Meadowgate.nwd" /log
   "C:\Meadowgate\events.log"
   ```

   If you're using Navisworks Simulate, you'll need to change the text to reflect the path:

   ```
   "C:\Program Files\Autodesk\Navisworks Simulate 2013\ ↵
   FileToolsTaskRunner.exe" /i
   "C:\Meadowgate\filetools.txt" /of "C:\Meadowgate\Meadowgate.nwd" /log
   "C:\Meadowgate\events.log"
   ```

FIGURE 12.5
Windows Run
dialog box

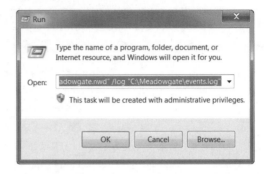

This command consists of three different switches. The /i switch references the input file, or in this case, the text file with the path to the files you're trying to append. The /of switch designates the output file. In this case, you're saving the output as an NWD file with the name Meadowgate. The last switch, /log, prompts Navisworks to create a log of the actions and save to the Meadowgate folder. When the command is executed, a new DOS window opens and Navisworks starts in the background. Depending on your system, this process may take a few minutes to run. The files listed in your text file will be appended and the subsequent NWD file will be saved to the Meadowgate folder along with the events.log file listing which actions were completed (Figure 12.6). Any errors encountered in this process will be listed in the log.

FIGURE 12.6
Batch utility log

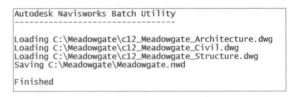

In this section, you explored using command-line switches to automate certain tasks outside the main Navisworks application. Using a simple syntax, repetitive routines or settings can easily be defined and executed.

Extending Navisworks to External Applications

When Navisworks is used in multidiscipline workflows, you can leverage the benefits beyond the core application by interacting with third-party applications. This section will explore a few of these opportunities by showcasing some little-known workflows and functions. Although these external applications provide additional value, they are in no way required to enjoy the benefits of Navisworks. These solutions extend the efficiency of Navisworks to a larger user base and provide greater interaction that can translate into a more streamlined process and additional ways to maximize your investment.

Interacting with NWNavigator

Navisworks Navigator, or Navigator as it's commonly referred to, is an AutoCAD Runtime Extension (ARX) plug-in that allows you to create a virtual session of Navisworks directly inside your CAD viewing window. This instance of Navisworks contains the same general navigation tools as the core application but allows you to swap camera views between your AutoCAD window and the dockable Navisworks window. You can easily import and export viewpoints between Navigator and AutoCAD and explore the models that are part of your design.

When Navisworks is initially installed, the application searches for any compliant version of AutoCAD (2004 or newer) and installs the NWNavigator ARX plug-in. In AutoCAD, you can open the command by typing **NWNavigator** in the command line. A dockable window will open in your AutoCAD window (Figure 12.7). You can expand the size of this window by dragging the borders or simply move it to another part of your monitor. Displayed across the top of this window is a series of toolbar commands.

FIGURE 12.7
Navigator displayed alongside AutoCAD

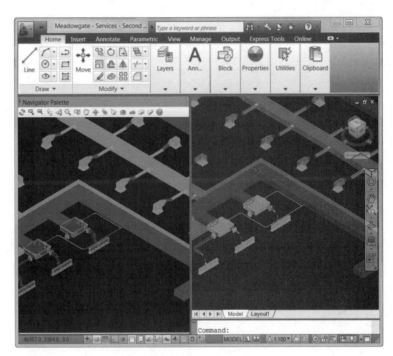

Table 12.4 lists the different commands in the Navigator window.

TABLE 12.4:   NWNavigator Overview

ICON	DESCRIPTION
	Clicking this icon updates the Navigator view to synchronize the views between the Navigator and AutoCAD windows. Every time the CAD model is updated, you need to resync the model by clicking this icon.
	Clicking this icon changes the current AutoCAD view to reflect the view in the Navigator window.
	Clicking this icon changes the Navigator window to reflect the current AutoCAD view.

TABLE 12.4: NWNavigator Overview *(CONTINUED)*

ICON	DESCRIPTION
	Clicking this icon selects the Walk mode, which allows you to navigate through the model on a horizontal plane.
	Clicking this icon activates the Look-around mode, allowing you to view the model from the current camera position.
	Clicking this icon activates the Zoom mode. Holding down the left mouse button and dragging forward or backward zooms in or out.
	Clicking this icon activates the zoom box, allowing you to specify an area to zoom in to.
	Clicking this icon selects the Pan mode. Holding the left mouse button, you can pan around the model in all directions.
	Clicking this icon selects the Orbit mode. With this tool activated, hold down the left button to rotate the camera around the model like a satellite.
	Clicking this icon activates the Examine mode. Holding down the left mouse button allows you to keep your camera stationary while moving the model.
	Clicking this icon selects the Fly mode. Holding down the left mouse button will trigger the camera. Move the mouse in any direction to change direction.
	Clicking this icon selects the Turntable command, allowing you to rotate the model on a common axis.
	Clicking this icon functions as the Zoom All command and shows the whole model.
	Clicking this icon shows the model in Perspective Camera view.
	Clicking this icon shows the model in Orthographic Camera view.
	Clicking this icon triggers the Help menu.

Let's examine the steps to use NWNavigator:

1. Open an AutoCAD-based platform (version 2004 or newer) with the ARX plug-in installed.

2. Open the file c12_Meadowgate_Ductwork.dwg.

3. Type **NWNavigator** at the AutoCAD command line. A new window will open inside the AutoCAD viewing window.

4. Click the icon to refresh the Navigator window.

5. To create the same AutoCAD view in the Navigator window, click the Get AutoCAD Viewpoint icon 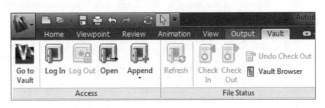.

6. Adjust the view in Navigator by using the navigation tools.

7. To update the AutoCAD view with the Navigator view, click the Set AutoCAD Viewpoint icon .

8. Close the Navigator window when finished to end the session.

HANDLING LARGE AUTOCAD FILES WITH NWNAVIGATOR

One of the main benefits of Navisworks is the ability to work with large datasets. When opened in Navisworks, raw data files are converted into the lightweight NWC format that allows for easy viewing of complex models. Using NWNavigator allows users to easily navigate large AutoCAD files without waiting for lengthy regeneration times.

Instead of navigating in the AutoCAD window, use the Navigator window to interact with extremely large CAD files and locate the proper camera angle. Then, use the Set AutoCAD Viewpoint command to update the AutoCAD view.

Leveraging Vault for Data Management

Navisworks 2013 allows you to access the data management capabilities of Autodesk Vault. Vault offers a comprehensive solution for managing the large volume of data that is generated during projects, including the standard NWF, NWD, and NWC formats. A vault is a repository where documents and files are stored and managed. Autodesk Vault is a data management system that offers file security, version control, and multiuser support. The Vault add-in is available with Autodesk Navisworks Manage and Autodesk Navisworks Simulate, and it supports connection to Autodesk Vault Basic, Autodesk Vault Workgroup, Autodesk Vault Collaboration, Autodesk Vault Collaboration AEC, and Autodesk Vault Professional.

Furthermore, Navisworks and Vault integration enables you to retrieve/save, check in/check out, control file versioning, and manage the relationship between NWF and design data. You can organize all of your files and keep them in one location for easy access. All file versions are retained, so you never misplace or replace past versions. The vault stores each version of a file, along with all the file's dependencies, giving you a living history of the project as you work on it. The vault also stores file properties such as the user name, date, and comments for rapid searching and retrieving.

To use the Autodesk Vault add-in, you need to install the Autodesk Vault 2013 client first. Once it's installed, a dedicated tab for Vault (Figure 12.8) will display in the Navisworks interface. Users can save and load standard Navisworks files in addition to appending all the standard formats that Navisworks currently reads.

FIGURE 12.8
Vault tab in the ribbon

When you save files back to Vault, the model hierarchy is retained so workflows between numerous offices can be maintained. Also, the Refresh command allows users to continually update source files and have those changes easily update and display in Navisworks. Lastly, users can add comments or notes to the files when checking in to ensure effective communication with all project members (Figure 12.9).

FIGURE 12.9
Vault's Check In
dialog box

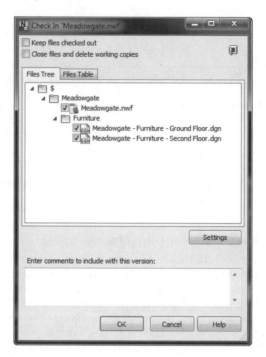

CONCEPTUALIZING EXTERNAL SCHEDULES IN NAVISWORKS

When you're building TimeLiner schedules, Navisworks can bring in schedule data from a variety of scheduling applications such as Microsoft Project and Primavera P6. In addition, schedule data can be created from scratch and exported. In a typical construction coordination process, the role of the scheduler is sometimes removed from the early planning and development procedures. As a result, conceptual schedules may be missing or inaccurate for preliminary 4D work.

To aid with this issue, schedulers can create their schedules in Navisworks using the TimeLiner tools and develop an accurate naming convention that can be exported to a dedicated scheduling application.

Once all the files have been appended in the main model, the scheduler can easily break the model down into specific objects by using search/selection sets that represent the individual schedule tasks. At this point, the sets start to define the naming convention for the project schedule. In addition to the flexible naming standards, the Sets window can easily be modified to change the hierarchy and order. This allows the scheduler to identify all the components in the model that need to be addressed in the schedule, but more importantly, this hierarchy becomes the root arrangement of the schedule.

Using the Add Tasks feature in TimeLiner, you can create a task for each defined search/selection set. By default, this feature uses the current date as the start date and increments each subsequent task by one day. You can also add tasks manually, and using the new TimeLiner Indent and Outdent features, you can create a new model hierarchy. Using the interactive Gantt chart in TimeLiner, you can easily modify the dates to reflect a more realistic timeframe. At any point during this process, you can run the simulation to display the current schedule in 4D. When discrepancies in the construction model are discovered, the SwitchBack tool allows you to quickly reference the original source file and make any necessary changes, such as breaking up the slabs into individual pours or parting a wall into individual components.

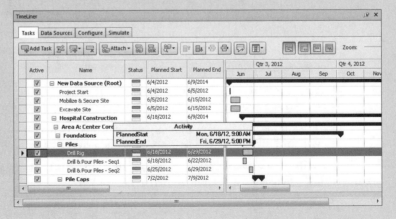

Once the conceptual schedule is complete and all facets of the project are fully understood, the schedule can be exported as a CSV or the newly supported Microsoft XML format and brought into a dedicated scheduling application for further refinement and updates. Later, you can reverse this process and reimport the fully validated schedule back into Navisworks. Since the task names were already defined from your initial search/selection sets, you can create a simple rule to map them to the appropriate objects in your scene.

This workflow provides a way to bridge some of the gaps and inefficiencies in the construction process by bringing the scheduler and other project team members together earlier in the process. This workflow also standardizes on a consistent naming convention so that as schedules and models are updated, they can quickly be linked in an efficient manner. For more information on these workflows, see Chapter 7, "4D Sequencing with TimeLiner."

Embedding Navisworks Files in Microsoft PowerPoint Presentations

Another novel way to use the Navisworks navigation engine is to embed this functionality into your PowerPoint presentations. Instead of having to switch between bullet points and the dynamic model, you can embed the ActiveX viewer directly into your slide deck so that your presentations become more interactive and enlightening. Let's look at the steps to complete this. You'll be using the file `c12_Meadowgate.nwd`. But first, you'll need the ActiveX controls for this functionality, so make sure they're installed.

1. Open Microsoft PowerPoint and make sure the Developer tab is unhidden.

2. Select the More Controls icon in the Controls panel (Figure 12.10).

FIGURE 12.10
PowerPoint
Controls panel

3. In the pop-up window, select Navisworks Integrated Control 10 MDI or Navisworks Integrated Control 10 SDI from the list and click OK.

4. Your cursor will change to a + sign. In your slide, drag the mouse to create a box that represents the outline of the area you want to display the Navisworks viewer.

5. The outline will contain eight grips that can be used to enlarge or reshape the viewer window. Right-click inside the outline and select Properties from the menu.

6. In the Properties window, enter the path to the NWD file in the SRC field (e.g., **C:\Temp\ c12_Meadowgate.nwd**), as shown in Figure 12.11.

7. Close the Properties window and press F5 to run in Slideshow mode.

FIGURE 12.11
PowerPoint
Properties window

FIGURE 12.11
PowerPoint
Properties window

8. After the control loads, you can interact with your model inside PowerPoint (Figure 12.12). To change the navigation mode, right-click in the viewer window and select Viewpoints ➤ Navigation Mode.

FIGURE 12.12
Power Point presentation showing embedded Navisworks viewer

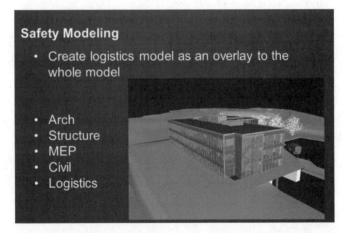

When saving the files, only the link to the model is preserved. It's a best practice to store the model in the same folder as the PowerPoint presentation. Also, when you save your slideshow, you'll need to save it as a macro-enabled presentation. Here are the steps to configure PowerPoint:

1. Click the Microsoft Office button (top-left circular button) and select File ➤ Save As (or just press F12).

2. Under Save As Type, select PowerPoint Macro-Enabled Presentation, give it a name, and click Save.

Examining Other Export Options

Besides the integration with third-party applications, Navisworks can export different file formats that can be saved as an FBX® file for additional rendering capabilities in Autodesk® 3ds Max®, DWF/DWFx export, or other tools, which can be viewed in Freedom and other model viewers. In all of these examples, the main benefit is being able to collaborate outside Navisworks to extend the value of the model to additional workflows and functions. In Chapter 2, you examined the Publish feature as a means to share NWD files securely. For the next series of exercises, you'll learn how to save the Navisworks model to additional formats that can be incorporated into these adjacent programs.

Exporting to Google Earth

Google Earth is a unique application that provides users with a virtual globe allowing users to search by address, enter coordinates or simply browse with a mouse. In Navisworks you can export your model to a specific set of coordinates and then open the model inside of Google Earth. This is useful since the model can then be compared against other 3D buildings, roads and even weather conditions. However you first need a few pieces of information to export to a specific location. To accurately align the Navisworks model, you need the latitude and longitude of the location you wish to place your model. In Google Earth this can be accomplished in numerous ways, however the easiest is to add up to three placemarkers that define reference points of the proposed model siting. These placemarkers are key to properly orienting and aligning your Navisworks model. To assist with exporting the model to the correct coordinates, Navisworks uses a KML Options editor to specify the Google Earth coordinates in tandem with the Navisworks model. The exported KML file contains the same model hierarchy including most geometry (triangles and lines) as well as limited colors. Due to limitations of Google Earth, viewpoints and hyperlinks may be adjusted on export.

Let's explore the interface in detail by selecting the Google Earth KML button in the Export Scene panel of the Output tab (Figure 12.13).

FIGURE 12.13
Google Earth Icon location

The KML Options editor contains several different functions (Figure 12.14). Let's break these down to get a better understanding.

In the options area at the top, there are two settings to configure. The first, Export Model Relative to Terrain Height is used to determine if the model is measured from the surface of the ground, or from sea-level. As a best practice, keep this box checked to measure from the actual surface of the ground. The second option, Collapse on Export, allows you to collapse the model hierarchy to different levels when exporting out. The four choices are:

◆ None -the whole model hierarchy is exported

◆ All Objects - all model objects are collapsed into one node

◆ Files - each distinct file is collapsed into one node

◆ Layers - all layers in the model are collapsed into one node

FIGURE 12.14
KML Options
Window

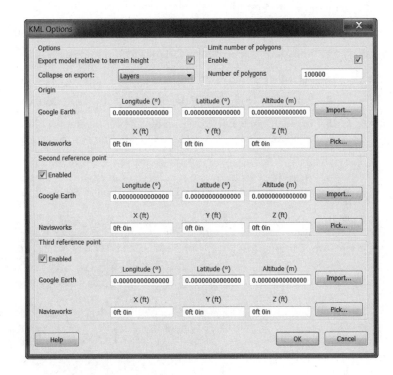

For simplicity, it's recommended that you use the Layers option.

Even though Navisworks can handle enormous files with relative ease, applications like Google Earth aren't meant to handle the sheer number of polygons (triangles) in your scene. To keep Google Earth from becoming overloaded, you should limit the number of polygons in your export. Select the enable checkbox in the Limit Number of Polygons area in the top right to restrict the amount of geometry exported. A good balance of 100,000 polygons yields good performance in Google Earth and maintains fidelity of the Navisworks model.

To align the Navisworks model, you need to specify the origin position of the Google Earth surface. At least one set of points must be defined, however up to three different sets can be referenced for greater accuracy. In addition to defining the Google Earth points, you need to specify the reference points from the Navisworks model. These points will always be positioned to exactly overlay the Google Earth position. In the first reference area, or Origin, you can manually enter the values of the Longitude, Latitude and Altitude, however to make this easier, you can also import a KMZ file. Recall when deciding where to place your model, you can create placemarkers in Google Earth that reference the origin and additional points and save those as KMZ files. To specify the Navisworks points, use the Pick button. When your cursor changes to a crosshair, you can select the appropriate point in the model view to capture the reference point.

Let's explore this workflow using the steps listed below. For this exercise we'll be using the model c12_Meadowgate_Earth.nwd. Since you're adding this to an existing site surface in Google Earth, it's a good idea to remove the civil file from your Navisworks model so that you only export the building.

1. Open the model and Google Earth KML options dialog box.

2. Make sure Export Model Relative to Terrain Height is checked.

3. Set Collapse on Export to Layers

4. Enable the Number of Polygons and set the value to 100,000

5. For the Google Earth origin point, select the import button and navigate to the file c12_Meadowgate_1.kmz. Select Open. The coordinates from that placemarker are now listed in the coordinate fields.

6. Select the Pick button to specify the Navisworks reference point. With the crosshairs, select the edge of the building as depicted in Figure 12.15.

FIGURE 12.15
Google Earth
reference locations

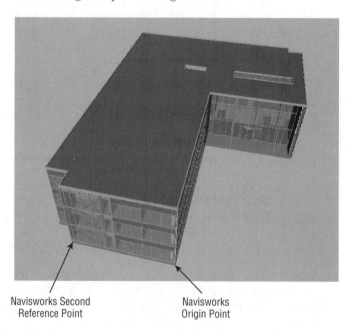

Navisworks Second   Navisworks
Reference Point   Origin Point

7. For the Google Earth second reference point, Select the Enabled checkbox and select the import button. Navigate to the file c12_Meadowgate_2.kmz. Select Open. The coordinates from that placemarker are now listed in the coordinate fields.

8. Select the Pick button to specify the Navisworks reference point. With the crosshairs, select the edge of the building as depicted in Figure 12.15.

9. Select OK and save the KMZ file.

10. Initiate Google Earth and open the previous saved KMZ file.

The Meadowgate model will be displayed in the town just outside Sheffield, England (Figure 12.16).

FIGURE 12.16
Navisworks model
situated in Google
Earth

FBX

FBX, or Filmbox as it's sometimes referred to, is another format that allows you to export your Navisworks scene and reference in other applications such as 3ds Max. This is useful if you want to take your model into a higher-end rendering solution than what the Presenter module provides. When exporting to the FBX format, all model primitives (triangles and lines), materials, viewpoints, and lights are supported with the exception of point clouds.

To export to FBX, follow these steps:

1. Open the FBX Options (Figure 12.17) by clicking the FBX button in the Export Scene panel in the Output tab.

FIGURE 12.17
FBX export options

2. Depending on the size of the model, you may want to limit the amount of geometry exported. Click the Enabled check box and enter the number of polygons to limit in the export.

3. To include Textures, Lights, and Cameras in the export, select the appropriate check boxes in the Include area.

4. In the Advanced Options area, specify the unit of measurement. Leave the FBX file format as Binary and specify the most current file version.

5. In the Texture area, click Embed to have the textures "baked" into the FBX file. If necessary, you can specify a separate location or the existing reference location.

6. Click OK and specify the filename and the location where you want to save.

With the FBX format, you can export your Navisworks scene and bring it into 3ds Max, Autodesk® Maya®, or similar rendering applications (Figure 12.18) to create high-end visualizations or advanced animations.

FIGURE 12.18
FBX export shown in 3ds Max

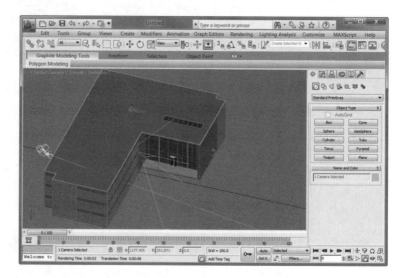

3D DWF/DWFx

Another format that is useful for sharing and viewing 3D models is the DWF/DWFx format. In Navisworks, users can export their scene to a DWF file for use in downstream viewers such as Autodesk™ Design Review™. Since your project team may be dispersed across a wide area, having access to multiple files allows all stakeholders to have access to the model. To export to DWF/DWFx, click the 3D DWF/DWFx button in the Export Scene panel in the Output tab. Specify the filename and location.

When you're working with DWF files, limited object properties are saved in the export process. Linked files and embedded 2D views do not export. The DWFx format is supported by the Microsoft XPS viewer, allowing you to view the model without downloading any additional software.

Customizing with the Navisworks API

An API is a set of specifications that allows users to program and automate existing functions in the program. Navisworks' API is designed to maximize the customization possibilities of the product and minimize the constraints upon using it creatively. Since this is a broad topic and mostly limited to developers, this section will provide a general overview of the API and is not meant to be an exhaustive technical guide.

The API is divided into three versions: .NET, COM, and NWCreate. In addition to the minimum system requirements for Navisworks, programmers will need Navisworks Simulate or Manage to be installed since no form of the API (plug-in or controls) will be supported in Freedom.

The .NET API is an ongoing enhancement to Navisworks and was substantially enhanced for the 2013 release to include functionality for customizing the Clash Detective functions. This is intended to replace the COM API in most cases. The main areas of this API are focused on plug-ins, automation, and controls. There are several advantages to implementing the .NET API for Navisworks:

◆ Programmatic access to Navisworks models is opened up to more programming environments.

◆ Integrating with other Windows-based applications, such as Microsoft Excel and Word, is made dramatically easier by using an application's native .NET API.

◆ The .NET API is designed for both 32-bit and 64-bit operating systems. Visual Basic was designed only for 32-bit operating systems.

◆ The .NET API allows access to advanced programming interfaces with a lower learning curve than those for more traditional programming languages such as C++.

Users of the Navisworks .NET API are able to do the following:

◆ Gain access to application information

◆ Gain access to model and document information

◆ Perform simple operations on Navisworks documents (open, save, execute plug-ins) without having to fully load the main application

The Navisworks .NET API is fully accessible by any language compatible with the Microsoft .NET Framework 3.5, such as Visual Basic .NET or Visual C#.

API controls that have been installed are typically referenced from the Add-ins tab in Navisworks (Figure 12.19). These controls cannot be accessed via keyboard shortcuts.

FIGURE 12.19
Add-ins tab in Navisworks showing custom plug-ins

The older COM interface also consists of three parts: Automation, which allows you to control the product from any COM-compliant language; the ActiveX control API, which allows you

to embed Navisworks functionality into ActiveX control containers; and Plug-ins, for extending Navisworks functionality.

A complete Navisworks model is accessed via a State object, which corresponds to a document in Windows terminology and contains the objects Navisworks users interact with, such as views, animations, and selection sets. The COM interface, in all three parts (Automation, ActiveX, and Plug-ins), lets you access the State object.

There is a lot of similarity between the APIs, in that they all provide access to the Navisworks internal state. In addition, there is a C/C++ API, called NWCreate, which is used for creating models.

The COM interface API is also programmable in .NET, although we recommend that you use classic VB. To assist with users who may have both .NET and COM controls implemented, a specific COM interop control allows you to run the COM API within the .NET Framework. However, since the COM API is being deprecated, most future development will focus on the .NET API.

Applications using the .NET API include the following:

- ◆ Plug-ins

- ◆ Automation

- ◆ Control-based applications

The Navisworks development team has produced a short video that describes the .NET API in detail. It is available on the Wiley download site and can be accessed from the `Chapter 12` folder under `c12_Recording.zip`.

In addition, there is a Developer Guide and several examples to assist users with configuring the API. The samples require that Microsoft Visual Studio or Microsoft Visual Express editions be installed. You can locate these samples and other documentation in the `API` folder. It is typically located here: `C:\Program Files\Autodesk\Navisworks Manage 2013\API`.

There are also some additional samples that can be downloaded from the `Chapter 12` folder under the name `c12_Samples.zip`.

The Bottom Line

Interact with Navisworks Freedom.   In addition to the core applications Manage and Simulate, Autodesk provides Navisworks Freedom as a no-cost viewer to extend the value of the model to users who may not have access to the core products.

> **Master It**   What file formats does Navisworks Freedom view?

Configure NWNavigator.   NWNavigator is a plug-in that allows you to create a virtual instance of Navisworks inside a session of AutoCAD.

> **Master It**   What is the benefit of using NWNavigator with large datasets?

Export to third-party applications.   Navisworks can export the model scene to external applications where adjacent workflows and benefits are realized.

> **Master It**   What are some of the different file formats that Navisworks can export to?

Chapter 13

Other Useful Navisworks Tools

At this point in this book, we've discussed the bulk of the Autodesk® Navisworks® tools and extra modules. This chapter looks at the other tools not previously mentioned that interface with other programs. We describe export tools, which give you the power to view and change Navisworks models in other programs. Tools that access external databases and files are also explored. Through the use of these tools, you can fully harness the ability of Navisworks to interact with other programs.

In this chapter, you'll learn to:

- ◆ Connect external data to object properties
- ◆ Use the Project Browser
- ◆ Reference external documents from the model

Model Data Tools

Navisworks allows you to import significant amounts of metadata from authoring tools; however, there are times when you may want to connect additional data sources to the model. Navisworks lets you connect these additional data sources to the model through the use of data tools. Most Open Database Connectivity (ODBC) connections are available in Navisworks.

Database connections are especially useful to clients with large existing databases. Rather than reinvent the wheel by embedding metadata into user-defined model properties where it is stagnant, you can create a dynamic link to the model through database connections. Utilizing these data connections enables Navisworks to stay agnostic to any one connection type and permits seamless integration with existing systems.

CONNECTING TO MICROSOFT OFFICE PRODUCTS

Navisworks can be installed either as a 32-bit or a 64-bit program. Although there are many performance reasons why you would want to install the 64-bit version, keep in mind some drawbacks. To connect to Microsoft Office products, you must have the correct drivers. If you are running any version older than Microsoft Office 2010, you only have 32-bit drivers. With 32-bit drivers, you can connect to Navisworks 32 bit but not Navisworks 64 bit. You cannot download and install the 64-bit Office drivers without first uninstalling Microsoft Office.

If you have Microsoft Office 2010 64 bit installed, you only have 64-bit drivers and may only connect to Microsoft Office programs with Navisworks 64 bit.

To connect to a data tool, click the DataTools icon on the Tools panel of the Home tab.

When you click the DataTools icon, a dialog box is displayed, as shown in Figure 13.1. In the center of this dialog box is a list of items with check boxes next to them. Each item on the list is an external reference to an ODBC link. If the check boxes are not selected, as shown in Figure 13.1, none of the links will be active.

The buttons on the right allow you to add, modify, delete, import, and export your data tools.

FIGURE 13.1
DataTools
dialog box

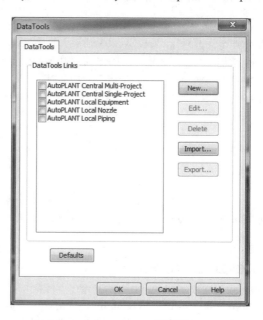

Click the New button to open a window to set up a new ODBC connection, as shown in Figure 13.2. There are many steps to configuring a new ODBC link, and we will walk you through the process.

FIGURE 13.2
Setting up a new
ODBC link

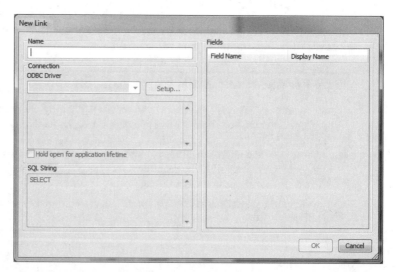

Name   This text box defines the name of the link. This name will show up in the DataTools main window. You can name the link using any characters, but you have to give the link a name before you can edit other options.

ODBC_Driver   This drop-down list is populated with ODBC drivers that are supported by Navisworks. The list includes AutoPLANT, Microsoft Access, Microsoft Excel, Microsoft SQL, Oracle, and many others. Select the driver in this drop-down list that corresponds to the database you wish to link to.

Setup   Setup is a button that allows you to define the location of your database. The options to configure Setup will change depending on the ODBC driver you selected previously.

The following figures show the various types of setup windows you will see. They include SQL Server Login (Figure 13.3), Select Data Source (Figure 13.4), ODBC Microsoft Excel Setup (Figure 13.5), and ODBC Microsoft Access Setup (Figure 13.6).

FIGURE 13.3

SQL Server Login
dialog box

To create a SQL connection, select an active server from the Server drop-down list shown in Figure 13.3. Configure the username (Login ID) and password as needed.

The SQL option is very useful when you couple it with the Autodesk® Revit® SQL DB link. Consider connecting the live Revit model information stored in a SQL environment to the Navisworks model to add information such as the operations and owner's manual. Having these added properties will bring additional needed resources to life-cycle management.

FIGURE 13.4

Data source
selection

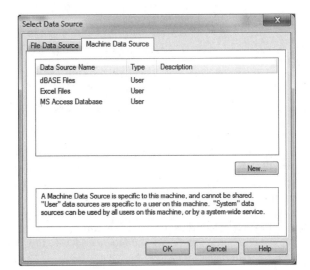

To connect to an existing ODBC connection, simply select the desired connection from the existing ODBC connections shown in Figure 13.4. To learn more about creating ODBC connections, contact your IT department or check resources on the Internet.

The ODBC link is useful if you work in an environment that uses active databases to share information that you wish to embed into the model. An example is connecting popular software such as Prolog to the model.

FIGURE 13.5
Connecting to Excel

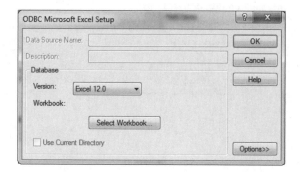

To connect to a Microsoft Excel spreadsheet, first select the Excel version from the drop-down shown in Figure 13.5. Click the Select Workbook button and browse to the Excel file you wish to link.

The Excel link is useful to connect existing Excel workbooks to a model. An example of data you could add is estimating data. You can add quantities, values, and even Construction Specification Institute (CSI) codes or Uniformat codes to the project. This allows users to quickly search model objects by estimating values.

FIGURE 13.6
Connecting to Access

To connect to a Microsoft Access tool, click the Select button in the dialog box shown in Figure 13.6 and browse to the Access database you wish to connect to. If your Access installation requires a username and password, use the Advanced button on the right to insert the correct username and password.

Connecting to an Access database can be an effective way to keep data in the model up to date with current facilities data. Models can be exported from Revit directly into a Microsoft Office database, allowing extra data to be added to the Navisworks model properties.

Back on the main ODBC setup screen (Figure 13.2), the window directly under the ODBC driver will populate with a string that will connect the Navisworks model to the database you selected. Any time you change the ODBC connection, this box will change. Only change the text in this box if you are confident in your connection syntax skills.

SQL String   In the SQL String box, you must create a SQL query line to obtain all the information you desire. Although creating a SQL string is outside the scope of this book, we'll provide some general suggestions.

SELECT * will select all the information in a table. Use the keyword FROM to establish the name of the table. Use the keyword WHERE to establish value constraints to obtain specific information relative to selections. Use %prop to reference Navisworks data. For example, %prop(Item, Name) will obtain information from the Item tab in the Properties window and look at the Name attribute.

Fields   The Fields side of the Edit Link window (shown in Figure 13.7) is an input window with the Field Name column and the Display Name column. The Field Name column of this panel corresponds to the name of a column in the database referenced by the SQL statement. The Display Name column of this panel allows you to define the name of the value that will display in the Properties window. It is in the Fields area that you define which properties from the referenced table you will add to the project.

To add a property to the model, double-click the Field Name column in the Fields panel and type the name corresponding to the column name in the table you are referencing with your SQL statement. This name must be entered exactly as it appears in the database. To add a new name for the column to display in your Navisworks Properties window, double-click the name in the Display Name column and change the value to your desired name.

By connecting the SQL statement to the Properties window, you can customize exactly what values you wish to display. In this manner, you can easily obtain special information for any object while maintaining the same link for the project.

Hold Open For Application Lifetime   The Hold Open For Application Lifetime check box determines whether the database link is opened for the duration of the Navisworks session. If this option is unchecked, Navisworks will open the database, obtain the information, and then close the database. Any changes made to the database will not be reflected until Navisworks is loaded again. If you select this check box, data will be constantly uploaded to Navisworks. If changes are made to the database, Navisworks will automatically enable the Hold Open For Application Lifetime option in order to obtain new information.

The remaining buttons in the main DataTools dialog box (Figure 13.1) are as follows:

Edit   The Edit button allows you to change the properties of any given data link. Select the link in the Data Links panel and click the Edit button. To apply changes, make sure you click the OK button. When you edit properties in this window, Navisworks will reopen the database to obtain all the information contained in your new property settings.

Delete   The Delete button allows you to delete any data tool's link. Select the data link you wish to delete and click the Delete button. This operation cannot be undone, so use caution. If you only want to not display the added properties, you can always uncheck the box next to the link.

Import   The Import button allows you to import previous ODBC settings saved in an XML file. The information includes the connection setting, the SQL string, and the added field names. The drawback is that you will most likely have to edit the ODBC Driver field in order to establish a connection on a different computer. Fixing this possible error is as simple as selecting the type of driver needed, such as a Microsoft Access driver.

Export The Export button allows you to export the settings for the selected data link. The information is exported as an XML file and contains the driver string, the SQL string, and the field name information. The Export tool can be very handy if you want to share this information with other teams in the form of an NWD file. The data tools links do not follow the NWD — the link information is part of your local Navisworks module. Exporting your setting and sending an NWF file with the database will allow all users to have the same information. Alternatively, you could publish your model and embed the data information in the model.

Defaults The Defaults button allows you to reset all links to their original state. Keep in mind that clicking this button will delete any new links you may have created. Clicking this button also restores any of the default links that you may have deleted. If you accidentally click this button, you can click Cancel to undo all changes made since you opened the DataTools window.

OK Clicking the OK button saves all changes to your local session of Navisworks.

Cancel Clicking the Cancel button will undo all changes that you have made since you opened the DataTools window.

Let's put all this together and connect a Microsoft Access database to a model, using the following steps:

1. Open c13_Data_Connection.nwd.

2. Click the Data Tools icon in the Tools panel on the Home tab.

3. Click the New button.

4. Type **Access** in the Name box.

5. Select Microsoft Access Driver (*.mdb) from the ODBC Driver drop-down list.

6. Click the Setup button.

7. Click the Select button, browse to the gatehouse.mdb file, and click OK.

8. Select the Hold Open For Application Lifetime option.

9. Type `SELECT * FROM Maintenance WHERE "Name"= %prop("Item", "Layer");` in the SQL String panel.

10. In the Field Name panel, type **Name**.

11. Type these additional field names: **Notes**, **Date**, and **Author**. Change the names in the Display Name column as you wish.

12. Check your settings against Figure 13.7. The only differences you should see will be in the box under ODBC Driver because the location of your file will vary from the location in the figure. Ensure the Hold Open check box below the new link is checked, and click OK until you close all the windows.

13. Click Saved Viewpoints in the project and select the brown object.

14. Open the properties of this item and observe the new tab in the Properties window called Access. This tab has all the properties you defined in the previous steps.

15. Change some values in the Notes column of the Access database and see how they affect the model.

FIGURE 13.7
Configuring an
Access link

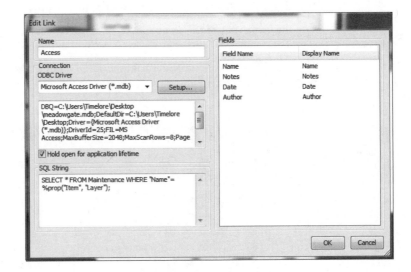

Let's try the exercise using Microsoft Excel for our data source:

1. Open c13_Data_Connection.nwd.

2. Click the Data Tools icon in the Tools panel on the Home tab.

3. Click the New button.

4. Type **Excel** in the Name box (this name is for your reference only and will define the name of the new tab in the Properties window).

5. Select Microsoft Excel Driver (*.xls, *.xlsx, *.xlsm, *.xlsb) from the Driver drop-down list.

6. Click the Setup button.

7. Click the Select Workbook button and browse to the meadowgate.xlsx file.

8. Ensure Version 12.0 is selected from the Version drop-down and click OK.

9. Select Hold Open For Application Lifetime.

10. Type **SELECT * FROM [Maintenance$] WHERE "Name"= %prop("Item", "Layer");** in the SQL String panel.

11. In the Field Name panel, type **Name**.

12. Type these additional field names: **Notes**, **Date**, and **Author**. Change the names in the Display Name column as you wish.

13. Check your settings against Figure 13.8. The only differences you should see will be in the box under ODBC Driver because the location of your file will vary from the location in the figure. Ensure the check box below the new link is checked, and click OK until you close all the windows.

14. Click Saved Viewpoints in the project and select the brown object.

15. Open the properties of this item and observe the new tab in the Properties window called Excel. This tab has all the properties you defined in the previous steps.

16. Change some values in the Notes column of the Excel workbook and see how they affect the model. Don't forget to save the workbook after you have made the changes. Navisworks will read only saved changes.

FIGURE 13.8
Configuring an
Excel connection

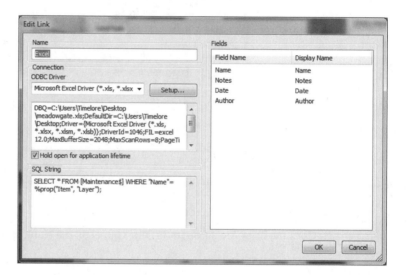

Using these data tools will allow you to increase the information you store in the Navisworks model properties. Many options exist for linking the data to your objects, and all will allow you to enhance the metadata that you can store. This added metadata can easily be updated, enabling users of the model to access ever-changing information.

The Project Browser in Depth

The Project Browser is a powerful feature of Navisworks that allows you to view multiple different models individually in Navisworks. Specifically, the Project Browser lets you view 2D DWF™/DWFx files along with 3D DWF/DWFx files. The ability to view both 3D DWF/DWFx and 2D DWF/DWFx enhances the information that you can share with all teams. The Project Browser is available in Navisworks Manage, Navisworks Simulate, and Navisworks Freedom.

Navigating the Project Browser

Let's review the various parts of the Project Browser. Open the Project Browser by clicking the View tab and, on the Workspace panel, clicking the Windows icon and choosing Project Browser. The Project Browser icon can also be found in the bottom right of the Navisworks window. The arrows at the bottom allow you to quickly toggle between different views, and the main window icon brings up the Project Browser. As shown in Figure 13.9, the browser consists of four areas: the top bar, the Browser pane, Quick View, and Properties.

FIGURE 13.9
The Project Browser
has four sections.

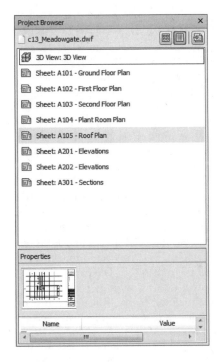

The top bar contains three icons: Thumbnails, List View, and Import Sheets And Models. The first icon allows you to toggle the Browser display to a thumbnail view. This view provides a small snapshot of each model in the project. This view helps you identify the contents of each file, even when the files lack good naming conventions.

The second icon on the top bar allows you to toggle the Browser display to a list view. This view provides the name of each file loaded into the browser and lists them in the Browser pane.

The third icon on the top bar enables you to import additional sheets and models to your project. These models can be of any format that Navisworks supports and can include 3D DWF/DWFx files.

The Browser pane lets you see which projects are loaded into the browser. Any file with a symbol like this has not been prepared and linked to all the other sheets. In this window, you can prepare, open, delete, append, and merge sheets.

Prepare Sheets/Prepare All Sheets   Each sheet or model that is added into the project must be prepared. When sheets are prepared, they are able to reference one another and link themselves together. To prepare a sheet, right-click the sheet and select Prepare Sheet or Prepare All Sheets. When you prepare a sheet, Navisworks creates an NWC file in the same directory in which the parent file resides.

Open Sheets   The Open Sheets function allows you to open any sheet and view its contents. To open a sheet, double-click the sheet name, or right-click the sheet and select Open. The sheet's contents open in individual views. You can select 3D or 2D files to view.

Searching among 3D and 2D Objects

Another important enhancement related to the Project Browser is the ability to search among 3D objects and 2D objects. If you select any object in the 3D environment, you can search for it. The results yield a list of drawings in which the object appears. Likewise, a search for any objects selected in the 2D environment will yield results in other 2D sheets as well as the 3D model.

To prepare your project, open a 3D DWF/DWFx file. Once this file has been opened, open the Project Browser and import 2D DWF/DWFx sheets that correspond to the 3D model. It is important that these sheets be prepared with vector properties. If you are using software such as Revit, be sure the views you export are rendered in wireframe. If a view is rendered with color or shading, the DWF/DWFx file will export as a raster image and will not have the properties necessary to select and query model elements.

Once you have loaded all your files in the Project Browser, you will notice the ⟁ symbol next to all of your drawings. This means your drawings are not yet prepared. Navisworks needs to create NWC files of each drawing just as it does for other file formats. If you have a DWF/DWFx file with multiple sheets combined into one, Navisworks will create a new NWC file for each sheet contained in the DWF/DWFx file.

To prepare all your drawings, right-click in the Browser panel and select Prepare All Sheets. This process may take some time depending on how large the DWF/DWFx file is.

To search for an object among sheets, select the object you wish to view. Right-click and select Find Object In Other Sheets And Models. When you select this option, a new tab will be created in the Project Browser window called Find Item In Other Sheets And Models. This tab will populate a list of each sheet that contains the object you searched for.

Let's put this feature to the test by following these steps:

1. Start a new project in Navisworks and open `c13_Meadowgate.dwf`.

2. Open the Project Browser.

3. Right-click in the Project Browser and select Prepare All Sheets.

4. Click any object in the model, right-click, and select Find Item In Other Sheets And Models.

5. Select one of the 2D sheets to view the object in 2D.

The power of the Project Browser allows you to quickly select an object in 3D and obtain detailed 2D information at the click of a button. Through this method, you can review 2D details instantly and mark revisions.

When you create viewpoints in a model, the viewpoints will only appear in the Saved Viewpoints window when the model that the view refers to is open. For instance, if you create a viewpoint in the 2D sheet A101, that view will appear only when you have sheet A101 selected in the Project Browser. In this manner, you can easily customize views specific to each sheet and model.

If you decide to export a viewpoints report as either XML or HTML, the viewpoints for the current model selected in the Project Browser will be exported. No additional viewpoints from other sheets or models from the Project Browser will be included in this report.

CLASHING WITH DWF/DWFx MODELS

Having the Project Browser can be especially useful during coordination. When a clash is found, you can quickly reference 2D views and mark up the drawing for an RFI. You can then reference the 3D view for more clarity and submit the RFI in minutes.

The drawback to using DWF/DWFx models involves the ability to use SwitchBack. NWC formats support SwitchBack, but the DWF/DWFx format does not. Your goal for the model should help you decide which format is best for you. If you are changing the model yourself, you should consider using SwitchBack; however, if you are identifying issues and only need to write an RFI, then consider using the DWF/DWFx format.

Mastering Links

Earlier in this chapter, you learned about data tools and the power they bring to object properties. Now, we are going to discuss the power of links. A link is a reference to another file that can be activated with a click. The Link tool in Navisworks lets you attach an outside file to any geometry in the model. This tool further allows for a customizable interface for controlling links on the screen as you navigate through the model. To view links in the project, click the Links icon 🔗 Links on the Display panel of the Home tab.

Links can be created in a number of ways. In this section, we will review how you can create links. Specifically, the types of links are hyperlinks, labels, Clash Detective, TimeLiner, viewpoints, redlines, and sets.

Creating Links

In Navisworks, you have the ability to create links to outside documents. There are two ways to create links. You can use either the Links panel on the Item Tool tab or the context menu. Three actions are available in the panel, as shown in Figure 13.10: Add Link, Edit Links, and Reset Links.

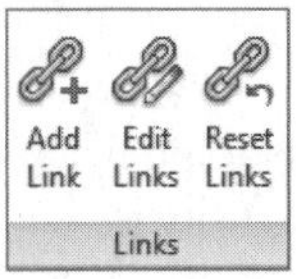

FIGURE 13.10
The Links panel

The Add Link button allows you to create the connection to an external document. To add a link, select an object or selection set and click the Add Link button. When you click the button, a dialog box will appear, as shown in Figure 13.11, containing the following options:

FIGURE 13.11
The Add Link
dialog box

Name   This text box allows you to create a name for your link. You can use any alphanumeric characters as well as symbols in this name.

Link To File Or URL   This area is used to define the path to your document. Select the ellipsis button next to the text box and browse to the document you wish to connect to. If you are connecting to an Internet website, copy the URL from the website and paste it in the URL text box in Navisworks.

RELATIVE VS. ABSOLUTE PATHS FOR LINKS

Advanced users can create a relative path rather than an absolute path to linked content. Doing so is important if you plan on sharing the document with other parties. If you have a project directory, create a folder called links. Place all your documents in the links folder. When you browse to this folder, instead of leaving the directory absolute, change key parts. Here's how:

◆ If the file you are linking is in the same directory as the Navisworks file, simply change the URL to match the name of the file.

◆ If the file you are linking is in a directory one step above the location of the Navisworks folder, change the URL to read ../foldername/filename.

◆ If the file you are linking is in a folder that is a subfolder of the Navisworks folder, change the URL to read subfoldername/filename.

Category   This drop-down list by default has two options: Hyperlink and Label. When you choose Hyperlink, an icon corresponding to the document's type will appear in Navisworks. If you select Label, a box with the name of your link will appear in Navisworks.

Another option is to type a new category into the text box. When you do so, a new category is added to the drop-down list. Creating your own category is beneficial because it allows you to categorize your links. Categorizing links lets you control the visualization of the links based on category and also lets you search and find specific links more easily.

Attachment Points   Attachment points allow you to specify where your link will appear. By default, links appear in the center of the object you select. If you choose a selection set, links will appear by default in the center of each object in your selection. When you click Add, you are able to choose where your links will appear. You can select as many points as you want.

The Clear All button allows you to clear all the points that you have added on the link and restore the link to the center of each object selected.

The Attachment Point tool is important when you wish to list the same information in multiple places or key places in the model. For example, suppose you have a wall that is 50 feet long and you wish to attach the maintenance information every 10 feet. You could add five points along that wall.

Editing Links

The Edit Links tool allows you to select any link and change its properties. To edit a link, you must first select an object in the project that has a link. When you click the Edit Links icon, the dialog box shown in Figure 13.12 appears.

FIGURE 13.12
The Edit Links
dialog box

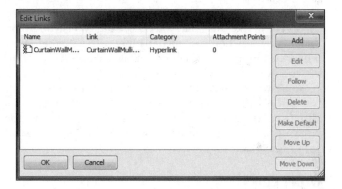

The main window displays all the links that are attached to the selected object. Here, you can select any link and modify it or add new links. Edit Links is basically the link manager in Navisworks.

Add   This button has the same functionality as the Add Link button described earlier.

Edit   This button allows you to edit the properties of a previously defined link. To use this button, select a link from the main window and click the Edit button. You can then change any of the properties associated with the link.

Follow   This button allows you to follow the link that you selected in the main window.

Delete   This button deletes the instance of the link selected in the main window.

Make Default   This button sets the link selected in the main window to be the default link displayed. When multiple links are linked to the same object, only the default link will appear in the center of the object. To allow for multiple objects to be connected to an object and to be displayed, make sure you add points for each link.

Move Up   This button moves the selected link up in the list of links. If you shift a link to the top, it automatically becomes the default link.

Move Down This button moves the selected link down in the list of links. If you shift a link from the top, it will no longer be the default link.

At any time, if you click Cancel, all the changes you made while the window was opened will be lost. If you click OK, your changes will be saved.

External Application Links

There are many instances when you will see some links in your model that you didn't explicitly create in Navisworks. These links come from external programs. If you create links in Revit, Autodesk® AutoCAD®, or other such programs, those links will be brought into Navisworks. The path of those links will remain the same as in the authoring program. It's important to note that these links are simply a connection to an external document. If you want to be able to view the external document, it is necessary to transmit the original document along with the model.

Bringing links into Navisworks through authoring software is a unique feature in Navisworks. You can easily have all the members of the design team or project team insert the operations and maintenance manual submittals into each of their drawings. Then, you can compile the drawings together in Navisworks and the model will be complete with all the links to the operations and maintenance manuals you need for facilities management.

Other external links that you may see in Navisworks that you did not make include viewpoints. Any viewpoints created in other external programs or views created in other programs will come through as viewpoints in Navisworks. Even fly-through videos will be converted to viewpoints in Navisworks. These viewpoints will show up in your model as links.

You can harness the power of links in other programs and bring special information to the Navisworks model. This unique tool is especially useful when members of the team involved with the creation of models keep links in mind early. With some forethought, submittals can be easily linked to the model. Viewpoints can also be created by the team to allow key areas to be highlighted and reviewed.

Other Links

Navisworks creates a number of links that are separate from document links. As mentioned earlier, viewpoints show up as links. Viewpoint links appear as icons displaying either the orthographic icon or the perspective icon. Navisworks also creates links for the following:

Each Clash Found with the Clash Detective Tool The clash icon ● changes color based on the status of the clash. Hundreds of these can appear in your project when you run the Clash Detective.

Each Set Attached to TimeLiner These links appear as by default as text. The links when selected will select the objects associated with the TimeLiner sequence. You can open the properties menu of these objects to see specifics from TimeLiner.

Each Redline Tag in Your Navisworks Model These links appear as an icon ◉ by default. When selected, the link brings you to the viewpoint the tag appears on.

Each Selection Set When you create a selection set, a corresponding link is created in the center of the selected items. When selected, the link will select all the parts of the selection set. The link displays as an icon ▣ by default.

All of these links can be leveraged to produce a model with the information you desire shown. The links are created for your benefit, and you can customize them to fit your needs.

Table 13.1 provides an overview of all of the different link icons available in your Navisworks scene.

TABLE 13.1: Link Icon Descriptions

ICON	DESCRIPTION
	Represents links that have hyperlink, label, or any user-defined category (and points to a web address)
	Represents links that have hyperlink, label, or any user-defined category (and points to an external file)
	Represents links with Clash Detective category (new clashes, demonstrated by a red circle)
	Represents links with Clash Detective category (active clashes, demonstrated by an orange circle)
	Represents links with Clash Detective category (reviewed clashes, demonstrated by a blue circle)
	Represents links with Clash Detective category (resolved clashes, demonstrated by a yellow circle)
	Represents links with Clash Detective category (approved clashes, demonstrated by a green circle)
	Represents links with TimeLiner category (task with attached items)
	Represents links with TimeLiner category (task with valid links)
	Represents links with TimeLiner category (tasks with broken links)
	Represents links with viewpoints category (Perspective Camera mode)
	Represents links with viewpoints category (Orthographic Camera mode)
	Represents links with tags category
	Represents links with sets category (selection sets)
	Represents links with sets category (search sets)

Managing Links

With all of the links shown in Navisworks, it is easy to create a model with too many links visible to see the model properly. Because of the sheer number of links that can be created, it is necessary to customize the way links are viewed.

CUSTOMIZING LINK DISPLAY

The first options for managing links in the project determine how all links are displayed. To customize links, choose Options ➤ Interface ➤ Links. In the main window, you have many choices to customize your links, as shown in Figure 13.13:

FIGURE 13.13
Options Editor
for links

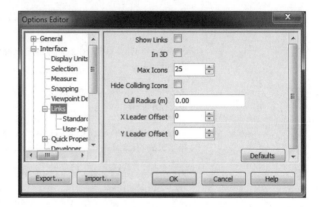

Show Links This check box toggles on and off the visibility of all links in the project.

In 3D This check box toggles on and off the 3D display of links. When this option is selected, links will float in space from the object they are connected to. They can be obstructed by other objects. When this option is not selected, the link will appear in 2D and will appear through geometry.

Max Icons This option assigns the maximum number of links that will be displayed at any time. By default, this option is set to 25.

Hide Colliding Icons This check box when selected will hide in the view any icons that overlap each other. When Hide Colliding Icons is deselected, overlapping links will appear in the scene.

Cull Radius This option controls how close you have to be for a link to appear. By default, this option is set to 0, which means all icons will appear. If you change the setting to 10 feet, then links will only appear if you are within 10 feet of them.

X Leader Offset This option controls how far in the X direction a link will be offset.

Y Leader Offset This option controls how far in the Y direction a link will be offset.

Import/Export These buttons allow you to import or export your link settings.

Using these values, you can set a culling range of 10 feet and a Max Icons setting of 25 to allow for easier viewing. These customizable options will change from project to project and allow you to take control of links in your scene.

ADDING LEADER LINES TO LINKS

In addition to toggling between 2D and 3D views of attached links, you can add leader lines, which help distinguish what objects the link is referencing. In the Links Options Editor, specify a value of approximately 40 for the X and Y Leader Offsets.

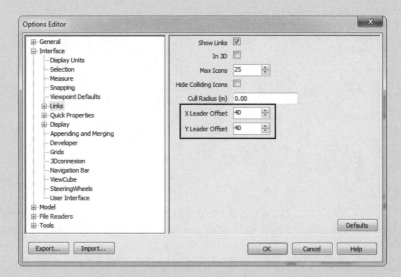

When links are displayed, they will be customized to show a leader line or arrow toward the attachment point of the object.

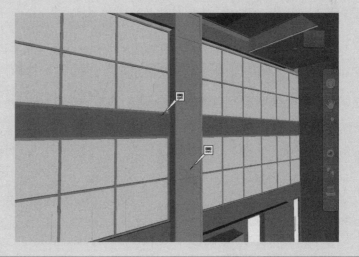

LINKS CATEGORIES

Earlier, we discussed global link options. The Standard Categories (see Figure 13.14) and User Defined Categories options allow you to specify the way each category is displayed. These options can be accessed by choosing Options ➢ Interface Links ➢ Standard Categories (or User Defined Categories).

FIGURE 13.14
Standard Categories
for links

Each category is listed along with its corresponding attributes. Each of these attributes can be customized so that you can display only the links you want to display and in the manner you desire:

Icon Type   This drop-down box lets you select text or an icon. If you select text, then the name of the link will appear in the model. If you select an icon, then an icon will appear that corresponds with the document's type.

Visible   This check box toggles on the visibility of the link. When checked, the links of the selected category will be displayed in the model. If this option is unchecked, the links will not display for that category.

Hide Icons Without Comment   This check box, if selected, will display only links that contain comments in their view. If no comment was tagged in the view, the link will not be visible. If this option is unchecked, all links of that category will display normally according to other link preferences.

The User Defined Categories global options differ slightly from the Standard Categories. The User Defined Categories option has a unique top bar that allows you to toggle views, as shown in Figure 13.15. The icons allow you to toggle to a grid, list, or scene view. A scene view will display only links that are available in the scene. The padlock icon means you cannot add or delete categories in this view.

FIGURE 13.15
Top bar of User
Defined Categories

Links not only allow you to connect to external documents, but they also give you the power to display the data you wish to display. Links are even searchable. Simply open the Find Items menu and search for **hyperlinks**. If you created user-defined categories, you can choose to search links by categories. All of these tools make Navisworks a great environment to connect to external documents at the click of a button.

Let's put this feature to the test by trying the following sequence:

1. Open the file c13_Links.nwd.

2. Select the topography in the model.

3. On the Item Tools tab, select the Links panel and click the Add Link icon. Alternatively, right-click the topography and select Links ➤ Add Link.

4. Type **Topo Update** for the name.

5. Browse for Topo Update.doc.

6. Type in **updates** for the category.

7. Click the Add button, and add a couple of attachment points on the topography where you want the links to appear.

8. Turn off all other links from the global options, with the exception of the user-defined category Updates.

9. Ensure links are activated by clicking the Links icon on the Display panel of the Home tab.

10. Select the link.

 Real World Scenario

LINKED SUBMITTALS

During construction, the model can be constantly updated with new information such as submittals. When submittals are linked into a model, the model becomes a useful tool for quality control during construction as well as for end-user life-cycle management. Life-cycle management is an added value that serves the owner of the building for the life of the building. When submittals are added to the model, the sixth dimension is created.

Contractors have found great value in connecting submittals to the model. During construction, the operations and maintenance submittals are added to the model after each is approved. By placing the submittals into the model, the team can quickly query the model for cut sheets of fixtures and get the information they need at the click of a button.

The project team is also working on the project with close-out procedures in mind. By adding the operations and maintenance submittals to the model, contractors are able to give owners a working model for their facilities management department along with the traditional set of binders.

The submittal data is key for life-cycle management. When there is a problem in the building, all the information in the submittals is needed to mitigate or fix the issue. Because all the information is located in a centralized place that is easy to navigate, professionals have the tools they need to keep the building operating efficiently. The files can easily be transferred in packages because of the power of relative links.

The following images depict a model at the completion of construction with all the submittal data linked in to allow facilities groups to quickly obtain the information they need to sustain the building.

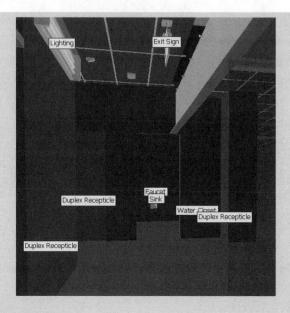

Source: C.W. Driver

KOHLER®

CAXTON™

Features

- *Vitreous china*
- *Undercounter*
- *With or without overflow*
- *Available with KOHLER Artist Editions designs*
- *Includes 52047 clamp assembly, unless specified*
- *15" (38.1 cm) x 12" (30.5 cm)*
- *17" (43.2 cm) x 14" (35.6 cm)*
- *19" (48.3 cm) x 15" (38.1 cm)*

UNDERCOUNTER LAVATORY
K-2209
K-2210, K-2211

ADA

Codes/Standards Applicable
Specified model meets or exceeds the following:

- *ADA*
- *ASME A112.19.2/CSA B45.1*
- *ICC/ANSI A117.1*

Colors/Finishes
- 0: White
- Other: Refer to Price Book for additional colors/finishes

Accessories:
- CP: Polished Chrome
- Other: Refer to Price Book for additional colors/finishes

Specified Model

Model	Description	Colors/Finishes	
K-2209	Lavatory, 15" (38.1 cm) x 12" (30.5 cm), with overflow, with clamps	❑ 0 White	❑ Other_____
K-2210	Lavatory, 17" (43.2 cm) x 14" (35.6 cm), with overflow, with clamps	❑ 0 White	❑ Other_____
K-2210-G	Lavatory, 17" (43.2 cm) x 14" (35.6 cm), with glazed underside, without overflow, with clamps	❑ 0 White	❑ Other_____
K-2210-L	Lavatory, 17" (43.2 cm) x 14" (35.6 cm), with overflow, without clamps	❑ 0 White	❑ Other_____
K-2210-N	Lavatory, 17" (43.2 cm) x 14" (35.6 cm), without overflow, with clamps	❑ 0 White	❑ Other_____
K-2211	Lavatory, 19" (48.3 cm) x 15" (38.1 cm), with overflow, with clamps	❑ 0 White	❑ Other_____
K-2211-G	Lavatory, 19" (48.3 cm) x 15" (38.1 cm), with glazed underside, without overflow, with clamps	❑ 0 White	❑ Other_____
K-2211-L	Lavatory, 19" (48.3 cm) x 15" (38.1 cm), with overflow, without clamps	❑ 0 White	❑ Other_____

Gearing Up for Your Next Project

In this book, we have covered how to use the various tools in Navisworks. This section includes useful tips to get you started on your next Navisworks project. The goal of starting a new project is to transfer as much of your work on previous projects to the new project, including document settings, clash settings, and Presenter maps.

When starting a project in Navisworks, consider importing all of the settings from a similar project. In this manner, you are not reinventing the wheel but harnessing the power of long hours spent in previous projects to the current project.

Another good practice at the beginning of a project is to make sure all files are located in the correct place and are displaying properly. It's important to check your scene statistics early on in the project to ensure that all objects are displaying properly. If they are not, the scene statistics will tell you which object enabler you are missing.

Check twice for the location of the individual files loaded into the project. The saying "measure twice, cut once" holds true in Navisworks. Make sure the files are in their correct place before running any analysis on the models.

It is suggested that, for a new project, you actually create a new database link instead of editing the old link. Since link information is stored with the local version of Navisworks and not in the NWD or NWF file, it is best to create a new database connection for the new project.

Getting a License   If you work on a copy of Navisworks that operates under a network license, you may need to check out the license. To do so, follow these steps:

1. Select the arrow next to the help symbol (?) ▾ .

2. Select About Navisworks.

3. Click the Product Information button.

4. Click the Borrow License button.

5. Select a date from the calendar.

6. Click the Borrow License button again.

The Bottom Line

Connect external data to object properties.   Model data tools allow you to connect external database links to object properties.

> **Master It**   How can you connect to an existing facilities management system that is Microsoft Access based?

Use the Project Browser.   The Project Browser allows you to access information from both 2D and 3D models. This can be especially useful in the field when you wish to access 2D data from a 3D model. Imagine being on the jobsite with a tablet PC, selecting any object you see in the building, and selecting the same object in 3D. Then, from the 3D model, you can quickly access the contract documents in the standard 2D views.

Master It   How can you find an object selected in a 3D model in other views? Give an example of when you would use this function.

Reference external documents from the model.   The Links tool allows you to reference external documents from the model. This can enhance the model's information significantly. You can use links during construction to attach submittal information to the model. This information can then be used for quality control.

Master It   How can you insert a picture into the model?

Chapter 14

Managing BIM Workflows

Understanding workflows in this industry is often critical to the success of a project. This chapter addresses a few different workflows for using the Autodesk® Navisworks® 2013 software in and around the construction environment. This chapter expresses the views of the guest authors in specific workflows tailored around their industries. Take this information as a starting point or reference to help you begin to embrace workflow changes of your own.

In this chapter, you'll learn to:

◆ Understand the importance of leveraging data shortcuts

◆ Know when and how to upgrade software during an active project

◆ Plan for BIM using project planning meetings

Leveraging Navisworks in BIM

The following scenarios describe the BIM (building information modeling) process in contractor and civil workflows. In all of these examples, Navisworks plays an important part in the overall solution and incorporates topics such as clash detection and 4D into the day-to-day operations. In some cases, the authors are sharing a glimpse of how they are using the fundamental tools in Navisworks and proposing new workflows to address areas such as facilities management or production planning.

In addition to the core functionality of Navisworks, the authors have expanded on best practices around model sharing, naming conventions, and project team interactions to address the data flow from authoring software such as Autodesk® Revit® and Civil 3D® applications to Navisworks and ancillary solutions such as project scheduling applications. While the core of this Mastering book focuses on the features and workflows of Navisworks, you must remember that BIM can be in NWD, RVT, DWG, or other format. In the following cases, Navisworks is an important tool in our assortment of BIM solutions, but the tools will work in harmony only when used in the proper amounts or order. Henceforth, you will see workflows that democratize the pivotal elements of BIM but also evangelize the benefits of Navisworks.

For this chapter, several industry professionals have graciously shared their vision and workflows around their specific industry challenges. While no specific example is the universal solution for all challenges, you should take time to understand that these concepts and workflows were developed over years of internal collaboration and real-world practice.

ABOUT THE CONTRIBUTING WRITERS: JOHN MACK, ART THEUSCH, AND ROBERTA OLDENBURG

John Mack has been in the construction industry for more than 25 years. During that time, he has held positions in project management, material ordering, and installation of piping and plumbing systems as a journeyman pipe fitter, project foreman, project general foreman, detailer, detailing manager, teacher, and 3D software developer. This wide variety gives John a unique advantage in his current role as VDC/BIM department manager at Herrero Contractors, Inc. John is the current president of the San Francisco Navisworks User Group and has been heavily involved with the group since its inception.

As a BIM specialist, Art Theusch is responsible for Building Information Modeling operations for The Christman Company. His responsibilities include BIM coordination with design teams throughout the construction process as well as with construction teams in the field. Through this collaboration, Art incorporates 3D collision detection and visualization, 4D sequencing, scheduling and phasing plans, 5D quantity and cost analysis, BIM-enabled facilities management, and Green BIM. In addition, Art has spoken on the topic of BIM at national conferences, in project interviews, and at college campuses including MSU, Georgia State University, Grand Rapids Community College, and Lansing Community College. Art has also been a featured speaker for many organizations, including AGC, CFMA (Construction Financial Managers Association), DMB (Department of Management & Budget), PEN REN (Pentagon Renovation & Construction), and IMAGINiT web presentations. Art is a graduate of Michigan State University, where he obtained a master's degree in Construction Management. In addition to his responsibilities at The Christman Company, Art teaches Building Information Modeling to the juniors, seniors, and graduate students in the Construction Management Program at Michigan State University. He currently teaches several of the BIM courses for the AGC of Michigan and Illinois. He has received his credentials in CM-BIM and LEED AP BD+C. He has also completed the internship requirements for the National Council of Architectural Registrations Boards. Art is currently on the AGC of America's national BIM committee, which is responsible for reconstructing the first two of four BIM training courses, which are a prerequisite to the CM-BIM certification exam.

Roberta Oldenburg serves as an integrated construction coordinator with Mortenson Construction in Brookfield, Wisconsin. In her role, she uses a variety of Autodesk software programs and innovative technologies to virtually design and construct buildings through BIM and 3D/4D models. Using these tools, she helps to manage the overall design coordination process through all phases of construction by working with owners, designers, and contractors. She has extensive experience coordinating the installation of mechanical systems in the construction of vertical facilities and has most recently utilized this expertise to implement the use of BIM technologies on horizontal construction projects. She recently has successfully worked with the Wisconsin Department of Transportation-SE Region on deploying VDC-BIM technologies on various transportation horizontal design-construction projects. Roberta earned a Bachelor of Science degree in Architectural Studies from the University of Wisconsin in Milwaukee. She is active in the industry at reaching out to local universities to further educate students on the use of VDC and BIM in construction and leads the SE Regions Civil 3D user group. She has recently spoken at several national conferences on the success and benefits of using BIM on horizontal construction projects.

Contractor Workflow with John Mack of Herrero Contractors, Inc.

Building information modeling, sometimes called virtual design and construction (VDC), is a set of tools and workflow concepts that offers our team opportunities to reduce waste and improve value to the overall project. When implemented properly, BIM can optimize and integrate otherwise fragmented workflows from design to estimating, to detailing, to fabrication, and to preassembly. Direct exchange of digital information allows content created by one upstream authoring application to be reused by downstream applications. This avoids waste by eliminating the conversion of information into printed documents and re-creation digitally for use in the downstream process. Given this potential, the Integrated Project Delivery (IPD) team will investigate and utilize BIM and lean delivery workflow concepts to the extent possible to increase quality and reduce rework.

The Projects

The two projects that are used for reference in this section are new hospitals for the same client in Northern California. They have an Integrated Project Delivery–style contract.

Statistics for hospital one:

◆ 1,000,000± sf

◆ 17 stories

◆ 555 beds

◆ 24 labor, delivery rooms

◆ 19 ORs

◆ 34 ER treatment rooms

Statistics for hospital two:

◆ 90,000± sf

◆ 6 stories

◆ 80 beds

◆ 5 labor, delivery rooms

◆ 4 ORs

◆ 12 ER treatment rooms

There is a unique opportunity on these two projects. Not only are they for the same client, but the same companies are on both projects, and in some cases the same people. All major trades for design consultants and contractors for both projects are colocated on a single building floor. Major trades include architectural, mechanical (wet and dry), electrical, plumbing, fire protection, and drywall. Other trades work in the colocation for only one to three days a week. There is a lot of sharing of ideas, successes, and failures between the two projects, thus giving us an advantage for trying new things.

Establishing Leadership

A leadership structure needs to be established for effective BIM utilization in projects. This structure needs to be evident at every level of the project team. The purpose of the structure is to facilitate the dissemination of BIM-related decisions; ensure that the process, standards, and protocols are being followed holistically; and provide support for the team as process questions arise. The leadership is made up of the following roles:

◆ BIM/VDC manager

◆ BIM core group

◆ BIM champions

BIM/VDC MANAGER

The BIM/VDC manager assigned to a project is typically from the Construction Manager or General Contractor (CM/GC) or, very rarely, the architect's staff. The BIM/VDC manager must have a strong understanding of BIM and VDC tools and processes. They must be up to date with all authoring, review, coordination, analysis, scheduling, and tracking software tools and technologies. The BIM/VDC manager keeps the BIM core group on target, assists the BIM champions in achieving their objectives, helps the modeling team with technical issues, and owns/maintains/updates the modeling guidelines for the project.

On large projects, this is a full-time position that often lacks hands-on tasks or measurable deliverables. On small projects, this may not be a full-time position and can be combined with other project tasks, such as model integration or leading the coordination process. The overall success of BIM/VDC use on the project is the measure of this person's performance. Very large projects may require two BIM/VDC managers.

BIM CORE GROUP

To aid in the facilitation and continuing implementation of the BIM program, a BIM core group must be formed. The BIM core group will consist of a member from each of the major stakeholders:

◆ Owner

◆ Architect

◆ CM/GC

◆ Owner BIM consultant (optional)

◆ Facility management director

Responsibilities of the BIM core group:

◆ Interface with project team

◆ Develop the BIM implementation plan

◆ Provide guidance to expanded IPD team

◆ Arrive at decisions by consensus

◆ Support overall project goals of integrating technologies with lean objectives and Target Value Design

◆ Address the contractual and legal concerns in data exchange as required

BIM CHAMPIONS OR MODELING MANAGERS

Each company will have a BIM champion or modeling manager assigned to the project. This person is the company's BIM/VDC guru. For large companies or those with more risk, this person is usually a manager and is not responsible for day-to-day production tasks. For smaller companies or ones with less risk, this person can be the actual person working on the project.

The BIM champions will meet once a week or as determined by project demands. The BIM/VDC manager will assign tasks to this group as set forth by the BIM core group. The champions will collectively work on the task by testing and then creating a workflow to have the task completed as part of the standard work on the project. Each task will be documented by one of the BIM champions. The collected results will be presented to the BIM core group and then the project team for sign-off or acknowledgement of accepted use on the project. This document will be part of the current best practices for the project team. It is the BIM champions' responsibility to make sure everyone at their companies who is working on the project has been presented with the goals and standard work processes set forth from this procedure and is using them on the project.

Creating the Vision

The first task for the BIM/VDC manager is to create the BIM/VDC vision for the project with the BIM core group. The vision is best created using mind mapping (see Figure 14.1) software to have something visual to share with the project team. The objective of this exercise is to list all the ways the team believes the model can be used to increase quality and reduce rework. Remember that not everything in the vision will be achievable; that is what the goals are for. The vision will provide a high-level look to help create achievable project goals. It will also challenge the team's ability to learn what items can become project goals. Hopefully, each project will try one new goal to expand the team's knowledge. See Figure 14.1 for an example of what was used on one of the hospital projects. Ideas for your team's vision can be taken from this document.

FIGURE 14.1
Example of mind map

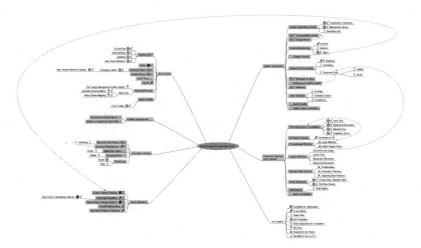

THE VISION STATEMENT

The vision statement sets the team's goals for the project. A project team's BIM/VDC vision statement should aim to position the team to outperform the competition. The vision statement should be a simple and creative reminder that the team can refer to during the life of the project.

Here are the sample vision statement (purpose) and mission (values) from one of our projects:

Vision Statement for BIM Team (Our Purpose) Provide the guidance for our team to streamline their processes by having the leading-edge building model(s) in order to increase the value of our client's future business needs.

MISSION (OUR VALUES)

◆ Have the team produce a BIM that reduces or eliminates duplicate work between architects, engineers, contractors, and trade partners.

◆ The BIM should be interoperable with as little translation or conversion required as possible.

◆ It should also be the primary data source for pricing, scheduling, specifying, coordination, and visualization.

◆ Keep in mind the client's main principles as we do our work:

   ◆ Use true collaboration.

   ◆ Optimize the whole.

   ◆ Fuse learning and action.

   ◆ Projects are networks of commitment.

   ◆ Maximize interrelatedness.

◆ Provide work-based processes for the team to create consistent and value-focused deliverables.

◆ Have a knowledge-based workforce.

SETTING GOALS

Look at the vision and start making a list of the achievable goals for your project. Create a matrix to help track the goals (see Figure 14.2).

FIGURE 14.2
Goals matrix

BIM/VDC Goal	Description of Goal	Measurable Objective	What Trades	Constraints	Core Acceptance	Completion Timeframe
Clash Detection	Achieve a clash free model environment	Zero clashes between models.	A, S, C, M, E, P, FP...	Need models from all trades	Yes	Start of construction, March 2011

Remember that the objectives need to have something measurable and have a completion milestone. Each accepted goal should be placed into an A3 sheet for sign-off from the BIM core group. The signed-off goals are what the BIM/VDC manager will guide the team to complete.

DEFINING GOAL TERMINOLOGY

Besides the goal of zero clashes, other users have adopted additional terms to describe this objective. Some of these include:

◆ Conflict free

◆ No constructability issues

◆ Fully coordinated

◆ Spatially coordinated

While the industry works out a universally accepted term for this goal, you can expect differences in consistency when describing this process.

Project Staffing

Each accepted goal will have a subset of measurable objectives. Each objective will have a skill set, toolset, and time frame for its completion. When creating the objectives that support the BIM/VDC goals, list the skill required, the level of competency with those skills, the title/position associated with the performance of the tasks, and the amount of time to be dedicated to completion of the objective. Providing this information for each objective will allow proper staffing to support the accepted goals for the project. It will also determine whether outside or temporary staffing is needed.

QUALIFICATION/SELECTION OF COMPANIES TO PARTNER WITH ON THE PROJECT

When setting the goals, each goal has trade participation called out. When selecting the consulting and construction teams for each trade, you should expect that they can clearly show their competence in each goal that they will be expected to work on. The typical statement "We do that all the time" does not prove competence. Take the time to have the team step you through how they plan to deliver. Ask them to map what their vision is for working with their trade counterparts. A simple presentation around a flow chart has proven to be an easy way to deliver this request. There should be a method of grading each company on its answer to attack each goal to allow the best possible choice to move forward in the interview process. Choosing by Advantages (CBA) is a good approach for this type of analysis.

CHOOSING BY ADVANTAGES

Most decision-making methods in use have limitations that result in flawed and less than optimal results. Choosing by Advantages is a tested and widely used decision-making system that enables project teams to make effective decisions by looking at the advantages of each option. CBA is an easy-to-use process that requires teams to focus on the attributes and advantages of the different alternatives. Not only will the CBA system allow you to make the best decision in any scenario, it will also make it easy to show why the decision was the correct one.

In his book *The Choosing by Advantages Decisionmaking System* (Praeger, 1999), Jim Suhr expounds the benefits of CBA as an improvement on more traditional weighing of advantages and disadvantages as well as reducing double counting and other mistakes.

CBA helps remove some of the drawbacks to simply using pros and cons in your decision making by developing critical thinking skills that:

◆ Clarify operational definitions

◆ Focus on advantage-based decisions and differences between critical attributes

◆ Anchor decisions in relevant data

◆ Base decisions on the importance of advantages

ESTABLISHING THE MODELING TEAM

The modeling team personnel may differ from the BIM champions from company to company. The modeling team consists of any individuals who are creating an actual model or creating any content to be placed in a model. It is the modeling team's responsibility to adhere to the goals and standards set forth by the BIM champions. The modeling team will deliver standard work material and help keep all IPD team members in alignment with the goals and standards established for the project.

QUALIFICATION TEST FOR MODELING TEAM

An additional requirement that may be implemented but has not yet been done is performing a qualification assessment for modeling teams. With help from the BIM/VDC manager, each trade would submit a detailed step-by-step workflow to show how their work is produced and delivered. The BIM/VDC manager would use this workflow to qualify the worker sent to perform work on the project. To be accepted to work on the project, the individual would have to show the BIM/VDC manager that they are capable of performing all the functions on their workflow. If they could not, they would not be allowed to work on the project. This requirement also provides a training guideline for each company, thus setting them up for success.

TO COLOCATE OR NOT TO COLOCATE?

Colocation means moving or placing things together. In construction, it means placing the project team in a single physical workspace, which is often referred to as "the big room."

There are many advantages to having a project team use colocation. The biggest advantage is access to project members. Occupying the workspace provides ample face-to-face contact and facilitates communication. Other advantages include shared resources such as a network for model files, resource information, office support, and supplies. The shared network is a singularly huge advantage on a project because it allows for real-time file sharing or as close to real-time file sharing as possible.

For network setup, you should look at a one-way trust environment. See Microsoft's paper "Domain Trust" at:

```
http://technet.microsoft.com/en-us/library/cc961481.aspx
```

A disadvantage of colocation is cost and finding a space to suit the need. The advantage of colocation for smaller projects does not outweigh the cost (at least not yet). For smaller projects, not colocating is the current standard. Although the team typically meets on a regular schedule in a single location, it does not have the advantage of being in the environment every day. For days outside the scheduled group meetings, a virtual big room is needed.

To set up a virtual big room, the team needs to take advantage of technology to use the Internet to extend the workplace to multiple places. Using web-hosting services such as GoToMeeting or WebEx allows for an interactive meeting with the attendees in the comfort of their own office or wherever they might be in the world. Currently, we are using these types of services to have online meetings, real-time review, a visual walk-through of models, clash detection, and many other tasks that require more than just a phone conversation.

The ideal virtual big room would have the following technology readily available to everyone on the project. The objective is to let people work from anywhere and attend collaborative meetings.

- A live microphone to talk to anyone on the project as needed.
  - Instant messaging or chat would be a less-desirable alternative.
  - IM or chat would be an acceptable addition to a live microphone.
- A web-hosting service account for immediate use by all team members.
- A daily time frame of three to four hours when all team members are available.
- A shared server on a cloud computer for check-in and checkout of all files for the project. No individual company's servers should be used for project documentation.
- Scheduled upload and download from the shared server so the user does not have to wait for files to open. The user can schedule the utility to check out the file prior to needing it for work.
- Videoconferencing capabilities—either HD codecs with large displays or, to replace/supplement the live microphones, Skype, HP SkyRoom, or other desktop/laptop videoconferencing applications.
- Depending on level of technological sophistication, a document camera as part of the videoconferencing system may be of value.

Selecting the Software

It is the BIM core group's responsibility to approve all software being proposed for use on the project. This will be done by research and various testing for compatibility with other modeling software being used on the project.

Each company should use what they are comfortable with, providing it meets the objectives set in the vision and goals. If the software does not meet the objectives, then either the company needs to come up with alternate software to meet the needs, or a new company needs to be placed on the project. Most companies base their training, standards, and production planning on their software choice, so dictating specific software maybe more harmful to a project than letting them use what they already know.

The first rule in upgrading and selecting software is this: *No company can upgrade modeling software on the project without the BIM core group's written approval!* Due to backward compatibility issues with many software applications, software updates need to be carefully coordinated by the BIM core group. Otherwise, significant downtime may be incurred as files become incompatible between team members.

First, the team needs to establish which software will be used to compile all models from all trades into one platform. Any software to be used for modeling on the project must at minimum have compatibility with the collaboration software choice. All companies modeling will need at least one copy of the full collaboration software on the project. It is optimal for every person modeling to have the software, but that can be costly. For those who do not have the full software, the collaboration software should have a free viewer available for published files.

The team on both of the example hospital projects chose Navisworks Manage (NWM) as the collaboration software. NWM was used in design for visual spatial planning. As the projects moved forward and the models grew more reliable, the clash detection part of the software was introduced. Clash tests were set up between every model to show where two items occupied the same physical space. This allowed the team to coordinate prior to the field installation. Each company was required to have, at minimum, one copy of NWM. Everyone was required to have Navisworks Freedom (NWF) installed on the workstations that did not have a full version of NWM. NWF is used for viewing published files from the full version, NWM. The CM/GC was responsible for facilitating, creating, and publishing the files for clash viewing. Software for creation of all models from all trades was compatible with NWM.

Stress Testing the Models

Stress testing the hardware and software is a piece of the model plan that is usually neglected but is important. This testing is designed see how much the hardware and software being used on the project can handle, or conversely it may reveal the need to upgrade.

Take a large area of the building and have each company place model objects in the area. The modeling does not have to make sense. The intention is to just get the amount of data that would occupy a model of this size for each trade. Then start putting the models together to see where the breaking point is. This testing should be done very early in the project by the BIM champions. The outcome of this test will illustrate which companies are capable of creating and opening the content needed to do their job. It will also determine the file size of the models, which will flush out the hardware selection for the project.

Selecting the Hardware

Hardware selection is tricky. Things to take into account when selecting hardware include the following:

◆ New technologies—Contact software vendors if help is needed to understand the level of hardware needed to meet project expectations. Be aware of new software builds and new software available to the team. Software requirements will play a large role in selecting the hardware. Minimum requirements usually do not fit the objectives for the project. Stress testing will help determine what requirements are needed to complete the project.

◆ Size of the building (ft²)—The size of the building is one of the components that will dictate the file size of the model. A bigger building means a bigger file size.

◆ Scope of what is to be modeled—The level of detail (LOD) for the modeled objects is one of the components that will dictate the file size of the model. A higher LOD or more data in model objects means a bigger file size.

◆ File size—The file size will dictate what hardware needs to be purchased; for example, it will determine the size and speed of the CPU, amount of RAM, size of the video card, size of the hard drive, speed of the hard drive, and speed of the bus.

◆ Number of disciplines modeling on the project.

◆ Number of models (files).

◆ Number of Revit users in one central file.

◆ Size of the shared network.

◆ The goals for the project.

◆ Life cycle of a lower-quality computer versus a higher-quality computer.

◆ Mobility of the user.

◆ Software intended to be used.

◆ 64-bit OS and modeling software—Note that this may have to supersede company guidelines and policies to achieve the project's target.

◆ Experience of team members.

The Workflow: Mapping the Current and Future Process

Creating a map of the standard workflow is often beneficial. In the first BIM champions meeting, the BIM/VDC manager will assign each trade the task of creating a flow diagram of their current workflow. The workflow will show how they create a model and documentation from the model, as well as how hand-offs between design and construction for that trade will be performed. This is done by using a simple flow diagram. Each trade will present the workflow to the BIM champions. The BIM champions will work with the trade to improve on this workflow by eliminating waste from the current state flow. The final workflow will be documented as standard work for the project. The BIM/VDC manager will refer to this document as the project progresses to be sure it is being used. If something changes, the BIM/VDC manager will have the trade modify the flow diagram document to reflect the change and have the trade resubmit the new flow for the record.

Level of Detail

Milestones with schedule dates are a necessity when creating a modeling plan. The first part of the modeling plan should be creating the LOD for each object to be in the model. At each milestone, an object will have a level of detail that it will carry with it. As the project progresses, the object will carry more data at each milestone until it reaches an agreed-upon maturity. Trade-specific rules for each project are good. An example of a trade-specific rule would be "No conduit under 1" to be modeled unless it is a rack with three or more conduits."

Figure 14.3 shows the detail of definition we used for one of the hospital projects. We placed the descriptor number on the matrix for each spec division for the project, for example, the detail level for cabinets:

- Level 000 for criteria design

- Level 200 for detailed design

- Level 300 for construction

FIGURE 14.3
LOD matrix

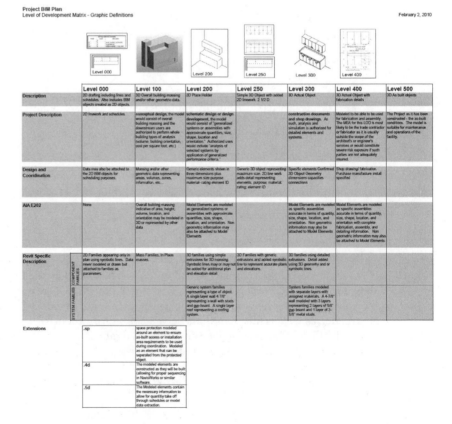

Project BIM Plan
Level of Development Matrix - Graphic Definitions

February 2, 2010

Figure 14.4 shows a sample LOD matrix with definitions.

FIGURE 14.4
LOD sample

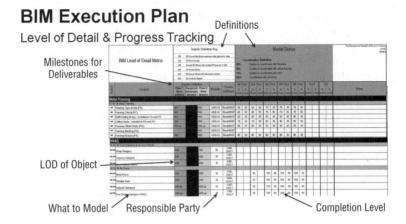

FIGURE 14.4
LOD sample

Sharing Model Files

Sharing model files is a necessity when using BIM/VDC on a project. The full project team must have access to the most current project information at all times, regardless of how complete/incomplete that information may be. Daily synchronization of information is the industry baseline at the time this chapter is being written. More often is desirable, although updates that are too frequent become burdensome.

Here is an example workflow for file sharing:

1. Create your file and store it on your server. Keep your working file on the server.

2. Clean the file:

   ◆ Models: Remove Xrefs and linked files.

   ◆ Drawings: Create DWF™ files.

   ◆ Documents: Create PDFs.

3. Post the file to the Autodesk® Buzzsaw® software. Behind the scenes, Buzzsaw Sync will automatically copy the file to the shared server. (This can be set up in your home office, too.)

4. Use the L drive while onsite to access shared files. When offsite, use Buzzsaw to access shared files.

Access to shared files is handled differently for a colocated team compared to a non-colocated team. Colocated teams must set up a shared project server that is accessible by all companies that work onsite, even those that are onsite only part of the time. Project collaboration software must be used for access by offsite team members or as the primary sharing mechanism for non-colocated teams. Simple FTP sites can fulfill simple file-sharing needs, but there are many collaboration platforms that offer more robust organization and management functionality for an integrated team. Buzzsaw, ProjectWise, Box.com, SharePoint, Vault, and Newforma are some of the popular systems used in the industry. In all cases, project information resides on a secured server that all project team members have access to, whether on or off the project site. Costs vary for the different platforms, and a detailed analysis of the ultimate cost to the project (including administration time, transfer rates, and useful features) should be performed before adopting a platform for a given project. The platform with lowest first cost is not always the one with lowest ultimate cost. Buzzsaw was the chosen platform on both of the hospital projects. Buzzsaw Sync is being used to synchronize between Buzzsaw and the shared server (see Figure 14.5).

FIGURE 14.5
Buzzsaw sample

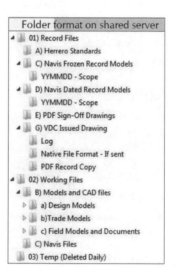

USING BUZZSAW SYNC WITH NAVISWORKS

With Buzzsaw Sync, users can synchronize from a local drive to the Buzzsaw cloud, upload models and files without interrupting their current workflows, and leverage Buzzsaw permissions to securely synchronize, exchange, and access information. This bidirectional workflow is useful when working with design and other source files as well as sharing Navisworks files. The following image shows a typical BIM workflow where Buzzsaw Sync is used to capture models from different geographically dispersed trade disciplines and host them in a common location for access to Navisworks.

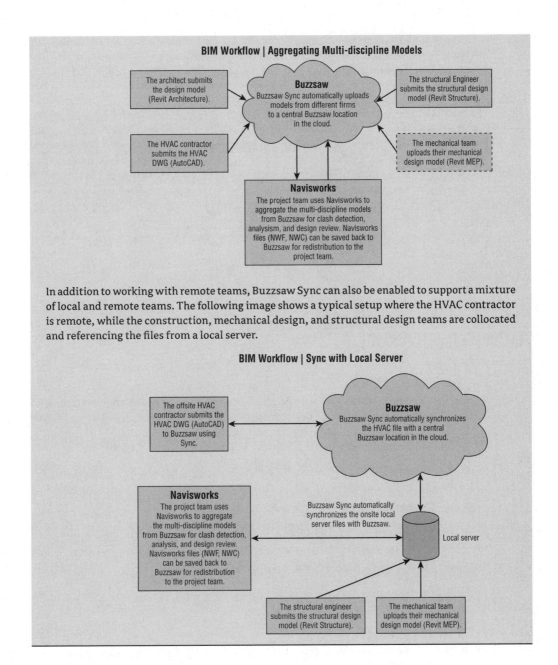

In addition to working with remote teams, Buzzsaw Sync can also be enabled to support a mixture of local and remote teams. The following image shows a typical setup where the HVAC contractor is remote, while the construction, mechanical design, and structural design teams are collocated and referencing the files from a local server.

File Naming

On large projects such as the hospital projects, having a project file-naming standard is required. Dates should not be part of the file naming when sharing with others. Most of the higher-end software allows for revision tracking, providing the filenames remain the same as updated files are posted over the top of older ones. This means no dates in filenames. A file can be highlighted and older versions listed as available for download and viewing. Figure 14.6, from Autodesk Buzzsaw, shows a highlighted file on the left and the Versions tab on the right showing all versions posted to the shared site using the same filename.

You can download any version of the file at any time by selecting the Versions tab. The file shown on the left in the folder tree is always the most recent file.

FIGURE 14.6

Buzzsaw Versions tab

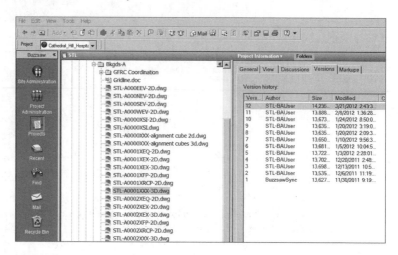

Here is a sample of the file naming used on the projects (see Figure 14.7 and Figure 14.8).

The Training Plan

Project-wide training will include items that companies are expected to do that would otherwise not be a part of their standard delivery methods or that are specialized items for the project. Project guidelines supersede any company guidelines.

The following list is suggested training to take place on the project:

- Using the web-based file-sharing site
- Using the shared server
- Understanding the project modeling standards
- Understanding the level of detail matrix
- Understanding the workflow for the specific project
- Cleaning up models prior to sharing them with others
- File-naming standards

Tracking Changes

Tracking changes in the model is important. Which trades should track changes and when (or at which stages of the project) need to be agreed to collectively by your BIM champions, not separately by each individual trade! Different trades and scopes will have different limitations on when and what to track dependent on the level of fluidity and complexity of their work in a given stage of the project.

On one of the hospital projects, the structural engineer tracked changes in a Word document and released this document simultaneously with the model. This is easily achievable for a trade such as structural because they have a limited number of objects in their model. Conversely, the architect is not able to track changes with the same level of precision early in the design; programming of the building is not stable enough to track every move. Once an area's programming is approved, the changes are minimal and can then be tracked. Because other trades' changes are often the result of changes by structural and architecture, tracking all their changes may not be necessary.

There are programs that can aid in documenting and finding changes. These programs take two versions of a file from the same area and provide a color-coded comparison. Autodesk Design Review has the ability to compare DWF documents and automatically color code changes for 2D sheet files. The Navisworks Compare feature can track changes in the solid models by color coding the discrepancies. There are many other programs that will compare two DWG™ format files using many different methods to accomplish the same function.

Whatever change process your team decides on should be documented and adhered to.

FIGURE 14.7

BIM file-naming example A

XX********.***	Project	
STL-	St. Luke's Hospital	STL-

XX********.***	Discipline	
A	All Disciplines	XX
	Architecture	A
	Civil/Site Work	C
	Electrical Construction	EC
	Electrical Design	ED
	Equipment	Q
	Exterior Curtain Wall	CW
	Exterior Panel	EP
	Fire Alarm	FA
	Fire Protection	FP
	General	G
	Infrastructure	N
	Integrated Model	IM
	Interior Design	ID
	Kitchen	K
	Landscape	L
	Mechanical HVAC	MH
	Mechanical Piping	MP
	Medical Equipment	ME
	Metal Gauge Framing	MF
	Plumbing Construction	PC
	Plumbing Design	PC
	Pneumatic Tube	PT
	Process Piping	D
	Security	SY
	Sheet Metal Flashing	SF
	Shoring	SH
	Structural Construction	SC
	Structural Design	S
	Tele/Data	T
	Vertical Transportation	VT

Sorted by Abbreviation	
Architecture	A
Civil/Site Work	C
Exterior Curtain Wall	CW
Process Piping	D
Electrical Construction	EC
Electrical Design	ED
Exterior Panel	EP
Fire Alarm	FA
Fire Protection	FP
General	G
Interior Design	ID
Integrated Model	IM
Kitchen	K
Landscape	L
Medical Equipment	ME
Metal Gauge Framing	MF
Mechanical HVAC	MH
Mechanical Piping	MP
Infrastructure	N
Plumbing Construction	PC
Plumbing Design	PC
Pneumatic Tube	PT
Equipment	Q
Structural Design	S
Structural Construction	SC
Sheet Metal Flashing	SF
Shoring	SH
Security	SY
Tele/Data	T
Vertical Transportation	VT
All Disciplines	XX

00***.***	Lower Floor	
00	All Levels	00
	Underground (below SOG)	UG
	Site (beyond building extents)	SI
	Parking Level 2	P2
	Parking Level 1	P1
	1st Floor	01
	2nd Floor	02
	3rd Floor	03
	4th Floor	04
	5th Floor	05
	6th Floor	06

00***.***	Upper Floor	
02	All Levels	00
	Underground (below SOG)	UG
	Site (beyond building extents)	SI
	Parking Level 2	P2
	Parking Level 1	P1
	1st Floor	01
	2nd Floor	02
	3rd Floor	03
	4th Floor	04
	5th Floor	05
	6th Floor	06

*******X**.***	Sector	
X	Entire Floor	X
	Area A	A
	Area B	B
	Area C	C
	Area D	D
	Area E	E
	Area F	F
	Area G	G
	Area H	H
	Area I	I
	Area J	J

FIGURE 14.8
BIM file-naming
example B

*********XX.***	User Options			Sorted by Acronym	
IN	All Components	XX		Acoustic Ceiling	AC
	Acoustic Ceiling	AC		Electrical Branch Conduit	BC
	Building Core & Shell	CS		Building Core & Shell	CS
	Building Exterior	EX		Communications	EC
	Building Floor Plan	FP		Lighting	EL
	Building Interior	IN		Lighting Clearance	ELC
	Building Sections	SX		Power	EP
	Communications	EC		Equipment Plan	EQ
	Electrical Branch Conduit	BC		Tele / Data	ET
	Elevation Plan	EV		Elevation Plan	EV
	Equipment Plan	EQ		Building Exterior	EX
	Feeder Conduit	FC		Framing Backing	FB
	Framing Backing	FB		Feeder Conduit	FC
	Framing Kickers	FK		Framing Kickers	FK
	Framing King Studs	FS		Fuel Oil	FO
	Framing Offset Walls	FW		Building Floor Plan	FP
	Framing Priority Walls	PW		Framing King Studs	FS
	Framing Typical Unit	FU		Framing Typical Unit	FU
	Fuel Oil	FO		Framing Offset Walls	FW
	Hanger and Seismic	HS		Hanger and Seismic	HS
	Lighting	EL		Building Interior	IN
	Lighting Clearance	ELC		Medical Gas	MG
	Mechanical Piping	MP		Micro-Phasing	MI
	Medical Gas	MG		Miscellaneous Metal	MM
	Metal Stairs and Railings	MS		Mechanical Piping	MP
	Micro-Phasing	MI		Metal Stairs and Railings	MS
	Miscellaneous Metal	MM		Plumbing	PL
	Plumbing	PL		Pneumatic Tube	PT
	Pneumatic Tube	PT		Framing Priority Walls	PW
	Power	EP		Reflected Ceiling Plan	RCP
	Reflected Ceiling Plan	RCP		Reinforcing Steel (rebar)	RS
	Reinforcing Steel (rebar)	RS		Storm Drain	SD
	Sanitary Waste and Vent	SS		Shoring	SH
	Security	SY		Site	SI
	Sheet Metal	SM		Sheet Metal	SM
	Shoring	SH		Slab Penetrations	SP
	Site	SI		Sanitary Waste and Vent	SS
	Slab Penetrations	SP		Building Sections	SX
	Storm Drain	SD		Security	SY
	Tele / Data	ET		Traffic Lanes	TL
	Temporary Power	TP		Temporary Power	TP
	Total Station Layout	TS		Total Station Layout	TS
	Traffic Lanes	TL		Underground Utilities	UU
	Underground Utilities	UU		All Components	XX

*********.XXX	Content Form	
	Not Used (Assumed 3D)	
	2D	-2D
	3D	-3D

If the files relate to a "special area" insert a short description at
the end of all related files (MFD004XIN-OR.rvt - Interior 4th
Floor Metal Framing for Operating Rooms). Make sure that
"special area modifier" is distributed.

Other Examples
Operating Room   -OR
Edge of Slab Coordination   -Slab Edge

*********.XXX	File Extension	
dwg	AutoCAD Drawing File	dwg
	AutoCAD Web Format File	dwf
	Industry Foundation Class File	ifc
	Navisworks Cache File	nwc
	Navisworks File	nwd
	Navisworks File	nwf
	Revit Drawing File	rvt

AUGI Script File Name   STL-A002XIN-A10-Central.rvt

For those using the AUGI Script for creating the Revit Local from Central, the file names will have the following end modifiers		
	Revit Vertical Discipline	
-A	Revit Architecture	-A
	Revit Structure	-S
	Revit MEP	-M
	Revit Version	
10	2010	10
	If Central File	
-Central	Central	-Central

Reliable Promises and Weekly Work Plans

To have a reliable promise, five elements must be present:

- Speaker (performer)—This is the person who will be delivering the work. Be clear that the speaker is making the commitment, not someone else.

- Listener (customer)—This is the person who depends on the speaker's performance. The action to perform on has already been requested.

◆ Conditions of satisfaction—Requests can be interpreted in ways that are not obvious to both parties. Make sure that there is no misunderstanding in negotiating the request.

◆ Future action—When a promise is made, sometime before the due date, an action will be performed to reach the desired conditions of satisfaction.

◆ Due date—This is a must when making a promise. The speaker needs to declare the date when the action will be complete. The listener can negotiate if the offered due date is not acceptable.

Many promises will be made on a project, and there must be a method of tracking them. Lean Construction Institute's Last Planner™ is a good documentation process that has helped to achieve desired results when tracking reliable promises. Refer to `http://www.leanconstruction.org/` for more information on Last Planner.

An element of the Last Planner is to keep a weekly work plan (WWP), as shown in Figure 14.9, to track the reliable commitments. Individuals are measured by their ability to complete an action on time. When items are not completed on time, the WWP tracks the reason. This allows the management to help the person having issues with completing work on time by providing a tool to help them become more reliable. Tracking the requests completed on time versus the number of requests is known as Percent Plan Complete (PPC).

FIGURE 14.9
Weekly work plan

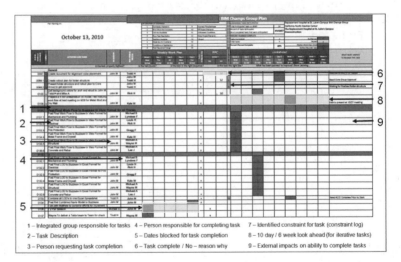

1 – Integrated group responsible for tasks   4 – Person responsible for completing task   7 – Identified constraint for task (constraint log)

2 – Task Description   5 – Dates blocked for task completion   8 – 10 day / 6 week look ahead (for iterative tasks)

3 – Person requesting task completion   6 – Task complete / No – reason why   9 – External impacts on ability to complete tasks

The Integrated Building Model

This is a virtual model of the building comprising 3D models from all trades. The most prominent software in the industry for compilation from multiple software platforms is Navisworks, and Navisworks Manage is a commonly chosen platform for such projects.

Integrated models have multiple purposes. In design, the primary use is visualization for space planning. In preconstruction, the primary use is clash detection or spatial coordination.

Generally, one person creates the integrated model by compiling the separate 3D working models into the single compiled platform. It is recommended that the person assembling the model also drive the model when it is used in group meetings.

To facilitate this process, there are some fundamental modeling rules that need to be followed. First, as mentioned in the "Selecting the Software" section of this chapter, all software chosen to produce working models for the project must be compatible with the chosen collaboration software. Second, either each model needs to be delivered in a format that is compatible with the collaboration software, or the person assembling the model needs the native software to make the extraction to a suitable format. It is preferable that the author of the working model provide a copy of the model in the native file format. The project team can then leverage this file for compilation and coordination in addition to sharing with the others on the team.

Once all the models are in the correct format, the person creating the integrated model will bring each trade in one at a time until all models for the area being assembled are in the integrated model. For vertical distribution, such as exterior skin, shafts, or elevators, the integrated model is multifloor with only that trade shown. For horizontal distribution, such as mechanical, electrical, piping, or fire sprinkler, the integrated model is assembled by floor. Once the vertical models are coordinated, they can be brought into each horizontal model for coordination.

These integrated models are congested and sometimes hard to read. To help read the integrated model, the person assembling will use the collaboration software to set each trade to a predetermined color, thus overriding the color settings from the original model. Figure 14.10 shows a sample color chart that is used for an integrated model.

FIGURE 14.10

Color coding

Spatial Coordination Color Code (NWD) October 11, 2011

Version 2

Element	Color
Architectural Walls	Pale Yellow (80% transparent) (255,255,175)
Architectural Ceilings	Black (50% transparent) (0,0,0)
Architectural Ceiling Components (Struts, Braces, Housings)	Black (20% transparent) (0,0,0)
Architectural Doors (Frames, Panels, Glazing Framing)	Burnt Orange (225,125,25)
Architectural Glazing (Windows, Glass Balusters, Glass lights in Doors)	Light Turquoise (80% transparent) (204,255,255)
Grid	Violet (127,127, 255)
Wood Framing	Tan (150,50,50)
Stairs	White (255,255,255)
Equipment, Furniture	White (255,255,255)
Concrete Slab, Mat, Deck, Roofs	Grey (25% transparent) (100,100,100)
Steel Beams, Columns, Shoring	Brown (128,70,0)
Viscous Dampers	Indigo (75,0,130)
Medical Gas	Salmon (255,128,128)
HVAC Exhaust	Pale Blue (128,128,255)
HVAC Supply	Green (0,128,0)
Mechanical Piping	Cyan (0,255,255)
Plumbing	Sea Greenish (64,128,128)
Pneumatic Tube	Pink (255,128,255)
Electrical Distribution	Yellow (255,255,0)
Lighting	Yellow (255,255,0)
Fire Protection	Burgundy (128,0,0)
Fire Smoke Dampers	Red (255,0,0)
Metal Framing 1 Hour Rating	Yellow (255,255,0)
Metal Framing 2 Hour Rating	Red (255,0,0)
Metal Framing No Rating	Green (0,128,0)
Metal Framing Critical Stud	Purple (0, 32, 96)
Head of Wall Mono-coat Layer	Yellow (255,255,0)
Head of Wall Track Layer	Purple (0, 32, 96)
Head of Wall Clearance Layer	Orange (255,165,0)

COLOR CODING WITH THE APPEARANCE PROFILER IN NAVISWORKS

Navisworks will display the model colors as they were configured in the source application. When overriding colors to reflect a common color code, you can use the Appearance Profiler to change numerous model objects consecutively.

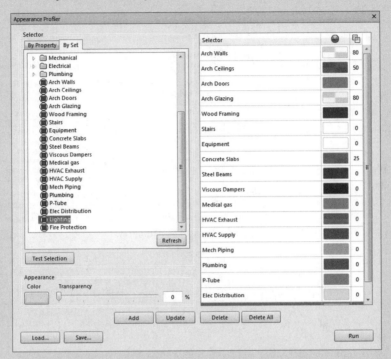

The Appearance Profiler allows you to set up custom appearance profiles based on sets (search and selection) and property values and use them to color code objects in the model to differentiate system types and visually identify their status. Appearance profiles can be saved as DAT files and shared among other Navisworks users. For more information on the Appearance Profiler, see Chapter 4, "Climbing the Selection Tree."

Model Tolerances

When we discuss tolerances between model clash tests, we generally assume the tolerance is zero. However, with slight variations in modeling and the exactness of Navisworks and other programs, we need to occasionally allow for greater tolerances to cut down on the number of false clashes. During construction coordination, tolerances can be defined and adhered to using the collaboration software. The software has the ability to manage tolerances between modeled objects. Figure 14.11 is a screen shot from one of the programs showing that the clearance or tolerance between structural and mechanical is 3 inches. If anything impedes a 3-inch space between the models, the clash system will report it as a clash.

FIGURE 14.11

Navisworks
Tolerance

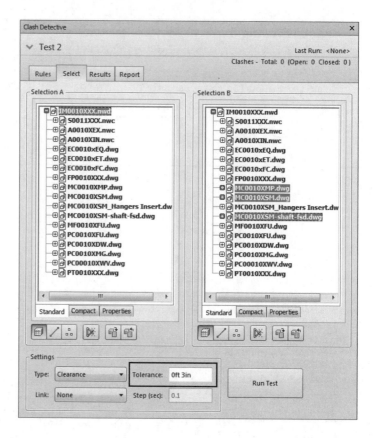

A separate tolerance can be set up between any two trades in the clash report. Figure 14.12 is a spreadsheet showing the tolerances between various trades. The numbers represented for each trade need to be negotiated and accepted for use on each project.

FIGURE 14.12

Tolerance matrix

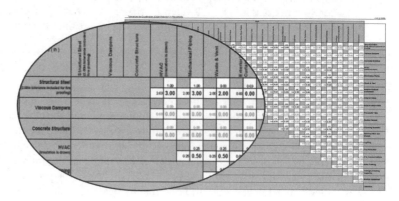

3D Spatial Coordination

Spatial coordination is used during the design of a building to aid with the visualization of all the modeled objects. For best results, an integrated model of what is available needs to be assembled. The model for an area of the building is displayed. Discussion about the area happens in a group setting to help the designers make decisions and to allow the owner to see the design intent. This is not the same as clash detection.

3D Clash Detection and Clash Avoidance

As the design matures and more models from different trades are completed, clash detection is the next step in the coordination process. It requires a much higher level of certainty than spatial coordination. The clash report will show where two objects occupy the same space or when an object breaches into the tolerance space. Then, someone volunteers (is assigned) to fix this issues.

For those using Navisworks Manage, tests are set up to run Clash Detective between each trade. Clash Detective tells when two (or more) objects are occupying the same space by means of a clash report. Figure 14.13 shows a sample of clash tests for a project. The highlighted clash test is for structural compared to HVAC. This clash report was run using the sample given earlier in the "Model Tolerances" section, where the tolerance between these two trades is 3 inches.

To be most effective, the project team needs to practice clash avoidance as they create their trade models. This is different from the traditional method where everyone draws and clash-detection software finds the issues. The result of the traditional process is fast initial production but with rework that sometimes results in multiple iterations for one area.

Using clash avoidance, the person modeling is responsible for looking at other trades that have already modeled in the area prior to commencing work. To get from the starting point to the first clash report will take longer, but overall, there is a time savings because of less rework. This also requires sequencing the trades for optimal impact. Due to the restrictive nature of these trades, large sheet-metal mains and graded plumbing systems should be completed before other MEP trades start. Other trades then work around these constraints. As a trade finishes their scope within a specific area, they let the team know they are finished. Others not yet finished will then work around them as well.

As this process progresses, later trades need to continue to work around the growing number of completed trades. If a trade comes into an area that is occupied by someone else, it is their responsibility to work around the object or start the negotiation for the space needed with the trade already in place. The building needs to be broken into small enough pieces to allow all trades sufficient workspace within the sequencing. Essential to this process is communication, communication, communication (see Figure 14.14).

4D Model-Based Scheduling

We use this action to show trade sequencing for installation. The ultimate objective for 4D scheduling would be to have the master schedule tied into the integrated building model to show the entire building sequence for all trades. Technology is available today to do this, but the time to assemble such a schedule is too great. Unfortunately, the technology and process have not developed enough to make this a value for a project. Until we can get further development of this action, we are only doing small areas of the building at a time this way. Figure 14.15 shows the time-based assembly of a bathroom core using 4D software.

FIGURE 14.13

Clashes

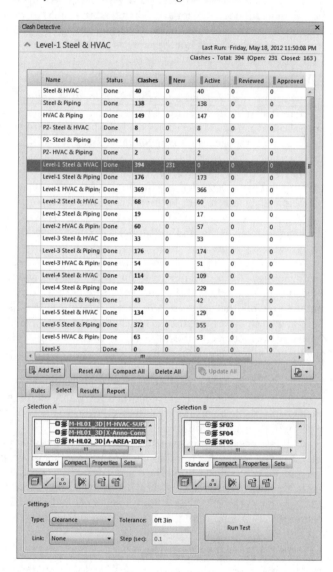

FIGURE 14.14

Clash avoidance

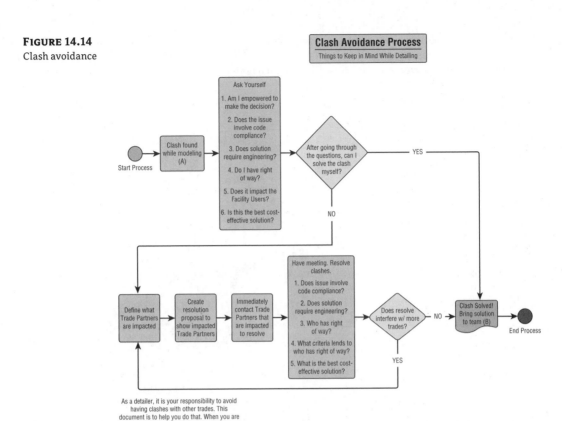

FIGURE 14.15

4D scheduling

4D Model-Based Production Planning

The software that mechanical contractors typically use has the ability to create production planning. The software leverages the data of the modeled objects to create patterns that are used to cut parts with plasma or laser cutting tools. The software can create fabrication sheets that are used to put together multiple parts into an assembly. After the assembly is done, the fabrication sheets are used for quality control, to track labor, shipping/receiving, and installation of the assembly. Not all the software used is this sophisticated, but having an actual model mocking the real installation will lead to better production. The integrated model can be used to help the field foremen schedule their work crews by using the model to simulate sequencing of the installation. The 4D simulations are used to visualize where the different crews should be at a specific moment. This is useful because it gives the project team a better glimpse into the dynamics of the construction site and provides opportunities to address conflicts earlier. Figure 14.16 and Figure 14.17 are two samples of how trades leverage the model for production planning.

FIGURE 14.16
Sample 1

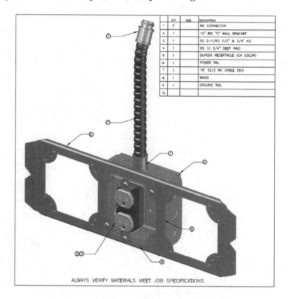

FIGURE 14.17
Sample 2

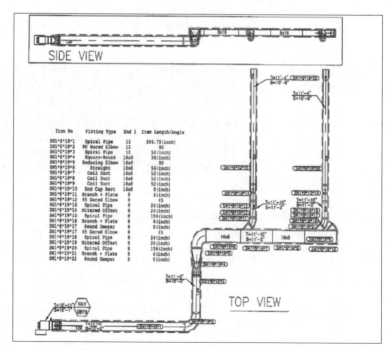

Facility Maintenance

This is a new area in the industry. A few companies use the integrated model to hyperlink modeled objects to the operations and maintenance (O&M) manuals and startup procedures. Even fewer use the integrated model to run the facility or to track maintenance of equipment. If the owner has the services to supervise the construction model after turnover, it can be leveraged for future upgrades to the facility. Working collaboratively with the project designers and contractors can determine what can be provided for facilities maintenance.

Contract Requirements

The adoption of BIM/VDC usage mandates that contractual risks change with the technology. Where there is risk, there is opportunity! A few contracts are starting to emerge in the industry that have BIM requirements. AGC ConsensusDOCS 301 and AIA E202 are two that are starting to be widely used.

Model Data Ownership

The model and the model data for the project are owned by the client, who paid for them. Model ownership needs to be stated in the contract for the project so there is no doubt about who is the owner of the model and all documentation derived from it.

The ultimate ownership of the data is with the owner, but there must be project team ownership of the data as it is being created. During the authoring, members of the project team have joint ownership of and responsibility for the data contained in the BIM. It should be noted that as BIM continues to mature, the courts will ultimately decide the ownership roles.

Testing New Technology or Ideas

Jeffrey Liker said it best in *The Toyota Way* (McGraw-Hill, 2004) with principle 8: "Use only reliable, thoroughly tested technology that serves your people and processes." Technology is pulled by construction, not pushed to construction. Pulling from construction to find the correct technology reduces overproduction. To test the new technology, set up a small test case on the project. If it works, then expand it to a larger group. If it does not work, make improvements and try again. For quicker success and a shorter duration for testing, talk to others who have completed work on similar ideas. Keep an open mind and always be willing to try something new.

Contractor Workflow with Art Theusch, The Christman Company

Building information modeling has quickly become one of The Christman Company's top strategies to address risk management on its job sites with its ability to coordinate two of the largest drivers in the construction process. Traditionally, the MEP trades account for 40 percent of commercial construction costs and also set the pace of the job, while the construction activities are notoriously the drivers of the schedule's critical path. Christman immediately recognized the opportunity Navisworks provides to control the coordination of these drivers in 3D. Like several other initiatives in the industry, BIM is not something that can be simply purchased and applied. It continues to be a process, involving the hard work of people and the need for management and organization. The benefits of BIM and 3D coordination are ultimately driven by the sound processes that govern the implementation within each project, all of which need proper planning.

Project Planning Kickoff

The planning for BIM begins as early as possible in the project; often, the first opportunity arises with our project planning kickoff meeting. During these meetings, the team sits with the designers, design plans, and the owner to discuss the deliverables, methods, and dates as a team. As the construction manager or general contractor, Christman uses this meeting as an effort to start our BIM execution plan (BIMx), a critical component of this kickoff meeting. As preparations are made for BIM to be integrated, it is necessary that a strong plan for how the model will be created is established and how it can be leveraged is discussed.

BIM Execution Plan

The purpose of the BIMx is to create a structure for integrating BIM into the planning processes. We always begin by setting our goals for the BIM. The two most crucial pieces of information to extract are what the owner anticipates receiving as a result of BIM and what we plan to use the model for. These goals drive the level of detail and the amount of information collected along the way. After we understand what the owner anticipates from both the design and construction teams, a BIM matrix is created. Figure 14.18 shows a chart, originally created by Penn State University, that serves as a great tool, outlining the various ways the team plans to leverage the model during design and construction.

FIGURE 14.18
BIM execution plan

X	PLAN	X	DESIGN	X	CONSTRUCT	X	OPERATE
	PROGRAMMING		DESIGN AUTHORING	X	SITE UTILIZATION PLANNING		BUILDING MAINTENANCE SCHEDULING
	SITE ANALYSIS		DESIGN REVIEWS		CONSTRUCTION SYSTEM DESIGN		BUILDING SYSTEM ANALYSIS
		X	3D COORDINATION	X	3D COORDINATION		ASSET MANAGEMENT
			STRUCTURAL ANALYSIS		DIGITAL FABRICATION		SPACE MANAGEMENT / TRACKING
			LIGHTING ANALYSIS		3D CONTROL AND PLANNING		DISASTER PLANNING
		X	ENERGY ANALYSIS		RECORD MODELING		RECORD MODELING
			MECHANICAL ANALYSIS				
			OTHER ENG. ANALYSIS				
		X	SUSTAINABLITY (LEED) EVALUATION				
			CODE VALIDATION				
X	PHASE PLANNING (4D MODELING)	X	PHASE PLANNING (4D MODELING)	X	PHASE PLANNING (4D MODELING)		PHASE PLANNING (4D MODELING)
	COST ESTIMATION	X	COST ESTIMATION	X	COST ESTIMATION		COST ESTIMATION
	EXISTING CONDITIONS MODELING		EXISTING CONDITIONS MODELING		EXISTING CONDITIONS MODELING		EXISTING CONDITIONS MODELING

Quality Analysis/Quality Check of Design Models

In order to use the model for 3D (clash detection), 4D (scheduling), and 5D (estimating), we discovered that we needed to learn the vast levels of information that can be stored within the model. The BIM team spent time with our estimators to further understand how a set of drawings is dissected. We learned that they perform their quantity takeoff similar to the process of building a building. They begin by quantifying the foundations, then the structure, and so on. As we developed our quality analysis/quality check (QA/QC) process, we decided to follow in similar footsteps.

From a high level, our QA/QC process begins with incorporating a template that sorts the model based on the assembly codes, which are identical to the Uniformat codes our estimators use to sort estimates. This process is typically implemented with our authoring software. With that in mind, our first order of business is to apply the appropriate assembly codes to all the families in the model. Upon completion of sorting the model, our template allows the estimators to filter through the presorted 3D views of the separate assembly codes. This helps our estimators quickly understand the systems of the building through the BIM software.

Past experiences involving the use of designers' models have led us to check several areas upon receiving the model. An example of such, and also a common starting area in the process, is ceilings. We have often noticed that the ceilings are not drawn as accurately as are necessary in order to be used for quantification during planning as well as coordination during construction. The second area we focus on is wall types, because we have found several unique challenges when reviewing the wall systems. For example, the naming conventions could be misleading or an incorrect system may have been drawn for the particular application.

Clash Detection of Design Models

It has also become our practice to run clash detection of the design models during the preconstruction process, which has served to assist our operations teams in recognizing the congested areas of the building prior to construction. We have also found that our feedback to the design team has been invaluable to the overall process. In several instances, we have been invited to lead the 3D coordination for the design teams. We have altered our focus of this specific coordination to better facilitate the needs of designers, providing a 3,000-foot view of coordination, rather than the detailed reviews that we facilitate with our trade contractors. Over time, our team has developed methods to tailor our effort with the designers so as to eliminate much of the amount of rework; the purpose of this effort is to help bring the design along, not to poke holes in the project.

Navisworks Timeline of the Project during Design

At Christman, we have been delicate in our approach to incorporating 4D scheduling. We have seen a tremendous value in using the models for site logistics. Our strategy has been a slow morphing phase between site logistics, with phasing, that is shown at strategic points of the schedule versus a full-blown 4D schedule.

A complete 4D schedule can become very time consuming; as the model and its schedule develop, a tremendous time investment may be required in order to link each of the moving parts. Our most successful attempts at 4D scheduling have come when we link the model at intervals when the both the model and the schedule have reached a pause in development. We traditionally see this happen in the late construction document stage of design as well as at the competition of 3D coordination with the trade contractors.

Several avenues for the incorporation of a 4D scheduled model into the trade contractor meetings have been explored. In order for this effort to be fruitful, the model and schedule both must be up to date. The trade contractors will quickly lose trust in the tool if it is believed to be inaccurate. When the model and schedule are up to date, we have seen the tremendous power of the weekly look-ahead. As we all know, schedules can change on a moment's notice, and having the ability to run "what if" scenarios with the trades input is priceless.

Prepping the Model for Bidding

As of recently, there has been increased desire from trade contractors to receive design models during the bidding phase. As this has grown, we have had to develop methods to protect the concerns of the design teams, because sharing the model can present several apprehensions. One of the most common concerns stems from the risk of the design being altered as well as our being held accountable for the quantities in the model. With the use of model release forms, we have been able to ease many such fears and risks. The most interesting solution we provided was to leverage Navisworks to create an NWD with an expiration date. The design team was ultimately very pleased with the solution. The model was set to expire one week after the bid and was also in a locked (non-authoring) format that would implode at the set date. This allowed the design team to share the information knowing that the contents would only be accessible for a short time. If the model were to fall into unauthorized hands after the bid, any sensitive information in the model would be inaccessible.

3D Coordination

3D clash detection has long been the easiest adaptation for BIM efforts on our projects, providing the necessary facilitation to reach our company's goal of incorporating BIM on all projects. This past year, we were able to encompass BIM on two-thirds of our jobs with the use of 3D coordination. From day one, we decided to act as the BIM coordinator for the MEP coordination efforts, because we believe that we can maximize our efforts and communicate the most about the building through the details of coordination. In addition, the MEP coordination effort impacts all the peripheral trade contractors, and we incorporate their involvement as recognition of the potential impact we may have on their construction sequence.

Creating comprehensive clash reports has been a constant evolution for the Christman BIM team. When we began running clash reports, we created elaborate Excel matrixes that were easy for the detailers to understand but did not mean much to the rest of the construction team. After many projects and several revisions to the methods, we developed the matrix shown in Figure 14.19. The bottom matrix describes how many clashes there are between the various systems—this matrix then feeds up into the data above. In addition:

♦ The Recent History chart shows how many clashes were found on a particular date, while the graph beside it shows these dates in blue with a red trend line. We use this chart to help us anticipate when we will complete the coordination of an area.

♦ The Clash Distribution pie chart shows what percentage of clashes each trade is responsible for.

♦ The Clash History is a stacked pie chart referencing backwards. This helps understand how each trade has progressed in the last few weeks.

♦ The last chart represents the percentage of Clashes Resolved. We created this report to help us understand who was performing as well as who was underperforming.

The information within the Clashes Resolved data proved to be some of the most valuable. We noticed that if the trades were scoring below 70 percent, we were usually facing several design issues that were preventing the trades from resolving their clashes from week to week. It was also noted that when the trades were scoring over 70 percent, great progress was being made toward completing an area.

FIGURE 14.19

Clash report

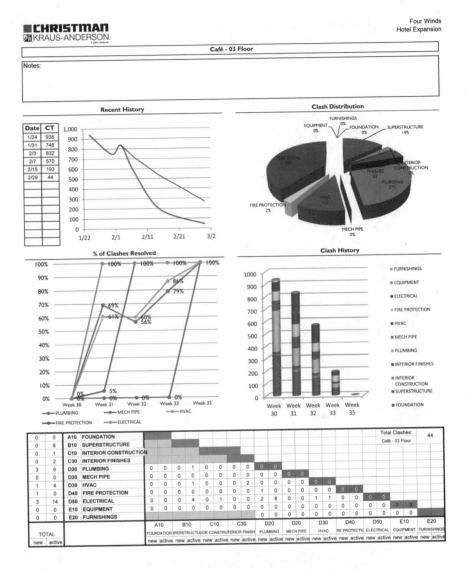

This document was sent out to the entire team on a weekly basis. This document helped the project managers and the superintendents understand what was going on in the coordination efforts. The interesting component is that the information and data were not new, but the software enabled us to package and communicate the information in different ways; with it, we were able to repackage and communicate the necessary messages to the entire project team.

To incorporate the richest 3D coordination, supplementing the architectural design model with several items has proven necessary and useful. For example, king studs and kickers can cause a great deal of struggle if they are not incorporated into the model. We have also begun to require several items, such as access door panels and door clearances, to be identified in the model. These may seem small, but if we are not watching out for the little foxes, they can ruin the comfort of the building for the owner.

Once the coordination process is complete, the model becomes a signed-off document that the trades must adhere to. The model lives on during the course of construction and is constantly referred to in order to assist trades in understanding why the specific coordination decisions have been made. On several occasions, we have had trades request to reroute systems; upon such requests, we will open the model to review the possibilities. In most cases, we found that another system was planned for the space and the contractor was unaware of those plans. Under the traditional process, it was a first-come, first-served mentality. The coordinated model has quickly become one of our best planning tools for construction.

Deliverables

As construction nears completion, we leverage Navisworks several times so we can inform the owner on the systems and components of the new building. There are several things that we can do with the model through Navisworks. We have found some of the simplest and easiest deliverables for owners have involved creating saved views of every room in the building. We have seen owners regularly use such information to review what's above a space, for example, before they send their team out to work above the ceiling. On another project, we required the trades to hyperlink specified construction documentation to the model, which turned the model into a digital filing cabinet for future repair work, allowing the owner to click equipment within the model and have all of the data at their fingertips. This saves hours of looking through manuals for the appropriate data to help them repair the system.

Recap

In recent years, building information modeling has become a major tool in risk management across a diverse array of construction management methods. The Navisworks programs, with proper time investments and planning, allow Christman to control overall coordination and MEP systems, two major factors during the construction process. As with many improvement methods, BIM is not implemented with the purchase; it must be organized and properly implemented through a great deal of time and planning invested. Ultimately, the impact of BIM is extremely profound on the methods of construction and provide overarching benefits to both Christman and its clients alike.

Civil Workflow with Roberta Oldenburg of Mortenson Construction

As new technologies are coming into play and people are seeing their benefits, it is becoming less of a question of whether you are going to use BIM than how you are going to use it. During the last decade, BIM has become a standard in the building industry, and over the last several years, it has started to move into the transportation industry. In the transportation industry, with the software encouraging designing in 3D, the days of looking at a 4,500-sheet set and imagining what the end product is going to look like are nearing an end.

As you plan for your project, you want to understand what the expectations are early on so that you are able to set up the project appropriately. What is the goal of doing BIM? Are you starting in the design portion, is it meant to be passed over to construction, or are you starting with the construction and reverse engineering? As the transportation industry moves in this direction, everyone is seeing a lot of the same struggles as in the building industry. This part of the chapter will focus on workflows and ideas developed from the implementation of several transportation projects.

Starting with the End in Mind

As we plan for our projects, we start with the end in mind. This allows a clear understanding of the desired deliverables. What is needed for a coordination model is different from what is needed for a 4D model, which is different from what is needed for Automated Machine Guidance (AMG). Understanding what the desired end result is will assist with what needs to be modeled and the workflow.

Many teams new to 3D modeling get overwhelmed with the thought of doing BIM. Since designing in 3D on the transportation side is relatively new to most firms, they are still learning how to use the software and manage the large files. Take a step back as a team and evaluate where the most value will be added on the project and start there. Find the best available areas of value (i.e., ROI) to use 3D models in design and construction. For instance, on a rural road, it may not make sense to do 4D simulations, but it would make perfect sense to model in 3D and extract the surfaces for AMG.

Following are some of the processes that can be used:

4D Simulation   This is tying a design or construction schedule to the model to simulate the construction process. Where you might find the most benefit is identifying the most complex area of a project (for example, replacing a bridge, tunnels, major interchanges, or areas that have an aggressive schedule). It is a great communication tool to help make critical planning decisions and identify sequence busts.

Constructability Reviews   Use these to identify potential issues prior to the start of construction. These would be done on areas that the team has identified as high risk. These may include structures or a detail of a complex system.

Visualization   Creating a visual representation of the project is one of the simplest forms of communicating to the team. Looking at a 3D image of the project allows for no misinterpretations because the entire team sees the same thing.

Earthwork Analysis—QTO   Using QTO allows the opportunity to take off quantities for design and construction documents. When drawings are set up with the appropriate information from the beginning, this is an easy step that will allow obtaining accurate quantities for bidding projects.

Site Utilization Planning   When planning for construction staging and equipment placement, this can prove to be a great tool to improve communication with the team and assist with maintaining safety.

3D Coordination and Design Review   Being able to understand coordination issues early on in the process saves time and money in the future. Navisworks Manage is used for clash detection to assist with this process.

Automated Machine Guidance   Automated Machine Guidance links sophisticated software with construction equipment to direct the operation of machinery with a high level of precision, improving the speed and accuracy of highway construction processes. Modeling the project allows the opportunity to use AMG and can be done on any size project.

♦ The idea is to choose what makes sense for the project to implement and learn from the experience. You should avoid duplicated efforts by converting 2D plans to 3D; start your design with 3D models.

♦ If you provide 3D models from designer to contractor, it will yield lower bids, reduce rework, reduce risk by more readily identifying areas of concern, reduce duplication of services, improve workflows, and increase coordination.

Building the Team

It is very important to get all stakeholders involved early on in the process because each person sees a different value that BIM can bring to the project. The team may consist of owners, project managers, designers, engineers, structural, contractors, consultants, maintenance, traffic, and so on. Collaboration is key in this process, and the goal is to work as a team to better communicate and resolve issues early on. There should be a BIM champion who will manage and coordinate this process.

Setting Standards

After the team has been established, the next step is to collaboratively set up standards that will be followed by all members. These would go into a BIM implementation plan that would identify the expectations and integrate the owner, designers, and contractors. This document would include owner deliverables, BIM innovations, software interoperability, level of detail, and downstream construction.

SOFTWARE INTEROPERABILITY

Making the decision early about what software is going to be used is key; unfortunately, in the current market, you'll likely be using multiple platforms. This isn't ideal but it is the reality of where the transportation industry is today. It is important that you understand what the interoperability issues are up front as you start a project because it is then easier to work through them.

Many times when you export from one program to another, model information such as object properties is unfortunately lost. We have been using Civil 3D, but in many cases, the design team has used InRoads. In the last project, just for the construction portion, we used Primavera, Navisworks Manage, Revit Structure, Civil 3D, Autodesk® MicroStation®, and InRoads, not to mention the software needed for scanning. Depending on what we were going to use the information for, there was a need to convert files using different methods.

DATA SHARING AND TRANSFERRING

The team will need to decide where the data is stored. If there are multiple teams, they will need to decide where to transfer the data as updates are done. In addition, most projects may have multiple consultants working on different parts of the project, which creates issues as to who should have access to the master design files. This is not just an issue for transferring files. It can also be an issue for data because there are various computer-aided engineering (CAE) tools that each discipline uses for design that may not be easily transferred from one program to another.

Naming Conventions

For file naming, it is best to come up with a system that will work for the team and to keep it the same throughout the project. An index should be developed for electronic files to reference as new team members are introduced; it should be all-inclusive and include survey data that is coming in. This is especially important when multiple platforms are being used because it would provide understanding of which drawings contain what information so that decisions can easily be made about which drawings to convert for use.

Level of Detail

When defining modeling standards, you need to ascertain the level of detail that is expected in the model and evaluate what is going to bring the most benefit to the team. This will be determined on a case-by-case basis for each project. The level of detail needs to be set before the project begins.

Creating the Model

When creating the model, there are a number of factors to consider. You need to identify the coordinate system, create data, understand data shortcuts, test the files, participate in meetings to coordinate stakeholders' needs, and break up the model for 4D.

The Coordinate System

Working in a civil engineering environment, everything is done in real coordinates, which is not necessarily the case with buildings. The first thing to do when starting a project is to ensure that you georeference the file. It is important to verify that each team is using the correct coordinate system to avoid issues later. Generally, we test this several times because we typically work with multiple platforms.

Creating Existing Data

To create the existing conditions, it is important to get the data. Data collection is being done several ways. In the past, it has been collected by photogrammetry. More recently, data is being collected by LiDAR (Light Detection and Ranging), which can be collected by aerial, static, and mobile. Conventionally, it can be collected with surveys and GPS. Getting the existing data is important when starting the design of the project.

After the data is collected, it is processed and then the traditional data is extracted for the team to work with. The information is typically handed over in DGN, DWG, or LandXML format. Generally, the files contain feature lines, points, surfaces, and symbols that are used to locate lights, trees, signs, bridges, and the like. That information is used by the design team as a reference for the new projects. Bringing that information into Civil 3D, we would then separate out the surfaces or create new surfaces for what we need. Recently, we have been using the information to create the existing bridges using Revit Structure to build them along with Civil 3D to extract pavement information. Existing utilities are being modeled off the existing as-builts, surveys by Diggers Hotline, potholing to confirm elevations, and sometimes ground-penetrating radar.

CREATING PROPOSED DATA

There are two ways to get this information. One would be to reverse engineer the design documents, which is not recommended. There are many cases in which the earthwork contractor reverse engineered the design files to use AMG for their work. The preferred method is to have the original design done in 3D by the design team. If the design is done in Civil 3D, the road surfaces can be transferred for the construction team and will lean up the process. There is much more to do than just the surfaces and roadways: drainage, electrical, fiber optics, water, lighting, signs, bridges, and structures, to name a few. There are plenty of opportunities to model the bridge structures in Revit, where the information can be exported for survey layout.

DATA SHORTCUTS

If you're designing in Civil 3D, it is important to understand the software, its capabilities, and how large the files can get. It is best to use data shortcuts and to lay out the plan before you start a project. When doing a 4D model and splitting up the surfaces to accommodate the schedule, you may get more than 100 surfaces. Setting up the data shortcuts will allow you to move more easily in the files and manipulate the surfaces.

COMPILING IN NAVISWORKS

It is important to test the files to make sure that they are being represented appropriately. This includes not only being able to view the file but also how you want it to be represented in the selection tree to make it easier to locate for coordination or linking to a 4D simulation. On one of the projects that I worked on, we reversed engineered the design documents, and it was important that the labels in the model were the same as those in the drawings. The model was given to the owner, contractors, and the consultants, and we wanted them to be able to identify any issues or concerns in the model and easily go back to the design documents. In addition, we made sure everything was georeferenced so that they could verify locations and elevations in Navisworks.

Following are some tips for working with files in Navisworks:

Civil 3D and Navisworks Compatibility   To take advantage of the Navisworks Navigator plug-in in Civil 3D, you need to install Civil 3D and any additional applications before installing Navisworks. If Civil 3D isn't installed first, you can go to the control panel and reinstall the Navisworks Exporter plug-in.

Viewing Surfaces   You must create styles with triangles. You will not be able to view any other surface styles in Navisworks. Another consideration is that if you turn off the surface in Civil 3D and refresh Navisworks, you will lose the surface in the selection tree and will need to relink it. You need to create a new surface style that has the Triangles setting turned on. Surfaces will not show up otherwise.

DWG vs. NWCOUT Command   The NWCOUT command will create an NWC cache file. This will retain the surface names, pipe networks, and the like, whereas the drawing file will not.

Corridor Solids   This tool in Autodesk Labs will allow you to create solids from your corridor design. You can easily add more regions to come in as solids for clash detection. This tool is great to break up the model for coordination and 4D simulations.

Units   When working with multiple platforms, it is possible that the units will not match up when brought into Navisworks, so it may appear that something is missing. You will need to grab the file and modify the transform units to ensure proper insertion.

COORDINATION

With buildings, there is a hierarchy of importance among the different systems. With transportation projects, you will find the same thing. It is important to get a list of the hot-button issues for the project managers so everyone can understand where the greatest concern is and incorporate it into the clash-detection model. Drainage is generally one of the systems that will take precedence. You can use clash detection to verify that there is adequate coverage of pipes. Coordinating the concerns into the process is key.

You can also use meetings to coordinate the project with the team:

◆ Kickoff meeting—The initial meeting should be set up with the contractor, designers, and owner or project manager. This will depend on whether coordination will happen during the design phase or construction phase. Include dates for posting drawings, a list of tasks and completion dates, QC dates, and each team member's responsibilities. This process would include how to break up the project into manageable areas to coordinate.

◆ Owner team/contractor meetings—These include updates on modeling progress. Issues that arise can be modeled and looked at closely in such meetings.

◆ Field coordination meetings—These involve working with contractors or staff that are using the tool.

BREAKING UP THE MODEL FOR 4D

Determining when the 4D simulation is desired will dictate whether the designer's schedule or the contractor's schedule will be used and to what level of detail the model will need to be broken into. It is important that you understand the production rates and how the contractor is going to build the project so the model can be broken up appropriately. Keep in mind that you can only break up the model into as much detail as the schedule has room for.

With the corridor model, you can modify and add regions in Civil 3D to accommodate the production rates in the schedule. The next step would be to export the file using corridor solids into a new file. If the subassembly was set up correctly, you will have different layers of the roadway and barriers that can be linked to the schedule.

The most difficult part is understanding how the excavation will be done to be able to create new surfaces and appropriate grading for each task. This is where it is very important to have set up your data shortcuts. To create these, you'll reference the existing and proposed surfaces to get the intramural surface. Remember to name them so that they are easily identified in the selection tree in Navisworks.

When using Navisworks, it is important to create selection sets based on the schedule's Activity ID. Create folders either by stage or by task to easily identify the Activity ID. In each folder, you will put the selection sets associated with that road (or other item) and link the objects. This process will affect the way it links to the schedule.

After importing the schedule, create a rule that will automatically link the selection sets (named per Activity ID) to the schedule. After the rules are in place and the task types are set up, you should be able to click the rule and link the selection sets.

This is only one way of linking the objects to the schedule, but it helps to organize the model for relinking an updated schedule. It makes it easier to search for tasks and change areas if need be.

The End in Mind

Start with the end in mind. How is this information going to be used after design and construction? Ideally, it will be transferred to maintenance and referenced for future projects. The idea is to have this be a life-cycle model where you start with an existing project; plan, design, construct, and maintain the information; and then reuse it to plan the next project. The ability to create a model out of 4,572 pages will give key decision makers the opportunity to see the project in its entirety and make educated decisions.

The Bottom Line

Understand the importance of leveraging data shortcuts.   Civil 3D has many tools to aid in the creation of objects.

> **Master It**   In Civil 3D, what is the most important reason to use data shortcuts (in terms of Navisworks)?

Know when and how to upgrade software during an active project.   It's always important to keep in mind when and how to upgrade software in a project.

> **Master It**   John Mack talks about the importance of upgrading your software on a project. What is the first step in the process for upgrading software?

Plan for BIM using project planning meetings.   Treating BIM like an actual project has its advantages.

> **Master It**   Art Theusch talks about project planning meetings. What would be the main goal for having a project planning meeting? (Think deliverables.)

Appendix A

The Bottom Line

Each The Bottom Line section in the chapters suggests exercises to deepen skills and understanding. Sometimes, there is only one possible solution, but often, you are encouraged to use your skills and creativity to create something that builds on what you know and lets you explore one of many possibilities.

Chapter 1: Getting to Know Autodesk Navisworks

Understand the ribbon. Knowing the locations of various tools within the Ribbon provides a good foundation for being able to quickly access items across the Autodesk® Navisworks® interface.

Master It Can you quickly locate Gravity and Collision?

Solution Gravity and Collision are located in a few different places. On the Viewpoint tab, in the Motion panel, you can access Gravity and Collision from the Realism dropdown. Also, these tools can found on the Navigation toolbar after you have activated the Walk tool. You can also use Ctrl+D for Collision and Ctrl+G for Gravity.

Use the Measure and Redline tools. The Measure and Redline tools are useful in Navisworks throughout a project, and having a basic understanding of these tools is essential.

Master It Locate two columns and use the Measure Shortest Distance tool. Can you create a viewpoint and convert this to a redline?

Solution After you have located and selected your columns, using the Select Tool (Ctrl+1), locate the Measure Shortest Distance tool on the Measure panel or on the Measure Tools palette on the Review tab. The distance will appear on the screen.

Using the Convert To Redline tool located on the Measure panel or on the Measure Tools palette of the Review tab, convert the measurement to a redline. Notice that a new viewpoint is created in the Saved Viewpoints palette.

Chapter 2: Files and File Types

Understand Navisworks file formats. Having a complete understanding of the different file formats is important. The 3D files are the building blocks for any successful Navisworks project. Take time to fully understand file formats before moving ahead.

Master It   What are the three native file formats that Navisworks uses? What is the advantage of using the NWF format rather than the NWD?

Solution   NWC, NWD, and NWF are the three native file formats. Using the NWF file format allows you to continuously update your model with changes made to the original source files while the NWD file format is a static snapshot of your model.

Open and append various files.   Appending and merging files is the proper way to create highly complex yet intelligent 3D models. Aggregating and sharing this information with a larger audience helps drive efficiency and increase project awareness.

Master It   How can the Merge feature complement the design review process with an extended team?

Solution   By simultaneously sharing the Navisworks model with numerous extended team members to capture markup information and comments, the merge feature allows you to consolidate this unique information without duplicating any elements into a single model.

Configure object enablers.   Not all files types are created equally. Proper planning and understanding of the various file types will help you identify where object enablers are required and configure the proper setup to ensure uninterrupted access.

Master It   How do you display a custom object in Navisworks?

Solution   Enabling Object Enablers allows DWG-based files with custom objects to display properly by acting as a translator to convert these objects into a format that Navisworks can read.

Chapter 3: Moving around the Model

Use the mouse to navigate inside Navisworks.   Learning to use the mouse to navigate is critical to understanding and mastering the tools in Navisworks. Almost every Navigation tool utilizes the mouse for navigation in some way. There are shortcuts for tools like Orbit, Zoom, and Pan that can aid in your navigation.

Master It   Explain the process for using the mouse controls with Zoom, Pan, and Orbit.

Solution   With a tool like Select selected, you can pan by holding down the middle mouse button, zoom by rolling the middle mouse button, and orbit by pressing the middle mouse button and selecting the Shift key.

Walk and fly through the model.   As with the Walk tool, learning the Fly tool is essential. While at first, this tool may seem difficult to understand, it has great potential for navigating large sites and covering great distances.

Master It   Where do you go to reset the roll angle of the Fly tool?

Solution   To reset the roll angle back to 0, click the Edit Current Viewpoint button on the Save, Load & Playback panel on the Viewpoint tab. Then change Roll Angle to 0. This will set your view back to a level aspect.

Understand the ViewCube and SteeringWheels. For some users, these tools can be difficult to master; others find them to be useful time-savers because of the heads-up type of use, meaning they're always on the screen, saving you the time of having to search for additional tools when using these tools. You also have the ability to utilize the two sets of tools together. Having at least a basic understanding will help improve your workflow.

Master It How can the ViewCube and SteeringWheels be utilized in conjunction with each other? Give an example.

Solution The ViewCube remains open while SteeringWheels is active. You can use the ViewCube tools to manipulate the view as needed. You can find Home view on both the SteeringWheels and ViewCube. Here's a quick example of using these tools together: say you're using the SteeringWheels to walk or orbit and you need to further adjust your view with the compass portion of the ViewCube. You can do so easily and then immediately return to your navigation.

Chapter 4: Climbing the Selection Tree

Create search and selection sets. The ability to break down your model into intelligent groupings is one of the key areas of Navisworks that help expand the benefits of coordinating large models.

Master It How are search sets created, and what other tools are required?

Solution Search sets differ from selection sets in that the model elements are identified by a search query. The Find Items tool allows you to search and filter results by object properties.

Export and reuse search sets. The strength of Navisworks lies in its ability to reuse search strings. This allows you to build a library of search criteria that will drastically cut down the amount of time it takes to configure new projects.

Master It How can a search set be reused on another project?

Solution All search sets can be exported as an XML file for reuse on future projects. Export the XML by choosing Search Sets from the Export Data area of the Output tab. On future projects, choose Import from the application icon menu and select the XML file. All search set data will now be accessible in the new model.

Navigate the selection tree. The selection tree maintains the list of all models in your current scene. In addition, there are numerous options for controlling visibility and selections.

Master It How do you change the color and/or transparency of one of the appended files?

Solution By right-clicking the file to modify, you can specify the color and/or transparency by selecting Override Item from the menu. You can also accomplish this by using the color and transparency settings in the Appearance area of the Item Tools contextual tab.

Chapter 5: Model Snapshots: Viewpoints, Animations, and Sections

Create and save animations.   Using real-world examples and adding realism to a project can give those involved a sense of depth and realism when participating in a project or when trying to get a point across. Animations combined with Navigation tools can be a great way to achieve success and clarity on a project.

Master It   You're working on a project and need to create a quick animation of a flyover of a large site. What are the steps involved for using recording and animation with Fly?

Solution   Plan what you want to record first, then follow these steps:

1. Go to the Viewpoint tab, and on the Save, Load & Playback panel, click the Save Viewpoint drop-down and select Record.

2. Select the Fly tool from the Navigation Bar.

3. When ready, click the Record button to start recording.

4. Click Stop when you want to end the recording.

Link sections.   While creating sections is vital to a project, sometimes you need to section them in more than one direction at a time. Linking sections together allows you greater flexibility to slice your model in more than one direction simultaneously.

Master It   How do you link top and left sections in Navisworks?

Solution   With Sectioning enabled, turn on Plane 1 and set it to Top. Turn on Plane 2 and set it to Left. Then select Link Section Planes. Now, the section planes can be manipulated together.

Save and edit viewpoints.   Viewpoints have a lot of uses. Some are created on the spur of the moment to capture a quick view, whereas others are created to maintain visibility states of objects or to store comments.

Master It   While working on a project, you have made changes (changed transparency, hidden items) to the scene, but before restoring the items to their original state, you want to save a viewpoint on the fly. How can you quickly save this viewpoint?

Solution   There are three ways to save viewpoints:

- Go to the Viewpoint tab, and in the Save, Load & Playback panel, click Save Viewpoint.

- Right-click anywhere in the Saved Viewpoints folder and select Save Viewpoint.

- Right-click anywhere in the scene, and select Viewpoints ➢ Saved Viewpoints ➢ Save Viewpoint.

Chapter 6: Documenting Your Project

Measure objects in the model.   Navisworks provides six Measure tools that allow for a variety of ways to calculate distances, areas, and angles.

Master It   Which tool allows you to measure multiple points and accrue the results?

Solution   The Accumulate measurement tool allows you to calculate the sum of several point-to-point measurements.

Align models with unknown coordinates.   Occasionally, models are appended with different coordinate systems and do not align properly in the model.

Master It   What tools are available to correct misaligned models?

Solution   If the distance the model is off is known or can easily be measured, you can override the model to align properly. However, if the distance is unknown, you can quickly align the model in place by using the Point To Point measurement tool to locate a common point on both models and specifying the Transform Selected Items command.

Use the Redline and Commenting tools.   Design reviews can easily be documented and communicated in Navisworks with the aid of the Redline and Commenting tools. These include any combination of text, linework, and tags.

Master It   What is the advantage of using the redline tag?

Solution   Redline tags allow you to mark any object in the model, whether or not it's part of a saved viewpoint. In addition to creating a numbered tag in the model view, tags associate comments with a status and create or update the saved viewpoint all in one action.

Chapter 7: 4D Sequencing with TimeLiner

Link your model to a project schedule.   Navisworks links to common scheduling applications as a means to add schedule data to TimeLiner.

Master It   What formats don't require an installed scheduling application to view their data?

Solution   Both MPX and CSV files can be accessed without a separately installed scheduling application.

Create a 4D sequence.   Navisworks creates 4D models by linking in schedule data to generate models that address the time and spatial aspects of a construction site.

Master It   What is the benefit of using a 4D model compared to traditional coordination efforts?

Solution 4D modeling allows for a better understanding of the project schedule by removing the limitations of traditional planning tools. This also helps you understand the full scope of the project and improve your project execution strategy. Finally, a 4D model helps foster enhanced communication by allowing all stakeholders to understand the project.

Automate schedule linking with rules. Rules allow you to automate the time-consuming portion of connecting schedule tasks to specific objects in your Navisworks scene. When working with models that contain embedded object properties, you can further leverage this data to assist with the linking.

Master It How do you attach objects to schedule tasks by using the object properties?

Solution Create a new rule and then map the internal object properties to a specific category and property by defining a custom rule description.

Explore safety and site logistics planning. Moving beyond static paper safety plans, a 4D model can identify potential safety issues and aid in the site logistics planning efforts.

Master It How can site logistics be better coordinated with a 4D model?

Solution Since a 4D model is dynamic, changes to the site or project schedule can easily be visualized and appropriate steps taken to mitigate the risk. This includes simulating equipment paths, worker areas, material laydown areas, excavations, temporary structures, and other items in flux.

Chapter 8: Clash Detection

Create rules to examine various clash outcomes. Rules for clashes can be a great asset and affect the outcome of a clash. Rules can help you filter specific objects, like items contained in a selection set, so that you're clashing only the specific elements needed.

Master It Rules are divided into two types: default and rules templates. What is the key difference between default rules and rules templates?

Solution Default rules have no options to change or customize. They are also set in Clash Detective by default. Rules templates are created with a base so that you can customize your own rules as needed by adding specific elements like selection sets or properties you want to filter out.

Select objects and geometry for clash detection. Navisworks provides the ability to import over 40 types of files, which means there could be all types of geometry for Clash Detective to try to clash. Therefore, you have the ability to change the geometry type to suit your needs.

Master It What are the three types of geometry that you can choose to clash against?

Solution Surfaces are the default clash option and clash the surface or 3D face of the selected objects. Lines clash items with center lines, usually used in conjunction with pipes. Points allow you to clash points, usually when clashing point cloud data from laser scans.

Interpret and use clash reports.   Clash reports come in various shapes and sizes and can be saved internally to Navisworks as well as externally. These reports have various uses: They can be imported into other software programs or databases, used with Microsoft Excel, or included as images inside Navisworks. Reports can also contain a great deal of customizable information that you can easily control.

Master It   Let's look at a specific aspect of creating a report. You have created an HTML report, but the images do not appear to be exporting. What could be a possible solution for your problem?

Solution   There are two possible fixes:

◆   Make sure the Image box is selected in the Contents area. Also make sure your Clash Type check boxes are selected.

◆   Don't save to your desktop, unless you save to a folder on your desktop. The report is creating images and another associated file, and it could be a great deal of information to manage, especially if you export several reports.

Chapter 9: Creating Visualizations

Add RPC objects to your model.   With RPC objects, you have a chance to improve the visual appeal of your model or scene for rendering. You can add furniture, trees, people, vehicles, equipment, or other items as needed. When rendered, they usually appear visually appealing and help augment a scene.

Master It   Adding RPCs can be quick and easy. What are the two ways that you can add an RPC to your model?

Solution   There are two distinct ways to add an RPC to the model. The first step is to get the RPC from the archive and into the palette (using double-click or drag and drop). Then use one of the two following methods:

◆   Select the RPC from the palette and drag and drop it into the scene. Wherever you release the cursor is where the RPC will be placed.

◆   Right-click the palette and select Add Instance, and then select a point where the RPC will be placed.

Determine which of the two graphics systems better suits your purpose.   Navisworks utilizes two distinctly different graphics systems, the Navisworks graphics system (Presenter) and the Autodesk graphics system. Each one has its own advantages and disadvantages; Presenter is the default system.

Master It   Explain the key difference between the Navisworks graphics system and the Autodesk graphics system.

Solution   To view some materials, lighting, and effects in real time, you will have to use the Presenter system. Many materials, lighting, and effects that are related to the Autodesk system do not appear in real time and you have to complete a render, even if you use Preview or Low Quality, for them to appear.

Use the rendering engine inside Navisworks. Navisworks contains its own rendering tools, which you can use to create realistic images directly from the model. These images can be exported as animations or image files and used for a variety of applications. Within Navisworks, you have access to several render styles.

Master It How many render styles can be combined in the palette to produce an accurate rendering?

Solution Ultimately, only one render style can be on the palette at a time. When you add another, it will replace the one you previously had. So, keep that in mind if you made changes on the palette. You might want to add the style to My Render Styles before adding a new one to the palette.

Chapter 10: Animating Objects

Create a simple animation. Navisworks can create both camera view and object animations or a combination of both. These animations can be created from scratch or leverage existing saved viewpoints.

Master It When working with object animations, what is keyframe animation and what is its advantage?

Solution A keyframe is a snapshot of a change to the model. When animating, Navisworks interpolates the frames (views) between each keyframe. This creates an easy-to-configure process yet yields a smooth and polished animation.

Manipulate geometry. Animating objects in Navisworks greatly enhances the realism of your model, but more importantly, it can be used to uncover potential coordination issues and act as a tool to keep all stakeholders up-to-date on the project.

Master It Name the five types of object animation manipulation.

Solution

- Translating (moving) the object
- Rotating the object
- Scaling the object
- Changing the color of the object
- Changing the transparency of the object

Export animations. Navisworks can export animations for use in marketing, education, and other areas.

Master It What are the two types of animation renderings that can be saved? What is the primary difference between the two?

Solution

- **Open GL:** This output shows the animation in the basic shaded model view with generic materials and lighting.

◆ **Presenter:** This output creates a more realistic view by incorporating materials, lighting, and textures. Also, this output takes significantly longer to render.

Chapter 11: Giving Objects Life and Action with Scripter

Manage scripts. Scripter gives you the power to quickly toggle on and off scripts. This ability allows you to have a single model with many scripts that can easily be configured for any group.

Master It How can you enable all scripts in a group?

Solution Select the check box next to the folder containing the group.

Create events. Events are rules that define special triggers. Users set off events by meeting the conditions set by the rules of the event.

Master It Which event would you use to open a door when you near it?

Solution Select the On Hotspot event for this scenario.

Create actions. Actions are the reaction the model has to the triggers defined by event(s). These actions allow you to control what the model will do in reaction to triggers you set.

Master It How can you lead a user to a special viewpoint in your project and start an animation in that scene?

Solution Create a viewpoint in the location where you wish to take your user. Select the Show Viewpoint action in the Scripter window and select the viewpoint you created. Then select the Play Animation action in the Scripter window and select the animation you wish to play.

Interact with the model. Interacting with the model brings to life real-world experiences in the model.

Master It How could you create a scenario where a door opens as you near it and human avatars exit the door as soon as the door finishes opening?

Solution For this scenario, you could create a number of scripts. One way would be to create two scripts. The first would have an event set to On Hotspot with the sliding door specified as the selection. The action would be set to Animation with the door opening. The second script would have the event set to On Animation with the door animation selected and the Trigger On set to Ending. The action for the second script would be set to Play Animation with human avatars walking out of the door.

Chapter 12: Collaborating Outside of Navisworks

Interact with Navisworks Freedom. In addition to the core applications Manage and Simulate, Autodesk provides Navisworks Freedom as a no-cost viewer to extend the value of the model to users who may not have access to the core products.

Master It What file formats does Navisworks Freedom view?

Solution   Navisworks Freedom only displays NWD and DWF™/DWFx/W2D files. However, the project browser and 2D DWF views are supported.

Configure NWNavigator.   NWNavigator is a plug-in that allows you to create a virtual instance of Navisworks inside a session of AutoCAD.

Master It   What is the benefit of using NWNavigator with large datasets?

Solution   Since Navisworks handles large files much easier than most design applications, NWNavigator can be used to quickly navigate large complex files. Using the viewpoint controls, users can quickly navigate to a specific view and re-create the same vantage point in their CAD display window.

Export to third-party applications.   Navisworks can export the model scene to external applications where adjacent workflows and benefits are realized.

Master It   What are some of the different file formats that Navisworks can export to?

Solution   3D DWF/DWFx — This is used in numerous free viewers including Autodesk Design Review.

FBX — This format is used to translate the model into a format that high-end rendering solutions such as Autodesk® 3ds Max® and Autodesk® Maya® can work with.

Chapter 13: Other Useful Navisworks Tools

Connect external data to object properties.   Model data tools allow you to connect external database links to object properties.

Master It   How can you connect to an existing facilities management system that is Microsoft Access–based?

Solution   Link to the database containing the maintenance log information.

Use the Project Browser.   The Project Browser allows you to access information from both 2D and 3D models. This can be especially useful in the field when you wish to access 2D data from a 3D model. Imagine being on the jobsite with a tablet PC, selecting any object you see in the building, and selecting the same object in 3D. Then, from the 3D model, you can quickly access the contract documents in the standard 2D views.

Master It   How can you find an object selected in a 3D model in other views? Give an example of when you would use this function.

Solution   Select the object in the 3D model, then select Find Item In Other Sheets And Models.

Reference external documents from the model.   The Links tool allows you to reference external documents from the model. This can enhance the model's information significantly. You can use links during construction to attach submittal information to the model. This information can then be used for quality control.

Master It   How can you insert a picture into the model?

Solution   Select the object you wish to host the picture and click the Add Link button.

Chapter 14: Managing BIM Workflows

Understand the importance of leveraging data shortcuts.   Civil 3D has many tools to aid in the creation of objects.

Master It   In Civil 3D, what is the most important reason to use data shortcuts (in terms of Navisworks)?

Solution   When doing a 4D model and splitting up the surfaces to accommodate the schedule, you may get more than 100 surfaces. Setting up the data shortcuts will allow you to move more easily in the files and manipulate the surfaces.

Know when and how to upgrade software during an active project.   It's always important to keep in mind when and how to upgrade software in a project.

Master It   John Mack talks about the importance of upgrading your software on a project. What is the first step in the process for upgrading software?

Solution   No company can upgrade modeling software on the project without the BIM core group's written approval

Plan for BIM using project planning meetings.   Treating BIM like an actual project has its advantages.

Master It   Art Theusch talks about project planning meetings. What would be the main goal for having a project planning meeting? (Think deliverables.)

Solution   The main goal would be to create a BIM execution plan during the meeting. The purpose of the BIMx is to create a structure for the integration of BIM into the planning process.

Appendix B

Best Practices and Supplementary Information

This appendix provides additional information on best practices for optimum model performance and supplementary material for advanced configurations. Several areas of this appendix have been reprinted with permission from Autodesk.

Optimizing Performance

Although Autodesk® Navisworks® 2013 doesn't require extensive amounts of system resources to function efficiently, several settings are available that optimize the performance of your session. This section provides an overview of the various settings and, where applicable, provides recommendations on best practices for optimum performance. However, because of the numerous differences between processors, video cards, RAM, and other components, you should experiment with these settings to determine what works best with your system.

The performance settings are located in two areas of the Global Options Editor. The first group of settings (Global Options ➢ Interface ➢ Display) controls the display of the model. Let's explore a few of these settings.

2D Graphics

You can adjust the level of detail of your 2D graphics, which means you can trade off between the rendering performance and 2D fidelity. From the Level Of Detail drop-down list, you can select from the following options:

Low Gives you lower 2D fidelity but better rendering performance.

Medium Gives you medium 2D fidelity and medium rendering performance; this is the default option.

High Gives you higher 2D fidelity but lower rendering performance.

Detail

Guarantee Frame Rate Indicates whether the Navisworks engine maintains the frame rate specified on the Speed tab of the File Options dialog box.

By default, this check box is selected, and the target rate is maintained while moving. When movement stops, the complete model is rendered.

If this check box is clear, the complete model is always rendered during navigation, no matter how long it takes.

Fill In Detail   Indicates whether Navisworks fills in any discarded detail when navigation has stopped.

Graphics System

Navisworks supports two graphics systems: Presenter Graphics and Autodesk Graphics.

Auto Select   By default, this check box is selected and Navisworks controls which graphics system to use. Clear this check box if you want to select the system yourself. Doing so enables the System drop-down list.

Hardware Acceleration   Select this check box to utilize any available OpenGL hardware acceleration on your video card.

If your video card drivers do not function well with Navisworks, clear this check box.

If your video card does not support OpenGL hardware acceleration, this check box is not available.

System   This drop-down list is available when you clear the Auto Select check box. Select from the following options:

Presenter   Supports the display of Presenter materials and uses Hardware or Software OpenGL.

Autodesk   Supports the display of Autodesk materials and uses Direct3D or Hardware OpenGL.

Three-dimensional models can use either graphics system; the Presenter system is the default option. However, 2D sheets can only use Autodesk Graphics and will not render without a Direct3D/OpenGL–supported graphics card.

Occlusion Culling   Select this check box to enable occlusion culling. This means that Navisworks only draws visible objects and ignores any objects located behind other objects. This option is useful when you are working with complex files because the hidden geometry will not be rendered, thus increasing performance.

Occlusion culling can *only* be used on a machine with an OpenGL 1.5–compliant graphics card. Also, occlusion culling is not used in a 2D workspace.

If your video card supports OpenGL, you can improve the graphical performance by turning on Hardware Acceleration and Occlusion Culling.

Using the Hardware Acceleration option usually gives you better and faster rendering. However, some graphics cards may not function well in this mode, in which case we recommend that you switch off this option.

Occlusion culling can significantly improve performance in situations when much of the model is not visible. For example, when you walk down the corridor of a building, the walls occlude most geometry outside the corridor. Other rooms are only visible through doorways or windows. Turning on Occlusion Culling dramatically reduces the rendering load in such cases.

Transparency

Interactive Transparency   Select this check box to render transparent items dynamically during interactive navigation.

By default, this check box is clear; therefore, transparent items are only drawn when interaction has stopped.

If your video card does not support hardware-accelerated OpenGL, selecting this check box can affect display performance.

In addition to the display settings, you can configure options for optimizing the model's performance. To access these options, choose Global Options ➤ Model ➤ Performance.

Memory Limit

Auto   Indicates whether Navisworks automatically determines the maximum memory that can be used. Selecting this check box sets the memory limit to the lowest of your available physical memory or address space, less that required for your operating system.

Limit (MB)   Specifies the maximum memory that Navisworks can use.

Merge Duplicates

These options improve performance by eliminating instances of duplicate geometry. Rather than storing every item in memory, if any items are the same, Autodesk Navisworks can store one instance of them and copy that instance into other positions. This is of particular benefit on larger models, where significant numbers of these duplicate geometries exist.

On Convert   Select this check box to merge duplicates when a CAD file is converted into the Navisworks format.

On Append   Select this check box to merge duplicates when a new file is appended to the currently opened Navisworks file.

On Load   Select this check box to merge duplicates when a file is loaded into Navisworks.

On Save NWF   Select this check box to merge duplicates when the current scene is saved in the NWF file format.

Securing the Global Options Editor

If you've made changes to the Global Options, you can save the options file as an XML file and easily reload it in case of any changes. However, since file units, preferences, and performance settings are housed in this section, it makes sense to secure the Global Options Editor. You can add another layer of security by locking down the Options Editor to prevent any unauthorized modifications.

You'll need to access the Options Editor through the DOS command window. Here's how:

1. Click the Windows Start button (lower-left corner of your screen).

2. Click Run.

3. Type **cmd** in the Open field and click OK.

4. A command prompt window will open. Click after the C:\ prompt.

5. Type **CD C:\Program Files\Autodesk\Navisworks Manage 2013** or the location of your Navisworks installation. You will now be in the Navisworks program directory.

6. Type **optionseditor.exe -l** (that's a minus sign following by the lowercase letter L). See Figure B.1. The Global Options Editor will open in Locked mode, allowing you to select which options to secure.

FIGURE B.1

Opening the Global Options Editor from the DOS command prompt

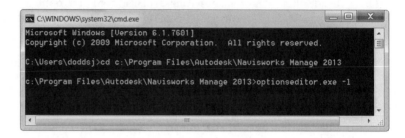

In the Options Editor dialog box, you can now select which options you wish to secure by clicking the appropriate check boxes, as shown in Figure B.2.

FIGURE B.2

Click the appropriate check boxes.

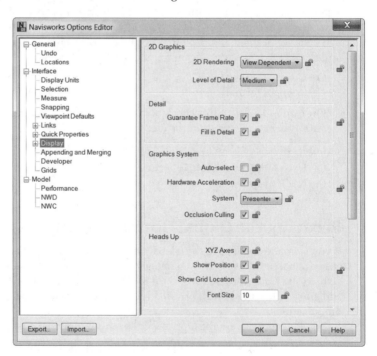

Save your settings as an XML file in a dedicated folder (e.g., C:/Global Options/Locked.xml). To have this file locked every time a user logs on, use the command-line switch tools covered in Chapter 12, "Collaborating outside of Navisworks," to reference this options file. To do

so, first right-click your Navisworks program icon and select Properties from the context menu. In the Shortcut tab, modify the Target line to read:

```
C:\Program Files\Autodesk\Navisworks Manage 2013\roamer.exe -options
"C:\Global Options\Locked.xml"
```

Modify your path and folder names as needed.

When the user opens Navisworks, any settings in the Global Options that were locked will be grayed out with a lock icon next to them (Figure B.3). This process makes it much easier to maintain project standards without worrying about users making changes.

FIGURE B.3
Locked Global Options appear grayed out with a lock icon beside them.

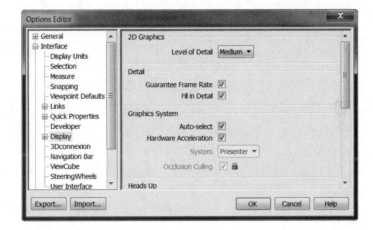

Supported File Types

Table B.1 lists the supported CAD formats.

TABLE B.1:   Supported CAD Formats

FORMAT	EXTENSIONS
Navisworks	.nwd, .nwf, .nwc
AutoCAD®	.dwg, .dwf
MicroStation (SE, J, V8, XM)	.dgn, .prp, .prw
3D Studio	.3ds, .prj
ACIS SAT	.sat, .sab
CIS/2	.stp
DWF™	.dwf, .dwfx, .w2d
FBX®	.fbx

TABLE B.1: Supported CAD Formats *(CONTINUED)*

FORMAT	EXTENSIONS
IFC	`.ifc`
IGES	`.igs, .iges`
Inventor®	`.ipt, .iam, .ipj`
Informatix MAN	`.man, .cv7`
JT Open	`.jt`
PDS Design Review	`.dri`
Parasolids	`.x_b`
Pro/ENGINEER	`.prt, .asm, .g, .neu`
RVM	`.rvm`
Revit®	`.rvt`
SketchUp	`.skp`
STEP	`.stp, .step`
STL	`.stl`
VRML	`.wrl, .wrz`

Table B.2 shows the supported laser scan formats.

TABLE B.2: Supported Laser Scan Formats

FORMAT	EXTENSIONS
ASCII laser file	`.asc, .txt`
Faro	`.fls, .fws, .iQscan, .iQmod, .iQwsp`
Leica	`.pts, .ptx`
Riegl	`.3dd`
Trimble	Native file not supported; convert to ASCII laser file
Z+F	`.zfc, .zfs`

Getting Help

From time to time, you may need the answer to a quick question. Navisworks provides an in-depth help guide that contains complete information on using the program. Becoming familiar with the help system will greatly improve your efficiency.

Click the Help icon ⑦ in the upper-right corner of the program or press F1. In the Help window, you use the left pane to locate information. The tabs above the left pane give you several ways for finding the topics you want to view. The right pane displays the topics you select.

The Contents tab does the following:

◆ Presents an overview of the available documentation in a list of topics and subtopics

◆ Allows you to browse by selecting and expanding topics

◆ Provides a structure so you can always see where you are in Help and quickly jump to other topics

The Index tab does the following:

◆ Displays an alphabetical list of keywords related to the topics listed on the Contents tab

◆ Accesses information quickly when you already know the name of a feature, command, or operation, or when you know what action you want the program to perform

The Search tab does the following:

◆ Provides a keyword search of all the topics listed on the Contents tab

◆ Accepts the Boolean operators AND (+), OR, NOT (-), and NEAR

◆ Accepts the wildcards *, ?, and ~

◆ Allows you to perform a search for a phrase when the phrase is enclosed in double quotes

◆ Displays a ranked list of topics that contain the word or words entered in the keyword field

◆ Sorts the results by any column heading: Title, Location, or Rank

Most topics in the Help system have three tabs above the right pane of the Help window. The tabs display different types of information.

Concept   Describes a feature or function. When you click the Concept tab, the Help Contents list in the left pane of the Help window expands and highlights the current topic. The Contents tab displays the Help structure for that topic. You can easily display nearby topics by clicking them in the list.

Procedure   Provides step-by-step instructions for common procedures related to the current topic. After displaying a procedure, you can click the Procedure tab to redisplay the current list of procedures.

Quick Reference   Lists reference information related to the current topic.

When you click a different tab, the topic remains the same. Only the type of information displayed—concept, procedures, or quick reference links—is different.

Changing the Third Person Avatar Figure

In addition to the large collection of Third Person avatars available within Navisworks, you can create your own. You can do so using any file that Navisworks can read, such as DWG™ or SKP files. To change your avatar, do the following:

1. Create a new folder in the `avatars` directory. This is typically located in the program installation folder: `C:/Program Files/Autodesk/Navisworks Manage 2013/ avatars`.

2. Open the file you that you wish to convert into an avatar in Navisworks.

3. Save the file you wish to use as an NWD in the new folder in the `avatars` directory.

4. Restart Navisworks.

5. Open your file and engage the avatar. In the Edit Viewpoint dialog box, select settings under the Collision area. Select your avatar from the Avatar drop-down list, as shown in Figure B.4.

FIGURE B.4
Choose your avatar from the Avatar drop-down.

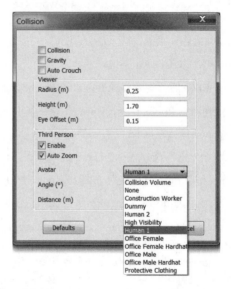

You may need to tweak the size by modifying the height, radius, and eye offset settings. When creating custom avatars, you might want to reference an existing avatar to set up the correct orientation of the model.

Selected Glossary

Navisworks has many terms that are used in this book as well as in the software. This section covers some commonly used terms and descriptions. We have also included terms that may relate to items outside Navisworks.

Display Terminology

Average Frame Rate   Shows the current measured frame rate, averaged over the last second.

Average Frame Time   Shows the time taken to render the last frame.

Average Triangle Rate   Shows the rate at which triangles are being rendered and is a measure of how well your graphics card is working.

Culling   A process for determining which items Navisworks should not draw during the rendering of a scene. Navisworks does a level of prioritized culling with the drop-out method of rendering interactive scenes, but you have a certain level of control over other aspects of culling, such as back face and near and far planes.

Drop-out   To maintain interactivity and guarantee a user-defined frame rate, Navisworks only renders what it can in the fraction of a second it has. The remainder is "dropped out," or not rendered. Navisworks prioritizes what is rendered and what is dropped out based on the size of the item's bounding box, the distance from the viewer, and the size on screen, so only the less-significant items in the scene are dropped out. Once navigation has ceased, the scene continues rendering until all items are visible.

Frame Rate   The number of frames per second (fps) that are rendered in the main navigation window. Navisworks guarantees a user-defined frame rate in order to maintain interactivity.

Export Terminology

Codec   These are terms specific to Navisworks that are used in relation to exporting. Codec stands for "compression/decompression" and is a program that compresses and decompresses animations when creating and playing back AVI files. Codecs are installed independently of Navisworks and are available when installed on your Windows system, and the same codec that was used to create an AVI file is required to play it back.

File Terminology

Cache files   When any native CAD file is opened or appended, Navisworks creates a cache file (NWC) if the Write Cache option is set. When the file is next opened or appended, Navisworks will read data from the corresponding cache file rather than reconvert the original data if the cache is newer than the original file. If the original file is altered, Navisworks will re-create the cache file when it is next loaded. Cache files speed up access to commonly used files. They are particularly useful for models made up of many files, of which only a few are changed between viewing sessions. Cache files can also be exported from some CAD applications where a native file reader is not available with Navisworks.

External references   External references (sometimes called reference files or XRefs) are shown in the Navisworks selection tree as an inserted group. Navisworks looks for the externally referenced files in the same place that Autodesk® AutoCAD® or MicroStation would.

Faceting factor   During an export from a CAD package to NWC format, or while Navisworks is reading a native CAD file, decisions must be made as to how a curved surface is reduced to flat facets. For most applications and file formats, you have control over the level of faceting that takes place. All items, no matter what their size, will use the same faceting factor and so have the same number of sides to curved entities. Therefore, you need to experiment a little with different values to account for the size that these items will appear on the screen.

Max facet deviation Maximum facet deviation is used in conjunction with the faceting factor to ensure that larger objects, with too large a deviation from the original, have additional facets added. If a difference greater than the entered value is found in a model, it adds more facets. The values are measured in the model units.

Navisworks document Navisworks document (NWD) files are useful when you want to take a snapshot of the model at a certain time. All the geometry and review information is saved into the NWD file and cannot be changed. Published NWD files can be password protected and time-bombed for security. These files are also very small, compressing the CAD data by up to 80 percent of the original size. NWD files are useful when you are issuing models for viewing by others with the Navisworks Freedom 2013 free viewer.

Navisworks file Navisworks files (NWF) are useful when you are using the native CAD files appended into Navisworks. They store the location of the appended files, along with any design reviews made in Navisworks, such as comments, redlines, viewpoints, animations, and so on. If a group of files is appended into a Navisworks scene and saved as an NWF file, then upon reopening this NWF file later (once the original CAD files have been changed), the updated CAD files will be loaded into the scene for review.

Shape Merge Threshold MicroStation shapes are polygons that can have three or more vertices. They're often used to model more complex objects, a process that can waste memory. So, Navisworks merges all shapes on the same level or in the same cell and with the same color into a "shape set" if these shapes have less than or equal to the number of vertices specified by the Shape Merge Threshold setting.

Selection Terminology

Composite objects A composite object is a group of geometry that is considered a single object in the selection tree. For example, a window object might be made up of a frame and a pane. If it's a composite object, the window object would be both the frame and the pane and be selected all at once.

Instances An instance is a single object, such as a tree, that is referred to several times within a model. This has the advantage of cutting down on file size by not unnecessarily repeating an object.

Item name The original CAD or Navisworks assigned identifier. Any item can have a name and this name will usually come from the original CAD package in which the model was created.

Item type Every item in Navisworks has a type. Examples of types are reference files, layers, instances (sometimes called inserts), and groups. Every CAD package also has a number of geometry types, such as polygons or 3D solids.

Selection resolution   The level in the selection tree at which you start selecting. You can cycle through items in the tree by holding down the Shift key during a selection.

User name and internal name   Each category and property name has two parts: a user-visible string, which is localized, and an internal string, which isn't and is mainly used by the API. By default, when matching names in the Smart Tags and Find Items dialog boxes, both parts must be the same, but you can use the flags to match on only one part. You can use Ignore User Name if you want to match something irrespective of which localized version is being used.

Viewpoint Terminology

Angular speed   The speed that the camera moves when turning right and left in any navigation mode.

Anti-aliasing   Improves image quality by softening the jagged-edge appearance of sharp lines. 2x to 64x refers to the extra number of frames that are required for the anti-aliasing process. The greater the number of frames, the finer the effect (with the consequent increase in rendering time).

Aspect ratio   Aspect ratio is the proportion of X-axis to Y-axis size. For example, when exporting a bitmap of a viewpoint, maintaining the aspect ratio would keep the proportion of the view even if the number of pixels is different.

Camera-centric   Navigation modes in which the camera is moved around the model.

Field of view   The field of view (FOV) of a camera is the angle that the camera can see. A large FOV will fit more into the view but will look distorted, and a small FOV will tend to flatten the view, tending toward an orthographic view. There are two FOVs in Navisworks: vertical and horizontal. Editing one will change the other, and the two are related by the viewpoint's aspect ratio.

Focal point   The focal point is the position in 3D space that the camera will zoom in to or rotate around in Orbit and Zoom modes.

Model-centric   Navigation modes in which the model is moved in front of the camera.

Roll   The roll of the camera is its angle around the viewing axis. This cannot be edited in a navigation mode where the viewport up vector stays upright (Walk and Orbit).

Saved attributes   Each viewpoint can optionally save the state of its hidden and "required" items, as well as any material (color and transparency) overrides. Then, on recalling the viewpoint, those same items are rehidden, remade required, and the materials reinstated. This can be useful in the creation of animations when you are dragging viewpoints onto an empty animation. This is also useful when you are creating viewpoints that section your project for downstream use in Navisworks Freedom.

Tilt angle   This is indicated in the scene's units below (negative) or above (positive) horizontal (0) at the base of the Tilt window.

Viewpoint up vector   The direction that Navisworks considers "up." This is maintained in the Walk and Orbit modes. This may be also referred to as "world up vector."

Clash Detective Terminology

Clash status   Each clash has a current status associated with it, and each status has a colored icon to identify it. This status is updated automatically by Clash Detective or can be manually overridden if desired. The statuses are as follows:

New   Clash found for the first time in the current run of the test

Active   Clash found in a previous run of the test and not resolved

Reviewed   Clash previously found and marked by somebody as reviewed

Approved   Clash previously found and approved by someone

Resolved   Clash found in a previous run of the test and not in the current run of the test, therefore assumed to be resolved

Clearance clash   A clash in which the geometry of item 1 may or may not intersect that of item 2 but comes within a distance of less than the set tolerance.

Duplicate clash   A clash in which the geometry of item 1 is the same as that of item 2, located within a distance of between zero and the set tolerance. A tolerance of zero would therefore only detect duplicate geometry in exactly the same location.

Hard clash   A clash in which the geometry of item 1 intersects that of item 2 by a distance of more than the set tolerance.

Intersection method   A standard Hard clash test type applies a normal intersection method, which sets the clash test to check for intersections between any of the triangles defining the two items being tested (remember that all Navisworks geometry is composed of triangles). This may miss clashes between items where none of the triangles intersect. For example, say two pipes are exactly parallel and overlap each other slightly at their ends. The pipes intersect, yet none of the triangles that define their geometry do and so this clash would be missed using the standard Hard clash test type. However, choosing Hard (Conservative) will report all pairs of items that might clash. This may give false positives in the results, but it is a more thorough and safer clash-detection method.

Severity   For Hard clashes, the severity of a clash depends on the intersection of the two items intersecting. Hard clashes are recorded as a negative distance. The more negative the distance, the more severe the clash. Hard clash severity depends on whether the Conservative or Normal intersection method has been applied. If Normal, the greatest penetration between a pair of triangles is measured. If Conservative, the greatest penetration of space around one item into the space around another is measured. For Clearance clashes, the severity depends on how close one item invades the distance required around the second. For example, an item coming within 3 mm is more severe than an item coming within 5 mm of the other. For Duplicate clashes, the severity depends on how close one item is to the other. When the distance between them is zero, it is more likely that this is duplicate geometry, whereas items that are farther apart are more likely to be different objects and therefore have a lesser severity.

Tolerance   Controls the severity of the clashes reported and the ability to filter out negligible clashes, which can be assumed to be worked around on site. Tolerance is used for Hard clash, Clearance clash, and Duplicate clash types. Any clash found that is within this tolerance will be reported, whereas clashes outside this tolerance will be ignored. So for Hard clashes, a clash with a severity of between zero and the tolerance value will be ignored, whereas for Clearance clashes, a clash with a severity of more than the tolerance value will be ignored because it is farther away than the distance required. Similarly, a Duplicate clash with a severity of more than the tolerance value will be ignored because it is likely to be a separate, yet identical piece of geometry. Keep in mind that if a material is 0.01 inches thick, such as ducting, and your tolerance in a Hard clash is set to 0.1 inches thick, you will miss all hits to that ducting.

Modeling and Other Terminology

3D A model drawn using a CAD system that has three dimensions, i.e., width, length, and depth.

4D The action of linking 3D modeled object to a line item in a schedule or tying any time relation to modeled objects.

5D The act of extracting quantities from CAD model files and tying the data to estimating software.

A3 problem solving report An A3 is a method of creating a report to share with others. The report is placed on a single 11″ × 17″ paper (A3 paper size). The intent is for person(s) it is directed at to be able to understand what the topic is within 30 seconds. The report is to have the following information:

1. Baseline or current state of the problem

2. Analysis or root cause of the problem

3. A list of advantages of each alternative that was reviewed

4. Proposal of the recommended solution

5. Action plan or path forward

6. Any visual aids that are needed on the page.

Automated Machine Guidance Automated Machine Guidance (AMG) incorporates the use of a three-dimensional computer model to move or place materials with greater precision.

BIM core group The BIM core group consists of a member from each of the major shareholders: owner, architect, CM/GC, and owner BIM consultant (optional).

Building Information Modeling Building Information Modeling (BIM) is the process of creating and organizing building data during its life cycle. Typically, it uses three-dimensional, real-time, dynamic building modeling software to increase productivity in building design and construction. The process produces the BIM, which encompasses building geometry, spatial relationships, geographic information, prefabrication information and quantities, and properties of a building and its surrounding property.

Choosing By Advantages Choosing By Advantages (CBA) is a decision-making process designed to place emphasis on the importance of an advantage of an alternative.

Disadvantages are not used, because a disadvantage of one alternative is an advantage to another alternative. Advantages are weighed by importance to the alternative.

Coordination   Coordination as it refers to BIM/VDC is the act or process of creating realistic BIM geometry in model files, combining these models into one integrated software platform. During the coordination process, proper spatial boundaries and clearances are adhered to in order to create an accurate integrated computer representation of the building from all participating trades, thus producing a clash-free model.

Detailing   Detailing is the act or process of creating shop drawings for fabrication and installation instructions assembled directly from the BIM.

Geospatial-geographic information systems   Geospatial-geographic information systems (GIS) use geospatial analysis in a variety of contexts. Use of the word *geospatial* in place of geographic analysis is incorrect.

Integrated building model   A 3D CAD model that consists of all available trade models for a building incorporated into one common file. This is sometimes referred to as a composite model.

Integrated project delivery team   "Architect, Owner and CM/CG agree to form an IPD Team to facilitate design, construction and commissioning of the project. The IPD Team members, including architect and architect's consultants, and CM/GC, CM/GC's subcontractors and suppliers, and owner, and owner's selected consultants and separate contractors will be expected to reasonably share information and cooperatively collaborate for the benefit of the project." — *Quoted from* **"Integrated Agreement for Lean Project Delivery Between Owner, Architect and CM/CG,"** *August 1, 2007.*

LIDAR   LIDAR (Light Detection and Ranging, also LADAR) is an optical remote-sensing technology that can measure the distance to, or other properties of, a target by illuminating the target with light, often using pulses from a laser.

Mind-mapping software   Mind-mapping software is used to create a diagram to show the relationship between ideas and information.

Photogrammetry   The practice of determining the geometric properties of objects from photographic images. Photogrammetry is as old as modern photography and can be dated to the mid-nineteenth century.

Virtual design and construction   Virtual design and construction (VDC) is the use of integrated multidisciplinary performance models of design-construction projects, including the product, work processes, and organization of the design-construction-operation team in order to support explicit and public business objectives. The term VDC is commonly misused in place of BIM during the design and construction process.

Index

Note to the Reader: Throughout this index, **boldfaced** page numbers indicate primary discussions of a topic. *Italicized* page numbers indicate illustrations.